DEMOCRACY IN INDONESIA

1950s and 1990s

edited by

**David Bourchier
and
John Legge**

Monash Papers on Southeast Asia No. 31
Centre of Southeast Asian Studies
Monash University

First published 1994
by the
Centre of Southeast Asian Studies
Monash University
Clayton, Victoria 3168
Australia

© 1994 David Bourchier and John Legge

This book is copyright. Apart from any fair dealings for the purposes of private study, research, criticism or review, as permitted under the Copyright Act, no part may be reproduced by any process without written permission. Inquires should be made to the publisher.

National Library of Australia
Cataloguing-in-publication data:
Democracy in Indonesia: 1950s and 1990s. Bibliography. Includes index. 1. Democracy - Indonesia - History. 2. Democracy - Indonesia. 3. Indonesia - Politics and government - 1950-1966. 4. Indonesia - Politics and government - 1966- . 5. Indonesia - History - 1950-1966. I. Bourchier, David. II. Legge, J.D. (John David), 1921. III. Monash University. Centre of Southeast Asian Studies. (Series: Monash papers on Southeast Asian Studies; no. 31). 320.9598

I.S.B.N...............0 7326 0561 X
I.S.S.N...............0727 6680

Typeset by
David Bourchier

Printed and bound by
Aristoc Press Pty. Ltd.
Glen Waverley, Australia.

Cover design by Vane Lindesay
Cover photograph credit: Stanley

For information on other publications from the Centre, write to:

The Publications Officer
Centre of Southeast Asian Studies
Monash Asia Institute
Monash University
Clayton, Victoria 3168
Australia

Contents

Contributors — vi
Glossary — viii
Preface — xiii

PART I: THE 1950s

1. The Case of the Disappearing Decade
   Ruth T. McVey — 3

2. Constitutional Democracy: how well did it function?
   Herb Feith — 16

3. Inevitable or Avoidable? Interpretations of the Collapse of Parliamentary Democracy
   Jamie Mackie — 26

4. On the Fall of the Parliamentary System
   Daniel S. Lev — 39

5. Human Rights and the *Konstituante* Debates of 1956-59
   Adnan Buyung Nasution — 43

6. The 1950s in New Order Ideology and Politics
   David Bourchier — 50

7. The Impact of American Foreign Policy
   George McT. Kahin — 63

8. Legacies of the 'Revolution'
   Robert Cribb — 74

9. The Indonesia Raya Dream and its Impact on the Concept of Democracy
   Y.B. Mangunwijaya — 79

10. 'Rowing in a typhoon': Nahdlatul Ulama and the Decline of Parliamentary Democracy
    Greg Fealy — 88

11. The Failure and Future of Democracy: conversations with a group of former revolutionary activists
    Anton Lucas — 99

PART II: PROSPECTS FOR THE 1990s

12 Democratic Prospects in Indonesia
   Harold Crouch 115

13 Rewinding 'Back to the Future': the Left and Constitutional Democracy
   Ben Anderson 128

14 The Impact of neo-Modernism on Indonesian Islamic Thought: the emergence of a new pluralism
   Greg Barton 143

15 Islam, Politics and Democracy in the 1950s and 1990s
   Abdurrahman Wahid 151

16 Pancasila Discourse in Suharto's late New Order
   Douglas E. Ramage 156

17 Gender Interests and Indonesian Democracy
   Susan Blackburn 168

18 Free from what? Responsible to whom? The Problem of Democracy and the Indonesian Press
   Paul Tickell 182

19 Challenging State Corporatism on the Labour Front: Working Class Politics in the 1990s
   Vedi R. Hadiz 190

20 Regionalism and Decentralisation
   Audrey R. Kahin 204

21 The Dilemmas of Decentralisation and Democratisation
   Ichlasul Amal 214

22 Ethnicity in Indonesian Politics
   Burhan Magenda 223

23 From Lower to Middle Class: Political Activities before and after 1988
   Arief Budiman 229

24 Party and Parliamentary Politics 1987-1993
   Michael R.J. Vatikiotis 236

25 Interpretation of the Current Scene
   Soetjipto Wirosardjono 243

26 A New Political Context: the Urbanisation of the Rural
   Kenneth R. Young 248

27	The Transformation of the Informal Sector: Social and Political Consequences *Hans-Dieter Evers*	258
28	The Inner Contraction of the Suharto Regime: a starting point for a withdrawal to the barracks *Ulf Sundhaussen*	272
29	Can all good things go together? Democracy, Growth, and Unity in post-Suharto Indonesia *R. William Liddle*	286
30	Democratisation in the 1990s: Coming to Terms with Gradualism? *Marsillam Simanjuntak*	302

Afterword

31	*Anthony Reid*	313

Index 319

Contributors

Ichlasul Amal, Dean of the Faculty of Social and Political Studies, Gadjah Mada University, Yogyakarta.

Benedict Anderson, Aaron L. Binenkorb Professor of International Studies, Department of Government, Cornell University, Ithaca, New York.

Greg Barton, Lecturer, School of Social Inquiry, Deakin University, Melbourne.

Susan Blackburn, Senior Lecturer in Politics, Monash University, Melbourne.

David Bourchier, Post Graduate student, Politics, Monash University.

Arief Budiman, Centre for Contemporary Indonesian Studies, Satya Wacana Christian University, Salatiga.

Robert Cribb, Senior Lecturer in History, University of Queensland, Brisbane.

Harold Crouch, Senior Fellow, Department of Social and Political Change, Australian National University, Canberra.

Hans-Dieter Evers, Professor of Sociology, University of Bielefeld, Germany. Visiting Fellow, Population Studies Centre, Gadjah Mada University, Yogyakarta.

Greg Fealy, Post Graduate student, History, Monash University.

Herb Feith, Reader in Politics, Monash University. Retired in 1990.

Vedi Hadiz, Post Graduate student, Asia Research Centre, Murdoch University, Perth.

Audrey R. Kahin, Cornell Modern Indonesia Project, Cornell University.

George McT. Kahin, Emeritus Professor, Department of Government, Cornell University.

John Legge, Emeritus Professor, Centre of Southeast Asian Studies, Monash University.

Daniel S. Lev, Professor of Political Science, University of Washington, Seattle.

R. William Liddle, Department of Political Science, The Ohio State University, Columbus.

Anton Lucas, Senior Lecturer in Asian Studies, Flinders University of South Australia, Adelaide.

Jamie Mackie, formerly Professor of Social and Political Change, Australian National University.

Burhan Magenda, Lecturer in the Faculty of Social and Political Studies, University of Indonesia and head of the Intellectuals Department in Golkar.

Y. B. Mangunwijaya, a Yogyakarta-based novelist, philosopher, pastor, architect and activist.

Ruth McVey, formerly of the School of Oriental and African Studies, University of London.

Adnan Buyung Nasution, Chair of the Indonesian Legal Aid Foundation, Jakarta, recently completed a Doctorate at Utrecht University, The Netherlands.

Douglas E. Ramage, Fellow in the Program on International Economics and Politics at the East-West Center in Honolulu, Hawaii. Fulbright Scholar in Jakarta from 1991 to 1993.

Anthony Reid, Professor of Pacific and Asian History, Research School of Pacific and Asian Studies, Australian National University.

Marsillam Simanjuntak, Head of the Public Affairs Research Group (GRUP), Jakarta and a prominent member of *Forum Demokrasi*.

Ulf Sundhaussen, Senior Lecturer in Government, University of Queensland.

Paul Tickell, Lecturer, Centre for Asian Studies, The University of Western Australia, Perth.

Michael Vatikiotis, formerly Jakarta correspondent for the *Far Eastern Economic Review* from 1989-91 and now ASEAN correspondent, based in Kuala Lumpur.

Abdurrahman Wahid, Chair of the Executive Board of Nahdlatul Ulama.

Soetjipto Wirosardjono, former secretary general of the Indonesian Bureau of Statistics, currently a Deputy Chair of the Institute for Applied Technology Research (BPPT) and a member of the editorial board of *Republika*.

Kenneth R. Young, Senior Lecturer, Department of Sociology and Anthropology, Monash University.

Glossary

abangan	The nominally Muslim or spiritually syncretic community or orientation in Java.
ABRI	*Angkatan Bersenjata Republik Indonesia*, the Armed Forces of the Republic of Indonesia.
aliran	Major socio-cultural group or orientation (such as *abangan, santri*).
arus sejarah	The forward flow of History.
asas tunggal	'Sole basis', compulsory recognition of the Pancasila as the sole ideological foundation for all social and political organisations.
BFO	*Bijeenkomst voor Federaal Overleg*, Federal Consultative Assembly, a co-ordinating body of the federal states established by the Dutch.
Cikini affair	The attempted assassination of President Sukarno in Central Jakarta on 30 November 1957.
daerah	Region, regional
Darul Islam	A movement which fought for the establishment of an Islamic state. Concentrated in West Java, Sulawesi and Aceh, it lasted from 1948 until its leader, Kartosuwirjo, was captured and executed in 1962.
Dewan Nasional	National Council, the advisory body formed 12 July 1957 to advise the newly appointed Karya Cabinet. It was this body which formulated the guidelines for Guided Democracy.
DPR	*Dewan Perwakilan Rakyat*, People's Representative Council.

DPRD	*Dewan Perwakilan Rakyat Daerah*, Regional People's Representative Council.
dwifungsi	The 'dual function' doctrine by which the Armed Forces claim a right to participate in social and political affairs as well as defence and security.
FBSI	All-Indonesia Workers' Federation, *Federasi Buruh Seluruh Indonesia.*
GAPI	*Gabungan Politik Indonesia*, Indonesian Political Federation. A union of nationalist groups in the 1930s.
GBHN	*Garis Besar Haluan Negara*, State Policy Guidelines.
Gerindo	*Gerakan Rakyat Indonesia*, Indonesian People's Movement, one of the nationalist groupings in the 1930s.
Gestapu	*Gerakan September Tigapuluh*, the 30th September (1965) Movement.
Golkar	The government's political organisation. Until 1988 the name was a contraction of *Golongan Karya*, Functional Groups.
Gotong Royong Parliament	The 283 member 'mutual cooperation' parliament formed by Sukarno in June 1960.
HIP	*Hubungan Industrial Pancasila*, Pancasila Industrial Relations, the official doctrine requiring harmonious relations between labour and capital.
ICMI	*Ikatan Cendekiawan Muslim Indonesia*, Indonesian Muslim Intellectuals Association, formed in 1990.
kabupaten	Sub-provincial district
keterbukaan	Political openness, *glasnost*
KNI	*Komite Nasional Indonesia*, National Committees (local representative bodies during the revolution).
KNIP	*Komite Nasional Indonesia Pusat*, the Central National Committee (1945).
Konfrontasi	Sukarno's 'Confrontation' with Malaysia

	(1963-66).
Konsepsi	Sukarno's 'Conception' or manifesto of government based on deliberation and consensus as an alternative to liberal democracy, promulgated 21 February 1957.
Konstituante	The Constituent Assembly, the product of the 1955 general elections entrusted with the task of drafting a new constitution to replace the Provisional Constitution of 1950. The Assembly was dissolved by Presidential Decree 3 July 1959.
Masyumi	*Majelis Syuro Muslimin Indonesia*, Consultative Council of Indonesian Muslims. One of the 'big four' political parties in the 1950s until its banning in August 1960.
MPR	*Majelis Permusyawaratan Rakyat*, People's Consultative Assembly. The 1000 member assembly which meets once every five years to elect the president and endorse government policy.
Musyawarah Nasional	National (Consultative) Congress, September 1957.
MUNAS	See *Musyawarah Nasional*
NU	*Nahdlatul Ulama*, Resurgence of the Islamic Scholars. One of the 'big four' political parties in the 1950s. After being forced into the PPP in 1973 it withdrew in 1984 over conflicts with the pro-government PPP leadership.
P4	*Pedoman Penghayatan dan Pengalaman Pancasila*, Directives for the Realisation and Implementation of Pancasila, the Pancasila Education courses begun in the late 1970s.
Pamong Praja	The territorial administrative corps
Pancasila	The Indonesian State Doctrine, consisting of five principles currently translated as: Belief in one supreme God; Just and civilised humanity; National Unity; Democracy led by the inner wisdom of unanimity arising out of deliberations among representatives; Social justice for the whole of the Indonesian people.
Panglima	Military commander

Pangreh Praja	Earlier name of the territorial administrative corps (*Pamong Praja*).
PDI	*Partai Demokrasi Indonesia*, Indonesian Democratic Party, created by the government in 1973 from nine Christian, nationalist and socialist parties.
pejuang	Revolutionary fighter
pemuda	Youth. During the Revolution the term acquired militant connotations.
Permesta	*Piagam Perjuangan Semesta*, Charter of the Common Struggle (Sulawesi Utara). Revolt came into the open in February 1958.
PID	*Politieke Inlichtingen Dienst*, Political Intelligence Service of the Dutch East Indies.
PKI	*Partai Komunis Indonesia*, Indonesian Communist Party, banned in 1966.
PKK	*Pembinaan Kesejahteraan Keluarga* or Family Welfare Guidance, a corporate style women's body set up by the New Order.
PNI	*Partai Nasional Indonesia*, Indonesian Nationalist Party. Established in 1927 under the leadership of Sukarno, and re-formed in 1945, it was amalgamated into the PDI in 1973.
PPP	*Partai Persatuan Pembangunan*, Unity Development Party, a broad Islamic coalition party created by the government in 1973.
PPPKI	*Permufakatan Perhimpunan-perhimpunan Politik Kebangsaan Indonesia*, Confederation of Indonesian People's Political Associations, a loose political grouping of the late 1920s.
priyayi	Petty aristocracy, integrated into the colonial civil service.
PRRI	*Pemerintah Revolusioner Republik Indonesia*, The Revolutionary Government of the Indonesian Republic, the rebel government proclaimed on the Outer Islands in 1958.
pusat	Centre, central
santri	The devout Muslim community or orientation.
SARA	*Suku, Agama, Ras, Antar Golongan*, the

	prohibition on inflaming ethnic, religious, racial or communal sentiment.
SBLP	*Serikat Buruh Lapangan Pekerjaan*, Sectoral Labour Unions.
SBSI	*Serikat Buruh Indonesia Sejahtera*, Indonesian Prosperous Workers Union, established in 1992 as a rival to the SPSI.
SPSI	*Serikat Pekerja Seluruh Indonesia*, the government-sponsored All-Indonesia Workers Union.
umat	The Muslim community of believers.

Preface

In December 1992 Monash University's Centre of Southeast Studies hosted a conference at which scholars from a wide range of disciplines and from a number of different countries focussed their attention on problems of Indonesian democratisation. Noting the existence of a renewed interest in Indonesia itself in the parliamentary experience of the 1950s, and recognising that new perceptions of the period form an important element in current political debates in Indonesia, the conference aimed to look again at the 1950s, to consider alternative re-interpretations of that period, to address some of the political, economic and social changes that have occurred since then, and, against that background, to reflect upon the possibility of democratic development in the future.

Clearly at the centre of a program of that kind must lie the classic study of the political experience of the 1950s, Herbert Feith's *Decline of Constitutional Democracy in Indonesia*, published by Cornell University Press in 1962, and indeed the conference was convened as a means of paying tribute to Herb Feith's central contribution to the scholarly study of modern Indonesia.

Herb Feith first went to Indonesia as a raw graduate from the University of Melbourne in 1951. Through the aid of Molly Bondan he had obtained a position as an ordinary *pegawai* (civil servant) in the Department of Information. Out of that experience the Volunteer Graduate Scheme was born. Herb was instrumental in bringing about an Inter-Governmental Agreement between the Governments of Indonesia and Australia for the employment by Indonesia of Australian graduates on ordinary Indonesian civil service salaries. (The VGS anticipated by a number of years America's not dissimilar Peace Corps experiment.) In 1954 Herb went back as one of the first volunteers under the scheme. He and other graduates who went to Indonesia in this way were able to achieve an intimacy of contact with Indonesian colleagues that was not remotely possible for ordinary diplomats in Southeast Asian countries, or for foreign experts under various aid schemes. The Volunteer Graduate Scheme has passed through a number of forms since then, but it lives on as the Australian Volunteers Abroad Program of the Overseas Service Bureau.

As a volunteer graduate Herb watched the political developments of the 1950s at close quarters. He observed the October 17 Affair of 1952. He observed the elections of 1955 and wrote about them for the Cornell Interim Reports series. His next move was to Cornell as a graduate student and his PhD dissertation eventually emerged as the classic and definitive study, *The Decline of Constitutional Democracy in Indonesia*. This work was very much in the political science tradition which characterised much of the post World War II study of modern Southeast Asia. The emphasis was on parties, political dynamics, skill groups, but also with a recognition of the more profound cultural configurations of Indonesian society. It was an authoritative and seminal work which set the agenda for much of the later study of Indonesia in the western world and also in Indonesia itself. And he coupled it with a profound and continuing engagement with the society under study.

He then came to Monash where he has taught Indonesian politics, supervised the work of several generations of graduate students and played a major role in the formation of the Centre of Southeast Asian Studies. An inspirational teacher and a person deeply committed to the subject matter he taught, it would be difficult to over-estimate the importance of his contribution.

Herb's retirement at the end of 1990 has not marked the end of his active involvement in Indonesian studies nor lessened the intensity of his engagement with Indonesia. The conference provided an opportunity for his colleagues and students, from Indonesia and around the Indonesianist world, to pay tribute to his teaching and scholarship.

*****

Indonesian Democracy: 1950s and 1990s — and the years in between — in four days was a tall order. We had initially planned to devote time to assessing different concepts of democracy, but it soon became apparent that this would bog us down and reduce the time available for our rapidly growing list of interesting speakers. Instead the organising committee decided that problems of definition were best left to individual speakers and that the conference should focus on the substance of Indonesia's political history, addressing several questions simultaneously. What really went on in the '50s? How did it appear then and shortly thereafter? Western observers in the post World War II world focused on new nationalisms, and the emergence of new states, on ideological conflict, and on questions of economic development and distribution. The methods used were those of the social sciences: economics, political science, sociology and anthropology. There was considerable confidence on the part of those observers. They had a sense that it was not, after all, so very difficult to understand the dynamics of other societies. And they displayed considerable optimism about the likely trend of events, an optimism that was to be followed by the disappointment of what, from this distance in time would appear to be unreal expectations.

How does all that look from the vantage point of the early 90s? And how do present-day perceptions of the past affect the way in which Indonesian and outside observers now view the present and the future?

Our concern, then, was focussed at several levels. What was it like then? How did observers see it then? Or rather, inevitably, how do they now *think* they saw it then? And how does a present backward look from the vantage point of the 90s get shaped by, and help to shape, current preoccupations?

It will be apparent that we had in mind a reflexive inquiry which not only looked back at past perceptions and at present ones, but which also looked at ourselves looking back and taking stock. Earlier observers constructed their own Indonesia. The conference was encouraged to deconstruct those constructions and to be sceptical, in consequence, about later constructions.

One possible difference between the perspectives of earlier observers of the 1950s and later ones is that, for the former, there was a sense of open texture in their perceptions of events, a sense that had this or that element been different, had this or that mistake been avoided, things could have worked out differently. Had governments been more stable, had regional grievances been addressed more quickly and effectively, had the Army acted differently, the outcome might have been different. It will be seen that they have not entirely lost that sense of missed opportunities. By contrast later observers, looking back after thirty or forty years, might well tend to feel a sense of determinism about the 50s, a sense that what happened was bound to happen. Imagined changes in the details of events wouldn't have made much difference to the main course of events. If that is correct, it might also be the case that, for all their sense of a fixed course of events in the past, later observers probably have a sense of open texture about the present. If certain choices are made, if the political game can be directed in a certain way, the course of the future may be shaped and directed.

The reflexive rationale of the program did not work out quite as originally envisaged but, in a number of papers, attention was paid not merely to current interpretations of the 1950s but to the way in which those interpretations reflect a preoccupation with present day issues. In the first section Ruth McVey undertakes a broad overview of the way in which judgments of the period have changed over time. There follow papers by Herb Feith himself, who gives a highly personal assessment of the way he now sees the period, and by Jamie Mackie and Dan Lev who were close observers of events at the time and who revisit here their earlier conclusions. They retain, perhaps, a perception of lost opportunities. Even in retrospect there is a sense that, with some imagined changes at critical points of the story, the outcome could have been very different. In broadly similar vein Adnan Buyung Nasution presents the fruits of his doctoral research on the constitution drafting process of the 1950s and shows how close the Constituent Assembly came to drafting a genuinely democratic instrument. He, too, notices where choices were made which determined the way events developed. But in identifying the tensions between those who sought constitutional definitions of human rights and constitutional provision to limit State power and those who preferred a more organic model of the State, he argues, perhaps, that the outcome was less open than Feith, Mackie and Lev suggest. Between them these papers help to indicate the main schools of thought into which current interpretations may be grouped.

David Bourchier then explores the image of the 1950s promoted by the New Order and describes how this depiction — emphasising the disjunction between 'anarchic' liberalism and Indonesian culture — has been used to serve the interests of the regime.

George Kahin presents the findings of his recent research into American intelligence gathering in Indonesia, and presents new and important conclusions about the way in which ill-conceived American policy in the 1950s was counter-productive and hastened the demise of parliamentary democracy.

Y. B. Mangunwijaya and Robert Cribb discuss the effect on the 1950s of aspects of the Japanese Occupation and the Revolution. And Greg Fealy challenges received views about the role of Nahdlatul Ulama during the parliamentary period.

Finally Anton Lucas taps the memories of survivors of the Revolution through interviews in which they now recall their expectations.

In the second section of the volume, attention is given to some of the changes that have taken place over the thirty or forty years that have followed the return to the 1945 Constitution and, against that background, to the prospects for democratic development in the future. Clearly it is not possible in a volume of this kind to present a complete political history of the period, and the papers in this section are intended, as it were, to take soundings at several points of time and to identify some of the more significant trends and to reflect the wide range of expectations of different observers.

Harold Crouch outlines what he sees as the main constraints affecting the possibility of democratisation. Ben Anderson considers the long term consequences of the crushing of the Left and the implications of that for Indonesia's radical conscience. Papers by Greg Barton, Abdurrahman Wahid and Douglas Ramage focus on the changing political role of Islam and consider, amongst other things, the success or otherwise of the Suharto government in 'deconfessionalising' politics, the development of pluralist tendencies in modern Islamic thought, and the emerging tensions within the ruling elite about the role of political Islam. Susan Blackburn then examines the nexus between gender and democracy and contrasts the position of women in the 1950s and under the New Order in a way which challenges many of the assumptions underpinning this book. Others examine the role of the media in assisting or resisting the emergence of a more open political system (Paul Tickell), and the pressures for political rights from an increasingly militant labour force in Indonesia (Vedi Hadiz). Three papers address questions of regional and ethnic difference and assertiveness (Audrey

Kahin, Ichlasul Amal and Burhan Magenda). Arief Budiman traces shifting patterns of opposition in the later 1980s and early 1990s while Michael Vatikiotis questions the depth of those changes. Soetjipto Wirosardjono examines the fluctuating interactions between Golkar and the Armed Forces and Ulf Sundhaussen reflects upon the future political role of the Army.

Ken Young and Hans-Dieter Evers identify significant changes in rural society which have implications for politics at the central level. Bill Liddle addresses the question of whether economic growth and democracy are compatible and returns to some of the issues raised in earlier papers — the changing role of Islam, the power, interests and intentions of the Armed Forces, the interests of business, changing class alignments including the growth of a more assertive working class and the prospects for political party development. But he confines himself to indicating possibilities rather than suggesting likely outcomes of current political processes.

Finally Marsillam Simanjuntak explores with subtlety the assumptions embedded in the gradualist approach to change and comes up with some uncomfortable conclusions. Where Ruth McVey's opening paper in this volume looks to no more than incremental changes in the direction of liberalising authoritarian rule Marsillam, at the end, doubts whether 'gradualism' can deliver any liberalisation at all.

****

A conference of this kind calls upon the help of many people. We are grateful, first of all, to the Centre of Southeast Asian Studies and to its Director, David Chandler, for agreeing to host the occasion and for assistance also from the Monash Asia Institute. The organising committee — Dita Axioma, Susan Blackburn, David Bourchier, David Chandler, Gale Dixon, Bob Hadiwinata, Barbara Hatley, Ariel Heryanto, John Legge and Ken Young — worked hard over a long period to plan the conference and to mobilise speakers.

For generous financial assistance thanks are due to the Vice Chancellor of Monash University, Professor Mal Logan who provided an initial seeding grant and made further contributions to costs of the conference, to the Australia-Indonesia Institute which provided fares for a number of Indonesian participants and which funded a very successful experiment in simultaneous interpreting, enabling proceedings to be conducted either in Indonesian or English, and to the Southeast Asian Regional Office of the Ford Foundation for supporting the travel costs of a number of Indonesian participants. *Tempo* and *Kompas* also made contributions to fares.

Organising assistance in Indonesia was provided by the Society for Political and Economic Studies (SPES) and its executive officer, Benny Subianto was an invaluable go-between providing a liaison between the organisation committee and Indonesian speakers. SPES, with the assistance of the Friedrich Neumann Stiftung, will bring out an Indonesian version of proceedings.

On the administrative side, Pam Sayers, Karin von Strokirch and Winnie Koh ran the office, saw to the innumerable problems of accommodation, transport, provision of papers and dealt with thousands of enquires. Lorrie Ryan of the Monash Asia Institute lent willing support.

John Legge
David Bourchier

Part One

THE 1950s

1

The Case of the Disappearing Decade

Ruth T. McVey

Indonesia's first postrevolutionary period has been something of a scholarly Sargasso Sea: an area of confusion in the historical mainstream from colonialism to the present, studded with insoluble or no longer relevant issues on which the academic may strand; a zone, therefore, to be avoided. So while Indonesianists have sounded the depths of the colonial archives, revisited the Japanese experience, and explored the further shores of the independence struggle, they have tended to tack gingerly past the 'weak-state interim of the parliamentary period'(Lev 1990:33) on the way to explaining how Indonesia has come to be the way it is.

New Order spokesmen have been even more emphatically negative: for them, the parliamentary period was a time of political chaos when, with particularist interests and alien ideas given free play, the hard-won unity of the independence struggle threatened to dissipate entirely. The irrationalities of Guided Democracy and the violence of its ending were, in this vision, not a negation of the experiment with constitutional democracy but a consequence of it.

That the present government should portray constitutional democracy in this way is understandable; after all, it is an authoritarian regime anxious to portray its discipline as essential to the nation's salvation. But since many academics working on modern Indonesian politics and history have been liberal foreigners, bound to the New Order neither by sympathy nor by compulsion, their shared wariness needs explanation. After all, the 1950s was the period in which Indonesian politics was most open and most clearly rooted in society; it produced the only really free elections the country has had and witnessed a wide-ranging debate about what the nation should be. Its experience was examined, at that time or shortly afterward, in some of the most significant investigations yet made of Indonesian society and politics. One might therefore have expected the 1950s to be a continuing point of reference; instead, the decade passed into an obscurity which only now may be ending.[1]

It seems to me the reason for the intellectuals' trepidation is in good part ideological — that is, it has been determined by an image of what Indonesia should be like. Overwhelmingly, the shared theme of both Indonesian political actors and foreign observers of the Indonesian scene has been that of the nation-state's realisation of itself. This great vision, the world historical metanarrative for most of the last two centuries, has had a particular urgency in Indonesia, a 'new nation' which had to win independence by arms and which had to create a sense of common destiny where none previously existed. Moreover, even though most of the first generation of those who studied the Republic were themselves non-Indonesian, they were closely bound by sympathy and ideological expectations to the national project, and their writings formed an intellectual framework for subsequent researchers. As a result, the theme of national destiny has set the bounds for analyses of Indonesia, very often subliminally and in fields not overtly connected with politics. It is worth examining the assumptions of this paradigm more closely, as they will tell us something not only about the way in which Indonesia's Constitutional Democracy has been perceived but also about the character of its present political elite.

In the world myth of nationalism, the achievement of nationhood has two aspects, which may occur as historical stages: the acquisition of formal sovereignty and the filling of that form with content. The first is relatively unproblematic; in Indonesia's case, it has usually been portrayed as a direct line of development from the first stirrings of national consciousness among a newly emerging intelligentsia to the accomplishment of the Revolution. The war of independence is the culmination of this stage and the heroic illustration of the project; it is also the last point at which history can be seen as relatively unambiguous. As a result, the Revolution has a legitimising function for the Indonesian political leadership and an attraction for the historian which other periods do not possess.

Once it became a question of filling the form of independence with content, political participants had to decide whether this was best done by stressing things which would make Indonesia the social, economic, and political equal of other nations (that is, those nations seen as setting the international tone) or whether it should be found by excluding that which was foreign to 'Indonesian-ness'. Generally, nationalists have claimed both goals; the crucial question has been the proportions of the mix and the manner of its presentation to the public. The initial post-independence assumption of both Indonesian political actors and their observers was that

---

1. The conference which occasioned this volume is one token of revived interest in the 1950s; we might also note that shortly before it Adnan Buyung Nasution presented a doctoral thesis in the Netherlands on the debates of the Constituent Assembly.

the first course should be emphasised. Summed up as 'modernity,' it had been an integral goal of the national movement from its beginnings. Moreover, the historical lack of a single high culture for the archipelago promised to make an emphasis on national roots both artificial and politically divisive. Nonetheless, as efforts to create a modern Indonesia ran into trouble, the second alternative grew in attraction. Above all, it avoided the frustrating and humiliating measurement of Indonesia's faltering efforts against other countries' apparent success.

This concept of the parliamentary period as an international merit test that was failed has been very influential, both among Indonesians and those who study them — indeed, it very likely contributed powerfully to the subsequent tendency of liberal academics to avoid the 1950s as a subject. For the political decision-makers of the time, the alternative was to claim that international criteria of performance did not matter, were alien, colonialist, and aimed at preventing the nation from discovering its true self. Instead, national values and momentum were sought by recalling (or inventing) appropriate moments of the pre-colonial past and, more particularly, of the Revolution. With the transition to Guided Democracy, the Revolution became mythologised as a cataclysm in which popular energies were fused to produce irresistible force; and the controlled reproduction of this dynamic condition was proffered as the way for the nation-state to revitalise self.

The argument between internal and external criteria for judging Indonesia's achievement took place among academic observers as well, most notably in an exchange between Herbert Feith (1982) and Harry Benda (1982). The latter, reacting to the dichotomy between 'problem-solvers' and 'solidarity-makers' that had formed the leitmotif of Feith's monumental *The Decline of Constitutional Democracy in Indonesia*, suggested that this criterion was too bound to the assumption that Indonesia must imitate Western experience. Granting that Indonesia would eventually 'modernise', he argued it would do so in its own way, after shedding its superficial trappings of Westernism. The task of the historian (and social scientist) was therefore to study the indigenous essences of Indonesia's culture and past, and see how these affected its present, rather than to measure the country against an alien and therefore largely irrelevant model. Feith rejected the extraneousness of the Western model,

> for any government of a complex partly modernised state, as Indonesia undoubtedly is, must concern itself with the efficient discharging of economic functions, and so sponsor various activities which it sees as culturally alien and *a priori* undesirable. (Feith 1982:28)

At the time, Benda's argument seemed to many academics the voice of realism, tempering liberal idealism's great expectations of the consequences of independence. The growing influence of this view was reflected in the subsequent tendency of analysts to explain Indonesian political behaviour primarily in terms of indigenous cultural values. Nowadays, however, we are more likely to respond to Feith's insistence on efficient management of the state apparatus and to agree that modernisation cannot be achieved by telling the world capitalist system to go away from the door. For analysts of the 1990s these are the preconditions of Southeast Asian economic growth, and they are also major legitimating claims of the New Order.

In another respect, however, Feith's position in *The Decline of Constitutional Democracy* diverges from the contemporary approach. He assumed that political democracy was integral to the modernising process and that state strengthening would emerge from cultural enlightenment rather than the other way round. In this, he shared the common Western assumption of the 1950s and much of the 1960s that modernisation was a matter of cultural change, of 'nation-building'. This vision assumed that through education, participation in the immediate levels of government, and the guidance of an elite capable of negotiating the differences between groups, the popular mass in developing countries would come to reject the blandishments of communism and the attraction of allegiances based on the 'primordial' attachments of religion and ethnicity, in favour of a common 'civic culture' which would provide a framework for political debate.

Both Feith and Benda shared an emphasis on the importance of culture — its persistence or its transformation — which is currently out of fashion. What matters now is not 'nation-building' but 'state-building', the creation of institutions that can enforce their will. It is the orientation of leaders, not the mass of the population, that counts; these must have the larger interests of economic growth and national power in mind. They must have the ability, willingness, and political machinery to carry out their program. In this vision, what stands in the way is not so much tradition as the short-sightedness of leaders and the presence of competing sources of power. Interest, not culture, is seen as the wellspring of action.

The theme of state-building arose, in Western political science, out of the concern for social order expressed seminally in Samuel Huntington's *Political Order in Changing Societies*; it reached its climax in the 'rediscovery' of the state in the 1980s and the argument that a strong state — one that was unbeholden to any important social group — was the essential condition of present-day industrialisation. Thus it is the state, not the nation, whose form must acquire content; the state can then stamp its mould on the population. The state deals with primordial loyalties first of all by suppressing them; they may then re-emerge in a highly controlled and re-directed form, as decorations on a centrally-composed theme of unity. The New Order has provided an excellent example of this approach in action.

Although the contemporary emphasis of theory regarding the strong state concentrates on its contribution to economic development, the initial focus was on the imposition of order, and this continues to be the overwhelming concern of the Suharto regime. This order, it is emphasised, is not simply that resulting from the application of force: it is the enforcement of rules. However arbitrarily its minions may act, the New Order seeks to portray itself as the defender of 'normality' and the 'rule of law', the umpire enforcing the ground rules for interaction between Indonesia's social forces.

The 'civic culture' which an earlier era saw as emerging from the consensus of a society learning from political participation now appears as a set of norms — the Pancasila[2] — formulated by the state and assigned to the population as its credo. The time when political norms were debated rather than imposed is portrayed, as we have seen, as an era of disorder and the incubator of violence. While one may refer to the negative example of the parliamentary period, it is best, in this vision, not to examine its details closely, for their airing may revive dangerous emotions and ambitions. The 1950s is, in short, a Pandora's Box whose lid must be kept firmly closed, a conclusion in which, for their own reasons, Indonesian intellectuals and foreign observers have until now concurred.

I should like to suggest that there is another way we can look at the parliamentary period, and that is as a time in which, in spite of — indeed, in part because of — political deadlock, economic decay, and social tension, Indonesia's leading groups began to achieve consciousness of their common interest as a ruling class. One means for this was the parliamentary experience itself, for though parliamentary democracy mobilised mass expectations it could not meet, it also provided an arena for discussion between elites which was vital for preserving the coherence of the state.

This is not to deny that leaders attempted to make or preserve their position by appealing to primordial or class feelings among the populace; all too clearly they did, the more so as faith in parliamentary democracy declined. But observers of postrevolutionary Indonesia have focussed on this centripetal impulse and ignored the limits which most such leaders placed on their own appeals for mass support. After all, it did not require Guided Democracy, let alone the New Order, to defeat the greatest challenges of that period. The Darul Islam[3] was a spent force by the end of it. Similarly, in spite of the inequity of economic and political weight between Java and the Outer Islands, there was very little real separatism. Only in South Maluku was there an effort to break away from the Republic; the 'regional' rebellions of the PRRI (*Pemerintah Revolusioner Republik Indonesia* - Revolutionary Government of the Republic of Indonesia) and Permesta (*Piagam Perjuangan Semesta* - Charter of the Common Struggle) were aimed at overthrowing the government in Jakarta, not at establishing separate states. They drew their main force from divisions within the military that had less to do with local interests than with the question of who headed the Army and how much power he had over his commanders. Even the most

---

2. The Indonesian State Doctrine, consisting of five principles: Belief in one, Supreme God; Just and civilised humanity; National Unity; Democracy led by the inner wisdom of unanimity arising out of deliberations among representatives; Social justice for the whole of the Indonesian people.

3. The Darul Islam movement fought for an Islamic state. Concentrated in West Java, Sulawesi and Aceh, it lasted from 1948 until its leader, Kartosuwirjo, was captured and executed in 1962.

disaffected of the civilian leaders were not willing to take the step which might have gained them vital foreign recognition and aid — the proclamation of a separate territorial state. For that matter the Indonesian Communist Party (PKI, *Partai Komunis Indonesia*), given the choice of pressing its interests at the possible expense of national schism, chose to back Nasution and Sukarno even though this meant accepting martial law and Guided Democracy: the communist leaders were too deeply imprinted with the priority of Indonesian nationhood and too sceptical that class appeals could win out over national loyalties to consider a course that might win Java at the cost of the rest of the archipelago.

When one considers the historical shallowness of Indonesian national consciousness, the weakness of actual central power, and the immediate economic and political advantages which regional elites could garner by setting up on their own, the absence of serious separatism is remarkable. It is proof of the extent to which the 'imagined community' of Indonesian nationhood had taken hold among the archipelago's indigenous elites,[4] and also of the only reluctantly conceded belief that centre-region differences could be mediated by parliamentary democracy. Similarly, the refusal of most Muslim leaders to reject the Republic's rule in spite of their failure to achieve a religious orientation testifies both to their assumption that Islamic goals must be pursued through and not against the Indonesian nation-state and to the fact that the parliamentary system functioned sufficiently well in negotiating secular-religious differences. We should not underestimate the importance of an adequately functioning mediating system for cementing claims to nationhood, however confused the country's politics may otherwise be. The Soviet Union and Yugoslavia show what happens to states which, though apparently authoritative, fail to convince their component elites that their interests are served by remaining together.

At the same time that Indonesia's experience of parliamentary democracy reinforced the conviction that the country should be one, it undermined — or at least caused to be thoroughly reinterpreted — another basic assumption of the independence struggle, namely that legitimacy rests on the popular will. To be sure, there had always been some reservations about this. Popular participation in politics had been debated almost from the outset of the Revolution, and much of the impetus for restricting it came from the most Westernised segment of the elite. The commitment of Feith's 'problem-solvers' to liberal democracy was distinctly tempered by the discovery that the populace did not share their ideas about what needed to be done. Worse, from the mid-1950s the common people showed a growing interest in communism. The problem-solvers found this repugnant ideologically, a threat to their economic and social position, and nationally dangerous because the

---

4. See Benedict Anderson (1983), especially pp.104-128. As an illustration, compare the difficulties Indonesia has experienced in persuading the East Timorese of their shared destiny.

PKI promised to remove Indonesia from the American sphere of influence, which they considered to be the country's inevitable and beneficial international environment. Consequently, they soon began to look beyond the framework of parliamentary politics for puissant support.

Other leaders, influenced by democratic convictions, calculations of partisan advantage, or fear that they would lose their basis for claiming social leadership, were more reluctant to find a non-parliamentary basis for power. But their doubts were already acute, and the economic and political pressures of the final years of the decade choked off what remained of the impetus for popular participation. Guided Democracy was something of a compromise, retaining the symbolism of the Revolution and the masses while restoring much of the power of the *pamong praja* (the territorial administrative corps) and entrenching military participation in all levels of decision-making.

One result of this was the gradual emergence of an anti-populist pole centred on the Army. It formed the political undertow to what Sukarno was pleased to call the wave of the Revolution; and when that wave broke in October 1965 it was strong enough to carry the country in quite the opposite direction from its surface momentum. Indeed, in some respects it swept politics back to the beginnings of postrevolutionary Indonesia: the reappearance on the political stage of such early problem-solving icons as Sumitro Djojohadikusumo and the Sultan of Yogyakarta proclaimed the resurrection of military-civilian affinities and agendas that had been suppressed but never eliminated.

Early observers of this alliance were more struck by its military component than the civilian, helped in part by the idea of the 'military as modernisers' which had taken hold among American political scientists anxious to justify the rising tide of third-world anti-communist military takeovers. As a result they were much more impressed by the Army's assumption of a special destiny in Indonesian politics than by what I think is the ultimately more important fact that the higher Army echelons became increasingly involved with relevant segments of the civilian bureaucratic and political elites.

We can see this in the social evolution of the officer corps. Though the postrevolutionary military had rusticated its least educated and cosmopolitan officials, throughout the 1950s its members had been generally of somewhat lower educational level and certainly had less social prestige than the equivalent ranks in the civilian bureaucracy. By the end of the decade, however, high *priyayi* families were increasingly linking themselves to the officer corps by marriage, as a source of protection and advantage and because they increasingly saw eye to eye on such issues as the threat of communism and the need to demobilise the population politically.

With the seizure and military management of Dutch enterprises, and Army participation in civilian administrative bodies under the State of Emergency proclaimed in 1957, officers gained experience and connections in economic and bureaucratic milieux. Nor was this the first involvement of many important officers with economic affairs. Suharto's career provides a rich illustration of the importance business connections had for financing Army commands both during the Revolution and the 1950s. What was most evident to observers at the time was the corruption and mismanagement produced by officers' involvement in economic affairs; what was perhaps more important for the New Order was the extent to which it helped to push bureaucratic and military elites towards a common appreciation of the problems the country faced.

Because of its rhetoric, its anti-Westernism, and the increasing favour which Sukarno showed the communists, we tend to remember Guided Democracy as a time of mass mobilisation. But it was not, except ceremonially; in practice the instruments for the elimination of popular choice were created (or revived from colonial times), while increasing economic decline and social unrest contributed powerfully to an unspoken but widening elite opinion that national decision-making needed to be freed from demands from below. Sukarno, of course, could not admit this, for his legitimacy rested on his claims to be the spokesman of the People; and the political left similarly needed to have the masses and the Revolution remain central to political justification if not to actual decision-making. But they, too, conspired to reduce popular participation to theatrics, in the interest of preserving national unity and preventing an open breach between military-led conservatism and populist radicalism. In the end they were hoist with their own petard: when, forced by economic disorder, revolutionary rhetoric, and popular impatience the break came, neither Sukarno nor the communists were willing (or perhaps thought they had a chance) to respond to the crisis save by further manoeuvrings among the elite.

I do not mean to imply by this that Guided Democracy's particular end was inevitable. Just as observers of 1950s Indonesia in this volume have noted that the defeat of Hatta and the problem-solvers did not seem assured at the time, and that the concatenation of events was decisive, so we cannot say that Guided Democracy was bound to collapse as it did. Rather, the point is that the spread of an elite sentiment on the need for popular demobilisation and for an authoritative regime centred on the Army was very important for undermining the Old Order and for the smooth construction of civilian-military cooperation in its replacement.

The 'strong state' that emerged from the wreckage of Guided Democracy was thus not built on new ground but on a consensus which had been slowly and painfully laid. It meant the new regime had a cadre of political, administrative, and military personnel whom experience had convinced that popular participation in politics must be strictly limited, the country must accede to the realities of world power and economic relationships, and that what mattered was the material accomplishment of 'development' rather than the realisation of a national essence or an international ideal. The power of Indonesia's 'strong state' rested not just on ruthless military suppression of opponents but on a broader elite consensus on what needed to be done.

One reason why the New Order appears so different from what preceded it is that the popular mass has vanished from the political stage. The violence with which it left has been taken as the sign of revolutionary upheaval, but while in certain respects the change was cataclysmic — certainly for those who were the victims of it — its systemic repercussions were more modest. We need only consider the very large number of politicians whose careers spanned Constitutional Democracy, Guided Democracy, and the New Order to remind ourselves that, at the elite level, more was conserved than was lost in the changes of regime. The order-threatening aspects of popular participation were exorcised by the massive and largely state-sponsored violence with which the communists were eliminated. From now on, the Army as national saviour would replace the popular will as a central source of legitimation. Replace but not eliminate, for we see the issue returning today.

Analysts of contemporary Indonesia have tended to deal with those social forces which act within the parameters of the system; and since the 'floating' mass of the population participates in politics only through the state ritual of elections, meaningful stirrings outside the ruling group appear to be restricted to segments of the educated and/or entrepreneurial elite. In the absence of any visible possibility of acquiring a mass following (about which, in any case, they have decidedly ambivalent feelings) these groups engage in a direct if highly unequal dialogue with the state.

The image of a small band of critics confronting the huge mass of the state has a particular poignancy in its recall of the beginnings of the nationalist movement.[5] It has also brought about something of a revival of the Benda-Feith debate, expressed with particular clarity in comments by Daniel Lev (1990) and William Liddle (1990) in a 1986 conference on the politics of the Indonesian middle class. Here Lev took a 'Feithian' position, arguing that the growth of educated 'middle strata' provided a force for change which would — given the present overwhelming presence of the Indonesian state in society — necessarily press for a reduction of state authority and an opening out of the possibilities for debate. A 'Bendaist' Liddle demurred, asserting the New Order's legitimacy in the eyes of those Indonesian social forces that count — especially the Army, whose leadership is enshrined in the system. The New Order has rewarded the middle class, he pointed out, and it will not really bite the hand that feeds it. Therefore '[President Suharto] and his colleagues have built a political system that will outlast their incumbency.'(1990:58)

Both these arguments stress interest rather than culture, state power rather than national coherence. Both centre on a confrontation between officialdom and a bourgeoisie which is increasingly influential but without real roots or interest in rural or working-class Indonesia. Which view, in another

---

5. See, for example, the article by Benedict Anderson in this collection.

generation, will seem the more 'realistic'? Or will their shared assumptions no longer seem addressed to the heart of the problem?

Only history will provide the answer to this, but we might discuss some of the points raised by the debate. To start with the most specific, let us consider the importance of the political character of the Indonesian Army, with its ideological self-consciousness, its insistence on its permanent centrality to political life, and its permeation of economic, administrative, and political structures. Certainly the Indonesian Army's view of itself and its place in society (which only emerged gradually, from the late 1950s) is different from that of the 'classic' military regime, where army takeovers are rhetorically conceived as temporary measures to save the nation and will be replaced by a return to barracks when the crisis passes. In fact, the Indonesian Army's self-assumed role is much more like that of an established communist party — perhaps not wholly by accident, given the TNI's long rivalry with and envy of the Indonesian Communist Party's organisation.

Nothing prevents a monolith of this type from presiding over capitalist expansion, as Deng's China shows. However, capitalism creates centres of power outside the state apparatus, which ultimately limit the autonomy and authority of the state and its ruling organisation. Moreover, in the long run monolithic organisations tend to become sclerotic and to lose touch with society at large. The problem is likely to emerge even earlier with an army than with a mass party, for the military lacks even a ritual connection with voices from below. Moreover, the fact that already many sons of military men choose non-military careers points to the likelihood that the Indonesian military will not encapsulate itself as a caste. It seems much more probable, assuming Indonesia's continuing capitalist development in a post-Suharto era, that the Army's special role will fade into rhetoric along with the revolutionary experience. Military leadership would then become increasingly embedded in a broader ruling class, and its interventions would be on behalf of larger alignments rather than the preservation of military prerogatives *per se*.

Certainly Liddle has a point that there are distinct limits to the amount of democratisation contemplated by the Indonesian 'middle class'.[6] The

---

6. 'Middle class' is a term much used and little defined by social scientists. In the volume in which the Lev-Liddle debate occurred, contributors used it to mean the bourgeoisie generally, members of the bourgeoisie who were not state functionaries, segments of the bourgeoisie which occupied 'middling' positions in the socio-economic elite, and so on. It is as much a cultural as an economic or political category, for it depends on a self-consciousness which gives rise to the perception of a distinction between civil society and the state. That is a very modern notion, and it requires the existence of both an elaborate administrative apparatus and a sizeable educated and relatively well-off urban population. On the whole, since — as we shall see below — 'middle-class' consciousness of a difference between state and social interests can extend into the upper levels of the governing elite, the middleness of the 'middle class' is not that crucial, and it might be clearer if we referred to a bourgeoisie, understanding this to include the salariat.

dialogue between liberal critics and the state has its David-vs-Goliath appearance because it takes place in an arena that has been cleared of other participants. The liberals are interested above all in increasing their room for expression, creating a space that is not dominated by the state. The concern some have to eliminate arbitrariness in the treatment of the population at large does not mean that they would wish to mobilise wronged groups to seek redress, even if this were allowed by the authorities. The Indonesian bourgeoisie has as little interest as the New Order state in re-opening the Pandora's Box of mass participation, primordial loyalties, and class resentment. What is likely to keep the Indonesian state an overwhelming political presence for some time to come is the fear that behind the façade of the strong state lies a weak one, and that any opening-up of political participation beyond the urban elite must be handled very carefully indeed.

Within these sharp limits, however, there is likely to be pressure towards constitutionalism. It is not just a matter of values received from abroad (though the force of world ideas is something that should not be underestimated). A developing capitalist economy creates both a greater demand for rule-based, rational administration and a pool of relatively well-off, influential, and educated people who are not dependent on the state for their livelihood but feel they should have a voice in how it is run. These may well be children of bureaucratic and military power-holders: for preference or for lack of availability, many offspring of senior officials do not pursue careers in state service. Increased contact between state and business, and the increased complexity of social and economic organisation, makes for a self-conscious ruling class whose interests stretch across the upper echelons of the military, government, business, and the professions, and for a growing demand for an authoritative forum in which these elite segments can negotiate their differences and determine their priorities. And the same process produces pressure for political representation for elites at more local levels.

Finally, although the extension of political participation to the mass of the population is likely to be undertaken very gingerly, with great concern not to repeat the mobilising of unsatisfiable demands, some form of representation and debate is necessary to state security as a source of intelligence on the political currents among the masses and a means of mediating between the population and its rulers. The more urbanisation and market relationships replace custom and patronage, the more urgent this becomes. In other words, constitutional democracy has its uses, and it is not accidental that it is a form identified historically with the development of capitalism.

But in considering the future prospects of Indonesian Constitutional Democracy, we need to bear some caveats in mind. First, the fact that government has a democratic form does not always mean that it has a democratic content. Constitutional form does not automatically fill with the ideologically appropriate content; on the contrary, often enough the purpose of adopting the form was to deflect pressures for providing the content. It is perfectly possible for a formally liberal democratic system to offer the mass of the population no real choice at all — the pre-Marcos (and post-Marcos?) Philippines provides an example. Similarly, constitutional democracy does not always mean social justice. It is possible for a highly authoritarian regime to be more conscious of the need to provide benefits to the populace than a democratic one: compare the rural development efforts of the New Order with, again, the Philippines. The Indonesian government's motive may have been based on considerations of state security rather than concern for the wellbeing of the multitude — perhaps the PKI's preeminent contribution, and no small one, was to convince military leaders that it was dangerous to ignore popular welfare entirely — but it has meant that something was done.

Academic observers often draw a sharp line between democracy and authoritarianism which in reality is not always there. In part this comes from the imposition of ideal types on a more ambiguous reality — the social scientists' mania for interring messy humanity in neat theoretical boxes — and in part from a tendency for Anglo-American concepts of democratic practice to dominate political scientists' thinking. But, particularly in a case like Indonesia's, the real changes in the foreseeable future are likely to be incremental shifts in behaviour and perception, the re-interpreting of existing institutions, and only in a very late stage (if indeed it seems necessary at all) a symbolic reformulation of rule.

In one respect the perception of outside observers has changed since the debate on Indonesian democracy began. Although the current enthusiasm for 'strong states', 'autonomous rulers', and 'developmental authoritarianism' may well prove a passing fashion, it is certainly true that the international model for modernisation no longer assumes that constitutional democracy (or its one-time alternative, communist totalitarianism) is a precondition. If anything it is viewed as an end product, obtainable when an authoritative elite has transformed the economy and society to such an extent that it can support the 'civic culture' which will enable responsible popular participation.

This fits well with the Indonesian bourgeoisie's 'Pandora's Box' caution towards democratisation; it is also a more realistic presentation of what has preserved Western democracies. To maintain social stability, Western elites have had to find ways to present the populace with choices that seem real but do not unduly disturb the existing order. People must be persuaded that there is no systemic alternative, that betterment will come only by perfecting established institutions. There must therefore be a high degree of social consensus, a blinkering-off of alternative visions, a reduction of debate to 'manageable' issues. Demands must be restricted to what is realistic (which is to say, what those who rule are willing to concede), for great and unfulfilled mass expectations have been the undoing of many democracies, including Indonesia's of the 1950s. All this is not just a matter of discipline and indoctrination, but also of the ability of rulers to apprehend and ameliorate conditions which the ruled find intolerable. The people must have reason to believe in the system, lest in desperation they transfer their faith to another. After all, when Pandora's Box was emptied of its disintegrative forces, what remained in it was hope: and hope, if allowed to escape, can be the most terrible threat to an established order.

References

Anderson, B.R.O'G, (1983) *Imagined Communities*, Verso, London.

Benda, H.J. (1982) Democracy in Indonesia, in B.R.O'G. Anderson and A. Kahin, (eds) *Interpreting Indonesian Politics: Thirteen Contributions to the Debate*, Cornell Modern Indonesia Project, Cornell University, Ithaca. (Reprinted from the Journal of Asian Studies, May 1964)

Feith, H. (1982) History. Theory, and Indonesian Politics: A Reply to Harry J. Benda, in B.R.O'G. Anderson and A. Kahin, (eds) *Interpreting Indonesian Politics: Thirteen Contributions to the Debate*, Cornell Modern Indonesia Project, Cornell University, Ithaca. (Reprinted from the Journal of Asian Studies, February 1965)

Lev, D.S. (1990) Intermediate Classes and Change in Indonesia: Some Initial Reflections, in R. Tanter and K. Young (eds) *The Politics of Middle Class Indonesia*, Centre of Southeast Asian Studies, Monash University, Clayton.

Liddle, W. (1990) 'The Middle Class and New Order legitimacy', 'Indonesia is Indonesia' and 'East Asian Political Development', in R. Tanter and K. Young (eds) *The Politics of Middle Class Indonesia*, Centre of Southeast Asian Studies, Monash University, Clayton.

2

Constitutional Democracy: how well did it function?

Herb Feith

In mid-1966, when General Suharto first opted for the term 'New Order' to describe the regime he was founding, the 'Old Order' against which he was defining it referred principally to the previous seven years, to what is usually called the 'Guided Democracy period'.

That association of the 'Old Order' with the Guided Democracy period was dominant for the next 15 or so years. The 'New Order' was depicted in antithesis to an 'Old Order' referring mainly to 1959-1965. Government spokespeople trained their fire on such 'Old Order' evils as the rising power and arrogance of the Communists, the bitterness of growing 'primordial' conflict and the 'lighthouse to the world' stances of a president who waged battle against imperialism and neo-colonialism abroad while allowing his own country to suffer economic rundown and administrative chaos.

But in the last 10-15 years that focus has gradually shifted. As it has become more difficult to think of Suharto's period of rule as new, it has become necessary to find new ways of describing the order he founded. The term 'New Order' continues to be used, but increasingly it has been supplemented and occasionally eclipsed by the term 'Pancasila Democracy'. Whereas there was previously an antithesis between the New Order and the Guided Democracy period immediately before it, the dominant antithesis today is between 'Pancasila Democracy' and the 'Liberal Democracy' of the period before 1959.

Since 1977 Indonesians have been going to government-run Pancasila courses. In that time they have heard bad things not only about the Guided Democracy period but also about the 'liberal democracy' which preceded it, usually said to date from December 1949 to July 1959. That 'liberal period' is depicted as one of pointless imitation of Western political forms, of persistently petty party bickering, of frustratingly deadlocked government, of primordial antagonism and religious-ideological polarisation that benefited nobody but the communists, and of rebellions that almost destroyed the country's territorial integrity.

But that conventional depiction has not gone unchallenged. In the last ten years or so people associated with opposition groups like the Petition of 50 have been telling another story about the 1950s : that ministers and senior civil servants lived simply and accessibly, that big-time corruption was rare, that the courts were independent of even cabinet ministers and top military officials, that the Afro-Asian Conference held in Bandung in 1955 was a triumph for Indonesia's good name in the world, that the elections of that year were honest and peaceful.

In view of these shifting judgements it is worth asking again how well or badly did the constitutional democracy of the 1950s really function.

A personal note on nostalgia and self-vindication

I am hardly an objective observer in relation to a question like that. Like most others of my age — I was born in 1930 — I am nostalgic about the years of my youth. I first arrived in Indonesia in July 1951 and spent over four of the next six years there. I had a wonderful time in those years and so I loved the Indonesia of the liberal period. Those feelings continue to shape my perceptions of that time, and so affect my preferences about the kind of country I would like Indonesia to become.

The nostalgia is, however, counterbalanced by my need to take account of what I have written about the period, especially my *Decline of Constitutional Democracy in Indonesia*. That book was written in 1959-61 — at a time when constitutional democracy seemed a lost cause all over the Third World — and it paints a fairly black picture. Much of it is about the way the people committed to the attempt to make constitutional democracy work were repeatedly frustrated and defeated. Much of it stresses the weakness of this group and the way they were often overwhelmed by the populist nationalism of the time, by the militant anti-colonialism of the *bekas pejuang* (the ex-fighters) of the Revolution. Much of it is about the ineffectiveness of government. Much of it reads as if the cards were stacked against constitutional democracy from the beginning.

In this paper, then, I am attempting to steer a course between nostalgia and self-vindication.

The record of Constitutional Democracy: the negative side of the ledger

It is amply clear that there are many respects in which Constitutional Democracy operated in dismaying, frustrating ways. The following are six examples, taken from the period before the system went into its terminal crisis:

1. The Natsir, Sukiman and Wilopo cabinets (September 1950 to July 1953)

were disappointingly short-lived, though they lasted longer than most of the eight cabinets of the 1945-49 period. Each of them fell with its longer-term policies unimplemented. The Hatta-ish policies of economic stabilisation and administrative regularisation which each of them pursued were unacceptable to a political public in which populist anti-imperialist passions ran high, a public which looked back nostalgically to the Revolution as a time of spirit, purpose and symbolically satisfying leadership.

2. After the abortive half-coup of 17 October 1952 the Army split into two blocs, one close to the Wilopo cabinet, the other close to President Sukarno, bringing the country to the brink of civil war.

3. In early 1953 President Sukarno, a figurehead president under the 1950 Constitution, engaged in an oratorical slanging match with the fiery Masyumi leader, Isa Anshary, on whether the replacement of the Pancasila by something more specifically Islamic would lead to Christian and Hindu areas splitting away. Consensus on the purposes of the state was undermined, with the President appearing as a partisan opponent of Islam.

4. The long election campaign of 1953-55 aggravated socio-religious and ethnic conflict in many urban and rural communities throughout the country, and especially *santri-abangan*[1] conflict in ethnically Javanese communities. The mood of that period — which prefigured the much fiercer conflict aggravation of 1963-65 when *santri-abangan* and right-left conflict were compounded by faster inflation and by land and succession issues — is vividly depicted in Clifford Geertz's account of a local religious official refusing to bury an activist of the small Javanist-leftist party, Permai.[2]

5. The PNI-led first cabinet of Ali Sastroamidjojo (August 1953-July 1955) allowed the election funding interests of its parties to distort macro-economic policy. It accelerated indigenisation of business in ways which generated a new level of inflation. It also aggravated the politicisation of the bureaucracy by sacking senior officials for their Masyumi and Socialist Party (PSI) sympathies. Its Masyumi-led successor, the Burhanuddin Harahap cabinet (August 1955-March 1956), then followed its example by sacking large numbers of PNI-sympathising officials.

6. Central authority came under challenge in a new way in 1954, when military commanders in some prosperous exporting regions of Sulawesi began to endorse smuggling operations in the name of the welfare of their soldiers. Local support for their actions reflected anger in those regions about the inflation and the increasingly unreal exchange rate. It also reflected a

---

1. *Abangan* = the nominally Muslim or spiritually syncretist community (or orientation) in Java. *Santri* = the devout Muslim community or orientation.

2. Geertz (1957). The way parties functioned in Javanese village society in the pre-election period (and the contrast with their roles in the villages of other ethnic communities) is brilliantly analysed in Geertz (1959). Recent research in Central Java suggests that villagers in some parts of this province now conflate the 1953-55 and 1963-65 periods, seeing them as all part of a single *jaman poyok-poyokan* (time of exchanging insults). See Pranowo (1991).

new anti-Jakartaism and anti-Javanism, and associated sentiments of anti-communism and anti-Sukarnoism.

Malfunctioning in the transition period

The most clear cut examples of the malfunctioning of the system come from its period of terminal crisis. In retrospect this period may be seen as beginning with the reappointment of A.H. Nasution as Army Chief of Staff in October 1955. This surprising and initially mysterious appointment prefigured a new possibility: that the President and the Army leadership, which had hitherto been pulling at the system of cabinets and parties from opposite ends, and thereby neutralising each other, might make common cause against the system.

Disappointment with the results of the 1955 elections, new ethnic and anti-Chinese movements, the President's promulgation, in February 1957, of his 'Conception' of government based on deliberation and consensus as an alternative to '50% plus one' majorities, the emergence of Hatta-sympathising regionalist movements in Sumatra and Sulawesi, and the dramatic takeover of Dutch business in December 1957 — all that came to a climax in February-March 1958, when a Padang-centred group associated with the regional movements proclaimed the Revolutionary Government of the Republic of Indonesia (PRRI), catalysing civil war.

In the following weeks Indonesia arguably came close to territorial breakup. That might have been the outcome if the covert CIA support for the Permesta counterparts in East Indonesia had been followed up by full-scale American endorsement. By the middle of 1958 the PRRI challenge had been substantially defeated and so the Sukarno-Army coalition emerged victorious. The defeat of the Hatta-sympathising forces set the stage for the transformation of the party and parliamentary system into 'Guided Democracy'.

In February 1959 the Army leaders persuaded Sukarno to move towards readoption of the authoritarian and rights-poor (but 'revolutionary') 1945 Constitution. In the following months the Sukarno-Army coalition tried to push that through the elected Constituent Assembly. That attempt failed, mainly because the Masyumi members of the Assembly were able to persuade the Nahdlatul Ulama members to join them in blocking it. Unable to win the necessary two-thirds majority in the Constituent Assembly, Sukarno re-enacted the 1945 Constitution by decree, dissolving the Assembly at the same time. With that action parliamentary democracy was formally ended.

In seeking to evaluate how well or how badly the system of parties and parliament functioned one can usefully distinguish the transition period of 1956-59 from the 1949-56 period. There are a few respects in which the system actually functioned better in the transition period than earlier. For instance coalition politics operated benignly in the period of the second Ali Sastroamidjojo cabinet (March 1956-March 1957), when the PNI (*Partai*

Nasional Indonesia, Indonesian Nationalist Party) and Masyumi cooperated once more and the tit-for-tat sackings of the two preceding cabinets (Masyumi and PSI officials being replaced by PNI ones by one cabinet, and PNI officials by Masyumi and PSI ones by its successor) were stopped. But in general the post-1956 period was one of aggravated malfunctioning, especially because of the way left-right and Java-Outer Islands reinforced each other in those years.

On the other side of the ledger, Constitutional Democracy worked well in many important ways. It had its benign balances, policy successes and positive dimensions of spirit.

Benign balances

1. The *Dwitunggal* (Duumvirate) of Sukarno and Hatta was a powerful symbol of national unity, and especially of unity between Javanese and non-Javanese, hub and periphery.

2. The *Pamong Praja* (territorial administrative corps) provided an important element of ballast in the system, as did the Secretary-Generals of Ministries and other key functionaries like Jaksa Agung Suprapto and Police Chief Sukanto. In provincial and *kabupaten* (district) government the professionalism and expertise of *Pamong Praja* officials countervailed the party-dominated and often youth-dominated provincial assemblies.

3. Governments made good use of foreign resources in several respects. It is true that there was little new foreign investment, except in oil. There was also a good deal of disinvestment, for instance slaughter tapping of rubber trees on the estates of foreign companies who believed they had no future in Indonesia. But many foreign companies were successfully forced to put Indonesians into senior staff positions. A lot of Indonesians got training and schooling in the outside world: Army and Police people in the US; Navy and Air Force people in the US and Eastern Europe; civilian trainees, undergraduates and post-graduates in the US, Western and Eastern Europe and Australia.

In addition good use was made of foreigners in various government agencies, not only of Dutch people who had been in Indonesia before 1949 but also of non-Dutch people from all over the world, including partisans of the revolutionary Republic like Molly Bondan, Poncke Princen, Carmel Budiardjo and Tom Atkinson, and UN experts, some of whom became Indonesia specialists e.g. Nathan Keyfitz and Benjamin Higgins.[3]

4. The system did reasonably well in accommodating the extremes of Right and Left. The communists were enabled to work within it and so were most of the militant Muslim groups, though this was not the case where Muslim militancy was compounded by regionalism, as it was in South Sulawesi (the

---

3. On the ways in which foreigners fitted into Indonesian government bodies in this period see Willner (1970 especially pp.278-288).

Kahar Muzakar movement, which became a rebellion in 1951) and Aceh (the Daud Beureueh-led rebellion of 1953).

Policy Successes
1. The governments of the period had major policy achievements in education and health and also in macro-economic policy, raising production, controlling inflation and raising export levels.
2. The cabinets and the Army were successful in winding down rebellions which had grown out of the Revolution, the Murba (Proletarian Party)-connected *Bambu Runcing* (Bamboo Spear brigade) or *Tentara Rakyat* (People's Army) of West Java, the PKI-connected *gerombolan* (gangs) of the Merapi-Merbabu Complex in Central Java and the Republic of the South Moluccas, and they made some progress against the Darul Islam of West Java.
3. Indonesia established a good name for itself internationally as a leading non-aligned state, partly because PSI and PNI influences were complementary in the fashioning of foreign policy. The major achievement was the Bandung Afro-Asian Conference of April 1955, arguably the Third World's first summit conference.

Positive dimensions of spirit
1. The press was very free, with a lot of variety, a lot of irreverent wit, especially in the cartoons and the *pojok* columns, a lot of subtlety and occasionally very penetrating analysis.
2. The courts enjoyed a great deal of independence, even in cases involving ministers, Army officers and party leaders.
3. Parliament as an institution attracted strong commitment, thanks partly to the leadership of its chairman, the PNI's Mr. Sartono. It got a lot of business done and relations with the executive were reasonable most of the time. Parliamentary debate was in some respects of high quality. The recent biographical research of Djin Siauw on his father, the Baperki[4] chairman and parliamentarian, Siauw Giok Tjhan, confirms that there were many friendships across party and ideological lines.
4. There was little inter-religious tension. I know of no church burnings except in some areas of Tanah Toraja controlled by the Kahar Muzakar group.
5. The Chinese minority was effectively protected against racist violence (at least until 1956).
6. The *pemuda* (youth) and *bekas pejuang* (definitely not *mantan pejuang*!) groups whom my *Decline* book treats as a problem for the functioning of Constitutional Democracy, played positive roles too, for instance former

---

4. Baperki = *Badan Permusyawaratan Kewarganegaraan Indonesia*, Deliberative Association for Indonesian Citizenship, a largely Chinese Indonesian organisation, founded in 1954.

Student Army people who worked as teachers and spreaders of the message of the Revolution in faraway parts of the country.

7. Partly because of the fast expansion of schooling, it was a period of rapid vertical mobility, with many people from the lower ranks of urban and village society rising rapidly (see Jaspan 1958).

8. The poise and confidence of political leaders and officials rose markedly from the early 1950s to the middle and later part of the decade.

Why then was Constitutional Democracy swept away? New themes and old in a long-running debate

If Constitutional Democracy worked reasonably well in these important respects, why was it swept away? That question will almost certainly continue to be a source of hot debate.

According to Rahman Tolleng, it is misleading to ask why Constitutional Democracy failed. It did not fail, he argues. It was killed off, by a Sukarno-Army coalition.

Rahman Tolleng's argument, put to me at a seminar at Yayasan SPES (Society for Political and Economic Studies) in Jakarta in May 1992, made me realise that my 1960s writing about the Constitutional Democracy period was conservative in a way that I had not previously appreciated. It is partly that I was attracted in the late 1950s and early 1960s to forms of social science analysis in which factors are more important than actors. In addition, I made too much of the 'legitimacy collapse' which set in in the middle of 1956, and gave insufficient attention to the dramatic changes of late 1957.

As Jamie Mackie argues in this volume, two relatively minor events of late November and early December 1957 — an adverse vote in the UN General Assembly on Indonesia's claim to West Irian and an abortive attempt to assassinate Sukarno — catalysed a third of vast importance, the snowballing seizure, first by PNI and communist unions and then by the Army, of the whole large remaining Dutch business empire. This action, followed by the sailing away of almost all ships of the KPM's inter-island fleet and the departure of almost all Dutch nationals, a total of 46,000, led to far reaching economic chaos but also to a dramatic change of political fortunes. At the time of the MUNAS (National Congress) in September 1957 the expectation was that the right coalition of Hatta and the rebel regional councils would be able to force Sukarno to a compromise. By the middle of December the wind had turned, with a prospect emerging that the left coalition of Sukarno, and Nasution's central leadership of the Army, would win out.

The ways in which the central question about the Constitutional Democracy of the 1950s is asked are manifestly important. The older pattern was to ask why it collapsed or disintegrated or why it was abandoned. Ulf Sundhaussen's paper in this volume, like his 'Indonesia: Past and Present Encounters with Democracy' (1986), reflects the older formulation, as does Bill Liddle's 'Indonesia's Democratic Past and Future' (1992). The new historiography, represented in this volume by Dan Lev, Buyung Nasution and Jamie Mackie, asks why it was overthrown, defeated, sabotaged or killed off.

Some versions of the new formulation imply that responsibility for the overthrow of the old system should be allotted primarily to the Army (or General Nasution, or Nasution and his Javanese fellow leaders of the Army, or Nasution and his mentor Prof. Djokosutono). Others imply that the more important instigator of the change was President Sukarno. All however agree that there was close cooperation between the two components of what became the ruling coalition of the Guided Democracy period.

All this has given an old debate new interest. But the older formulation of the key issue remains central. Stated more less neutrally, the question is: why was the system swept away?

Here too it is possible to discern a central disagreement between two clusters of thinkers. On the one hand are historians and students of Indonesian culture, many of them with a principal focus on the history and culture of the Javanese, who argue that the 1950s attempt to institute a constitutional democracy was doomed from the start because only a handful of Western-minded political leaders were committed to it, a fact which reflected the weakness of liberal and social-democratic ideas in the Indonesian nationalist movement. In this view, classically argued by Harry Benda (1964), Constitutional Democracy ran against the grain of Indonesian history.

That position is complemented by that of many economists and other developmentalists, Indonesian and non-Indonesian, who argue that attempting to institute a constitutional democracy in Indonesia in the 1950s was pointless and historically premature because the central task of any society at that level of development or material-technical complexity is development and the overcoming of mass poverty. The implication here is that constitutional democracy, whatever its merits, is likely to be a brake on economic development.

Over and against these two positions is the argument of a varied group of Indonesians and non-Indonesians who see constitutional democracy as culturally possible in the 1950s and now, and historically relevant in both periods, and who argue that the experiment with constitutional democracy failed for various contingent reasons.

The range of factors adduced here is large. Some writers have stressed that independence was achieved at a time when only a handful of Indonesians had had experience of senior positions in a modern state. Others have emphasised that the Dutch had provided Indonesians with almost no experience of representative institutions.

It has also often been argued that Indonesia's party system failed because it was not a two-party system. That had sometimes been seen as connected with the fact or presumed fact that it was Dutch-modelled. Was the *aliran* pattern not an adaptation of the long-established *verzuiling* ('pillarisation') of Dutch party life? In addition proportional representation has been said to be a cause of the malfunctioning of the party system of the 1950s.

Some writers are interested in the comparative lack in the 1950s of a strong single party. Indonesia had neither the one-party-dominance structure provided for India by its Congress Party (the product, it has been argued, of a relatively enlightened colonial policy in which representative institutions were built early) nor the totalitarian structure of communist Vietnam (that communism sometimes being traced back to the harshly repressive character of French colonial rule).

My own emphasis was and remains on the weakness of the state vis-a-vis society and of the roots of this in the fact that Indonesia achieved its independence by revolution. The immediate predecessor of the 1950s period was a turbulent period of social and economic as well as political change, which followed a turbulent and far-reachingly disruptive Japanese occupation. That background meant that the immediate post-1949 period generated predispositions to militant politics of many kinds, nationalist, communist and Muslim.

Let me end with a brief word about the connection between interpretations of the end of Constitutional Democracy of the 1950s and arguments about democracy and constitutionalism today.

As I see it there are four main streams in current Indonesian political thinking. Seen as a right-left continuum or arc they are: integralism, developmentalism, critical pluralism and radical democracy (see Feith 1991; Feith and Castles 1988).

The Benda position that the Constitutional Democracy of the 1950s ran against the grain of Indonesian history and culture, is characteristic of today's integralists. A version of it is presented in Nugroho Notosusanto's writing, notably in the final volume of *National History of Indonesia* (1977), which David Bourchier discusses in this volume, derived forms of which are widely used in Pancasila courses and in the high school subject *Pendidikan Sejarah Perjuangan Bangsa* (Historical Education in the Struggle of the Nation).

The argument that constitutional democracy was abandoned because it was historically premature in a country as poor as Indonesia then was is characteristic of today's developmentalists, or the more conservative of them, and it, too, is part of the reigning orthodoxy.

On the other hand radical democrats like Arief Budiman and Indro Tjahyono, or critical pluralists like Abdurrahman Wahid and Goenawan Mohamad are more commonly attracted to explanations which stress contingent factors to explain why the Constitutional Democracy of the 1950s was defeated. They tend to believe that things could easily have worked out differently in the late 1950s.

That optimistic view is also attractive to some of the less conservative and more actively democratic of the developmentalists. This group includes Sarwono Kusumaatmadja, whose strategies for democratisation are examined in Bill Liddle's paper in this volume and the Army reformer General Soemitro, whose thought is discussed in Lane (1991).

References

Benda, H.J. (1964) 'Democracy in Indonesia', *Journal of Asian Studies*, May 1964.
Feith, H. (1962) *Decline of Constitutional Democracy in Indonesia*, Cornell University Press, Ithaca.
_____ and Castles, L. (eds) (1988) 'Pengantar Edisi Indonesia' (Introduction to the Indonesian edition) 'Pemikiran Politik Indonesia, 1945-1965', LP3ES, Jakarta.
_____ (1991) Democratisation in Indonesia: Misleading Rhetoric or Real Possibility? in D.J. Goldsworthy (ed) *Development and Social Change in Asia*, Centre of Southeast Asian Studies, Monash University, Clayton.
Geertz, C. (1957) 'Ritual and Social Change: A Javanese Example', *American Anthropologist*, Vol.49, No.1 1957.
_____ (1959) The Javanese Village, in G.W. Skinner (ed) *Local, Ethnic and National Loyalties in Village Indonesia*, Yale University Southeast Asian Studies.
Jaspan, M.A. (1958) *Social Stratification and Social Mobility in Indonesia*, Djembatan, Jakarta.
Lane, M. (1991) *'Openness', Political Discontent and Succession in Indonesia: Political Developments in Indonesia, 1989-91*, Centre of the Study of Australia-Asia Relations, Griffith University.
Liddle, R.W. (1992) 'Indonesia's Democratic Past and Future', *Comparative Politics*, July 1992
Notosusanto, Nugroho (1977) *Sejarah Nasional Indonesia*, vol.VI, Balai Pustaka, Jakarta, (2nd edition)
Pranowo, B. (1991) *Creating Islamic Tradition in Java*, doctoral dissertation, Department of Anthropology, Monash University.
Sundhaussen, U. (1986) 'Indonesia: Past and Present Encounters with Democracy' ms later published as Indonesia, in L. Diamond, J. Lintz, S.M. Lipset (eds) *Democracy in Developing Countries*, Volume 3: Asia, Adamantine Press, London 1988.
Willner A.R. (1970) The Neotraditional Accommodation to Political Independence: The case of Indonesia, in L.W. Pye (ed) *Cases in Comparative Politics*, Little Brown & Co, Boston.

3

Inevitable or Avoidable? Interpretations of the Collapse of Parliamentary Democracy

Jamie Mackie

Why did Indonesia's attempt at parliamentary democracy in the 1950s fail? And what lessons can we draw from that episode about the prospects for movement towards a more democratic system of government in the 1990s? The first of these questions is much easier to answer than the second; but there seem to have been so many reasons why the odds were heavily stacked against the success of the democratic experiment that it is easy to slide unwittingly towards a myth that it was bound to happen. Yet if we adopt anything like an inevitability argument we have to ask what reasons there are for optimism that things have changed sufficiently since then to justify hopes that democracy might somehow take root in present-day circumstances, since they are even less encouraging in some respects, given the entrenched power of ABRI (*Angkatan Bersenjata Republik Indonesia*, the Indonesian Armed Forces) and its utter lack of enthusiasm for the ideals of the democratic reformers.

The next section of this paper will look into some of the implications of the question, 'Was it inevitable?', with special reference to the relevance then and now of the lack of deep-rooted democratic traditions in Indonesia and the sorts of value systems that sustain them. Then we will turn to Feith's explanation of why the parliamentary system collapsed, then to the events of the crucial years 1957-59, noting several occasions when events might easily have taken a very different turn. Finally, I will look at some of the lessons of the 1950s for the prospects of democracy in the 1990s.

Was it inevitable?
In a review article on Feith's book, *The Decline of Constitutional Democracy in Indonesia*, Harry Benda (1964) charged him with having addressed the wrong question: 'Why on earth did anyone seriously expect democracy to succeed in Indonesia, when all her past history and cultural traditions had pointed in the opposite direction?' The call by the nationalist leaders in the 1930-40s for more representative forms of government, parties, elections and parliaments was prompted more by tactical considerations, according to Benda, than any real conviction or commitment to democracy, or to the beliefs and values that usually accompany them. The democratic rhetoric and institutions of the colonial rulers had simply constituted the most successful formula to use in prising concessions out of them, as well as in winning support among opinion makers in the Netherlands or USA or Australia.

That is all true enough. But should we simply accept Benda's view as the last word on the subject? The main question to be asked here is whether the failure of parliamentary democracy in the 1950s really was as inevitable as has sometimes been suggested, simply because there was so little fundamental commitment to the institutions and values of democracy, or whether it might have been avoided if events had turned out just a little bit differently? I want to advance the latter case, that if the forces supporting Hatta had won out over President Sukarno in the power struggle that was being fought out through 1957-58, the *denouement* or regime crisis of Feith's story, as I believe they very nearly did in 1957, the later course of Indonesian history might have been very different indeed. It could have meant no shift to Guided Democracy in 1959 (or a very different type of regime, not Sukarno's creation but Hatta's), no *Konfrontasi* against Malaysia in 1963-65, no hyper-inflation in the 1960s and the opportunities it provided for the PKI to surge towards the gates of power in 1963-65, no Gestapu and hence no New Order.

Whether or not that was really a possibility we should take a sceptical attitude to explanations of the success or failure of democracy solely or primarily in terms of basic value commitments or cultural and political orientations towards authority, deference to hierarchy, individual freedoms, rights of dissent, or preference for consensus over party contestation, or community solidarity over minority views. These arguments are frequently heard in relation to the disillusionment with democracy that developed in Indonesia in the 1950s (and in several other countries besides Indonesia, at that time). If we reject the view that the failure of democracy in Indonesia was due mainly to the lack of such value commitments, what alternative explanation can be given for the collapse of parliamentary government and the party-based political system in the late 1950s, so soon after the 1955 general elections. My own answer would be that the odds against the success of that system were very high in the circumstances then prevailing, and were made higher by several sudden twists in the way events turned out in the course of the power struggles of 1957-58, as we shall see below. But with a bit more luck, or less bad luck, things might have turned out very differently.

Feith's explanation

The best explanation anyone has yet given of the events of 1956-59 is to be found in chapters 10-11 of Feith's *Decline*. The history of the 1950-59 years, he says, was:

> the story of the political failure of the Hatta group of leaders, a generally Western-oriented group who were in power in 1949 partly because Indonesia had needed to seek Western diplomatic support in order to win its independence.... Among this group there were some with value commitments to constitutional democracy, and most had commitments of interest.

This group, the core leaders (many of them PSI members or sympathisers) among the 'administrators' in Feith's illuminating administrator vs. solidarity-maker dichotomy, exerted a dominant influence on government policies in the years 1950-53, trying to tackle basic administrative, military and economic problems with some degree of success, but not enough to create 'a new rule-based politics' and to stabilise the postrevolutionary situation of ferment and high expectations.

> But they failed. The property basis of their power was always weak. And the military basis of it, the fact that their supporters had preponderant control over the army, was to be proved destructible.... They antagonised a powerful group of former revolutionaries, the men who stood to lose wherever appointments were made or credits dispensed on the basis of training or ability ... rather than on the basis of services to the cause of the Revolution. And they antagonised many of the same men by their efforts to make the whole process of government rule-based; for the ex-revolutionaries demanded that the state should have momentum and mystique. For all these reasons the Hatta group were eventually overwhelmed by opposition. In the middle of 1953 they were forced out of government power.

At the very end of his book, Feith quotes from Hatta's 'Past and Future' speech in order to contrast the views of those who wanted the national Revolution to be 'dammed up' and of those who wanted to 'use or fan political unrest' against them.

> In the last analysis constitutional democracy was defeated by the way in which the contest between these two views was resolved.... Both the battle itself and its outcome were important in bringing about an end to constitutional democracy. Neither a rule-based government nor a largely coercion-free government could be maintained for long in the face of persistent, and persistently restimulated, revolutionary ferment.

No one could fairly accuse Feith of being either an inevitabilitarian or a reductionist in his explanation of the decline of constitutional democracy or the defeat of the more strongly committed supporters of democratic institutions in Indonesia at that time. But he was trying to single out what he saw as the most deeply rooted set of factors relevant to the explanation, even though he would have admitted that a multifactoral explanation had to be given. Class-based explanations were obviously unconvincing, but he did not rush to the opposite extreme of invoking a 'cultural' explanation; instead he tried to give a quasi-structuralist account in terms of skill groups, backed up also by an emphasis on the political and social ferment of the times, the unrest and heightened expectations engendered by the revolutionary struggle for independence.

The 1957-58 turning-point

After the event, it is easy to tell the story of the course of events between the parliamentary crisis of early 1957 and the military showdown that occurred in February-March 1958 as if there were a remorseless inevitability to it all. That was not at all the way it looked to be at the time, however, nor does such an interpretation stand up to closer scrutiny today. On the contrary, it was widely believed throughout most of 1957 that the regionalist forces opposing Sukarno and Nasution had the highest trump cards in their hand and would ultimately win out in the politico-economic struggle being played out, because the Outer Islands produced nearly all of Indonesia's export produce and crucial foreign exchange earnings, without which the Jakarta government (and Java, which was heavily dependent on imports and had little export potential) would soon collapse (van der Kroef 1958; Mackie 1958). Inflation began to accelerate soon after the change of government and the rupiah depreciated steadily at a more alarming rate than ever before — for which President Sukarno was now more directly responsible than previously, although even less successful than his predecessors in finding remedies. No progress was being made towards resolving the regional crisis either by political or military pressures or by negotiations and compromise, for the extent of the barter trade in 1957 was steadily increasing, thereby enriching the regional authorities while depriving the central government of more and more foreign exchange revenue, without which it could not survive indefinitely.

Until December 1957, the basic political dynamics of the situation seemed to indicate, if anything, that the central government would eventually lose out in the protracted tug-of-war that was being fought out, unless it could mount a successful military attack on West Sumatra and North Sulawesi. But such an attack seemed to be out of the question for a number of reasons. One important one was that Nasution's position as Army Chief of Staff was highly controversial among top Army officers, another that the deep factional and divisional rifts within the Armed Forces created serious doubts about the degree of obedience and moral authority he or the central command could rely on in a crisis situation.

Throughout 1957, it was the central government (under Djuanda as Prime Minister from April onwards) that was the more conciliatory party and the regional authorities who remained intransigent and unwilling to compromise, being confident in their superior economic strength. Only at the *Musjawarah Nasional* in September 1957, one of the major highlights in the course of events over that year, did they appear even remotely willing to do so. But they made no significant concessions even then, or over the next two months, when the ever more rapidly deteriorating economic situation seemed to be working inexorably in their favour. At the end of November, however, quite out of the blue, the political situation changed dramatically as a result of three almost simultaneous events — a flare-up of anti-Dutch hostility after an adverse UN vote over the status of West Irian, the attempted assassination of President Sukarno (the 'Cikini affair'), followed by a series of snowballing 'take-overs' of all Dutch enterprises by labour unions and the official expulsion of Dutch nationals during the course of the next week.

Those events marked a sudden lurch to the left in the trajectory of Jakarta-level politics, precipitating the chain of events which led eventually to the decision by the regional rebels (and some Masyumi leaders who had joined them, Sjafruddin Prawiranegara and Natsir, most notably, as well as Professor Sumitro of the PSI) to force a showdown with the pro-Sukarno forces in the form of the proclamation of the PRRI-Permesta rebellion in February, after earlier issuing an ultimatum calling on the President to appoint a Hatta-led anti-communist cabinet.

Nasution was able to take advantage of the sense of emergency and crisis that had built up over the previous ten weeks to muster the forces he needed to mount an amphibious expedition against West Sumatra in March, later against North Sulawesi also, both of which quickly overcame the local resistance much more quickly than anyone had expected. By the middle of 1958 the regional rebellions had been effectively defeated (although it was to be another three years before the leaders surrendered) and the political situation completely transformed. Sukarno and Nasution were now riding high, but Hatta and his supporters were rendered virtually impotent. Most important of all, the Army leadership was now firmly in the saddle, after resolving the regional crisis that the parties and parliament had been unable to tackle effectively.

It is easy to imagine, however, that this could all have turned out very differently if events had taken a slightly different turn at any one of several points. I will mention just four such moments, without much elaboration. First, if the attempted assassination of Sukarno at Cikini had not occurred on the day after the UN vote on West Irian, at the end of November, at a time when tensions and tempers were running high for a number of reasons, the sharp swing to the left would probably not have happened. It is unlikely that the labor unions would have been able to push through the take-overs of Dutch trading enterprises, plantations and above all the crucially important KPM inter-island shipping line in the way they did over the following week, largely under PKI influence and instigation, in defiance of orders by the cabinet and Army leadership (acting under Martial Law powers) to desist.

The Army finally stepped in to put the Dutch enterprises under its own control simply to forestall the unions and the PKI; but nationalisation was an almost inevitable next step which had become politically unavoidable by then. The elimination of the Dutch economic stake in Indonesia was certainly a major historical turning point and it was a key factor in precipitating the anti-communist challenge from the regional rebels which crystallised into the political-military showdown of January-February 1958. Yet it was neither planned nor inevitable that events would turn out that way.

Second, if the PRRI leaders and their Masyumi-PSI supporters had not made the disastrous miscalculation in the following weeks that they must force a showdown by launching an open challenge to Sukarno in the form of the PRRI ultimatum, there would have been no need for the invasion of West Sumatra, so the regional dissidents' position of strength vis-a-vis the government would probably have been maintained well into 1958, as the national economy deteriorated exponentially. The belief that because of the lurch to the left the entire country was slipping rapidly towards economic chaos and political disintegration apparently triggered the decision by the PRRI leaders to challenge Sukarno openly. That turned out to be a fatal mistake, for it now became much easier for Sukarno and Nasution to mobilise the Armed Forces to crush the regional rebels, something that they could not have achieved a few weeks earlier.

Third, but going back in time a little, it can be argued that events might easily have taken a radically different turn at or soon after the National Congress (*Musjawarah Nasional*) in September 1957. If Hatta and the regional leaders had taken a more uncompromising stand against Sukarno at that meeting, instead of agreeing, as he finally did, to a meaningless but politically damaging (for him) joint statement holding out the possibility that he might be induced to work towards a restoration of the old Dwitunggal arrangement, the fact that the National Congress had simply failed to yield any significant results would have been starkly apparent.[1] Sukarno would then have come under great pressure in the weeks that followed to find another strategy to deal with the regional challenge, either by offering real concessions to the *daerah* or by trying to mobilise the Armed Forces against them, something that had not been possible previously and was unlikely to have changed significantly since then. As it happened, the Committee of Seven, established at the National Congress to resolve the military leadership problem, was reportedly moving by the end of November in a direction that

---

1. Apart from the symbolically important announcement in the National Congress final communique about the 'reuniting' of Sukarno and Hatta in their agreement to work towards the restoration of the *Dwitunggal*, the only substantive outcome of the entire meeting was a decision to set up a Committee of Seven to try to work out a formula to resolve the problems that had arisen over the military leadership since Nasution's reappointment as Army Chief of Staff in late 1955. Hatta and the Sultan of Yogya were both on that Committee, so the political balance was evenly spread.

might have led in due course to the removal of Nasution as the price to be paid for restoring Army discipline. We can only guess at how events might have developed if it had reached any sort of decision that would have represented a political setback for Sukarno and Nasution, except that it would surely have made the PRRI rebellion of February 1958 less likely rather than more. But after the turbulent events of early December nothing more was ever heard about the deliberations of that Committee.

Fourth, and going even further back in time, it can be argued that the reappointment of Nasution as Army Chief of Staff in November 1953, by Sukarno and in the face of opposition from the Masyumi, which was then the major party in the cabinet, was one of the precipitating factors in the entire military crisis that developed through 1956-57 and which had a lot to do with the regional revolts (Feith 1962:442-4,520ff). If that had not happened, as is easily conceivable, the later course of events could well have been profoundly different.

Clearly then there were a number of elements of sheer chance, coincidence and accidents of judgment or timing which influenced the course of events over the six months or more prior to the PRRI rebellion. Things might easily have turned out very differently and there was certainly nothing preordained about the final outcome. Yet the defeat of the PRRI-Permesta rebels and the pro-Hatta elements (as loosely defined) in Jakarta who were sympathetic to them was unquestionably a key factor in the demise of parliamentary democracy at the hands of Sukarno, Nasution and other advocates of a strong executive power under the 1945 Constitution.

The inevitability argument

The most carefully argued formulation of the argument that the events of 1957-58 were in some sense inevitable was set out in two rather similar articles by Bruce Glassburner and Hans Schmitt in the early 1960s, not long after they had both returned to California after teaching in the Economics Faculty at the University of Indonesia. They had been there throughout the 1957-58 regional crisis and the collapse of the parliamentary regime. Schmitt's argument focussed on monetary policy and its impact on various social groups. Essentially it boiled down to the following linked propositions:

i. Inflation and the undervalued exchange rates of the 1950s hurt exporters (mainly the Outer Islands) and benefited importers (Java, and Jakarta in particular).

ii. The Masyumi represented the former politically and the PNI-NU-PKI group the latter. Traders tended to align with Masyumi, bureaucrats with the PNI group.

So the political polarisation that had been developing from 1952 onwards seemed to be linked, and could be completely explained, in the last resort, in terms of the interest groups on both sides and their policy preferences. There was therefore a striking consistency and a kind of inexorable historical logic leading both sides towards the clash that reached its climax in 1957-58.

A second strand in this argument (and in Glassburner's, later) was that the anti-inflationary policies being pursued by Trade and Finance ministers upholding the Masyumi/export-sector interest in having a stable currency regime worked also to the benefit of Dutch capital, which still dominated the big plantation sector, banks and commercial houses handling the bulk of export and import trade. The Jakarta elite became increasingly divided during the 1950s between 'those who preferred foreign dominance to monetary chaos' and 'those who would risk financial stability to rid the economy of Dutch control' (Schmitt 1963:181). That dichotomy was more or less identical with Feith's administrator/solidarity-maker dichotomy, but with an even more compelling economic logic behind it. Schmitt's basic reasoning ran as follows:

> It was the uneven incidence of the burden of inflation which determined what indigenous interest groups backed each party.... Had the Dutch withdrawn or been expelled earlier, perhaps the need for inflation — and therefore the inducement for rebellion — might have been less.

Glassburner (1971:98) told the same story within a less iron-clad framework of determinism and inevitability, although he finally came to much the same conclusion. His approach differed from Schmitt's in that he rejected the latter's attempt to demonstrate a logical or historical necessity behind what happened; in fact, he claimed that the line of division between the two camps had not been as sharply defined as Schmitt depicted it. In a later account, co-authored with Ken Thomas (Thomas and Glassburner 1965), he allowed far more for the contingent and the unforeseen, stressing the unpredictable, almost accidental character of the events of December 1957. These gave rise to the nationalisation of Dutch enterprises which the PKI and other leftist forces were able to bring about, despite the fact that there had been no prior cabinet-level discussion of, or planning for, such an outcome, or even prior intent on the part of the ministers primarily concerned, who were aghast at what happened.

It was not inevitable that the takeover of Dutch enterprises would occur when and as they did, although once they had occurred there was a kind of fatal logic behind the spiral of events that then led on to the PRRI challenge to Jakarta and the long-delayed military showdown between centre and regions. It is therefore easy and tempting to say that what happened in Indonesia in the late 1950s simply had to happen. From there, it is also easy to slide on to the conclusion that democracy was bound to fail — and that is an argument I believe we should reject as simply fallacious. It often seemed, indeed, that there was a sort of zany inexorable logic to so much of what happened in that period, particularly in the two months prior to the PRRI rebellion. But the failure of democracy didn't have to happen. It happened because the people who were fighting for the cause were outmanoeuvred at that time by people who were not committed to it, for very much the reasons that Herb Feith has delineated. But it could easily have gone differently, regardless of the Glassburner-Schmitt argument for the inevitability of another part of the story.

Lessons for the 1990s

The lessons to be learnt from a closer examination of the various reasons for the collapse of parliamentary democracy in Indonesia in the 1950s will depend largely on the kinds of questions we ask about what happened then and our intentions in asking them. If we want to believe that its collapse was unavoidable and that the only solution to the problems facing Indonesia in 1957-58 was either military rule or the kind of 'strong government' that Sukarno and Nasution proposed after the defeat of the PRRI-Permesta rebellion in the form of a return to the 1945 Constitution, then we are likely to argue, as Sundhaussen (1989) has done, that the civilians who were leading the political parties had failed to cope with the threats to national unity and that democracy had proved an unsuitable form of government for Indonesia. Such arguments have almost become part of the national mythology since than, a key element in the justification of the Army's prominent role in the government. Like all myths, it needs clear-eyed reassessment from time to time. The alternative argument advanced by Lev that parliamentary democracy was deliberately undermined by the advocates of 'strong government' is perhaps overstated, but at least it deserves serious examination. There may be an element of truth in it, but how much? In both cases, the assessments we make of their truth or falsity will colour our attitudes to the possibility that a more democratic regime might work better in the very different circumstances of the 1990s.

Myths such as the notion that democracy was not suitable for Indonesia, or that the party politicians were solely to blame for what went wrong then, not the military leaders in the *daerah* or the *pusat*, are still thrown up at advocates of even the most moderate steps towards a more pluralistic or participatory system of government ('You don't want to take us back into that sort of chaos, do you?'), as if there could be no doubt about the validity of those interpretations of what went wrong between the 1955 elections and 1959. My argument here is that there must be a reconsideration and reinterpretation of those events at a time like the present, or many such. Was it in fact 'democracy' as such that was to blame for the problems that arose in the late 1950s — and, if so, which feature of 'democracy' — or was it that a parliamentary system was then in use rather than the presidential system created by the 1945 Constitution; hence that was the source of weak executive authority? This is a complex analytical question which depends on both the definitions we attach to those terms and on the adequacy of the historical data we select as relevant to the story we tell.

That sort of reinterpretation will have to be carried out mainly by the younger generation of Indonesians, particularly the historians and political scientists, who will be engaged in formulating and debating the most appropriate form of government to be created in the years ahead, in accordance with their visions of Indonesia's future. An outsider can do little more than draw attention to some of the historical problems relevant to these debates and the implications of the arguments advanced on both sides. The conclusions or lessons to be drawn about them are ultimately for Indonesians to determine. Two of the myths in common currency about the decline of constitutional democracy are worth considering briefly here as examples. One is that the parliamentary and party system was too divisive for a society which put great stress on social harmony, the politicians excessively self-seeking, corrupt and lacking in concern for the national interest; hence Sukarno and the Army had to step in to uphold the national interest and provide firm government. The other is that 'liberal' democracy was not in accordance with Indonesia's *kepribadian nasional* (national identity) and value systems; so it had to be modified by the creation of 'Guided Democracy'.

There is a grain of truth in both these arguments, but only a small grain. It cannot be denied that the mobilisation of party support in rural areas prior to the 1955 elections was widely regarded as excessively divisive and alarming by villagers unfamiliar with the process. Whether that was really true, or an adequate reason to swing to the opposite extreme of depoliticisation of rural areas, as in the 'floating mass' doctrine of 1972, is a matter that we need to reconsider now that elections are no longer a novelty, as they were then. Likewise, the *koehandel* ('horse trading') of political party leaders in the 1950s was certainly regarded as self-seeking, corrupt and destabilising in comparison with the sense of idealism and self-sacrifice that had inspired the preceding years of struggle for independence. Yet that had enabled Sukarno and the Army leaders to sweep the parties aside. The political arrangements which were then introduced have not proved much better in those respects, however, under the Old Order or the New, merely less open and accountable.

In conclusion, I want to summarise what I consider to be the most important conclusions to be drawn from my interpretation of the events of the late 1950s and their relevance to the debate about any future democratisation in Indonesia in the 1990s.

First, the immediate cause of the regime crisis which led to the collapse of the parliamentary system in the late 1950s was the threat to national unity posed by the regional rebellions. Their defeat by the Army in 1958 brought about a major shift in the power balance which decisively weakened what I have called the pro-Hatta forces and cleared the way for the advocates of strong central authority to impose the 1945 Constitution upon the Constituent Assembly. Nothing like that is likely to occur today, not even the kind of succession crisis that might conceivably arise at the end of President Suharto's time in office, which is unlikely to amount to more than a minor scuffle within the elite.

Second, the collapse of confidence in parliamentary democracy in 1956-57 was precipitated by that regime crisis because of the failure of the parliament, parties and cabinet to resolve the challenge from the regional dissidents whose aim was to overthrow the Ali Sastroamidjojo cabinet. It was the belief that party-based government was intrinsically weak, divisive, unstable and incapable of solving the nation's economic problems, that the cabinet's fall became a full-scale 'regime crisis', as Feith called it, leading over the next two years to martial law, nationalisation of the Dutch enterprises and the 'return to the 1945 Constitution' in July 1959. The situation today is almost the reverse. The shortcomings of the New Order political system today stem not from any failures of the political parties and parliament but from the excesses of authoritarian and bureaucratic control. The executive arm of government is very strong under the 1945 Constitution, but the legislative and representative arm has been greatly weakened. There is a lot of scope for strengthening the latter without going back to the bad old days of 1957-58. So it is appropriate that, in their efforts to strengthen the parties and parliament (*Dewan Perwakilan Rakyat* or DPR) the advocates of greater democratisation should re-examine the experiences of the former parliamentary system as a guide to the future.

Third, the roles played by Sukarno and the Army in pressing for substantial changes in the political system, culminating in the 1958-59 drive to 'return to the UUD 1945' were crucially important in undermining popular support for the parliament and parties at that time. But in the 1990s the situation is again very different. Although the excessive power of the government and the weakness of the representative bodies mandated by the Constitution are widely regarded as the major problem, the calls for reform are mostly of a gradualist rather than of a fundamental character. Even President Suharto and senior military leaders have supported the case for some movement in that direction. A regime crisis is less likely to arise over demands for democratisation than over the succession to Suharto.

Fourth, the lack of consensus within both the cabinet and the society more broadly in the late 1950s was undoubtedly a major factor behind the collapse of popular support for the institutions and practices of parliamentary democracy. Feith was right to draw attention to that as one of the key factors underlying the chain of events he was trying to explain. It was easy for Sukarno to exploit the prevailing disillusionment with 'liberal democracy' in his Konsepsi speech and his earlier 'Let's bury the parties' speech' after his return from China, where he was much impressed by Mao's one-party rule. In the 1990s, however, there is broad consensus now on a wider range of basic issues than there was then. There is nothing like the deep polarisation of political life that had developed in the late 1950s between the pro-Sukarno parties and their opponents, but a variety of cross-cutting political alignments.

Hence the prospects for progress towards a more democratic or representative type of political system, however that may be defined, are more favourable today in all these respects. As we have seen, the factors which caused the collapse of democracy in the 1950s are not now posing threats comparable with those that crippled the post-election government in

1956-57. It is authoritarian rule that is being called to account for its inadequacies in the 1990s, not democratic government.

Moreover, the socio-economic problems that crippled Indonesia's governments of the 1950s in their efforts to achieve 'development' under extremely difficult conditions (and at a time of unrealistically high expectations) have largely disappeared since then, mainly because of the New Order's successes on that front. The momentum of growth that has been achieved should be much easier to maintain in the years ahead, either by a more democratic government or an authoritarian one, despite the many problems still to be overcome.

Finally, a larger and more self-conscious urban middle class is slowly emerging, increasingly like the new middle classes in South Korea, Taiwan and Thailand which have spearheaded the drive for democratisation there in recent years, although Indonesia has still the smallest and weakest such class in the region, both economically and politically. We should be careful to avoid jumping to the conclusion that there is some causal correlation between the growth of a middle class and the pressures for democratisation. Many other factors come into the equation also (see Crouch and Morley 1993). On the other hand, it will almost certainly become increasingly difficult for any Indonesian government, whether authoritarian or semi-democratic, to disregard middle class demands for greater openness, accountability, fairness, participation, regularity in legal and administrative procedures and so on, as the economy becomes more complex and prosperous. Whatever progress in that direction may occur in the 1990s will probably be gradual and incremental, a widening of 'democratic space' under pressure from the middle class and professionals, as in Thailand and Taiwan, rather than a dramatic regime change, as in 1957-59. If we can achieve a deeper understanding of the reasons why democratic institutions failed to resolve the problems facing Indonesia in the late 1950s, we will be better able to demolish the myths that have become prevalent about the unsuitability of all forms of democratic government which the opponents of reform are still using to resist that progress.

References

Benda, H.J. (1964) 'Democracy in Indonesia', *Journal of Asian Studies* (May 1964) [reprinted in B. Anderson and A. Kahin (eds) 'Interpreting Indonesian Politics: Thirteen Contributions to the Debate' (Cornell Modern Indonesia Project, Ithaca, 1982)]

Crouch, H. and J.W. Morley (1993) The Dynamics of Political Change, in James W. Morley (ed) *Driven by Growth: Political Change in the Asia Pacific Region*, M.E. Sharp, Armonk, New York.

Feith, H. (1962) *Decline of Constitutional Democracy in Indonesia*, Cornell University Press, Ithaca.

Glassburner, B., (ed) (1971) *The Economy of Indonesia: Selected Readings*, Cornell University Press, Ithaca.

Mackie, J.A.C. (1958) 'Indonesia, the Search for Stability', *Australia's Neighbours*, 3rd series, Nos.87-88

Schmitt, H., (1963) 'Post-Colonial Politics: A Suggested Interpretation of the Indonesian Experience', *The Australian Journal of Politics and History*, No. 9, Vol. 2, 1963.

Sundhaussen, U. (1989) Indonesia, in L. Diamond, J. Linz & S.M. Lipset (eds) *Democracy in Developing Countries*, Volume 3: Asia, Adamantine Press, London.

Thomas, K., and B. Glassburner (1965) 'Abrogation, Take Over and Nationalisation: The Elimination of Dutch Economic Dominance from the Republic of Indonesia', *Australian Outlook*, Vol.19, No.2, 1965

van der Kroef, J.M. (1958) 'Disunited Indonesia', *Far Eastern Survey*, 27 (4-5)

4

On the Fall
of the Parliamentary System

Daniel S. Lev

Whatever else it did, the disintegration of party government in Indonesia early in 1957 ignited a blaze of interesting and useful analysis, producing new knowledge and provocative perspectives, deeper understanding of just about everything Indonesian except the original problem: why did the parliamentary order fail? Nearly everyone who took the question seriously defined it as complex — fortunately, for had it been thought simple, some of the fertile research that followed might not have been done. As there is no need to worry about that any longer, maybe we can return to the problem defined simply and therefore amenable to simpler answers. Defined simply, the problem is less 'What caused the collapse?' than 'Who caused the collapse?' 'What?' raises more interesting and subtle questions, but 'Who?' is more precise and, incidentally, forces us to look more sceptically at our answers to 'What?'

My own simple (and only slightly diffident) answer to the simpler question is that the Army did it. Why? In part because it could, but also because it had compelling interests in a quite different political system. There is little question that from March 1957 onwards the Army was directly involved, nor that after February 1958 Nasution and those around him took the principal initiatives to which everyone else, including Sukarno, had to respond. But when we read backwards from these years in Kahin and Feith especially, it is clear enough how politically active the Army was from the start. And if we then place the officer corps in the foreground rather than in the shadows of parliamentary politics, it is relatively easy — admittedly in the light of what we know happened later — to see the Army not as a gradually evolving political force that was drawn reluctantly into play, but rather as one that was ambitious, interested, assertive, and engaged from the beginning.

For whatever reasons — upward mobility, the revolutionary experience, the ideologising influence of the Darul Islam campaigns, local pressure on military resources — Army leaders evidently conceived their organisation politically almost from the start, as a kind of estate that was wrongly (even wrongfully) disenfranchised, but entitled to a share of political authority and much else. Nasution proclaimed the Army's middle-way, now the *dwifungsi*, in 1958, when reality needed a name and Djokosutono supplied it, but the essence of the formula must have existed at least by October 1952 and probably earlier. Contempt for the parties and civilian leadership may have generated a conviction not only that civilians had no right to dictate terms to the Army, but that the officer corps could do a better job of running the country. Emphasising this point alone, however, dilutes the solution. Were officers simply reacting to a bad situation, or did they, individually and collectively, also have distinct interests to pursue, making it more likely that they would act consistently rather than merely grumble and occasionally lash out?

In and out of Indonesia, much of the rumination about why the parliamentary system failed runs suspiciously parallel to the public reasoning of Sukarno, Nasution, and even Suharto, who draws on both. I wonder whether we haven't bought too easily into what are, essentially, their rationales. Guided Democracy (and the New Order) raised two basic issues about the parliamentary system: that it had no cultural roots in Indonesia and that the party system was divisive, exacerbating serious conflicts over religion, class, and ethnicity. Even if true, these charges do not fully explain why Sukarno and the Army acted as they did, or at least they imply a rather benign effort on their part to save the country. But were the accusations accurate, or was reality more mixed and ambiguous, as one would expect?

For all that the faults of the parliamentary system have entered into the canon in discussions of modern Indonesian political history, the internal weaknesses of it were less impressive than the power of those who wanted to bring it down. After 1950 parliamentary government in Indonesia worked no more problematically than in a few other countries where it survived. If so, why was it not possible to rework political institutions, if this was necessary, within a still constitutionalist framework? (This question naturally raises others, not yet altogether satisfactorily answered, about the survival or collapse of constitutionalist systems, and not only in new states.) In Indonesia, a standard answer has been that the party system was not only divisive but the parties themselves were barely committed to parliamentary values. The Constituent Assembly (*Konstituante*), for example, was and still is held responsible for subordinating the pressing need for a new, permanent constitution to its debilitating compulsion to debate the merits of Islam and the Pancasila.

Yet a closer look at the work of the Constituent Assembly — which Buyung Nasution makes available in his dissertation at Utrecht — demonstrates persuasively that this accusation is not true. During the troubled years 1957-1958 the Constituent Assembly came near to completing a constitution in which careful attention was paid institutional relationships, control over executive authority, and civil rights; and it was these 'liberal' concerns, not the grand (yet possibly negotiable) ideological confrontation, that preoccupied the Assembly through most of its short life until early 1959. Was it the possibility that the Constituent Assembly might actually produce a constitution that moved Nasution to force the issue of restoring the 1945 Constitution? Maybe, but the more relevant point here is that the Assembly's deliberations provide ample evidence that there were no constitutionalist values around.

What was lacking, though it may not have made a difference, was enough courage among party leaders in early 1957 and thereafter to put up a determined (or even interesting) defence of the parliamentary system. The ease with which all parties but the PKI gave up in 1958 indicated, as much as anything else, not so much a weak commitment to Republican values as an utter collapse of confidence, deeper perhaps than that of Fourth Republic France, but in the face of an opposition that had little or no constitutionalist inclinations at all, and, in the case of the Army, one that had a great deal at stake in a non-parliamentary system.

The cultural analyses that have been brought to bear on this history obscure the battle of interests involved. By doing so, moreover, they tend to ease Sukarno and the Army off the hook of responsibility, as if they were playing foreordained roles, or, in Sukarno's case at least, a role that made more sense to local, particularly Javanese, values than anything the parties had to offer. Isn't this reasoning a bit post hoc, however, and doesn't it distract attention from the distinct advantages to be gained by overturning the parliamentary order, advantages which Army leaders had the wherewithal to pursue consistently?

If this rings true at all, then maybe the figures of Sukarno and Nasution need to be reassessed. Both have been taken more at face value, and treated more respectfully and delicately, than perhaps they ought to be. Sukarno was in the more difficult, usually defensive, position, but his defences may have been limited by a lack of political imagination and a constricted political vision, which led him to fall back on the model of colonial institutions he publicly castigated. And if Hardi is right, Sukarno too lacked confidence, fearing that he would make a mess of the economy and perhaps much else. But in the main, after early 1957, Sukarno was the weaker party in his relationship with the Army, constantly caught up by military initiatives and pressures over which he had relatively little influence. In some ways, he was a reluctant cover for the Army's political power, incomparably more obstreperous, noisy, and posturing than Thai kings after 1932 but, as it turned out, not all that much more effectual.

As for the Army, its sources of strength in lasting organisation and brute force were also sources of political vulnerability, so long as Sukarno or anyone else could try to manipulate cleavages in the officer corps. Nasution most likely understood this better than most before Suharto took command. If the evidence of what he achieved counts at all, he sought strategically not only to clear political and economic space for the officer corps, but to lay claim to this space.

These objectives were possible only to the extent that the competitive interests of the parties, and their ideological claims to priority, were eliminated in favour of a centralised bureaucracy and a command economy into which officers could be injected more or less at will and by right. Hence Nasution's outspoken defence of the *pamong praja* against the intentions of Law 1/1957, his sequestration of the spoils of nationalisation in 1958, and the adoption of the corporatist concept of functional groups to displace the party system as the primary principle of political mobilisation. Resuscitating the 1945 Constitution, which (*pace* Hardi) was Nasution's project, was exactly in the same line. After 1965, other obstacles gone, Nasution's purpose was vindicated, consolidated, and elaborated even as Nasution was waved aside.

5

Human Rights and the *Konstituante* Debates of 1956-59

Adnan Buyung Nasution

Universal human rights, democracy, and the constitutional state with provisions effectively limiting and governing its exercise of power, have been considered in Indonesia, since the 1950s, as western concepts, not in harmony with Indonesian culture and identity. In Indonesian culture the interests of society are more important than those of the individual and, following from this, particularistic rights take precedence over universal human rights which adhere to human beings by virtue of their common humanity. Consequently open conflict is considered inappropriate, opposition is regarded as taboo and the ballot has been replaced by deliberation leading to the formulation of a consensus by a wise leader.

These ideas are advanced not only by the authorities of the Guided Democracy Period (1957-1966) and the Pancasila Democracy period (1966-the present) but are also to be found in much of the scholarly literature by Indonesianists such as MPM Muskens (1969) Ann Ruth Willner (1970) Harry Benda (1972) Brian May (1978) Merle Ricklefs (1981) David Reeve (1985) and Kenji Tsuchiya (1987).

The cultural argument confuses what is, or what may happen, with what is right. This kind of argument ignores the fact that in the struggle for Indonesian independence (since the beginning of the century and during the national revolution from 1945-49) as well as in the post independence period to the present, democratic aspirations have always existed alongside tendencies towards authoritarian rule.

The main purpose of my recent research has been to document the struggle in Indonesia to establish a constitutional state based on a recognition of fundamental human rights. This effort was expressed most clearly in the period when powerful authoritarian forces were in the course of acquiring power. Shortly after that seizure of power, limited democracy (whether in the form of Guided Democracy or Pancasila Democracy) *appeared* to be generally accepted.

The focus is on the Constituent Assembly (*Konstituante*) which, in modern Indonesian historiography, is either ignored or regarded as of little importance and, in any case, is seen as having failed (Muskens, 1969; Dahm, 1971; Boland, 1971; Nugroho Notosusanto, 1977; Pluvier, 1978; May, 1978; Caldwell and Utrecht, 1979). By contrast, I see the Constituent Assembly as representing the high point of the struggle for constitutional democracy in Indonesia, following the Proclamation of Independence of 17 August 1945 and Vice-Presidential Decree No. X of 16 October 1945, together with the steps taken to implement these.

The Vice-Presidential Decree, which was fully accepted by President Sukarno, represented a correction to the absoluteness of presidential power under the 1945 Constitution, by giving the Parliament co-legislative powers with the president. Subsequently, in November this was followed by the acceptance of the principle of ministerial responsibility to the parliament together with a multi-party system based on the acceptance of basic human rights, especially those of freedom of opinion, freedom of expression and freedom of assembly and organization.

The general election for the Constituent Assembly was held in 1955 by which time Indonesia's *external* freedom was established, when, that is to say, her freedom from colonial rule and the recognition of her sovereignty was secure. The mandate of the Assembly was to draft a new and definitive constitution which would guarantee *domestic* freedom for every Indonesian citizen. The Assembly was composed of 544 members and it sat continuously from 10 November 1956 till 2 June 1959.

Constituent Assembly discussion of the many basic subjects to be discussed in plenary sessions, the highest forum of the Assembly, were prepared in a variety of committees. My research has been directed especially to the Minutes of Plenary Sessions running to nearly 10,000 pages. These covered debates in 1957 about the basic philosophy of the state, debates about basic human rights in 1958 and debates about a return to the 1945 Constitution in 1959. The proposal for a return to the 1945 Constitution came from the Government and was advanced by President Sukarno. This represented the second governmental intervention in the constitutional debates. The first intervention occurred in 1958 when Prime Minister Djuanda pressed the Constituent Assembly to speed up its work.

The Government's proposal for a return to the 1945 Constitution was voted on three times and rejected. The Constituent Assembly then went into recess and the Chairman announced that he would enter into discussions with the Government. Political parties were then experiencing considerable pressure from the Army and from supporters of the concept of Guided Democracy who sought the dissolution of the Assembly and the introduction of the 1945

Constitution by Presidential Decree. In the end, three of the four major parties, the Indonesian Nationalist Party (PNI), the Indonesian Communist Party (PKI) and the Muslim Scholars' Party (Nahdlatul Ulama or NU) — gave their support, as the small nationalist parties had already done. The third and last governmental intervention in the debates of the Constituent Assembly — the Presidential Decree of July 1959 dissolving the Assembly and implementing the return to the 1945 Constitution — thus obtained the formal support of the existing political constellation.

The third governmental intervention must be seen in the context of the development of the idea of Guided Democracy, which was initially President Sukarno's concept, and which then secured the support of the Army which was becoming a political force in its own right.

Debates about the formal basis of the state related to Pancasila and Islam and to social and economic questions. The discussion demonstrated the degree to which procedural values, that is to say ethically valid methods of reaching goals, were sacrificed to ideology or fixation on substantive goals (ideals of social perfection). This was in spite of the fact that it is precisely the presence of ethical procedures which characterises a constitutional state based on the acceptance of human rights and on controls over the exercise of executive power and that all parties had committed themselves to these procedures. In the debate about the basis of the state, two state concepts were advanced, that of the *integralist state* which was legitimised by reference to Indonesian culture and the Pancasila ideology; and the idea of an *Islamic state*. Both of these were, in important respects, in conflict with the idea of a constitutional state. Both concepts rejected the distinction between the state and society, even though this distinction is essential if limitations on government authority and popular controls on state power are to have any substance at all.

Supporters of the integralist state use cultural arguments, i.e. that the state must be in accordance with the culture and identity of the Indonesian people, where the interests of society are more important than those of the individual and where the ties binding society together are like those of a family. According to this view human rights and problems of power ought not to be raised as issues. By contrast, acceptance of human rights together with controls over state power by representatives of the people are the very hallmarks of the constitutional state.

The Islamic state, as proposed in the Constituent Assembly, had its origins in the idea of absolute truth and perfection derived from the Qur'an and ordained by God. The Qur'an pertains not only to individual devotion (*ibadah*) but also prescribes principles and rules governing social life including the life of the State (*muamalah*). The Islamic state places religious truth above all, and so restricts the fullness of the right of every person to freedom of thought. That right, however, is a basic requirement of a constitutional state, that is to say a state which is freely consented to by all citizens for the protection of their human rights.

The fact that many supporters of a constitutional state (whether nationalist or Muslim) also desire an integralist or an Islamic state, indicates an inconsistency in their perceptions, caused by conceptual weakness, or by lack of understanding of the meaning of constitutionalism.

The debate about the basis of the state was above all an ideological confrontation between differing philosophies based on premises each of which, to their followers, appeared to represent an absolute truth. Their respective advocates, arguing from these premises, tried to convince their opponents but succeeded only in convincing themselves and those who already agreed with them. There was no possibility of compromise between the two sides and the debate merely sharpened the polarisation and feelings of enmity between them.

The debate about the principles of human rights differed in two important respects from that concerning the basis of the state. First, while the latter was abstract in character, and removed from the practical problems of establishing an administrative framework, the former was concrete and directed towards the protection of fragile humanitarian values, the problem of the weak and disadvantaged — workers, women and minorities — and towards restraining the misuse of power by the government and by powerful groups within society. Second, while the debate about the basis of the state was marked by ideological conflict and centrifugal tendencies, the human rights debate tended to be centripetal, resulting in a fundamental consensus about the values being discussed. A consensus about human rights and the manner of implementing them universally was attained through debate among members of the Assembly representing a wide range of outlooks, including those based on religion, conceptions of the human essence, Indonesian culture, social development, the independence struggle and the history of humanity. There was agreement not only about general individual rights and particular citizens' rights but even about the use of human rights as a standard against which undemocratic policies and illegal practices, including those which stemmed from colonial or pre-colonial days, might be judged. Human rights were also seen as a normative guide to the development of social and economic policy and the growth of democracy in Indonesia.

In the Constituent Assembly debates there were a number of differences of opinion concerning: a) freedom of religion, especially the freedom to change religions and whether religious laws ought to be applicable to marriage; and b) the possibility that giant capitalist concerns and the very rich might misuse human rights principles. Some speakers categorised those of Chinese descent as belonging to the very rich without regard to whether they were Indonesian citizens. But these differences of opinion did not detract from the fundamental agreement about the importance of including guarantees of rights in the Constitution. A Masyumi member explained this matter with great clarity in the following metaphor. If one thinks of the Constitution as a river, human rights constitute the water which flows in it. Without human rights all that is left is a dry and winding river bed. Similarly, the chairman of the Constituent Assembly, Mr Wilopo, summed up the view of the Plenary session that the section containing human rights was one of the most important sections of the draft Constitution, because constitutional government, desired by the Indonesian people, was a government limited by law and by the protection of human rights.

On the last day of the human rights debates, 10 September 1958, the Plenary Session agreed to a list of 19 human rights. The session also gave to the Constitutional Preparatory Committee (whose authority was thus radically extended) the task of formulating a list of human and civil rights for inclusion in the Constitution. This Constitutional Preparatory Committee reported on the results of its work on 8 December 1958. A decision about the formulation of 22 rights was reached after they received the required two thirds majority support, meaning that both the Pancasila coalition and the Muslim coalition in the Committee backed it. The Constituent Assembly therefore had effectively endorsed the 22 rights, and if the Plenary Session had been allowed to reconvene, the 22 rights articles, supported by these two groups, would certainly have been carried by acclamation.

The fact that 13 other rights did not get past the drafting stage in the Preparatory Committee does not detract from the fundamental consensus which had been reached. Besides, the disagreements about these 13 articles concerned only their formal philosophical rationale (whether deriving from God or from humanity) and how explicit the wording should be. Finally and most specifically, if freedom of religion was to be spelt out explicitly, as the non-Islamic parties wanted, this could appear to be in direct conflict with concrete Islamic law. Had the Plenary Session been able to consider this problem it would probably have decided to adopt a compromise formulation concerning the 13 rights which would be acceptable to both the Pancasila group and the Muslim coalition. In this way, the whole Declaration of Human Rights, augmented by other rights, would have been incorporated in the definitive Constitution.

Even at a time when anti-western sentiment was at its height, fundamental agreement could be reached about human rights. Indeed, there is no doubt that consensus on the question of human rights was the clearest achievement of the Constituent Assembly. The list of rights accepted by the Assembly can therefore be seen as representing the substantive constitutional values of the Republic of Indonesia. It was a *Proclamation of domestic freedom* by Indonesian citizens, on a par with Indonesia's declaration of *external* freedom, the Proclamation of 17 August 1945.

As Prime Minister Djuanda stated in the name of the Government on 27 May 1959, after a stormy human rights debate, the human rights articles agreed to in the Plenary Session were binding on the President and the future government. The Presidential Decree of 5 July 1959, which did not concern itself with human rights, did not in the least reduce the validity of the decisions of the Constituent Assembly.

It is worth comparing the debates about the to return to the 1945 Constitution with the earlier constitutional debates in the 'Constituent Assembly' of 1945 — that is to say, the *Badan Penyelidik Usaha-usaha Persiapan Kemerdekaan Indonesia* (the Investigating Committee for the Preparation of Indonesian Independence) in June and July 1945. There are some striking differences. In the earlier debates only Hatta and Yamin spoke of human rights and about guarantees against the misuse of power by government. Other members agreed with Supomo and Sukarno, who argued that, in an integralist state as embodied in the 1945 Constitution, human rights and guarantees ought to reflect family values and the customary laws governing life in Javanese villages. It was thus abundantly clear that they were blind to the problems of state power.

By 1959 people had learned from the post-1945 experience. Although the Pancasila group and the NU expressed support for a return to the 1945 Constitution, the great majority rejected the government's proposal to return to that Constitution without amendment. Members of the nationalist, communist and Islamic parties criticised the idea of Guided Democracy and pointed to the danger of dictatorship if the 1945 Constitution was adopted in its original form. They demanded constitutional guarantees against the misuse of power. Prime Minister Djuanda later proposed, as a concession, that the human rights already accepted by the Plenary Session, which, as mentioned above, were constitutionally binding, ought to be enshrined in the Bandung Charter as an amendment to the 1945 Constitution.

On the other hand there was some similarity between the debates of June and July 1945 and those of May and June 1959, namely in the attitude displayed by the Islamic parties. In June and July 1945 the Muslim group did not shift in the slightest from its demand for the inclusion in the 1945 Constitution of articles concerning Islamic teachings (although, ultimately, in the deciding session on 18 August 1945, the Islamic group agreed to Hatta's proposal to drop these articles.)

Again in 1959 the coalition of Islamic parties held firmly to the demand for the inclusion of the words 'with the obligation to follow Islamic law for the adherents of that religion' in the Preamble to the 1945 Constitution. They were of the view that, unless this demand was accepted, they would not support the proposal to return to the 1945 Constitution. It was clear from the result of the vote on the Muslim proposal that the Pancasila faction rejected it and the proposal failed. In turn, the Islamic group voted against the proposal to return to the 1945 Constitution, preventing the achievement of the two thirds majority necessary for it to be carried.

According to constitutional law there was no obstacle in the way of the Constituent Assembly reconvening and proceeding to draft a new and definitive constitution. This is why, at the end of the sitting devoted to the proposal to return to the 1945 Constitution, the Chairman adjourned the Assembly and entered into discussion with the government. There was a proposal to discuss the status of the Constituent Assembly, but it was then agreed to continue this after the recess. But the Assembly never met again because on 5 July it was dissolved by Presidential Decree.

The continuation of the struggle to establish constitutional government has much to learn from the events of 1959.

References

Benda, H.J., (1972) Democracy in Indonesia, in *Continuity and change in Southeast Asia: collected journal articles of Harry J. Benda*, Yale University Southeast Asia Studies, New Haven.

Boland, B.J., (1971) 'The struggle of Islam in modern Indonesia', *Verhandelingen van het Koninklijk Instituut voor Taal-, Land- en Volkenkunde*, vol 59 1971

Caldwell, M. and E. Utrecht (1979) *Indonesia, An Alternative History*, Alternative Publishing Co-operative Ltd, Sydney.

Dahm, B. (1971) *History of Indonesia in the twentieth century*, London, Pall Mall.

May, B. (1978) *The Indonesian Tragedy*, Routledge and Kegan Paul, London.

Muskens, M.P.M. (1969) *Indonesie, een strijd om nationale identiteit: nationalisten, Islamieten, Katholieken*, P. Brand, Bussum.

Notosusanto, N. (1977) *Sejarah Nasional Indonesia*, vols. V and VI, Balai Pustaka, Jakarta. (2nd edition)

Pluvier, J.M. (1978) *Indonesie : kolonialisme, onafhankelijkheid, neo-kolonialisme : een politieke geschiedenis van 1940 tot heden*, Socialistiese Uitgeverij Nijmegen SUN, Nijmegen.

Reeve, D. (1985) *Golkar of Indonesia: An Alternative to the Party System*. Oxford University Press, Singapore.

Ricklefs, M. (1981) *A History of Modern Indonesia*, Macmillan Asian History Series, London and Basingstoke.

Tsuchiya, K. (1987). *Democracy and leadership: the rise of the Taman Siswa movement in Indonesia*, [translated by Peter Hawkes] University of Hawaii Press, Honolulu.

Willner, A.R. (1970) The Neotraditional Accommodation to Political Independence: The case of Indonesia, in L.W. Pye (ed) *Cases in Comparative Politics*, Little Brown & Co, Boston.

6

The 1950s in New Order Ideology and Politics

David Bourchier

'The only reason people want to be masters of the future', muses a character in Milan Kundera's novel *The Book of Laughter and Forgetting*, 'is to change the past. They are fighting for access to the laboratories where photographs are retouched and biographies and histories rewritten' (1981:22). These words were written in the gloomy aftermath of the Soviet invasion of Czechoslovakia, but the general point — that control over state archives allows governments the potential to remould the past in their own image — is much more widely applicable. While the New Order government may not go to the extent of air-brushing 'non-persons' out of old photographs, it has nevertheless devoted considerable energy and resources to constructing and propagating a version of the past designed to preserve and justify present power structures. Official constructions of the past are, I want to suggest, a vital part of the New Order's ideological armoury.

My main concern in this paper is to examine the way in which the period of parliamentary democracy in the 1950s has been officially represented in the New Order period and the political reasons for this. The basic argument of the paper is that the primary function of 'the 1950s' has been as a symbol of the fundamental lack of fit between political liberalism — and, by extension, 'Western' political ideology as a whole — and Indonesia's 'national personality' or *kepribadian bangsa*. In the language of the New Order, the fifties stand for Westernism, national disintegration, economic backwardness and chronic political instability, the mirror image of the New Order's accent on indigenism, national unity, development and political stability. In practical terms, the fifties serve as a stick with which to beat those calling for the separation of powers, regional autonomy, parliamentarism, an expansion of political rights or press freedom. Official rhetoric about the period, I suggest, has become more significant in recent years as the government has come under increasing pressure to respond to 'liberal' type arguments from its critics.

Constructing history

Pada masa liberal timbul semacam anarki
(Department of Information pamphlet)[1]

Official history is propagated in Indonesia by official speeches, on television, through films and, most transparently, in the state-controlled education curriculum. Krishna Sen (1988) and others have written about the extremely important role of popular historical films such as *Enam Jam di Jogya* and *Pengkhianatan G30S/PKI* in constructing mythologies around the person of Suharto and affirming the current constellation of power in Indonesia. I want to concentrate here on government-prescribed history in schools and universities.

History is taught in two separate subjects: *Sejarah* (History) and *Pendidikan Sejarah Perjuangan Bangsa* (History of the National Struggle). Both are compulsory and together they account for more hours than any other compulsory subject in the senior secondary school curriculum (Leigh 1991:24).

The 'History of the National Struggle', usually referred to in Indonesia as PSPB, was introduced into the curriculum from kindergarten to tertiary level in 1985 on the initiative of the then Minister of Education and Culture, Nugroho Notosusanto. While the subject matter — Indonesian history — is much the same as the mainstream History subject, the objective is different. PSPB was introduced as part of the broader framework of ideological education, and in this sense is more closely allied to the Pancasila education courses such as PMP and P4[2] than with History. Its purpose, according to the 1983 Broad Guidelines of State Policy (1983), is 'to extend and develop the soul, spirit and values of 1945 to the younger generation'. Curriculum materials issued by the Department of Education explain that the 'values of 1945' consist of 1. the Pancasila and the 1945 Constitution and 2. the identity of the Indonesian National Army (TNI) as the Army of Struggle (*Tentara Pejuang*) which is equated with the Dual Function of the Armed Forces (*Dwifungsi ABRI*). The stated purpose of PSPB is not the learning of history as such but the use of historical episodes as a means of inculcating in students Pancasila values such as 'cooperation' and 'togetherness' as well as martial values such as 'heroism', 'bravery', 'willingness to sacrifice' and

---

1. *Sinopsis Derap Persada Nusantara*, Departemen Penerangan RI, NPD 79/10/07/1991. It means 'In the liberal era there arose a kind of anarchy'.

2. PMP = *Pendidikan Moral Pancasila* (Pancasila Moral Education) P4 = *Pedoman Penghayatan dan Pengalaman Pancasila*. ([Course on the] Directives for the Realisation and Implementation of Pancasila).

so on.

Although teachers are made aware of the dividing line between PSPB and History — the former emphasising value formation and the emotions rather than the intellect — there is a great deal of overlap in the subject matter and source materials for the two topics. In fact the prescribed texts for both topics were edited by the military historian Nugroho Notosusanto. The 'standard' history text for all levels of education for the period from the Japanese occupation to the present is volume VI of Nugroho's *National History of Indonesia* (*Sejarah Nasional Indonesia*). This book is periodically revised and updated, the fourth and most recent edition having been published in 1984. The source book for PSPB is *30 Years of Indonesian Independence* (*30 Tahun Indonesia Merdeka*) edited by Nugroho and published by the State Secretariat. This profusely illustrated book in four volumes is essentially a 'lightweight' version of volume VI of *National History of Indonesia*. Both of these books are explicitly issued as *buku babon* or canons for history teachers and for the producers of myriad smaller, cheaper primers.

While these are of course not the only historical writings produced by or available to Indonesians, their status as standard texts both determines the way millions of young Indonesians learn about history at school and provides a valuable indicator of how the New Order's top ideologues believe history ought to be presented.

The official texts, predictably enough, hail the achievements of Suharto and the New Order and contrast them with the turbulence and strife of the 'Old Order'. What is most striking about their coverage of the period between the declaration of independence and 1965 is the prominence given to the exploits of the military. The central and unmistakable message of both the text and the photographs is that ever since 1945 the military have been the true guardians of the Indonesian State and ideology. They have stood by to provide leadership whenever the State has been threatened by regional revolts, religious fanaticism, communist subversion and the incompetence of self-interested civilian politicians.

The military slant in school history books is perhaps most evident in their treatment of the Revolution, which they refer to as the 'War of Independence.' Far more weight is given to the armed struggle in the Revolution than to the diplomatic negotiations with the Dutch. In the secondary school primers on the Revolutionary period, only about 10% of total page space is devoted to the negotiations. Most egregious is the omission of any discussion in Nugroho's *National History of Indonesia* of the Emergency Government of Sjafruddin Prawiranegara (Biadlawi 1992). This is clearly calculated to convey the impression that Sukarno's and Hatta's arrest following the Dutch capture of Yogyakarta on 19 December 1948 signalled the abdication of civilian responsibility and leadership in the Revolution which passed to the Army under the Generalship of Sudirman.

The clear picture one gets from school history texts is that civilian politicians contributed very little to the Revolutionary struggle and at times undermined it. The first great mistake was Hatta's 3 November 1945 Decree which paved the way for the free formation of political parties. This is often referred to as a 'dark day' in the history of the Republic (e.g. Tugiyono & Soegiono 1991:101). The signing of the Renville and Linggajati agreements by civilian negotiators in 1947 and 1948 are both construed as naive and ultimately damaging to the cause of independence. Much is made of the forced withdrawal of Siliwangi troops from West Java as a result of concessions made in the Renville agreement. In one history primer students are instructed: Answer these questions briefly and correctly!: 'What is your attitude towards negotiations as a means of struggle?' and 'Supposing you were 17 in 1946, what would you do to give substance to independence?' (Lubis et al. 1990:105-114). The correct answer is clearly not 'Train to become a diplomat' or 'Join a political party'.

Civilian negotiators are also implicitly blamed for the less than spectacular results of the Round Table Conference in the Hague in 1949. The federal formula which the negotiators agreed to is frequently described in history texts as part of a Dutch ruse to 'divide and rule' Indonesia and ultimately to reoccupy their colony. The compromises of the Round Table Conference embodied in the federal Constitution are described as having been preserved in the Provisional Constitution of 1950 which provided the legal framework for the years of parliamentary democracy. 'It can be concluded' says *National History of Indonesia*, 'that the 1950 Constitution still bore the marks of these compromises' (Poesponegoro & Notosusanto 1984:212)[3]

Having clearly identified the early military's heroism, sacrifice and struggle (the 'values of 1945') as having been responsible for Indonesia's victory in the War of Independence, the schoolbook histories then judge the 1950s by the same standards. Needless to say, the compromises, debates and horse-trading that go with any parliamentary system do not measure up. In a 1984 'guidance session' (*pengarahan*) for prospective PSPB teachers, a senior Education Department official summed up the period of 'liberal democracy' as:

> a system of government which was not in tune with the character of the Indonesian nation which gave rise to instability of government marked by constantly changing cabinets which made development very difficult. Divisions became apparent. Domestic security disturbances occurred...
> (Kutoyo 1984)

This is precisely how the period is represented — as a turbulent and rather alien time, when Western influences were strong and the Indonesian nation had lost its way, lost sight of its true identity. While all was clearly not well during the 1950s, these examples reflect a conscious and coordinated effort to present the period in an unfavourable light.

---

3. The words '*kompromi*' and '*sifat-sifat kompromistis*' are used, denoting the negative aspect of what is otherwise held to be a positive value in Indonesian political life.

Most schoolbook representations of the 1950s concentrate on four issues: the rapid rise and fall of cabinets, the regional rebellions, the 1955 elections and Indonesia's success in building solidarity among third world nations. The rise and fall of cabinets is usually treated in a cursory way, with the emphasis on the *existence* of inter-party rivalry and power struggles rather than on the actual issues and debates of the time. In the 1977 edition of Nugroho's *National History of Indonesia*, only seven lines are devoted to the party politics of the years 1950-1955. The politics of the period between 1955 and 1957 does only slightly better with seventeen lines.[4] Little or no attempt is made in any of the standard accounts to differentiate the political parties: they are portrayed as collectively guilty of narrow-minded intolerance and self-interest.

The lion's share of page space in most schoolbook accounts of the 1950s is devoted to the regional rebellions and 'security disturbances' in various parts of the archipelago. The standard Year 3 junior high school history primer, for instance (Ananta 1989), devotes only two paragraphs of its section on the 1950s to parliamentary politics and twenty three to the revolts in West Java, North and South Sulawesi, the Moluccas, Aceh, South Kalimantan and in North, South and West Sumatra. Year 3 pupils are required to know the details of twelve different rebellions which occurred between 1950 and 1959. See Figure 1.

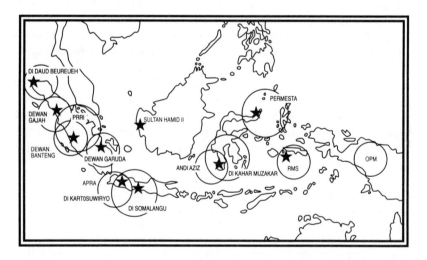

Figure 1. This map from a Year 3 text, paints a picture of chaos from one end of Indonesia to the other during the 1950s.[5]

---

4. The coverage in the 1984 edition is much more comprehensive, but this is not reflected in the primers which the vast majority of students actually use.

5. Tugiyono & Soegiono (1991:121). Note that the OPM in Irian Jaya is included on the map, although this group was not formed until 1969.

The stress given to the revolts and their suppression is such that some texts (e.g. Kansil & Julianto 1991:57) label the period between 1950-1959 not the liberal era but *Masa Survival* (The Age of Survival). The relatively expansive and detailed attention given to regional rebellions shifts the focus from civilian politicians to the Armed Forces command, which again plays the role of hero and guardian of national integrity. Military involvement in some of the regionalist movements is mentioned, but this is blamed on the corrupting influence of competition between the political parties (e.g. Nugroho 1977). The authors of the 1984 edition of *National History of Indonesia* accuse politicians of attempting to 'divide and rule' the Armed Forces in an attempt to break their strength and subordinate them to civilian control (Poesponegoro & Nugroho 1984:456).

The treatment of the 1955 elections is interesting. While taking some pride in the fact that they were orderly and widely praised for their fairness, most history texts (e.g. Kansil & Julianto 1991:61; Tugiyono & Soegiono 1991:112-113) represent them primarily as an attempt by the government to stabilise the political situation rather than as an exercise in democracy. The failure of the elections to put an end to instability is taken as evidence that the liberal democracy of the 1950s 'was indeed not in tune with the essence, the spirit and the values of 1945 of the Unitary Indonesian State as proclaimed on 17 August 1945' (Chaniago *et al.* 1989:58). According to one school text (Ananta 1989:46), the reason the elections did not create stability was 'because the liberal democratic system was still in place.'

The last years of parliamentary democracy are depicted as a period of deepening turmoil and paralysis on the part of the parties in the Constituent Assembly on one hand and the gradual reawakening of the spirit of 1945 on the other. There is no hint that the assembly made any progress towards formulating a new constitution. All that is said is that it was deadlocked and failed to carry out the task that was entrusted to it. Meanwhile 'national unity was being torn to shreds for the sake of the self-interest of various groups and parties' (Chaniago 1989:60-61). Again, the military and their allies — the group that Nugroho refers to as 'bearers of the 1945 spirit' (*golongan yang berkepribadian 1945*) — step into the breach.

The period of Parliamentary Democracy is described in such a way as to make the return to the executive-heavy 1945 Constitution and '1945 values' seem the inevitable and obvious remedy. The continuing political and economic turmoil after 1959 is attributed to Sukarno's impure implementation of the 1945 Constitution and the Communist Party's efforts to dominate the political scene, sow conflict in society and divide the Armed Forces. If the trouble with the 1950s was that politics was being played by the wrong rules, the Guided Democracy period is depicted as a time when the rules were right but their implementation was corrupted by Sukarno's personal ambition and the persistence of ideologically driven party politics. 30 September 1965, is represented as the climax of the turmoil and confusion summed up by the term 'Old Order'. The assassination of the six generals and Suharto's swift action to take control of the capital is covered in graphic detail and highlighted as the great watershed in Indonesia, both politically and ideologically. While the Pancasila may have been formulated some time in 1945 (the inclusion of two possible dates in some texts serves to cast doubt over Sukarno's authorship) PSPB teachers are instructed to treat 1 October (1965) — *Hari Kesaktian Pancasila* or the 'Sacredness of the Pancasila Day' — as the most important date in the calender of state rituals (Beberapa Penjelasan... 1984).

No single person has been more influential in shaping New Order historiography than Nugroho Notosusanto. His career illustrates well the interplay between political power, history writing and state ideology. In the late 1950s Nugroho was known as a writer of short stories, many of them based on his observations as a teenage fighter in the Revolution. Nugroho studied history at the University of London in the early 1960s and later wrote a doctoral dissertation at the University of Indonesia about the Japanese-created Peta Army (in which Suharto and most other senior military officers had served during the occupation). In 1964 he began working as a historian for the military, lecturing at several institutions including the Army Staff and Command School, the Air Force General Command School and the National Defence Institute. Shortly after the 1965 coup, while Chief Historian of the Armed Forces, Nugroho wrote an account of the coup called *40 Days of Failure of the G-30-S*. After the circulation of the detailed 'Cornell Paper' on the coup which disputed the official version of events, Nugroho was instructed by the Commander of the Army Staff and Command School to prepare an English language book to rebut its claims. This account, *The Coup Attempt of the 'September 30 Movement' in Indonesia*, was co-authored with military prosecutor Ismail Saleh and was first published in early 1967. As well as the general history texts discussed above, Nugroho wrote several books about the military and politics in Indonesia and about the origins of the New Order, all of which are highly supportive of the military's *dwifungsi* doctrine (e.g. Nugroho 1975, 1985a and 1985b). Recognition of his position as a key theorist of *dwifungsi* came in the form of an honorary commission as an Army colonel in 1968, which was later upgraded to brigadier-general. When the implementation of *dwifungsi* came under challenge from reformist elements in the Army in 1980 it was Nugroho who was called upon to head an expert committee designed to shore up the orthodox position (Jenkins 1984:191-195). In 1982 Nugroho was installed as Rector of the University of Indonesia and the following year was appointed Minister of Education and Culture, where he supported and oversaw the implementation not only of PSPB courses but also the rapid expansion of Pancasila education courses. He died in June

1985, while still in office.[6]

Nugroho was cherished by the military because he was able and willing to construct and sustain arguments which provided historical justification for their claim to a permanent role in government. The fact that he was a civilian who appears to have shared the military leadership's abhorrence of civilian supremacy made him an even more precious asset. By putting him in charge of writing the 'master text' on Indonesian history and later, the entire education system, the New Order leadership were doing their best to convince the public at large and the younger generation in particular that the only alternative to the present system of rule was anarchy.

This project has had only limited success. Barbara Leigh (1991) and James Siegel (1986) have both drawn attention to the highly structured formality of history teaching in Indonesian classrooms and the implicit recognition on the part of both students and teachers that what is being taught bears no direct relationship to the lived history of their parents and grandparents but is rather 'part of the set of knowledge contained in textbooks and activated when speaking Indonesian' (Siegel 1986:145). In a paper given at an Education Department seminar in Semarang in 1990, a tertiary level history teacher (Suwitha 1990) strongly criticised the dullness and narrowness of the PSPB syllabus and complained that this had made history teachers a particular target of ridicule among students. Another indicator of the failure of school students to internalise the lessons they learn in history classes is the extraordinary drawing power of Sukarno's image among the young. Twenty one years after Sukarno's death the New Order authorities still fear him enough to have felt compelled to reintroduce a ban on displaying his portrait during the 1992 election campaign.

The New Order's representation of history has also come in for public criticism from historians. More than one of the team of historians who, under Nugroho's guidance, compiled the original 1974 edition of *National History of Indonesia* resigned, alleging 'political intervention' in the preparation of the book (Biadlawi 1992). Historians and others have also attacked later editions on a number of counts, including their playing down of the role of political parties and belittling the achievements of President Sukarno (*Editor* 15 August 1992; Atmakusumah 1992).

Demands for political rights

If the main concern of the New Order's ideologists during its first couple of decades was to 'de-Sukarnoise' Indonesian political discourse, their main target for the past six or seven years has been the rights-oriented arguments of political liberalism.

---

6. Nugroho also served as curator of the Armed Forces Museum in Jakarta and as deputy Executive Chairman of the Central Heroes Development Body, the organisation which nominates candidates for National Hero status to the President. Almost half of the 51 heroes proclaimed between October 1965 and 1984 were military (Mengenal Pahlawan... 1984).

As has been well documented elsewhere, the rapid expansion of both an urban industrial working class and a professional middle class, especially in the past decade, has contributed to a big increase in the level and scope of political demands. Huge numbers of factory workers have engaged in industrial action in the past few years demanding the right to organise, the right to strike and an end to the routine abuse of labour law by employers. Middle class groups, meanwhile, resentful of the pattern of arbitrary, personalised decision making which has characterised the political and micro-economic management of the New Order, have pressed for political rights (including press freedom and the right to form political associations) as well as for effective mechanisms to curb the power of the executive (such as an independent judiciary and a stronger legislature). Support for such measures is evident across a broad spectrum of middle class groups and has even been voiced by the regime's appointees in parliament (see e.g. *Media Indonesia* 18 February 1991). Although the actual term has usually been avoided, it seems clear that these demands belong to what is essentially a *liberal democratic* political tradition.

President Suharto, better than anybody, understands the incompatibility between these kinds of demands and the continuation of the New Order State's hitherto almost unbounded capacity to manage and regulate political life in Indonesia. One major initiative taken by the New Order's ideologists to counteract demands for political rights, finely documented by Marsillam Simanjuntak (1989), has involved the resurrection and incorporation into state ideology of Supomo's concept of the 'integralist State' (*staatsidee integralistik*). A key element of integralism is the idea that individuals have no more rights vis-a-vis the State than a limb has rights vis-a-vis the body of which it is an integral part. Marsillam argued that this concept derives not from indigenous political philosophy as has been claimed by the New Order, but rather from conservative 19th century German legal philosophers who were totally opposed to the idea of popular sovereignty.

Another strategy in the defence of statism against liberal democratic demands — which, I should stress, have been fed not only by domestic structural changes but also by the global rise in the stocks of liberal democracy — has been the elaboration of the argument that liberal conceptions of human and individual rights are fundamentally untenable in Indonesia. Part of this argument stresses culture, i.e. that liberal values reflect 'Western' individualism and 'dichotomistic thinking' which are out of tune with the communally-oriented Indonesian sensibility. While this argument is frequently used in dialogue with the outside world, it has a limited lifespan domestically. How long, after all, can one keep telling Indonesian critics that they are un-Indonesian?

The other part of the argument, which has always been a vital part of New Order rhetoric but which appears to have become even more so in the past few years, says that any step down the path of political liberalisation is a step back towards the chaos of the 1950s. This argument has been used frequently in response to calls for the separation of powers, for more regional autonomy, for more authority for the DPR, for more independence for political parties, for more freedom for trade unions and for the application of international standards of human rights. In December 1992 Interior Minister Rudini lectured members of the Indonesian Muslim Intellectuals Association (ICMI, *Ikatan Cendekiawan Muslim Indonesia*) that any move to turn ICMI into a political party would revive the turmoil of the liberal 1950s (*The Straits Times*, 9 December 1992).

Re-evaluations

As calls of this kind increase, and the signs are that they will, the regime's representation of the 1950s will, I suggest, come under greater scrutiny than it has done so far. There have in fact already been some critics who have openly questioned government's rhetoric about the period and even advocated a return to liberal democracy. In August 1990 retired general and key figure in the Petition of 50 group, Ali Sadikin, gave an important speech in which he said that the passing of the Cold War and the worldwide trend towards the acceptance of popular sovereignty, pluralism and human rights should allow people to re-examine the period between 1950-59 in a new light. He argued that the inter-party conflicts at the time were an indication not of the inappropriateness of liberal democracy for Indonesia but rather of the inexperience of the politicians of the time and the polarising pressures of the Cold War. Sadikin argued that after 45 years of independence, Indonesians were now mature enough to come to terms with pluralism. Sadikin's dissident colleague Slamet Bratanata took a similar line, stressing as well the under-rated economic performance of several of the governments in the 1950s. Bratanata (1990) also highlighted the ironic fact that many of those in the government who condemn the period as being liberal and Western were themselves 'prize proteges of the West'.

Former commander of Kopkamtib, retired general Soemitro, has also been campaigning in the past two years for a return to what he calls 'normal politics', or democracy 'without any qualifications' (1989). Although he has on occasion said that this meant a return to the situation before 1959, he has also expressed reservations about allowing parties to form as freely as they did then (Interview, 25 March 1991). Chris Siner Key Timu, a member of Sadikin's group, has proposed that the problem of too many small parties being elected to parliament could be overcome by adopting a system similar to Germany's, whereby a party would need at least 5% of the vote to gain representation (Interview, 26 March 1991).

The procedures adopted at the time of the 1955 general election have also been adopted as a point of reference by critics of the New Order's electoral practices. A draft publication by the Body for the Protection of Political Rights (1992) contrasts the intimidation, violence and vote manipulation which characterised the 1992 elections in many areas with the 1955 election, which it maintains, with good reason, was 'the only truly free, secret, honest and just election' to be held in Indonesia.

By far the most comprehensive re-examination of the 1950s, however, which has already succeeding in forcing the debate about the period into the political mainstream, is Adnan Buyung Nasution's mammoth study (1992) of the workings of the Constitutent Assembly between 1956 and 1959. As I have mentioned above, the received wisdom about the Constitutent Assembly, the elected body which met to formulate a new constitution to replace the Provisional Constitution of 1950, is that it did very little for three years other than get bogged down in arguments about the appropriate relationship between religion and the State. Nasution shows that this was not the case, and that in fact the Assembly was very close to completing a highly democratic constitution when Sukarno decreed its dissolution in July 1959. Nasution's work also challenges the notion that the commitment of the elected civilian politicians to democracy and human rights was weak, arguing that these ideals were vocally propounded in the Constituent Assembly and have a solid and authentic foundation in Indonesian political history. It is too soon to assess the impact of Nasution's dissertation, but one indication of the continuing political sensitivity of the historical issues it raises is that the Commander of the Armed Forces General Try Sutrisno publicly denigrated it for 'attacking the 1945 Constitution' (Indonesian Legal Aid... 1992).

The 1950s, I have tried to show, play an important role in the ideology of the New Order. Their principal role, as they have been constructed in officially sponsored history books, is to provide a negative example of the application of liberal political philosophies in Indonesia and thereby help to preserve the present constellation of power from a rising tide of demands for political rights and freedoms. As Indonesia's middle and working classes grow, and pressures for change increase, interpretations of national history, particularly the question of civil-military relations in the early years of the Republic, will, I suggest, remain intensely political.

References

Beberapa Penjelasan mengenai Peristiwa dan Tokoh Sejarah sehubungan dengan PSPB, in *Laporan Teknis kepala Subdit pembinaan SLB pada upacara pembukaan penataran kepala dan guru SLB/A angkatan I dalam pengembangan bidang studi PSPB, 27 Feb 1984 di SLB/A Pembina tingkat Nasional*, Lebak Bulus, Jakarta.

Ananta, Bagas Prama (1989) *Sejarah Nasional Indonesia* (Untuk Kelas 3 SMP) PT Intan Pariwara, Klaten.

Atmakusumah (1992) 'SNI VI: Buku Politik', *Editor*, 15 August 1992

Badan Perlindungan Hak-hak Politik Rakyat (1992) n.p. Jakarta. 93 page manuscript.

Biadlawi, Masduki (1992) 'Meninjau Sejarah yang Berbau Kekuasaan', *Editor*, 15 August 1992

Bratanata, Slamat (writing as 'Abdullah') (1990) 'Looking at ourselves again', *Indonesian Observer*, 31 October 1990

Chaniango, A. K., Eddy Jusuf, St. Negoro (1989) *IPS Sejarah*, Kelas 3 SMP, Ghalia Indonesia, Jakarta.

Indonesian Legal Aid Foundation Press Release (1992) Human Rights Day, 10 December 1992

Jenkins, D. (1984) *Suharto and his Generals: Indonesian Military Politics, 1975-1983*, Modern Indonesia Project, Cornell University, Ithaca, N.Y.

Kansil, C.S.T. and Julianto (1990) *Sejarah Perjuangan Pergerakan Kebangsaan Indonesia* (For PSPB and PMP at senior high school and tertiary level) Penerbit Erlangga, Jakarta. (1988 edition)

Ketetapan-Ketetapan MPR Republik Indonesia 1983, Rapi, Surabaya, 1983

Kundera, Milan (1981) *The Book of Laughter and Forgetting*, Alfred A. Knopf, New York [Trans: Michael Hein]

Kutoyo, Sutrisno (compiler) (1984) *Beberapa pokok pikiran tentang Kerangka dasar dan materi PSPB*, Departemen Pendidikan dan Kebudayaan, Dirjen Pendidikan Dasar dan Menengah, Direktorat Pendidikan Dasar, Proyek Pembinaan Sekolah Luar Biasa Jakarta, Tahun 1983/84, in *Laporan Teknis kepala Subdit pembinaan SLB pada upacara pembukaan penataran kepala dan guru SLB/A angkatan I dalam pengembangan bidang studi PSPB, 27 Feb 1984 di SLB/A Pembina tingkat Nasional*, Lebak Bulus, Jakarta.

Leigh, B. (1991) 'Making the Indonesian State: the role of school texts', *RIMA*, Vol.25/1 Winter 1991

Lubis, H., Asmid Kamal Chaniago, Gatot Suraji, S. Harijadi Judya, Sudamadji, Jacobus Rinussa, St. Negoro (1990) *Pendidikan Sejarah Perjuangan Bangsa*, (Berdasarkan GBPP SMTP 1985) Untuk Kelas 1 SMTP, Yudhistira, Jakarta. (6th printing 1990)

Mengenal Pahlawan Bangsa, CV Teguh Karya, Solo, 1984

Nasution, Adnan Buyung (1992) *The Aspiration for Constitutional Government in Indonesia; A socio-legal Study of the Indonesian Konstituante 1956-1959*, PhD dissertation submitted to the Rijksuniversiteit in Utrecht, Utrecht.

Nugroho Notosusanto & Ismail Saleh (1968) *The coup attempt of the 'September 30 Movement' in Indonesia*, P.T. Pembimbing Masa, Jakarta.

_____ (1975) *The National Struggle and the Armed Forces in Indonesia*, Department of Defence and Security, Centre for Armed Forces History, Jakarta.

_____ (1977) *Sejarah Nasional Indonesia*, vol.VI, Balai Pustaka, Jakarta. (2nd edition)

_____ (1985a) *Tercapainya Konsensus Nasional 1966-1969*, Balai Pustaka, Jakarta.

_____ (1985b) *Pejuang dan Prajurit: Konsepsi dan Implementasi Dwi-fungsi ABRI*, Sinar Harapan, Jakarta.

Poesponegoro, Marwati Djoened and Nugroho Notosusanto (1984) *Sejarah*

Nasional Indonesia, vol.VI, Balai Pustaka, Jakarta. (4th edition)

Sadikin, Lt-Gen (Ret) H. Ali (1990) 'Kebhinekaan dan Kedaulatan Rakyat', a speech given to welcome the 45th anniversary of Indonesian independence, Jakarta, 14 August 1990

Sen, K. (1988) Filming 'History' under the New Order, in K. Sen (ed) *Histories and Stories*, Centre for Southeast Asian Studies, Monash University, Clayton.

Siegel, J.T. (1986) *Solo in the New Order: Language and Hierarchy in an Indonesian City*, Princeton University Press, Princeton.

Simanjuntak, Marsillam (1989) *Unsur Hegelian dalam Pandangan Negara Integralistik*, unpublished Master of Laws thesis, Faculty of Law, University of Indonesia, Depok.

Soemitro (1989) 'Aspiring to Normal Politics', *Far Eastern Economic Review*, 6 April 1989

Suwitha, I Putu Gede (1990) *Pendidikan Sejarah Perjuangan Bangsa (Sebuah Pengalaman Mengajar)* Paper to Seminar Sejarah Nasional V, Semarang 27-30 August 1990. Departemen Pendidikan dan Kebudayaan, Direktorat Sejarah dan Nilai Tradisional, Proyek Inventarisasi dan Dokumentasi Sejarah Nasional

Tugiyono Ks. & Soegiono (1991) Bahan acuan kegiatan Belajar-mengajar dengan pendekatan CBSA *IPS SEJARAH* untuk SMP, Kelas 3 semesta kelima, Kurikulum 1975 yang disempurnakan, C.V. Baru, Jakarta.

7

The Impact of American Foreign Policy

George McT. Kahin

The intrusion of American power in Indonesia during the 1950s was heavy, and some of the effects are still evident. This can, perhaps, be better appreciated if one first briefly notes the considerable extent to which American power had already shaped the political character of events in Indonesia from 1945 to 1949, for, in important respects, it then laid the foundations and conditioned the prospects for the course of Indonesian politics in the 1950s. But I must emphasise that these intrusions of American power were sometimes inadvertent and unintentional while others were very much intentional and carefully calculated, albeit often based on faulty intelligence.

An obsession with the potential spread of communism was the overriding consideration in the US during both these periods. But in Indonesia, as in Vietnam, during the first post-war years, that concern was rooted primarily in **Europe** — not in Southeast Asia. In order not to risk undermining the cooperation of France and the Netherlands in containing the growth of communist power in Europe, Washington quietly gave them both the tangible means for their military campaigns to re-establish control over their former Southeast Asian colonies. Without the modern weaponry, troop transport and massive financial assistance provided them by the United States, neither of these colonial powers would have been able to take over from the British after their brief post-war occupation. Without it neither France nor the Netherlands would have been able to hold on for very long even in those limited areas into which the British forces had shoehorned them, and in both Indonesia and Vietnam the struggles for independence would almost certainly have been much shorter and the attendant suffering and loss of life much less.

And it is plausible to argue that, had most Indonesian leaders not been conscious of the immense shadow cast by Anglo-American might standing behind the Dutch — and been convinced that these powers would play a decisive role in shaping the post-war world — the agenda for socio-economic change in the Republic would have been considerably more progressive than it in fact became. Today many Indonesians seem to be unaware that the leaders of their revolution were nearly all adherents of some variant of socialism — with even the dominant wing of the largest Islamic party, the Masyumi, regarding themselves as 'religious socialists'. Perhaps this lapse in historical memory reflects the same official New Order interpretation of history that shies away from referring to the period 1945-49 as a 'Revolution' and prefers the less politically evocative term 'struggle for independence'. But there is little doubt that worry over antagonising the leading capitalists powers was a significant factor in putting a damper on the inclination of the Republic's leaders to espouse a more radical socio-economic program.

The similarity of the roles of the US in Indonesia and Vietnam during the first three years after the end of World War II is striking, and if it had not been for the Madiun rebellion the parallel would undoubtedly have lasted longer. But once the Republic had confronted and defeated Indonesian communist forces the Dutch could no longer persuade American congressmen that Sukarno and Hatta were dangerously influenced by communism and liable to lead their country into the Soviet sphere. So dramatic was the American turn around as a consequence of this revelation that within a few weeks of the Madiun debacle an agent of the newly formed CIA was flown into Yogyakarta, where he recruited members of the Police Mobile Brigade and arranged for their being flown out through the Dutch blockade to the United States for training. And it took the Republic's crushing of the Madiun rebellion to induce Washington to pursue a role in the United Nations that was supportive enough of the Republic to be really effective.

In assessing the Madiun factor, it is also important, I think, to appreciate the American role in unintentionally helping to bring that rebellion about. It is not, I believe, at all clear what the course of Indonesia's history might have been had not Prime Minister Amir Sjarifuddin felt betrayed and humiliated, and had not his political credibility been undercut by the United States, when, in the early months of 1948, it inadvertently — but quite effectively — pulled the political rug out from under him by reneging on its pledge to ensure that the Netherlands would carry out its obligations under the Renville Agreement. How Amir sought to salvage his political career is a long story and too complicated to deal with here. But it can be plausibly argued, I believe, that had the American officials not so undermined him, the Madiun rebellion would probably never have occurred.

The 1950s

It is with some reluctance that I venture into the 1950s, for Herb Feith long ago covered them so well in his superb *The Decline of Constitutional Democracy in Indonesia*, a comprehensive and enormously insightful political study that has stood the test of time and still remains the classic in its field. What I shall attempt to do in this paper is simply to add a bit to the American dimension of the story, especially the 1957-8 period, drawing on data that was unavailable to him but which Audrey Kahin and I have discovered in the process of researching our present study of this period.

With the Eisenhower administration the Indonesian leadership had to cope with an American foreign policy approach even more Manichean in its orientation than was Truman's. Its principal architects, John Foster Dulles and the new CIA head, his brother Allen, saw Indonesia's international stance as a 'naive neutralism' that advantaged the communist camp in the cold war even if it did not actually presage entry into it. And this bias — largely shared by Eisenhower — affected Washington's attitude towards the dispute over West Irian. Despite the usually knowledgeable reporting of its ambassadors in Jakarta, the Eisenhower administration never did show any real understanding of how heavily the West Irian issue weighed on the political scales in Indonesia. This not only adversely affected Indonesian-American relations but had repercussions which significantly influenced the course of Indonesian domestic politics.

But to understand the Indonesian policies of Eisenhower and Dulles, it is essential to appreciate their retrospective evaluation of what they saw as America's great defeat by the communists in China. Both men attributed the communists' triumph in China to the Truman Administration's over-emphasis on trying to maintain China's full territorial integrity in the face of the communists' growing strength. It would have been more realistic, they held, to have temporarily abandoned the most vulnerable areas, while preserving the strength of Chiang Kai-shek's armies in more easily defended territory — pending an aggressive roll-back against them later — after communist governance had sufficiently alienated the populations in the areas they had occupied. This assessment was clearly expressed in the oral marching orders Eisenhower and Dulles gave Ambassador Hugh S. Cumming Jr.

According to Cumming's notes, Eisenhower cautioned him that 'the problem of unifying such a country [as Indonesia] would be a very great one, particularly since they had no tradition of self-government, [and] that as against a unified Indonesia, which would fall to the communists, and a break-up of that country into smaller segments, he would prefer the latter.' Dulles argued along the same lines, but in greater detail.

Not for more than three and a half years after Cumming's arrival in Jakarta in October 1953 did the Eisenhower Administration feel that conditions warranted application of this formula. But there were two major developments that finally brought them to do so. First, was Sukarno's attitude towards communist China after his trip there in October 1956. While he was not attracted to Mao's political system, he applauded his success in rebuilding China's economy and felt that the new China had lessons in economic development to offer that were highly relevant to undeveloped economies such as Indonesia's.

For Ambassador Cumming, who had long congratulated himself on what he believed to be his close rapport with Sukarno, and on having arranged his successful visit to the United States only a few months before, the Indonesian President's reaction to China was a great humiliation, and he acknowledged later that this was a watershed in his attitude towards Sukarno. Upon taking up a new post in Washington at the beginning of March 1957 he actively nourished the anti-Sukarno prejudices that the China trip had already engendered in the minds of President Eisenhower and Dulles.

Presumably as is the case with many ambitious servants, Cumming, having sensed his bosses' prejudices, was inclined to reinforce them. Dulles appointed Cumming as director of his department's intelligence arm, and then as State's liaison with CIA. Soon after, when Dulles charged Cumming with the responsibility of vetting all incoming departmental cables and deciding which should reach his desk, he acquired considerable influence in the department.

But more important than this 'China factor' in raising the concern of the Eisenhower administration about Indonesia's political prospects were the striking gains of the PKI in the provincial elections on Java in mid-1957. While in the 1955 elections for parliament the PKI had won 20.6% of the votes on Java, it garnered 27.4% of the Java-wide vote in the provincial elections held in July and August of 1957. This increase served to reinforce Washingtons's perception that, though Java might be drifting toward communism, the outer islands, where the PKI had been relatively weak in the 1955 elections, were on the whole, bastions of anti-communism.

With his brother Allen head of the CIA, Secretary of State Dulles was more inclined to respect that agency's reporting on Indonesia than that from the Jakarta Embassy, now headed by Ambassador John Allison. And on Indonesia, as with most other areas of the world, Eisenhower usually followed the advice of John Foster Dulles. The tendency to discount Allison's reporting was clearly increased by the views of Hugh Cumming. Increasingly in disagreement with the Jakarta Embassy, he helped sustain Dulles' own growing belief that Sukarno was, as the head of the CIA's Far Eastern Section reported in mid-1957, 'beyond redemption' and leading his country towards communism.

The unreliability of the CIA's reporting was also clearly evident in its representation of the movements for greater regional administrative and financial autonomy which by early 1957 had begun to develop in some areas outside Java. As Feith pointed out, these were based in large part on valid local grievances against the central government, and especially on the fact that most of the foreign exchange their exports earned benefited Java rather than their own areas. And in some, particularly West Sumatra, there was dissatisfaction with insufficient representation in the central government. But in every case the genesis of these regional assertions of autonomy was also strongly attributable to the ambitions of senior local military leaders who saw their own positions threatened by the efforts of General Nasution's central Army command to achieve greater consolidation and centralised control over regional commanders, and by his attempts to accomplish this through their often long overdue transfers to other posts.

Despite some wishful thinking in Washington, at this time none of these movements repudiated Sukarno as President of the Republic, displayed any intention to break with the Jakarta government, or registered any effect on the balance of power there. But during 1957 — still heeding the CIA and its agents in the field rather than the generally sober and accurate reporting of Allison's embassy — the Eisenhower administration listened attentively to the wild assessment of CIA Director Allen Dulles when he reported to the National Security Council in mid-March 1957 that 'the process of disintegration has continued in Indonesia to a point where only the island of Java remains under the control of the Central Government. The armed forces of the outlying islands have declared their independence of the Central Government....'

It was this sort of intelligence that gave rise to the calculation in the Eisenhower Administration that these regional movements could provide fulcrums for applying leverage on Jakarta in accord with American interests. This soon led to a radically new and covert level of US activism aimed at strengthening the regional military leaders and encouraging them to take a firmer stand in their demands for political change in the central government. Acting on the recommendations of Washington's recently established Interdepartmental Committee on Indonesia, headed by ex-ambassador Cumming, the US National Security Council (with Eisenhower and the two Dulles brothers present) on 23 September 1957, authorised a new two-level policy towards Indonesia. Ambassador Allison was to conduct 'official diplomatic relations' as usual in Jakarta while at the same time a new covert policy, of which he remained largely unaware, was to be executed concurrently. The essence of the covert mandate proceeded from the CIA's premise that 'the Communists on Java have not only a relative but also an absolute majority (remember that the actual figure was 27.4%) and that the trend cannot be reversed by any action we might take.' The NSC then stipulated that

> we wish to strengthen the dissident regional elements so that in their negotiations with the Central Government they will be negotiating from a position of strength and the government one of weakness; that failing successful negotiations, and should the regional elements break away, we will have laid the groundwork for strengthening the outer islands; that in the event of a civil war the anti-Communist forces will have greater strength; that time is running in favour of the Communists and against us.

This call for prompt action was soon met by CIA agents in Indonesia, now fully authorised to encourage and build up the strength of the dissident regional military leaders. Within just over a week a CIA agent arrived in Bukittinggi to turn over to Colonel Simbolon funds for the support of the troops who had accompanied him there after an Army coup had deposed him in North Sumatra. Soon afterwards Simbolon and a few officers from the staff of Lt. Colonel Husein, the central Sumatra commander, were invited to accompany this agent to the CIA station in Singapore. There, this agent recalls, Simbolon and these officers 'played up the anti-Communist act because they knew we were interested in that' and Simbolon announced that his Padang group 'were intending to revolt against the Jakarta government and that they needed money and arms'. More funds and the promise of arms delivery to Padang were quickly given, and arrangements were made for some of Simbolon's entourage to remain behind for training in radio communication.

Over the next five months the US provided the rebels in Sumatra with sophisticated communications equipment and modern arms for 8,000 men. Initially this was done discreetly — indirectly or over the beach via US Navy submarines. They also took out some of Colonel Husein's soldiers for training at various American military facilities in the western Pacific. In this effort to deliver arms and provide training to the dissident regional military, several American allies were gradually drawn in, most importantly the Chinese Nationalist government on Taiwan and the Philippines.

This external support further strengthened the dissident military leaders on Sumatra and Sulawesi, but did not prove sufficient to enable them to apply enough pressure on Sukarno and the Jakarta government to meet Washington's expectations. Two events at the end of November 1957 increased political polarisation within Jakarta, drove a deeper wedge between Sukarno and the Eisenhower administration, and quickly led to a substantial escalation in the level of American intervention.

First, senior American officials found that the Indonesians had not been bluffing when they promised that Dutch properties would be seized and the Dutch expelled if, once again, the Netherlands refused to negotiate the West Irian issue. Almost immediately after 29 November, when the UN Assembly — primarily because of a lack of US support — failed to muster the minimum two-thirds majority to permit even debate of the West Irian issue, a bitter Sukarno, refusing to accept the national and personal humiliation he saw as inherent in this Dutch victory, encouraged the Indonesian Army, and labor unions, to seize all Dutch properties, and most Dutch residents were ordered to leave. As a consequence, the Indonesian economy was badly shaken, and the Army as an institution greatly strengthened, gaining access to an enormous reservoir of patronage.

More unexpected, and with a heavy impact on the country's political life, was the very nearly successful attempt at Cikini, thirty six hours later, to assassinate Sukarno. This was understandably a traumatic event for him, and it resulted in a much sharper cleavage between him and the country's major Muslim political party, the Masyumi, members of whose youth organisation certainly played a part in the assassination attempt. The leaders of the party itself were not involved but it was plausible that Sukarno should assume they were. A campaign of harassment and intimidation with his certain knowledge if not instigation now drove three senior Masyumi leaders, Mohammad Natsir, Sjafruddin Prawiranegara, and Burhanuddin Harahap — along with Colonel Zulkifli Lubis — to seek refuge in Colonel Husein's now largely autonomous province of West Sumatra.

The effects of the Cikini incident on Sukarno, on Indonesia's domestic politics and on Indonesian-American relations should not be underestimated. Not only did it deal a decisive blow to Sukarno's already strained relationship with the Masyumi, thereby seriously skewing Indonesian domestic politics, but it also gravely undermined his trust in the United States. Initially he had seen just the Masyumi and Colonel Lubis as behind the assassination attempt, but his belated discovery, some two months later, that the United States was covertly arming his opponents in Sumatra and Sulawesi brought him to believe that the CIA was behind the Cikini plot, and that it remained out to get him. That conviction he continued to hold for many years to come, probably until his death. If this belief may have seemed unreasonable to some, it did not to the US Senate's Select Committee on Intelligence, when in 1975 it looked into the possibility of CIA roles in assassinations and assassination attempts against heads of state.

The combination of the Cikini affair and the takeovers of Dutch property so polarised political forces in Jakarta that Washington's existing plans for applying pressure there through strengthening dissident colonels in the outer islands now appeared much less promising. By 7 December 1957, the two Dulles brothers and Eisenhower had agreed that, if US aims were to be realised, a much more direct level of US intervention was required. They secretly planned a major naval expedition to Indonesia. Accordingly, the US Chief of Naval operations radioed the Commander in Chief of the US Pacific Forces

> Indonesian situation may become critical. Sail ... one cruiser, one destroyer division, all US amphibious forces available Philippine area, with embarked Marines plus necessary logistical forces. Keep out of sight of land if at all practical. Forces to be prepared any contingency including evacuation US personnel and landing Marines to protect lives and property in Indonesia especially Java and Sumatra....

In explaining this sudden move to his Under Secretary of State Dulles said
> what he would like to do is to see things get to a point where we could plausibly withdraw our recognition of the Sukarno government and give it to the dissident elements on Sumatra and land forces to protect the life and property of Americans; use this as an excuse to bring about a major shift there....

This rationale for the US naval action was to remain in place and serve as a major guide for US Indonesian policy for at least another five months.

Effective use of this naval force required access to Singapore's air and naval bases, and it had been confidently assumed in Washington that America's staunch Atlantic ally would of course make them available. But apparently no one had bothered to warn London, and to Secretary Dulles' great surprise, as the armada approached Singapore, the British baulked, and it was ignominiously obliged to turn around and steam back to Subic Bay. Three months later when the US undertook a second sally, the British had been consulted and Singapore's facilities were made fully available.

When the three Masyumi leaders who had fled Jakarta arrived in Padang during the second week of January 1958 they had not previously known of the colonels' ties with the CIA and they were surprised to find that they and their chief civilian ally, Sumitro Djojohadikusumo, already had well developed sources of external funding and military support, including air cover.

These Masyumi leaders were quite prepared to join with the colonels and Sumitro in demanding a change in Jakarta, whereby Sukarno would be left as a figurehead. with real power in the hands of a cabinet led by Hatta and the Sultan of Yogyakarta. But they were opposed to the colonels' fall-back position of a full break with Jakarta and the establishment of a counter government for all Indonesia if the first plan failed. And they strongly resisted the idea of a military government proposed by Colonel Lubis, or the possibility voiced by some that an independent State of Sumatra be established. But their influence was diminished by the firmness of the outside commitments the colonels and Sumitro had made and their belief that the United States would soon grant them de facto recognition, a status that both Washington and London were then seriously contemplating. But having associated themselves with the camp of rebellion, the Masyumi leaders realised that they too had crossed the Rubicon.

The Padang military leaders, on 10 February 1958, issued a proclamation demanding that Sukarno return to his constitutional position and rescind all past unconstitutional actions, and that Hatta and the Sultan of Yogyakarta form a new cabinet. Prime Minister Djuanda was given just five days to meet this ultimatum, which expired the day before Sukarno's return from abroad; otherwise unspecified steps were threatened. Secretary Dulles promptly encouraged them when, the next day, he made a public statement denigrating the Sukarno government and implicitly approving of the rebels' actions.

Undoubtedly heartened by Dulles' statement, Colonel Husein, on 15 February, announced the formation of a temporary counter-government for all Indonesia, Pemerintah Revolusioner Republik Indonesia (PRRI), which would serve until Sukarno returned to his constitutional position and appointed a cabinet led by Hatta and the Sultan of Yogyakarta.

Hatta and the Sultan, as well as Djuanda, were stunned and outraged at what they considered to be a rash, foolish, provocative, and utterly unnecessary move by the leaders in Padang and Minahasa. Moreover, the growing perception that the United States stood behind the rebels tended to undermine their patriotic credentials. Ironically, given Dulles' objectives, it was the PKI that drew maximum advantage from this widely held view.

The directness of the rebels' confrontation with Sukarno, and the fait-accompli with which they presented him upon his scheduled return on 16 February, removed almost any possibility for compromise. The country was now militarily as well as politically and geographically fully polarised and this fitted the strategy the Eisenhower administration was bent on pursuing.

On 23 February 1958, the commander of the US 7th Fleet ordered South an even more formidable task force than that which had been frustrated in trying to reach Singapore two months before. Arriving there just a few days after a second and stronger public statement of Dulles excoriating Sukarno's government and generally interpreted as a call for its displacement, the arrival of this armada was bound to make a strong impression.

It certainly acutely worried Prime Minister Djuanda and General Nasution, especially because, even before the ships arrived, the American Chargé, Sterling Cottrell, suddenly demanded that US forces be permitted back into central Sumatra — Colonel Husein's bailiwick — in a 'protective' move to safeguard American personnel and property at the Caltex oil installations there. Djuanda and Nasution correctly saw this as a ruse to get American troops positioned in a way which could advantage the rebels, and they concluded that all the US needed was a pretext.

Consequently they felt that every effort had to be made to pre-empt an American move into the oilfields. Secretly Nasution's existing schedule to send government troops to the east coast of central Sumatra was drastically speeded up to fit this new situation. With very limited logistical facilities his troops managed to get to the oilfields before the US Marines and demonstrated that they were perfectly capable of protecting American lives and property there.

Nasution's lightning attack caught American military and civilian officials every bit as much by surprise as it did the PRRI military commanders. Use of the Pekanbaru airfield had been second only to Singapore as pivotal in American planning. The strategy by which Eisenhower and the Dulles brothers had set such great store was now a shambles, and they now had to develop a new one. This was to provide the rebels with air cover while continuing to maintain as heavy a flow of weapons to them as possible. Nasution recognised the critical importance of air cover, and that with it the rebels would be a much more formidable foe. Consequently, as he had done with the Caltex fields, he drastically advanced the scheduled attack on Padang to preclude any possibility of its airfield being used. To provide air cover for General Yani's invasion forces Nasution had been able to spare him no more than two combat planes, but their bombing and strafing was enough to intimidate Colonel Husein's forces who promptly withdrew to the interior.

With the fall of Padang and then of Bukittinggi on 4 May, the rebels on

Sumatra were henceforward obliged to confine their operations largely to the level of protracted guerrilla warfare, a struggle which they were able to sustain for another three years, albeit with diminishing success.

But in the eastern theatre of rebellion, headquartered in Menado, there was sufficient time — and intervening geographic space — for the United States to put substantial air cover in place before Nasution could marshal the logistical resources — naval and air — to move against Colonel Sumual's Permesta forces, which had a good airfield at Menado and an even better one on Morotai. Moreover, both fields were close to those in the southern Philippines which were a short flight from the major American base at Clark Field. Through it were funnelled arms, planes, and American and Taiwanese pilots from other bases on Taiwan. Nasution felt he had to husband what little power he had primarily for the defence of Java, which — with good reason — he believed Sumual was preparing to bomb. And so the balance of airpower in Indonesia remained overwhelmingly in favour of Sumual.

The American and other foreign pilots that the CIA had rounded up for the rebels went on bombing and strafing sprees well outside Sulawesi, attacking European oil tankers and cargo ships along the east Kalimantan coast, sinking the Indonesian Navy's flagship, with all hands lost, as well as bombing government outposts in southern Sulawesi and Ambon. So heady was the rebels' reaction to the mastery of the air with which the CIA had endowed them that Colonel Sumual now laid plans for an attack on Java in the neighbourhood of the capital.

In the meantime, the new American Ambassador, Howard Jones, came to realise the foolishness and political counter-productivity of the Administration's policy of forceful intervention. He soon found a Washington ally within the US military establishment. These officials had become progressively worried over indications that the Indonesian Armed Forces were very serious about carrying out their threat to turn to the Soviet bloc for the ships, military planes and weaponry which the United States had for so long refused to sell them.

But it took an exceptionally dramatic event to get the Eisenhower administration to acknowledge that their old policy had to be abandoned. This occurred on 18 May, with the shooting down over Ambon and capture of Allen L. Pope, an American pilot working for the CIA on detached duty from the US military. Jakarta now had incontrovertible proof of direct American involvement in support of the rebels.

A partial disengagement of American support to the rebels in both Sumatra and Sulawesi did now begin, not as rapidly as Jones and the government leaders in Jakarta would have liked, but sufficient to impress Jakarta and lead to its renewed disposition to try and reach a settlement with the rebels. Washington's abandonment of the rebels was not complete, however, for there was still a strong enough minority voice in Washington which advocated 'keeping all options open' to insure that some military supplies continued to reach rebel pockets well into 1961.

But by the end of the third week of May 1958 the senior members of the Eisenhower Administration had concluded that their gambit in building up and using the leverage of the outer island colonels to contain the growth of communist power in Indonesia was failing, and that their best bet was to work through General Nasution and the central Army leadership to achieve this.

Marking this turning of the tide in American policy were token shipments of US military equipment and spare parts, the first of which was flown into Jakarta on 15 August 1958, and paid for out of President Eisenhower's Contingency Fund. This was more important psychologically and politically than in substance. Thereafter, however, there was a continuing, if somewhat spasmodic, increase in the flow of US weaponry. But as late as mid-July 1960, the Pentagon acknowledged the amount reaching Indonesia from the 'Iron Curtain Countries' was still greater than the total coming in from 'the West.' And even as late as that the general in charge of the US arms program for Indonesia stated privately 'as of now the US is still playing both sides'.

When Colonels Simbolon and Husein secretly made their own separate peace with General Nasution in mid-1961, leaving their Masyumi colleagues and Lubis high and dry and holding the bag, Washington's disposition to rely on Nasution was, of course, even stronger. Moreover, largely because of Jones' reporting, the Eisenhower administration was even more reluctantly concluding that containment of communist power in Indonesia meant not only supporting Nasution and the central Army leadership, but also required, for the time being at least, trying to get along with Sukarno instead of attempting to oust him.

Overall, as a consequence of the Eisenhower administration's heavily interventionist policies, the political landscape of Indonesia and the possibilities for its political development had been considerably altered. Some of these consequences I have already alluded to and others will be obvious enough.

Most obvious was the fact that the US had induced regional leaders to go **much further** than they had ever planned themselves in this break with Jakarta. Indonesian society was left considerably more polarised than it had been before this American intrusion. The country's major Islamic party had been so discredited that it emerged politically emasculated and the political future of its most gifted leader ruined. The NU which had sat on the sidelines, had benefited. The Socialist Party was weakened by Sumitro's involvement in the rebellion. The PKI somewhat increased its strength. The Army emerged much stronger, not simply militarily but as a major political force. Sukarno emerged marginally stronger.

From the American point of view this intervention had proved to be heavily counter-productive, and that is undoubtedly one reason why it is still so difficult to get many of the relevant documents concerning this US role declassified.

8

Legacies of the 'Revolution'

Robert Cribb

The struggle of 1945-1949 delivered political independence to Indonesia, but historians are still not agreed on the broader impact which those years of fighting and negotiation exercised on the politics of the 1950s, although they suggest for the most part that it was substantial.

We have, of course, the view expressed in Kahin's *Nationalism and Revolution in Indonesia* (1952) that the Revolution's main positive contribution, aside from the actual achievement of independence, was a reinforcing of Indonesian self-confidence and self-reliance which cut the ties of colonial dependence more effectively than a peaceable and gradual transfer of power. This view, to which Feith's *Decline of Constitutional Democracy* (1962) also seems to subscribe, implies that the decline of parliamentary democracy in the 1950s was a consequence of baleful legacies of the Revolution: political tensions had sharpened both because of the violent conflicts between Indonesians during the war of independence and because the impending departure of the Dutch meant that the character of independent Indonesia seemed about to be set. In addition, there was the physical destruction of infrastructure, which placed unmanageable economic burdens on the new system, and the issue of western New Guinea, which distracted the public and politicians from the serious business of government.

In opposition to this view, we have the argument, expressed most eloquently, though with little mention of the 1950s, in Anderson's *Java in a Time of Revolution* (1972), that the Revolution largely failed and that its direct impact on the broad development of Indonesian politics in the 1950s was thus minor; in this view, over-reliance on diplomatic dealings with the outside world during the independence struggle turned the Revolution into a mere transfer of power which left the structures and assumptions of the colonial state relatively intact. Paradoxically, however, this interpretation also stresses the role of the 1940s by explaining the fall of the parliamentary system as a delayed return to the goals of the Revolution and a shedding of colonial legacies.

And third, we have what might be called the 'time-bomb' view of the independence struggle: that the 1940s had little immediate impact on the politics of the 1950s, but that they had left a long term problem (or conceivably a blessing) in the form of a self-confident and politicised Army, whose experience in the 1940s provided the underpinning for intervention in politics which led initially to Guided Democracy and ultimately to thorough military domination of the polity under the New Order. This view emerges especially from the writings of McVey (1971 & 1972) and Sundhaussen (1982) on the Indonesian military.

Each of these interpretations rests, of course, on its own broader assumptions about the nature of Indonesian politics, but there are a number of ways in which a closer look at the period 1945-1949 can shed light on the validity of each argument.

First, we have, I think, over-estimated the destructive effects of the 1940s on the Indonesian economy and administration. The Japanese occupation and the armed struggle which followed it were, of course, deeply disruptive, but we need to remember that the extent of the fighting in Indonesia was limited throughout this period. The Japanese advanced rapidly and the Dutch applied scorched-earth tactics only on a limited scale; the Japanese military governments in Indonesia neglected physical infrastructure and ruthlessly exploited Indonesian labour, but shortage of personnel and distance from Japan meant that the Japanese intervention was distinctly less intrusive than in, say, Korea or China. The Japanese defeat and surrender in Indonesia, too, was accompanied by relatively little destruction, and what we loosely call the Revolution or the war of independence was in reality a long, fractious ceasefire punctuated by brief bouts of heavy fighting. This is not, of course, to say that the economy emerged unscathed from the 1940s, but rather that, given the vastly greater extent of destruction elsewhere in Asia and Europe, we should not give undue emphasis to the weakening effects of war in Indonesia.

This warning applies particularly to our understanding of the Indonesian bureaucracy. Studies of the Japanese occupation and the Revolution have shown that the capable, professional bureaucracy of the colonial era suffered significantly during these periods: the combination of public humiliation of officials and growing opportunities for corruption during the occupation added to resentment of the intrusive actions of government employees during the colonial period to create the environment in which social revolutions exploded along the length of Sumatra and Java in the aftermath of the Japanese surrender. Although the social revolutions were for the most part defeated, they have received such detailed study that we have tended to take as given that they succeeded in their immediate goals of displacing and destroying the local bureaucratic infrastructure.

This conclusion is not borne out by the history of the latter part of the Revolution. On Java, at least, by 1947 local administration in many regions was in the hands of regional defence councils (*Dewan Pertahanan Daerah*) in which defence, coordination of food supplies, financial policy and other key areas were decided jointly by civilian Residents and regional military commanders. The balance of power between civilian and military groups varied from region to region according to personality and strategic circumstances, but everywhere, as far as I can tell, the military depended both for supplies and for the cooperation of the people on the organisational capacity and popular standing of the civilian bureaucracy. The importance of the civilian administrative structure is indicated most strongly by the structure of Nasution's Java Command, which explicitly incorporated the civilian bureaucracy as a key element in mobilising mass support for the army guerrilla struggle.

There is even, I think, good reason to argue that the Revolution strengthened the civilian bureaucracy in some respects. The adversity which brought capable and dynamic young officers to the forefront of the Armed Forces had a similar effect in sections of the bureaucracy. The social revolutions, the hardship and disruptions of the independence struggle and the demand for difficult political decisions winnowed many less capable time-servers from the administration, leaving the civilian bureaucracy, far more than the military, trim, efficient and ready for the tasks of national reconstruction after 1949. The tragedy for the bureaucracy was not the destruction of the 1940s but the politicisation of the 1950s, which saw the bureaucracy swollen to unrecognisable proportions by political appointees from successive cabinets, leaving the capable old guard outnumbered and isolated.

A second area of misunderstanding lies in the common view of the parliamentary system as a legacy of colonialism, and more especially of the negotiations for the transfer of power in the course of 1949. The parliament of the 1950s was a hybrid in membership and structure. It drew its members from the various parliamentary institutions of the original Republic of Indonesia and from the federal BFO (*Bijeenkomst voor Federaal Overleg - Federal Consultative Assembly*) states; its procedures were drawn partly from external Dutch and American models and partly from those of the KNIP, which was influenced in turn by the Japanese-sponsored Chuo Sangi-in and by the colonial era Volksraad. Even more important, however, it was heir to a significant tradition of nationalist assembly, from the Youth Congresses and the PPPKI (*Permufakatan Perhimpunan-perhimpunan Politik Kebangsaan Indonesia* - Agreement of Indonesian People's Political Associations) of the 1920s to GAPI (*Gabungan Politik Indonesia* - Indonesian Political Federation) in the 1930s, and to the experience of popular sovereignty during the Revolution, when the KNIP and its Working Party were a forum for robust democratic exchange. Although the notion of a parliament is a Western one, the parliament of the 1950s was no more alien to Indonesian cultural and political traditions than any of the new state's other institutions, including the Army.

The parliamentary system, moreover, served the important role of postponing the struggle over Indonesia's national identity which had been brewing throughout the history of the nationalist movement. The stalemate between rival political forces in parliament, for which the 1950s has often been criticised, was precisely what Indonesia needed in the aftermath of the independence struggle when betrayal and privation had sharpened political antagonisms. It was no colonial inheritance which destroyed the parliamentary system, therefore: rather, the secular shift towards the left and towards Java in the balance of power in parliament after the 1955 elections destroyed the basis of the stalemate under which the Masyumi, the PNI and every other party could rely on thwarting the will of its opponents, without necessarily ever getting its own way.

A third area in which important and illuminating research has clouded our understanding of 1950s parliamentary democracy relates to the military. Neither the Kahin/Feith liberal interpretation of the direction of Indonesian politics, nor the culture-based approach which was a hallmark of Indonesianist studies in the 1960s and 70s, was geared to explain the military's intervention in Indonesian politics. The historical research which has now investigated this question has focussed primarily on the Revolution: this, we have been told, was the period in which the Army developed its sense of administrative separateness from the civilian administration, when it came to believe that it was a separate creation from the civilian institutions of the Republic, when it developed a sense of self-reliance, when it established its credentials as the sole reliable defender of the nation by organising to resist the Allies in 1945 and the Dutch in 1948/49 and acquired a corresponding contempt for timorous civilian politicians, and when it developed its profound antipathy to communism (and to political Islam). The 1950s, by contrast, was a time which vindicated, rather than created, these opinions, incubating attitudes created by the Revolution rather than shaping the military's basic beliefs.

None of this is entirely untrue, but it is no more than a partial picture of the Army's experience during these years. The Army's creation in 1945 was tightly intertwined, especially at regional level, with the seizure of power from the Japanese by civilian local national committees (*Komite Nasional Indonesia*). The Army was not the only significant armed force to defend the Republic after 1945 but rather shared the field with a host of irregular armed units; the Army's performance in the field, moreover, was generally dismal until 1949. Army units dallied with collaboration with the Dutch after the so-called first Police Action of mid-1947 and the first commander of the Army in West Java actually deserted to the Dutch. The Army, moreover, was not administratively separate from or independent of the civilian bureaucracy during the Revolution: vast amounts of logistical support came to the Army both through Amir Sjarifuddin's Department of Defence and through the regional civilian administrations. And finally, the Army itself was so deeply divided — from the front line right up to the High Command — that one can never talk of an 'Army' view in this period. We can certainly say that the Revolution left a wealth of military experience out of which military ideologists such as Nasution and Simatupang were able to create a powerful and plausible myth of Army devotion and grievance, but the Revolution as a whole does not point inexorably in the direction of eventual military rule.

In this brief paper, I have argued that three of our common assumptions about the impact of the Revolution on the parliamentary democracy of the 1950s are mistaken or at least over-stated and that the keys to the demise of the parliamentary system lie in the 1950s, not in the 1940s. The irony is, of course, is that hardly any serious research on the parliamentary democracy has been carried, since the 1950s themselves; we know far less on the whole about the parliamentary period than we do about the Revolution. Until this problem is remedied, the 1950s are likely to remain opaque.

References

Anderson, B.R.O'G. (1972) *Java in a Time of Revolution: Occupation and Resistance*, Cornell University Press, Ithaca, NY.

Feith, H. (1962) *The Decline of Constitutional Democracy in Indonesia*, Cornell University Press, Ithaca, NY.

Kahin, G. McT., (1952) *Nationalism and Revolution in Indonesia*, Cornell University Press, Ithaca, NY.

McVey, R.T. (1971) 'The Post-Revolutionary Transformation of the Indonesian Army', *Indonesia* 11 (April 1971)

_____ (1972) 'The Post-Revolutionary Transformation of the Indonesian Army', *Indonesia* 13 (April 1972)

Sundhaussen, U. (1982) *The Road to Power: Indonesian Military Politics 1945-1967*, Oxford University Press, Kuala Lumpur.

9

The Indonesia Raya Dream and its Impact on the Concept of Democracy

Y.B. Mangunwijaya

'A nation of coolies and a coolie among nations' (Sukarno) needs time to grow into the maturity of a free nation and a nation of free persons. Indonesia had achieved her political independence thanks to a handful enlightened intellectuals who, before the World War II, had pioneered the nationalist movement in a very gentlemanlike way. Our Indonesian historian, Professor Sartono Kartodirdjo, has pointed out in his many works that no peasant rebellions against colonial rule had ever gained victory. The independence struggle proved, however, that peasants (Indonesia was and is still an agrarian society) revolting against the Dutch (a rich industrialised nation and, according to the Dutch themselves, a genius in colonial administration) had successfully overthrown alien rule thanks to the helping hands of a relatively small number of intellectuals, whose eyes, ironically, were opened by the Dutch themselves.

Only afterwards, during the short interregnum of the Japanese, did the masses (relatively still a few, particularly the schooled youth) and the other strata of the Indonesian elite come to understand the true relations between the natives and the white lords. This was due to the manipulation by Sukarno and Hatta of the unexpected Japanese occupation. Only then did the common people become inspired by the fire of their leaders. The youth in particular underwent military training from the Japanese Army. These militaristic young people, trained by Great Japan, became the first seeds of the future Indonesian Armed Forces; but more important, also the first seeds of the whole political, economical, social, military, and cultural engineering of the

New Order.

Sukarno had no military training, He was an intellectual, a civilian leader with human values. Yet he did have a deeply hidden militaristic trait - that of the Javanese *ksatria* (knight). The *ksatria* ideal sparkled brightly in his soul and in that of the many *priyayi* as well. It was a feudal ideal, linked with the idea of *Indonesia Raya* (Great Indonesia). A second aspect of Sukarno's message was his desire for the ending of the coolie and *babu* (maidservant) mentality of the nation. But being free as a nation, and being recognised by other nations as free, does not automatically achieve a third aspect of Sukarno's message: the ending of *l'exploitation de l'homme par l'homme*, a theme he continually emphasised.

The Indonesian nationalists of the 1928 generation — the generation of founding fathers who formulated the Pancasila and proclaimed independence and adopted the 1945 Constitution — formulated five fundamental goals for the Indonesian struggle: a unified (not feudal) state replacing the Netherlands Indies; a nation, based on the rule of law; the rejection of a capitalist economy; the adoption of a cooperative system on the basis of the indigenous *gotong royong* (mutual help) spirit; the improvement of the lot of those Sukarno called the *marhaen*s, not a Marxist proletariat but the 'little people' of Indonesia. But there were differences within the leadership of that generation about how these goals were to be achieved. The Javanese Sukarno, like all Javanese *priyayi*, still dreamed of Indonesia Raya. On the other hand were the anti-fascist, democratic Minangkabaus, Hatta and Sjahrir, whose dream was of a free nation state ruled by democratic laws and reason.

Taught by humanistic Dutch teachers

It is important to notice that Sukarno, Hatta and Sjahrir were educated by the Dutch. It is also important to distinguish between the Dutch colonial Government and the actual Dutch teachers with the liberal outlook appropriate to the heirs of the former Batavian Republic, which had fought over 80 years for its freedom from Spain. Of course the educational system of the Netherlands Indies was colonial in nature, but the teachers as individual persons were generally enlightened and humanistic civilians in their methods and spirit. Even a subversive, anti-colonial novel like *Max Havelaar*, written by a rebellious former employer of the Dutch Administration, was prescribed Dutch literature for Dutch high schools, attended by Indonesian pupils. The professors and lecturers of the Academy of Law in Batavia once wrote a public letter to the Governor General to protest against the imprisonment of Sukarno.

The Dutch colonial system naturally aimed merely to produce the employees needed by the Administration, but in practice the Dutch teachers trained the pupils to think critically, to explore, to create, to become mature men and women with a free democratic spirit, with a sense of responsibility, albeit in a framework of a liberal bourgeois society, but also with its ascetic and ethical code of a hard working mercantile society. Soon these critically thinking Indonesian pupils discovered the cruel colonial and capitalistic system of their rulers, who exploited their native countrymen in a greedy manner. But at the same time they internalised also the virtues of their western lords and the right attitudes of a noble meritocracy as against the dark practices of feudalism and the hedonistic lives of their native kings and lazy nobility.

They internalised also the ideals of modern democracy for an enlightened society, the principles of the rule of law, the brave pioneering of adventurous merchants and explorers, smart inventors, the spirit of honest work, and fair play, the heroic spirit of Dutch and other freedom fighters — all virtues and attitudes which fascinated the young elites, who mentally were pulled out from their feudal traditions into the freedom of the modern democratic West. Finally they were inspired by the idea of nationalism and the struggle for independence. Sukarno-Hatta-Sjahrir as leaders were very different in their concepts of nation-building, but they shared Dutch teachings about how to run a state and society democratically within the spirit of the rule of law.

Through his western education Sukarno was able to discover and appreciate the modern trends of the new times. Nevertheless he remained traditional within the old *priyayi* ethos, strolling with one leg on traditional paths (he never had studied abroad) and was emotionally bound to the inherited dreams of a lost grand past of Java's or Indonesia Raya's history before the West came. Hatta and Sjahrir on the other hand, being Sumatrans and true *perantau* (emigrants) had inhaled the new spirit of the modern humanistic world of their teachers and of democratic societies.

But it was Sukarno who had the masses in his hands, sharing with them the dreams of being heirs of great kingdoms defeated by foreign political superiority but undefeated in the spiritual and magic realms. Especially in the quest for identity Sukarno could appeal to the imagination and frustrations of the masses. A hidden but continuing Messianic longing on the part of the masses appealed to his charismatic, charming personality.

It was understandable that, after the recognition of the Republic, fierce debates came up about whether the Revolution, (a transitional disorder in Hatta's eyes) was over or not.

Sukarno held firmly that colonialism and imperialism were not yet dead. Mohammad Hatta, to avoid a serious split in the nation, was persuaded to resign and democratic Soetan Sjahrir was pushed from the scene. Essentially Sukarno was right, always insisting that imperialism and colonialism were not dead, but only dying. But Hatta too was right, arguing that even the struggle against neo-imperialism and neo-colonialism should be carried out methodically in an ordered and competent way, not by means of slogans and demagogic manipulation of the masses. It was the old classical controversy of the decades before the World War II, between Sukarno's strategy of *machtsvorming* (the mobilisation of the power of the masses) and Hatta-Sjahrir's conviction, that struggle primarily requires trained leaders and

emancipated cadres, who know how to fight and for what purpose.
But after the Japanese set foot in the archipelago changes came.

Taught by the Japanese masters

The political and social engineering of the Japanese occupying forces was very harsh, but their propaganda units were smart and enchanting. Although three and a half years of occupation were too short a time for the changing of a whole society of coolies and *babu*s into determined fighters, the Japanese made a very great impact on the whole life and attitude of Indonesians, and especially on the young. The Japanese rulers, recognising the small numbers of occupying forces as compared with the very large area of Indonesia to be ruled, had to rely on the services of native leaders. This give-and-take policy between the Japanese rulers and Sukarno, with his love for mass demonstrations, was convincing and they joined in it without wavering. But for democratic and anti-fascist Hatta such co-operation was very painful. Together, however, they managed to mobilise the masses to become determined supporters of the independence movement.

The short interregnum of the Japanese however had created a new force for the future by the intensive training of a great number of military and paramilitary young people, who were fascinated by the Japanese example of how the East could defeat the lords from the powerful West. These young cadres, trained by Japanese military instructors, had never enjoyed the academic and humanistic education of their fathers and grandfathers of the 1908-1928 Generation. The ideology within which they were taught was the Japanese military *bushido* with its lessons about how to challenge Western superiority without losing self-identity and the pride of national greatness. This suited very well the dreams of their pupils: Great Indonesia. Pre-eminently it was Sukarno himself, who personified this nationalistic pride and determination.

So Sukarno and his Javanese admirers, recalling to mind the greatness of ancient Majapahit in her golden age (thanks to the lectures of their Dutch teachers), electrified by Multatuli's *Max Havelaar* novel (again, thanks to their Dutch teachers), but fairly comprehending the miserable fate of their coolie and *babu* brothers and sisters, and moved by the struggle of their Asian comrades in India and the Philippines for independence, generously understood their historical destiny of pioneering the freedom of their colonised country.

The Humanistic Strategy in the Revolution

The Indonesian nationalists of the pre World War II generation had one common trait in spite of differences. They were all more or less anti-fascist in attitude. It is therefore understandable that this humanistic, democratically educated, generation should be puzzled as to how to cope with the alien ethos of their Japanese masters. While Sukarno and Hatta held public positions under the Occupation, Sjahrir and Sjarifuddin remained as underground opponents of the Japanese, and at the end of the Occupation were concerned about charges of collaboration that might be levelled against those leaders and about the effect of Japan's military and para-military training of Indonesia's militant youth.

After the defeat of Japan there were those who believed that armed struggle was the only way to achieve independence. Against the mainstream Hatta and Sjahrir preferred the path of negotiation and diplomacy. And Sjahrir saw that without Sukarno and Hatta as supreme leaders the Revolution would run aground. In that context the idea was developed of Sukarno becoming a constitutional president with a prime minister and a cabinet responsible to KNIP (National Indonesian Central Committee). The choice of a democratic and constitutional system was a pragmatic and realistic choice, made during the first phase of the Republic's existence. It was not based on ideological notions drawn from an alien, Western liberal philosophy but was adopted to meet the needs of the moment. Through it Sukarno and Hatta were saved from possible Allied charges of collaboration and it enabled Sukarno to perform his role of mobilising the masses in support of the Revolution while Hatta, Sjahrir and the cabinet coped with the foreign powers and the Dutch. It was an emergency mechanism, adopted by consensus, within which the revolutionary energies of the people could be used, but in an ordered way.

Armed resistance to the Dutch was necessary, too, but ultimately the decisive battle was fought and won in the diplomatic field by the civil leaders.

The emergence of the Japanese-educated generation of leaders

A difficult question remains. Why did the parliamentary democracy, which gained such a great victory, fail after the recognition of the Indonesian State? The problem is a complex one. The most popular answer, first put forward by Sukarno (who actually was saved precisely by that system) was that parliamentary democracy was an imitation of Western models and couldn't fit into the Indonesian way of settling things.

Perhaps Sukarno was right, in the sense that he understood the human condition of his countrymen. A nation of former coolies and a former coolie among the other nations has a particular cultural and social infrastructure and mentality, A huddling-together people is always unhappy if its members have their own personal opinions. Free decisions and self-determination, the building-blocks of a democratic society, depend on strong personalities with individualistic attitudes.

Collectivist peoples need a strong leader who knows what the people need. In this sense Sukarno was more realistic than Mohammad Hatta and Soetan Sjahrir. Sukarno's Guided Democracy was right in principle, but only as an emergency measure, not as a guiding star for the future. In the long run it kills the exploring mind and the creative energies of the people, and it perpetuates a system and an atmosphere wherein indigenous feudalism, fascistic and colonial behaviour can flourish abundantly like weeds in the rainy monsoon. The New Order essentially goes along the same lines as Sukarno, creating a special sort of guided democracy, but a more feudalistic one, with something approaching a kingdom-like structure.

Meanwhile the generation of leaders with a humanistic touch and a democratic education has faded away. The militaristically trained youth in due course became the leaders of the nation. This had a mighty impact on a collectively-minded nation with its traditional dreams of a Greater Indonesia but also with the tormenting realities of underdevelopment and dependence on the still powerful neo-colonial and neo-imperialistic world structures.

Like the militant revolutionaries of the Choshu samurai clan who defeated the Tokugawa shoguns and started the Meiji Restoration, the Indonesian nationalists under Sukarno's anti-capitalist policy, had to face the mighty political, economic and cultural intervention of the powerful West, which continued to dominate the Indonesian archipelago. In this situation the pupils of the Japanese samurai were determined to build up the dreamed of Indonesia Raya through more or less the same methods which had enabled the Japanese, a hundred years ago, to overcome their scientific and technological underdevelopment. After the fall of Sukarno, the Indonesian samurai proceeded at full speed to follow the Japanese example. They were convinced of the need for a unified grand policy of a tightly disciplined Indonesia incorporating, like the famous Japan Inc., a concentration of all political, economical, cultural, ideological, scientific, technological and military powers in a single coordinated all-controlling system: a nation state and, simultaneously, a big national enterprise, mobilised and centrally guided in a military or paramilitary fashion.

We can thus see a clear parallel between the social engineering system of the New Order with its *dwifungsi* (dual function) of the Armed Forces, and the Japanese strategy of a special blend of military and civil government. It is not a matter of simple imitation of Japan, but many institutions and policies have sprung, consciously or unconsciously, from the Japanese way of thinking and operating.

First we see the military flavour of the whole society. Uniforms, marching, parades, mass sport and entertainment with typical militaristic ceremonies of glamour and national pride everywhere. Military discipline begins very early — in the kindergarten — and continues to university level. The art of fighting, according to the *Karate* or *Taekwondo, Judo* or *Pencak Silat* codes flourish among the youth. The language of command and obedience are common. Instructions, briefings, regulations, orders, commands and the like are part of daily life. Asking questions, worse, criticising, is taboo or is regarded as alien and disturbing to the Indonesian tradition of harmony. One is expected to march in line within ordered ranks, not in an, individualistic, liberalistic or 'western' style, with initiative and freedom. All kinds of initiatives and operations, meetings and discussions, research and scientific workshops require official permission. All sorts of professions are incorporated in an officially recognised, single professional organisation. The Nation is to be a big enterprise, powerful enough to face the superpowers or the multinational corporations.

There is something to be said for this style. A worldwide, systematically operating, menace must be met in a systematic way. Indonesia Incorporated, therefore, followed relevant models from the outside world, especially that of Japan, whose example had impressed the youth of those days, who have now become the leaders of the nation. Consciously or subconsciously the way of Japan in its different phases became the dominating example of the path the New Order should follow. It provided a model for dealing with development under one system of centralised planning and militaristic coordination.

The most 'useful' heritage from the Japanese rulers undoubtedly is the efficient infrastructure of the social engineering of the masses, namely the formidable Japanese *Tonari-kumi* system, developed by the Japanese in support of their war effort. The Japanese had not enough troops to control effectively the vast area of Indonesia, so the *Tonari-kumi* system of neighbourhood associations was created to control every aspect of life, depriving subversive groups of the opportunity to organise in secret underground networks and meetings. The *Tonari-kumi* controlled and reported all activities of its members. In this way a very small army or police unit could easily control a very large area.

Afterwards it was consolidated more efficiently, during the Revolution and its aftermath, into the *Rukun Warga* (RW - Citizens Associations) and the *Rukun Tetangga* (RT - Neighbourhood Associations), the cells of Indonesian society, and of the daily activities of the masses, in which people enjoy mutual help, but without which nobody can act legally. It is a useful brotherhood system. but at the same time an extraordinarily efficient instrument for controlling a whole society. This RT-RW system, its connecting SISKAMLING (*Sistem Keamanan Lingkungan* - Environment Security System) and the HANSIP (*Pertahanan Sipil* - Civil Defence Corps) was implanted by the Japanese, and proved very effective and reliable from the independence struggle until now. Improved and perfected by the New Order, this system has now become taken for granted as an instrument of the whole IPOLEKSOSBUDHANKAMLING (*ideologi-politik-ekonomi-sosial-budaya-pertahanan-keamanan-lingkungan* /ideological-political-economic-social-cultural-defence-security-environment) engineering of Indonesia Incorporated, Indonesia Raya.

In fact, this system contributes much solidarity and much real help for the daily life of the masses. The poor and the weak can survive only if they are united in an effective mutual-help-living-together closed village structure. In a still agrarian traditional village it is not a problem. For poor city-dwellers however, the RT-RW organisation is becoming a necessary substitute for the lost agrarian village system of mutual help. All aspects of life, child-care, youth-care, young-people-care, women-care, work, recreation, feast-celebrations, religion, relieving the poor, housing, water-supply, electricity, toilets, security, environmental cleanness, birth, even birth-control, marriage, death. In short all dimensions of life are supported and their burden relieved by the RT and RW. Nobody within the RT-RW, poor as he or she may be, need fear a hopeless existence; everybody knows that his or her dead body will be decently carried to the grave with the due prayers.

On the other hand, it is an integral part of a totally directed society. The 'Royal' Indonesia Incorporated has a controlled lifestyle held in a rigid feudal (often nepotistic) frame of traditional harmony, with everybody and everything in its own place and time, a cell of the Indonesian version of Japan after the Meiji Restoration, with the *zaibatsu*s (mammoth sized monopolistic financial cliques) as core agents, allied with the bureaucrats, the military, the technocrats, and recently even with the *bingos* — big non-governmental organisations.

Other parallel positions / organisations, created by the Japanese are for instance:

Japanese	Indonesian
Goshi	KORAMIL military commander at the village/subdistrict level
Keiboodan	HANSIP civil defence at the village/subdistrict level
Seinendan	PRAMUKA scouts, or young pioneers
Fujinkai	PKK, Darma Wanita, etc. organisations for housewives
kinrohoshi	*kerjabakti* prescribed unpaid labor for the community
Yamato Damashii	Pancasila the official state- and lifestyle ideology
Gunsai	Dwifungsi ABRI

But the most influential novelty brought by the Japanese is the entire fabric of social and cultural engineering, with its atmosphere of uniforms, marching, inspection ceremonies, parades, unification of professional organisations, military and paramilitary language, attitude and behaviour, security surveillance, and a whole set of commands and chains of instructions, directed in uni-language formulations with prescribed official interpretations, indoctrination etc.etc., often in a benevolent way and useful, but too often fascistic and communistic in performance and spirit.

The basic questions

What are the prospects then of democracy in Indonesia? Government officials, the dominating party and even intellectuals will take a very defensive or angry attitude when foreigners or critical countrymen assert that there is no democracy in Indonesia. Maybe it would help the dialogue if we were to talk about facts, for instance: the actual place of the (Indonesian) human person within the (Indonesian) society and state; about whether the dignity of citizens, regardless of gender, skin, religion, wealth or poverty, ethnic groups, notables or peasants, high or low status, is really held in high esteem, whether their voices are heard, their aspirations honoured. Is the Republic of Indonesia really much better for the little men and women, the peasants, the factory workers, the pupils in schools, university students, low governmental employees etc. than would have been the case had the Netherlands Indies still existed?

Maybe such a comparison is futile, if we are seeking to deal only with realities. But these were precisely the questions which Sukarno, Hatta and all the pioneers of the independence movement had in their minds and actions.

All those questions finally lead to the more important core questions, which require further studies in depth about the cultural and spiritual foundations of the Indonesian man and woman, their perceptions and concepts of person and society, about what the Indonesians call freedom, choice, justice, truth, fair, peace, self-determination, progress, development, obedience, rights and duties and responsibility. Only then can we consider the possibility of democracy.

10

'Rowing in a typhoon' Nahdlatul Ulama and the Decline of Parliamentary Democracy[1]

Greg Fealy

In Indonesian political historiography of the 1950s and 1960s, the traditionalist Islamic party, Nahdlatul Ulama (NU), was usually subject to highly critical interpretations. It was commonly portrayed as opportunistic, politically unsophisticated, venal, and inordinately accommodationist. Notorious for its frequent and usually expedient changes of policy, the Party was seen as bereft of principles and consumed with protecting its own narrow material and political interests. There were few more striking examples of this than NU's acquiescence and apparent collaboration in the dismantling of parliamentary democracy in the late 1950s, a political system it had long claimed to uphold.

Despite the ubiquity of such critical assessments, very little research has been conducted into NU's political thinking. The great intellectual curiosity which Indonesianists of the 1950s and 60s showed for organisations such as the PKI, PNI, Masyumi, Muhammadiyah, PSI and the like, did not extend to NU, even though it was the third largest party after the 1955 elections, and had participated in all but one cabinet (that of Wilopo) during the period of Parliamentary and Guided Democracy between 1950 and 1965.

Two reasons may be offered for this scholarly neglect. It can be argued that serious study of NU during the 'Old Order' has been undermined firstly

---

1. I would like to thank Dr Abdullah Saeed of Melbourne University for his clarification of several aspects of Islamic jurisprudence, and Professor Merle Ricklefs and Dr Herb Feith for their valuable comments on this paper.

by a secular bias which disregarded religious aspects; and secondly, by a pro-modernist inclination which drew scholars rather to a study of such organisations as Masyumi, Muhammadiyah and Persis and which discounted traditionalist Islamic beliefs.[2] This paper will endeavour to redress several aspects of this academic neglect by examining the role of Nahdlatul Ulama in the decline of parliamentary democracy and transition to Guided Democracy. Particular attention will be given to the Party's religious and political ideology, perhaps the least studied aspect of NU. Following a discussion of the origins of NU's religio-political thinking and its perceptions of democracy, the paper will consider the Party's approach to the political crises which it faced in the late 1950s.

Religio-political ideology of Nahdlatul Ulama

For the great majority of its leaders, members and supporters, NU is primarily a religious organisation, with political, social, and economic functions being of secondary importance. Formal leadership is in the hands of *kiai* (religious teachers)[3], whose authority rests upon their reputation as Islamic scholars and spiritual leaders. The milieu of the *kiai* and his followers is the *pesantren*, or the traditional Islamic boarding school. Until the late 1950s, these schools were overwhelmingly rural and almost exclusively devoted to classical Islamic studies. Instruction was centred on the Arabic-script *kitab kuning* (literally, 'yellow books') which most commonly contained commentaries on orthodox Sunni legal texts, and especially, *fiqh* (Islamic jurisprudence). Understanding the canons of traditional Islamic law and its methods of reasoning and application were regarded as essential elements of *pesantren* education. Within *pesantren*, and usually also within the local Muslim community, *kiai* command deep loyalty and obedience. Indeed, it is the relationship between *kiai* and their followers which forms the basis of Nahdlatul Ulama. Despite its large supporter base,[4] power within NU unquestionably resides with a relatively small number of *kiai*.

Theoretically, NU members may follow any one of the four Orthodox Sunni law schools, but in practice they adhere almost exclusively to the

---

2. As Keddie (1972:5-6) has noted, the academic neglect of traditionalist Islam is commonplace across the Muslim world.

3. In theory, the words '*ulama*' and '*kiai*' are almost synonymous. In practice, however, the latter term is sometimes given as an honorific to men not learned in Islamic studies. Hence, within NU a distinction is often made between *kiai* who are regarded as *zuama* or leaders, and those held to be genuine religious savants.

4. Government statistics in 1961 showed NU to have 522,413 formal members, the largest number of any political party. (The second largest party was the PKI with 468,814 members). In 1965, NU's official membership had climbed to 2.76 million, though the Party claimed a total of 5.33 million 'registered' members. *Siaran ke-17*, PBNU, 20 April 1961:1-2; 'Laporan Tambahan Daftar Anggota NU', PBNU, 11 February 1965, and 'Hasil Pendaftaran Anggota', PBNU, 6 April 1965, from Koleksi NU, Arsip Nasional, Jakarta Selatan, items 171 and 262.

teachings of the Syafi'i school. The bearings of NU's political thought derive largely from these sources. In general, the Syafi'i school places great emphasis on caution, moderation, and flexibility. Its followers are enjoined to avoid disorder and confrontation, and to strive for consensus and unity within the *umat* (community of believers). It is also noteworthy, given the predominance of Javanese *kiai* in the NU leadership, that such principles correspond closely to Javanese cultural ideals of order, balance and harmony, whether in personal or community life.

NU's attitudes to the state and government, and its consequent ordering of political priorities, draws heavily upon the precepts set forth by the great medieval Sunni thinkers such as al-Mawardi, al-Gazali and al-Baqillani. Writing against the backdrop of political turmoil which accompanied the various challenges to the Abbasid caliphate in the tenth and eleventh centuries, these scholars stressed that a key concern of *ulama* was safeguarding the *umat* from oppression and internal division. Only in an orderly and peaceful community could Muslims properly attend to their religious obligations, and thereby achieve fulfilment on earth and bliss in the hereafter. For the medieval *ulama*, a strong and stable state was a necessary condition to achieving this ideal of an orderly and pious society. It followed from this that leaders of the *umat* must be obedient to the state, even a despotic one, for authority was vastly preferred to anarchy.[5] Whilst *ulama* could advise and even admonish a government or ruler, civil disobedience and rebellion were proscribed except in cases of unacceptable state interference with the religious affairs of the *umat*. This irenic and accommodatory approach to politics became a hallmark of Sunnite political philosophy and practice, and is also reflected in the behaviour of Nahdlatul Ulama.

Aside from shaping NU's political behaviour, Islamic precepts also influenced the Party's perceptions of democracy. As with other political parties elsewhere in the Muslim world, NU accepted the basic democratic ideal of popular sovereignty but sought to redefine democracy according to Islamic law. Within the Qur'an and Hadiths were numerous injunctions bearing close resemblance to widely-accepted Western notions of democracy, including the ideas that consultation and deliberation (*syura*) should occur between the ruler and ruled, that community consensus (*ijma*) should be sought, and that equality (*musawat*), justice (*adil*) and upholding of rights (*hak*) should be present in Muslim society. Classical institutions such as *majlis al-syura* (consultative council) and *bay'ah* (contract or oath of appointment of the Caliph) were also capable of reinterpretation to justify representative parliaments and the right to elect governments.[6]

---

[5]. A frequently quoted aphorism from the medieval scholar, Ibn Jama'a, states that forty years of tyranny from a ruler are better than one hour of anarchy (Rosenthal 1958:44).

[6]. See the discussions in Enayat (1982:125-32); Esposito (1991:141, 285-86); and Iqbal (1983:252-60).

There was, however, a crucial difference between Islamic democratic ideals and those of Western liberal democracy: whereas the latter were centred around man, the former were centred around God. In an Islamic democracy, nothing should contradict God's Law, the *Syari'ah*, nor offend sacred Muslim axioms, regardless of majority opinion. Thus, in a democratic Islamic state, the right to free speech and action, as well as the scope for legislation, will be subject to restrictions not found in secular liberal democracies.[7] This desire for subordination of popular will to religious law was spelt out by the Rois Am (President-General) of NU, K.H. Wahab Hasbullah, when he declared in 1954 that his Party wanted the Indonesian state to be 'based on the *Syari'ah* and democracy that accorded with Islamic teachings' (*Duta Masyarakat*, 17 August 1954).

The influence of Islamic precepts upon NU's notions of democracy is evident in various reforms to the Western-style Provisional Constitution of 1950 proposed by the Party during the early to mid-1950s. Firstly, rather than the existing Prime Ministerial cabinet and figurehead Presidency, NU advocated a system of presidential cabinets in which the president (or vice-president) would lead Cabinet and share responsibility for governing with the Ministry. Such a system would be in keeping with Islamic principles that the head of state be fully accountable to the people for government actions. This would also promote a strong executive as exemplified in Muslim history by the governance of the Prophet Muhammad and the early caliphs. Secondly, NU wanted a bicameral legislature to replace the existing single-chambered parliament. Whilst the lower house would remain a popularly elected parliament, the upper house, or Senate, would comprise regional representatives and Islamic scholars who would have the final decision on all legislative matters. The justification for investing *ulama* with veto powers was that their knowledge of God's Law ensured that no legislation could be passed that was contrary to the *Syari'ah*.[8]

Aside from dissatisfaction over the existing cabinet and parliamentary structure, there was much about the 1950 Constitution which met with NU's approval. The Constitution's declaration that the Indonesian state should be based upon belief in God, its strong charter of civil and legal rights and guaranteeing of religious freedoms, and its requirement of cooperative

---

7. Despite a scarcity of documented discussions within NU of the relative virtues of Islamic versus Western liberal notions of democracy, NU *kiai* were certainly aware of the debate. Many senior *kiai*, via magazines, books, and personal accounts from the Middle East, followed the writings of Islamic scholars such as Rashid Rida and Muhammad Abduh.

8. 'Program Perjuangan' section 1, articles 8 & 10. Also, *Abadi*, 17 August 1954; *Mestika*, 17 August 1954; and Achmad Siddiq, 'Djalan-Tengah dari Dua Sistem' (Working Paper for 1956 Party Conference, Medan, 24 December 1956), Koleksi NU, Arsip Nasional, Jakarta, batch no. 252. Interestingly, although frequent mention was made by NU *kiai* of implementing the *Syari'ah* in Indonesia, references to reinstating the Jakarta Charter (which obliged the state to oversee adherence to Islamic law amongst Muslims) as the Preface to the Constitution were scarce prior to the late 1950s.

organisation of the economy and state regulation of national production and resources were all attractive features for NU. Also, in practical political terms, the democratic system enshrined in the Constitution was viewed as essentially fair and even-handed, allowing parties to compete for power without undue hindrance, and making provision for a popularly elected Constituent Assembly to formulate a permanent constitution.

Thus, NU had a genuinely ambivalent attitude to the provisional Constitution. As Muslims, they desired a political system that more fully reflected Islamic principles, and yet, as Indonesians, they recognised the need for a constitutional democracy acceptable to all the Republic's major political groupings, be they Muslim or non-Muslim. In such a situation, the Party regarded compromise as necessary and inevitable. 'NU seeks neither to nationalise Islam nor shift Indonesia to Mecca', a Party spokesman said (Nur A. G.N, in *Mestika*, 17 September 1954). NU was satisfied it could realise its short term political aims through the 1950 Constitution, and its longer term objectives of Islamic democracy through the electoral process and the Constituent Assembly.

NU during the transition to Guided Democracy

The transition from parliamentary to Guided Democracy which occurred between 1957 and 1960, was marked by a succession of crises. The critical events in this process were the announcement of Sukarno's 'Konsepsi' in February 1957, the installation of the extra-parliamentary Kabinet Karya in April 1957 and establishment of the National Council a month later, the proclamation by Presidential Decree of the 1945 Constitution and concomitant dissolution of the Constituent Assembly in July 1959, and finally the dissolution of the elected parliament in March 1960 and its replacement by an appointed Gotong-Royong Parliament in June. In each of these crises, NU decided against taking a stand to defend the existing system of liberal parliamentary democracy, preferring instead to back the proposals of Sukarno and the military.

To understand Nahdlatul Ulama's behaviour during this period, it is necessary to examine closely the Party's leadership. In the late 1950s and 1960s, NU was dominated by *kiai* and politicians notable for their pragmatism, circumspection and willingness to compromise. The pivotal figure in this group was K.H. Wahab Hasbullah, the most senior *kiai* in Nahdlatul Ulama, and a driving force behind the founding and development of the organisation. He was not only a respected religious scholar, but also an astute and charismatic political leader. More than any other person, Wahab shaped NU's flexible and highly practical approach to politics. The other key figure was Idham Chalid, who, from late 1956, occupied the strategic position of Party General-Chairman. A protege of Wahab during the early 1950s, Idham was a wily, cautious and popular leader within NU. Throughout the latter part of 1950s, Idham and Wahab, together with others such NU Secretary-General, Saifuddin Zuhri, K.H. Masykur, Zainul Arifin and Djamaluddin

Malik, conceived and implemented most of NU's policies and tactics.

The theoretical basis for the actions of the Wahab-Idham group was the general *fiqh* principle of *maslahat* (benefit). This was a contextual approach to Islamic law aimed at securing benefit or preventing harm in a manner concordant with the *Syari'ah*. According to al-Gazali, any actions to protect religion, life, intellect, lineage and property constituted *maslahat*; anything inimical to them was *mafsadah* (harm). Preventing *mafsadah* was also considered to be *maslahat*. In arriving at a decision, the *ulama* could calculate the net benefit or harm accruing from a particular action.[9] Additional to these calculations were a range of more specific *fiqh* principles upon which *kiai* could draw to further assist the decision-making process. The three most frequently cited by NU during the late fifties were:

(1) avoidance of harm must take precedence over the seeking of benefit;
(2) when confronted with a choice between two potentially dangerous alternatives, the course of least risk must be chosen;
(3) that which is unable to be fully achieved should not be fully abandoned (that is, partial success is acceptable).

It was largely on the basis of *maslahat* considerations, and, more particularly, the first two rules listed above, that NU acquiesced in the move away from a liberal democratic system. In terms of potential harm or risk, both to Party and *umat*, the NU leadership perceived there to be two major threats. The first was that of retaliation from President Sukarno and the Armed Forces. From late 1956, political power and authority had been ebbing away from the parties and parliament, and was increasingly concentrated in the hands of Sukarno and the Army. Both were determined to use their enhanced power to force structural change to a political system which they believed had failed the Republic's needs. Rejecting their proposals would not only be futile but also extremely hazardous. Parties seen to be frustrating change could easily be labelled 'counter-revolutionary' and become targets of intimidation and oppression. Were this to occur, NU's religious as well as economic and social activities would be imperilled. In any case, for NU and the other political parties to assume an oppositionist role would be to invite even more authoritarian and repressive measures from the President and military, with even greater damage to Indonesian democracy.

The second major concern was that if Nahdlatul Ulama refused to participate in the new political system its place would be taken by its opponent, the PKI. With the progressive exclusion of Masyumi from national politics following its involvement in the regional rebellions of 1956-1957, only NU's continued participation could prevent a further undermining of Islam's political influence and growth in the power of the Communist Party.

---

9. One of the most lucid English-language discussions of *maslahat* and *mafsadah* matters in *fiqh* is in Kamali (1989:339-58). See also Enayat (1982:148-49).

For these reasons, the NU leadership argued that it was much better for NU to safeguard itself, the *umat*, and the country by acceding to the wishes of Sukarno and the Army, and then endeavour to use its position within the political system to preserve as much as it could of democratic institutions. Such a course would also fulfil the third above-mentioned *fiqh* rule that partial success is better than none at all.

Maslahat had another important influence on NU's decision-making process: it permitted mutability. With each change in a political situation or fresh development in a crisis, new reckonings of harm and benefit would be made, and earlier positions reconsidered. Not for NU the rigid consistency of Masyumi: that brought only confrontation, brinkmanship and an escalation in danger.[10] In NU, judicious flexibility was a virtue, and the keeping open of options, a favoured strategy. As Idham Chalid told a Party gathering in 1959, 'NU always seeks, as far as possible, to adapt itself to the [prevailing] times and events, and never propounds something which is absolute or unconditional' (Idham Chalid 1959:102-3) The Party's frequent changes in policy on a variety of issues — something which confused and angered many outside observers, and further encouraged accusations of opportunism and desultoriness — were due, in large part, to recalculation of *maslahat* and *mafsadah* in the light of new developments. Two prime and oft-criticised instances of this were NU's flat rejection, then conditional acceptance, of Sukarno's Konsepsi, and later, its reneging on an initial undertaking not to participate in the Kabinet Karya. Both backdowns resulted from a belief that new factors altered the harm-benefit equation, thus requiring a reversal of prior decisions. In a fluid political situation such as during the late 1950s in Indonesia, there was always a strong likelihood of shifts in NU policy.

A final characteristic of Nahdlatul Ulama's decision-making which deserves comment was its reactiveness. In each of the crises of the late 1950s and early 1960s, NU's leadership was reluctant to take the initiative in publicly advancing their views, preferring instead to wait and monitor events before committing the Party to a particular course. In this regard they tended to follow events, not lead them. At no time was this more evident than immediately following President Sukarno's decree of 5 July 1959. Instead of risking a public statement which might later prove inexpedient, the NU leadership adopted a policy of silence (*bersikap diam*) lasting several weeks.

NU's concern with expediency, its reactiveness and inherent caution is captured in the remarks of Idham Chalid to the 1962 Party conference in Solo. Explaining the accommodatory policies pursued by the NU executive board during the transition period from parliamentary to Guided Democracy, he likened the Party to a boat in a tempest:

---

10. Rejection and implied criticism of Masyumi's hardline policies by NU leaders is commonplace in the Party's literature. See, for example, the speech of Idham Chalid in Fadhali (1969:13-30) and *Siaran ke-7*, PBNU, Jakarta, 1 July 1957, section 7.

> Our nation is being buffeted by a tremendous typhoon of revolution, a revolution which will tear down, crush, and, if need be, destroy anything seen to be blocking its path or impeding its aims.... The entire populace has no other choice besides participating in the revolution or standing on the side of the counter-revolution. [The NU executive board was mandated] to safeguard the Party boat, to continue rowing as far and as strongly as possible.... Truly [we find ourselves] 'rowing in a typhoon'.... Just a little incautiousness or negligence, just a little misunderstanding of the wind direction, just a little bad steering that fails to adjust to the roll of the wave, and certainly the ship will go under with all its load...[Our Party] has accommodated that situation...and placed itself in the safest possible position.... (Idham Chalid 1962:2-3)

Although preservation of NU and the *umat* was clearly the ultimate concern of the Wahab-Idham leadership, other elements also contributed to the decision to accept Guided Democracy. As noted above, since the early 1950s NU had advocated strong executive government and especially presidential cabinets. By the late 1950s, with the nation racked by regional rebellions and recurring political and economic crises, the case for bolstering the executive seemed all the more persuasive. It was, the Party leadership deemed, an 'emergency situation' in which a new, more authoritarian system of government would be better able to restore order and unity to the Republic than had the old regime (Chalid 1959:103). Hence, amid the anxiety of the events of July 1959, NU found some cause for optimism. The restoration of the 1945 Constitution had enhanced the relative power of the executive, and the installation of the Kabinet Kerja had seen the President assume direct leadership of the Ministry. In addition to this, the appointment of a new Gotong-Royong Parliament in 1960 had brought the partial fulfilment of another of NU's proposals from the early 1950s: that of *ulama* involvement in the legislative process. Sukarno's nomination of a group of religious scholars to the parliament, albeit without veto rights, was regarded within the Party as a progressive step.

The NU leadership's perception of consultation and deliberation was not just confined to formal state institutions such as cabinet, parliament, the National Council and the National Planning Board. Almost as important were the informal and personal consultations which took place between Sukarno (and to a lesser extent, the Army), and key NU leaders like Wahab, Idham, Saifuddin Zuhri, Zainul Arifin and Masykur. NU placed great store upon having access to, and a degree of influence within, the ranks of those who held power in Indonesia. As politicking became increasingly focussed upon the President, NU intensified its efforts to maintain good relations with him. It was the firm belief of the Wahab-Idham group that Sukarno sought and respected their advice, and in turn, would endeavour to protect the interests of NU and the Islamic community.[11]

Although much of the discussion in this paper has been centred on the dominant Wahab-Idham group, opinion within Nahdlatul Ulama was by no means monolithic. Indeed, PBNU's accommodationist response to the gradual dismantling of parliamentary democracy provoked heated, and occasionally rancorous, debate within the Party throughout the late 1950s and early 1960s. Criticism of Party policy was based on a variety of arguments, including religious law, the inalienability of democratic rights and anti-communism. Foremost among the internal critics was K.H. Bisri Syansuri, the second most senior *kiai* in the NU organisation (and Wahab's brother-in-law). An ulama noted for his deep religious learning and eschewal of practical politics, Bisri's approach to Islamic jurisprudence differed markedly from that of the accommodationists. Whereas the latter took a broad view of decision-making, interpreting Islamic law within the context of political and social conditions, Bisri was a strict textualist seeking rigorous application of specific religious laws, regardless of other considerations. Bisri, often with support from other Party notables like K.H.M. Dachlan and K.H. Achmad Siddiq, used *fiqh* precepts such as *ghasab* (arrogation of another's property or rights) to argue against Sukarno's increasing usurpation of democratic rights.

Another critic was the outspoken young politician, Imron Rosyadi. One of the few NU leaders with a sound grasp of Western political thought, Imron was a consistently staunch opponent of the drift away from parliamentary democracy.[12] Following the dissolution of the elected parliament in March 1960, Imron and Dachlan became two of the leading members of the Democratic League (*Liga Demokrasi*), a short-lived organisation which campaigned for the restoration of a genuine parliamentary system in Indonesia. Critics of NU's accommodationism were also numerous among the Party's more trenchant anti-communists, who believed that the implementation of Guided Democracy had favoured the PKI and its allies. Such a view was especially common within NU's young men's organisation, Ansor, and its veterans' association, Ikabepi. These pro-parliamentary democracy, or in some cases, anti-Guided Democracy, forces within NU, occasionally won compromises from the Wahab-Idham group, but rarely forced a total change of policy.

---

11. Of all the NU leaders, Wahab had the best relations with Sukarno, and would seem to have, at times, acted as a spiritual adviser to the President. Based on interview material from K.H. Muslich, Jakarta, 26 August 1991; Ibu Wahid Hasyim, Jakarta, 19 November 1991; and Hasyim Latief, Sepanjang, 23 November 1991.

12. See, for example, *Sin Po*, 24 May 1957; *Abadi*, 19 June 1957; and *Duta Masyarakat*, 26 May 1960.

Conclusion

This paper is not intended to serve as an apologia for Nahdlatul Ulama's political behaviour during the late 1950s and early 1960s. Rather, it is an attempt to make judgments which are sensitive to the value system and mental horizons of the group scrutinised, at the time concerned.

The *pesantren*-educated *kiai* who led NU during the late 1950s knew little or nothing of the writings of Jefferson, Rousseau, Bentham, the two Mills, or any other Western thinker who helped to shape modern perceptions of what democracy should be. Rather, the intellectual realm of the *kiai* was the writings of the great classical *ulama* and the traditional Islamic sciences. The *kiai* held these texts to be the product of centuries of accumulated scholarship and wisdom regarding the best manner to enact the Will of God. The teachings of these treatises taught *kiai* to value realism over idealism, flexibility over rigidity, and authoritarianism over anarchy. That was the way for a Muslim leader to serve the community of believers and God. Political expediency amounted to religious virtue.

As much as Nahdlatul Ulama's accommodationism irritated Western scholars, the fact remains that the organisation's religio-political ideology, based on its understanding of Islamic jurisprudence, discouraged it from taking bold action to prevent the decline of Western-inspired parliamentary democracy. Indeed, the Party was unwilling to place at risk its central function of defending and fostering Orthodox Islam in order to protect a liberal democratic system that it had long regarded with ambivalence. Under the cautious and pragmatic leadership of Wahab Hasbullah and Idham Chalid, the safeguarding of NU and the traditionalist *umat* was always the primary concern, and the fate of democracy secondary.

It can further be argued, as Ken Ward (1974:100) has done, that NU's flexible and accommodatory stance has served the organisation and its Muslim constituency well. NU emerged from the tumult of the late 1950s as by far the strongest Islamic party. Through its domination of the Ministry of Religion it was able to expand and upgrade the network of *pesantren* and provide valuable opportunities to its younger, more talented members. Its cooperation with Sukarno not only helped it avoid the execration and eventual banning which befell Masyumi, but also enabled NU to position itself to resist and later help to eliminate the PKI. The remarkable resilience and adaptability of Nahdlatul Ulama is in no small measure due to its capacity to make politics serve its religious objectives.

References

Aboebakar (ed) (1957) *Sejarah Hidup K.H.A. Wahid Hasjim dan Karangan Tersiar*, Panitya Buku Peringatan Alm. K.H.A. Wahid Hasjim, Jakarta.

Chalid, I. (1965) *Islam dan Demokrasi Terpimpin*, Api Islam, Jakarta.

_____ (1962) 'Laporan Ketua Umum Pengurus Besar Partai Nahdlatul 'Ulama Dalam Muktamar ke XXIII di Sala', 26 December 1962, Solo (From Koleksi NU, Arsip Nasional, Jakarta, batch no. 2.)

_____ (1959) Address to the Thirty-fourth NU anniversary, 30 January 1959, in PBNU (1960) *Buku Kenang-kenangan Mu'tamar ke-22 Partai Nahdlatul 'Ulama*, PBNU, Jakarta.

Enayat, H. (1982) *Modern Islamic Political Thought*, Macmillan, London.

Esposito, J.L. (1991) *Islam and Politics*, Syracuse University Press, New York.

Fadhali, A. (ed) (1969) *NU dan Aqidahnja*, Tohaputra, Semarang.

Haidar, A. (1988) Perpolitikan Nahdlatul 'Ulama, 1945-1965: Ditinjau dari Segi Pemikiran Politik Sunni, Masters Thesis, Fakultas Pasca Sarjana, IAIN Syarif Hidayatullah, Jakarta.

Iqbal, J, (1983) Democracy and the Modern Islamic State, in J.L. Esposito (ed) *Voices of Resurgent Islam*, Oxford University Press, New York & Oxford.

Kamali, M.H. (1989) *Principles of Islamic Jurisprudence*, Pelanduk Publications, Selangor.

Keddie, N.R. (ed) (1972) *Scholars, Saints and Sufis: Muslim Religious Institutions in the Middle East Since 1500*, University of California Press, Berkeley and Los Angeles.

PBNU (1960) *Buku Kenang-kenangan Mu'tamar ke-22 Partai Nahdlatul 'Ulama*, PBNU, Jakarta.

Rosenthal, E.I.J. (1958) *Political Thought in Medieval Islam: An Introductory Outline*, Cambridge University Press, Cambridge.

Ward, K. (1974) *The 1971 Election in Indonesia: An East Java Case Study*, Monash University Centre of Southeast Asian Studies, Clayton.

Zuhri, S. (1979) *Sejarah Kebangkitan Islam dan Perkembangannya di Indonesia*, Al-Ma'arif, Bandung.

11

The Failure and Future of Democracy: conversations with a group of former revolutionary activists[1]

Anton Lucas

Democracy is indeed a beautiful system. You can become president. You can choose whatever work you like. You have the same rights as others. And democracy means that I don't have to bow my head or be respectful to the president or cabinet ministers or other important people. This is a real victory for democracy. And you can do whatever you want as long as you keep within the law. But if you don't have money you won't be able to do a thing. In democratic countries you can buy whatever you like. But if you don't have the money, all you can do is gaze at the goods you want. This too is a kind of victory for democracy.
        Pramoedya Ananta Toer (1951:8-9)

People who don't have money these days have difficulties. Pak Harto has lots of money, that's the difference with Bung Karno. He didn't even own a house.... That's his success, he has money. Can you blame him for that? No, you can't. That's the way things are these days.
    Wahyono Sunarto (Interview in Jakarta on 26 July 1992)[2]

It was with a sense of apprehension that I embarked on fieldwork for this paper, taking up a suggestion of Lance Castles that I should seek the views of a group of key informants in my 1970s study of the early revolution on

---

[1]. The people interviewed for this paper were active in the revolution in Pekalongan residency on Java's north coast, the site of the author's research on the 'Three Regions Affair' (1991).

[2]. For biographical details see Lucas (1991:278)

Java's north coast, concerning the 'failure and future' of democracy in modern Indonesia. Except for two (Kadarisman and Wadyono), I had not seen any of the group for 16 years, and there was one informant, Suryono Darusman, whom I had never met. So I faced a number of difficulties and concerns in seeking to re-establish contact with them.

Firstly there was the minor difficulty of finding again the individual members of this group now in their late seventies. I had a current address list from Kadarisman Soerjodiwirjo who confirmed who was still alive from his own group of former activists of the Tegal branch of prewar nationalist students' association, *Indonesia Moeda*, who during the Three Regions affair of 1945 had called themselves the Nine Brothers (Lucas 1991). These were Ali Warsitohardjo, Suryono Darusman, Mustapha Tjokrodirdjo and Soesmono. In Tegal there was also Moelyono, the former chairman of the Pekalongan region branch of the Indonesian Socialist Party (PSI). From Brebes there was ex-*pemuda* leader Wahyono Sunarto, an admirer of Mohammad Hatta. The group of ten informants also include the former commander of the TKR/TRI in Pekalongan, Wadyono and two leftists, Soewignyo a member of the early PKI exiled to Boven Digul, and Karyaputra (a pseudonym). A member of the postwar PKI, Karyaputra was included because he was of a similar generation and local experience (Surabaya Gerindo) to the local communists in the *Tiga Daerah*. As informants these ex-activists were fairly evenly spread between the *kabupaten* town of Tegal (Kadarisman and Moelyono), the provincial capital Semarang (Wadyono, Mustapha Tjokrodirdjo, and Susmono) and the national capital Jakarta (Wayhono Sunarto, Soewignyo, Suryono Darusman and Ali Warsitohardjo). They were not so evenly spread as to ideology. Seven of the ten considered themselves followers of either Hatta's or Sjahrir's socialism (although in the 1955 election several voted for the PNI). The absence of an Islamic nationalist reflects the fact that most of the activist *kiai*s who were elected to positions of bureaucratic authority in 1945 were older than the urban based *pemuda* leaders in 1945, now in their mid to late seventies. None are now still alive, including the charismatic K.H. Abu Sudja'i, the *pesantren*-educated *Bupati* of Tegal from 1945 until 1947 who died last year.

Democracy has had a rocky road in Indonesia. During the Revolution the presidential-type constitution adopted in 1945 was operated by agreement in a parliamentary manner, with governments formed on the basis of support within the Central Indonesian National Committee (KNIP). After the transfer of sovereignty, the parliamentary system was embodied in the Provisional Constitution, adopted in 1950, and lasted until it was replaced by a return to the 1945 Constitution in 1959.

This paper discusses the perceptions of the parliamentary experience held now by these groups of ex-revolutionaries and then goes on to describe some of their views about democracy under the New Order and lastly their agendas for the future. All the informants in this study have constructed their lives around their experiences of the prewar nationalist movement, during the Japanese occupation, and the revolution of 1945-1949. Their views on democracy thus echo this past, as well as reflecting their own careers during the years since the revolution.

Memories of Parliamentary Democracy

> The 1950-59 period is perhaps the most interesting in Indonesia's history. It was like an open air stage where different political ideologies fought with each other. Civilian politicians were weak, and the role of the military was strengthening.... This was going on against the background of the struggle between the two worlds of capitalism and socialism, the colonised world, the new and old colonisers. (Hardoyo 1990)

Looking at the careers of ex-activists in this study, the 1950-57 or '59 period is significant from the point of view of their own careers either in politics, the civil service or business. Wadyono left the Army and with his PNI and military connections, with his Chinese high school friend ran a successful 'Ali Baba' trading company in Semarang. Ali Warsitohardjo studied land reform at the University of Wisconsin in 1951-52 and returned to work in agrarian affairs in the Department of the Interior, Sunarto was in the Jakarta municipality Department of Information, Soewignyo in the Education Ministry's community (non formal) education program. Karyaputra was studying at the Institute of Marxism in Peking, while Suryono Darusman was working as a diplomat in Africa and Eastern Europe, Kadarisman in municipal government in Tegal, and Mustapha Tjokrodirdjo worked as an architect's draftsman in Semarang.

The metaphor of an open air stage for the period of Parliamentary Democracy is a powerful one for all the ex-activists in this study but particularly for the ex-PSI informants. Banned in 1960, the party had competed openly in the campaign leading to the 1955 national elections. Thus Pekalongan region PSI leader Moelyono could recall that the PSI did better in Brebes *kabupaten* (immediately to the west of Tegal) than in any regency in Central Java. Similarly other informants recall with some relish their experiences during this time of populist politics. Sunarto remembers making speeches during the 1955 national election campaign explaining the nature of voting by secret ballot to assembled *kampung* dwellers. He would start his speech by asking the (mostly male) assembled *kampung* dwellers:

> How many unmarried girls are there in this *kampung*?...You can only choose one for your wife, right? Well, it will be the same in the election. You can only choose one party too...it's a private choice, like choosing a wife. (Interview in Jakarta on 29 July 1992)

Susmono another former Tegal activist who joined the political affairs section of the provincial government in Semarang in 1950 recalls the role of his section as adviser to local officials (*bupati*s and *wedana*s), who were all still Dutch trained *Pangreh Praja*. 'We wanted them to think in a more political way, to give people more freedom for political activities'. During the same period Susmono was also involved in contacting Darul Islam supporters in Pekalongan and Banyumas residencies 'because the government wanted to study the political goals of the Darul Islam movement'. (Interview in Semarang on 21 October 1992)

Then there was the change from the informal political style of the Yogya revolutionary period to the more remote Jakarta style of politics. The move of the Republican capital back to Jakarta bought a sense of isolation from government, as compared with the Yogya revolutionary days:

> Jakarta was different from Yogya. People who became ministers drove around in cars in Jakarta. In Yogya ministers were friends, like you and me. H.M. Erningpraja was the Minister of Labour in Yogya. We were in MULO together in Cirebon, he went on into politics. He was driving home from tennis in Jakarta, he stopped his car to talk to me. Sarino Mangunpranoto who was in Sabupri [agricultural workers union] was also like that, even when he was a minister in Jakarta, and I worked as an information officer for the city administration. [But] the solidarity of the Yogya days had changed. (Interview with Wahyono Sunarto in Jakarta on 26 July 1992)

Ali Warsitohardjo, who worked in agrarian affairs in the Ministry of the Interior throughout the period and so was a close observer of the political process, including the national elections of 1955 commented:

> The elections of '55 established [the principle of] upholding the People's choice. We had learnt about liberal democracy from Sjahrir. With the Working Committee and the KNIP we had felt what liberal democracy was like. The positive thing about liberal democracy was that there were many proposals from the regions which came to the parliament, although people also insulted each other in parliament. From a government point of view, before draft laws were presented to parliament, the ministerial council (*dewan menteri*) would discuss them. The needs of individual government departments were discussed by the *dewan menteri* who were party members. So ministers discussed things with their own parties before the *dewan menteri* discussed them. The process was a two way traffic. It was a bottom up approach, not top down like now. But its weakness was that it was a slow process. (Interview with Ali Warsitohardjo in Jakarta on 27 July 1992)[3]

A lawyer by training (although he never finished his degree because of the Japanese occupation) Ali Warsitohardjo was secretary of the seven man Republican committee which, together with the Dutch-sponsored federal RUSI (Republic of the United States of Indonesia) committee, formed a joint

---

3. Born in Jepara in 1914, Ali Warsitohardjo graduated from the Law School in Jakarta and was treasurer of the prewar tertiary students association PPPI. During the Japanese occupation Ali was appointed clerk of the Tegal *landrecht* or local 'native' court. During the Revolution he was arrested by the Dutch and imprisoned after the first military attack from 14 October 1947 until 15 June 1949. He then worked on the joint RUSI-RI committee (as secretary of the RI delegation) which wrote the 1950 Constitution, and was secretary of the PPPPSU (*Panitya Penyelenggara Pembentukan Propinsi Sumatera Utara*) a body formed to integrate the three federal states of North Sumatra into the Republic. In 1951-52[1] he studied land reform at the University of Wisconsin, and worked in agrarian affairs becoming secretary of the land reform division in 1967.

body which wrote the 1950 Constitution, under which the Indonesian government operated until Sukarno dissolved the Constituent Assembly in 1959.[4] To those who see Parliamentary Democracy's weakness in constitutional terms Ali Warsitohardjo has this to say:

It makes me annoyed when people ridicule the 1950 Constitution. Its effectiveness depended on having a national election. The cabinets and the parliament of 1950-55 were appointed from people whom the Dutch had used. They weren't chosen in a general election. So don't judge the 1950 Constitution by political events before 1955. The 'test case' for the 1950 Constitution is the period 1955-59. My conclusion about this period is that the parties didn't have a chance to develop themselves. Don't blame the system. The parties had no time to make a program. Don't forget that both the 1945 and the 1950 Constitutions have the same Preamble and the same Pancasila. (Interview with Ali Warsitohardjo in Jakarta on 27 July 1992)

What caused Parliamentary Democracy's failure?

Parliamentary Democracy didn't work. [There were] too many parties, too many opinions, too many ambitions. (Interview with Suryono Darusman in Jakarta on 12 November 1992)[5]

When former activists recall the period 1950-1959 they see its failure in political terms, as a failure of the parties to agree on a political process. Secondly they see its failure in cultural terms, in the negative influence of Javanese culture on the political process. We will first look at the failure of democracy in political terms.

Informants often ask the question 'How democratic was the system then anyway?' and their answer is usually that even under Parliamentary Democracy the system was not all that democratic. Parliamentary Democracy is today considered to be a period when there was more freedom of political expression, but for at least one informant this was not the case. Left-wing intellectual Karyaputra does not agree with this view of Parliamentary Democracy. He says that, beginning very early in the 1950s, when the federal states set up by the Dutch were dismantled and incorporated into the

---

4. The other Republican members of the Committee for the Preparation of the Constitution of the Unitary State were Deputy Prime Minister Abdul Hakim (Masyumi), Mr Hardi (PNI), Sakirman (PKI), Koesnan (Labour Party), Djohan Sjahroezah (Socialist Party) and Kasimo (Catholic Party). The federal delegation was headed by Professor Soepomo (the RUSI Justice Minister) and Abdul Wahab Suryodiningrat, a RUSI cabinet minister. See also Feith (1962:93)

5. S. Darusman was born in Payakumbah, West Sumatra, in 1919 but was brought up in Jakarta. During the Occupation he moved to Tegal, where he was appointed head of foreigners registration for the Tegal municipality. Head of the Tegal security force which replaced the *Pangreh Praja* run police force during the *Tiga Daerah* affair, in 1947 he went to Singapore on a mission to obtain weapons and supplies for the naval base in Tegal. His Singapore experiences are recounted in Darusman (1991). An older brother Maruto Darusman was amongst those executed in December 1948 in the aftermath of the Madiun Affair. After serving as ambassador in Moscow, and chief of political affairs in the Department of Foreign Affairs (1976-79), he retired in early 1982.

unitary Republic, Indonesian democracy was '*demokrasi minta idzin*' (asking permission democracy), or in Javanese '*demokrasi nyrimpeti*'. This was because of the military's role:

> Sukarno never banned anyone from speaking [in public]. He never banned anyone from criticising him, although he took action on that later on. But newspapers with views ranging from left-wing to extreme right-wing were allowed then. So that's a difference with today. Another comparison is with the role of the military. Today the military is in power and is dominant. Before the military was *nyrimpeti*. *Nyrimpeti* means to prevent someone from walking, or tripping them up by putting obstacles in their path. That's what the military did then. Parliamentary Democracy was in fact *nyrimpeti* democracy... on the practical political level you had to get permission for a public meeting from KMK, it was called the Municipal Military Command (*Komando Militer Kota*). Without their permission you couldn't hold a meeting. Maybe nationally the cabinet did not restrict public meetings, but locally the KMK did. (Interview with Karyaputra on 5 November 1992)[6]

On the failure of political processes, the elections of 1955 were flawed in several ways. Sunarto who worked as an information officer in the Jakarta city administration, and saw the working of the 1955 election campaign from the grass roots, has this to say about the 'failure' of Parliamentary Democracy:

> Everyone wanted to be a leader [in the 1950-'59 period]. There was an expression '*jual sapi*' [cow trading] which meant that people only wanted to be leaders, they wanted status. This was the result of colonialism. Because everyone felt inferior, everyone [at that time] wanted status, everyone was looking for opportunities. Indonesia was not ready yet. ...The essence of democracy is that people want to talk things through, but during that time PKI, PNI and the religious parties had their own versions of democracy. There was no common view about democracy. No-one wanted to compromise. The PNI was for social democracy, the people had to play a part, the PNI wanted to represent the people. While for the religious parties democracy was for religious people, it was the same for the other parties. In a way it's like the DPR now, in making a decision the people are never consulted, it's just 'DPR democracy'. Why? Because members do not represent the people, they represent the party. Look at the Traffic Law, the DPR should have looked at the impact on the people first. (*Ibid.*)[7]

For those campaigning in the regional areas for the smaller parties during

---

6. Karyaputra was born in Surabaya in 1923. His father, a hotel employee who organised a strike of his fellow workers in 1929 was an admirer of the early PKI leader Semaun. He joined the Surabaya prewar Gerindo youth, during the Japanese occupation was in the Heihō and after the Revolution he went to Europe then China were he studied for five years at the Institute for Marxism in Peking. Karyaputra worked in left wing intellectual circles in Indonesia until the Coup of 1965. He returned from Buru island prison camp in 1979.

7. At the time of this interview many voices were criticising the Indonesian parliament for accepting the government's Traffic Law, with its heavy fines for minor traffic offences, without debate on its impact on bus and taxi drivers. The legislation was eventually postponed by the President (see *Inside Indonesia*, No 32 September 1992, pp.24-26).

the 1955 election campaign, there are some parallels with the democratic process, and the political forces which dominated it. The leader of the Pekalongan residency branch of the PSI during the 1955 election makes a comparison between the dominance of the PNI at the village level in 1955 and Golkar (*Golongan Karya*, Functional Groups) in recent Indonesian elections:

> We felt very sad [during the 1955 election campaign] because we were faced with the [the situation where] people were quite clearly living under the tyranny of the PNI via the village headmen. Because all the village headmen, all the *camats* [subdistrict heads] were PNI... The poor people were scared of the village headmen. Those with some education [who worked for the government] weren't scared but were reluctant, because they knew they wouldn't get a promotion if they joined the PSI. They wouldn't lose their jobs, but they would never be promoted. But not only that. I didn't get a promotion for several years either, but the government also tried to find fault in my work so that I could be dismissed from my job. (Interview with Moelyono in Tegal on 30 October 1992)[8]

For PSI leader Moelyono the situation of the PNI at the village level in the '55 election was similar to that of Golkar in the New Order elections, even without the doctrine of the floating mass which prevents parties from campaigning below the subdistrict level. So if villagers (in Central Java) were under the 'tyranny' of the PNI in the 1955 national election, was the system of Parliamentary Democracy so very democratic?

While Moelyono thinks that the level of education was higher in the 1950s among politicians than it is now because many more people in the '50s had had a Dutch education, people traded political support in the parliament for jobs of high status; this was referred to as *jual sapi* (Moelyono says it comes from the Dutch expression *koehandel* 'cow trading' (or horse trading in English) (Feith 1962:183). Now in Indonesia there is a New Order equivalent of '*jual sapi*', according to Moelyono:

> In the regions it's different — not like before. *Koehandel* now is about furthering one's career, gaining promotions. For example for a local police officer to become a *camat*, there is a rate, an amount which has to be paid to the *kabupaten*, 5 million rupiah...Actually this is not *koehandel*, it's bribery... (Interview in Tegal on 30 October 1992)

Indeed an often heard story from informants and their families is how much money nowadays one has to pay for appointments and promotions

---

8. Moelyono was born in 1918, his father was an assistant *wedana* in Pekalongan regency, but he refused a career in the *Pangreh Praja*, the elite administrative corps. After graduating from MULO in Tegal in 1938, he enrolled in the Pharmacists' Assistants School in Batavia, graduating in 1941. During the Japanese occupation his uncle, Mr Besar Martokoesoemo, then mayor of Tegal, got him an appointment at the Kardinah hospital where he worked until being forced to resign in 1959, because of his PSI commitments. Detained by the Dutch three times for his Republican sympathies during the military occupation of Tegal, he became leader of Pekalongan residency branch of the PSI until its banning in 1960, when he went into private pharmacy practice.

throughout the entire bureaucracy. Payments for promotions and permanent appointments are now a common practice in all levels of the government.

Cultural factors in the failure of democracy

All my informants tended to explain the failure of democracy in Indonesia in terms of the negative influence of Javanese culture on the political process. In thus seeing Javanese culture in negative terms they differ from those like Sukarno who also gave a cultural explanation but who saw democracy, not Indonesian culture, as the problem.[9] The most often quoted Javanese aphorisms which describe these negative cultural traits are as follows:

1. *Ngrimo ing pandum*: this describes what an early PKI ex-Boven Digul informant described as Javanese '*feodal*' attitudes.[10] According to Soewignyo the aphorism means whatever is given from above is gratefully accepted by people of lower political or social status or in Indonesian '*apa yang diterima disyukuri*'. He describes this as 'a weakness of our (Javanese) culture', a kind of fatalism (Interview with Soewignyo in Jakarta on 25 July 1992; biography in Lucas (1991:279-80). People who hold this view explain the lack of opposition against authority in terms of *ngrimo ing pandum*. An example from PSI leader Moelyono:

> *Ngrimo ing pandum* is like... as an example if I don't get a promotion, well, I just accept it, and I don't protest. Or if there is a distribution of rice [to government employees] that is not enough, I am just *ngrimo ing pandum*. That's *feodalisme* which is an obstacle particularly in the southern part of Central Java while it's not a problem in West Java and East Java. But isn't your wife from Central Java?
> **Interviewer**: Yes, but she is not *ngrimo ing pandum*.
> **Moelyono**: Maybe she is bored with being *ngrimo ing pandum*. It's lower class people like me who have to be *ngrimo ing pandum*. This is the centre of local government here [and] a *camat* would be reluctant to talk frankly to the *bupati* or his representative. That is *feodalisme*. If someone is right but says it too strongly his superior gets angry and then has a grudge. And the grudge lasts for seven generations. (Interview with Moelyono in Tegal on 30 October 1992)

Moelyono actually dwells at length on a list of Javanese attitudes which he says are barriers or obstacles to the implementation of democracy. People, he says, are reluctantly embarrassed (*pakewa*) to oppose their superiors in public. Officials who are confronted will feel insulted, and have feelings of revenge towards those in opposition. Human rights exist in Indonesia, but they are limited. 'Don't offend anyone. If you offend someone you will certainly be defeated.' (*Ibid.*)

---

9. I thank John Legge for this insight.

10. I have retained the Indonesian *feodal* and *feodalisme* here because it seems to me to mean something different from the English words feudal and feudalism which refer essentially to social formations, while Indonesians more often use *feodal* to describe an attitude.

A variation of *ngrimo ing pandum* or what Moelyono calls Javanese feudalism is *pejah geseng nderek Bung Karno, pejah gesang nderek Golkar*, or 'dead or alive you follow Bung Karno, dead or alive you follow Golkar'. In other words you follow whoever is in power. Ali Warsitohardjo's comment about having to leave behind *semangat nyuwun inggih* (agreeing with everything one's superiors say) in order to be true to the spirit of the Revolution, is relevant here.(Interview in Jakarta on 27 July 1992).

2. *Mikul jero mendem duwur* is an expression of President Suharto according to Wadyono. Meaning literally 'hold up high and bury deep down' it refers to the traditional Muslim custom of burying the dead. In Muslim funerals in Indonesia the dead are wrapped in special white burial cloths and placed in an open wooden framed bier (or coffin in middle class urban families) which is carried shoulder height from the house where people have paid their last respects, to the cemetery. The body is supposed to be carried high (on the shoulders of the pall-bearers), and buried deep in the ground. Wadyono says this aphorism applies to Javanese *kawula-gusti* or servant master relations, which decree that one should praise (hold up) a leader's qualities and forget (bury) their faults. Karyaputra says that President Suharto is saying people should respect older people and keep silent about things which they don't agree with. Both Wadyono and Karyaputra also imply this aphorism reflects Suharto's undemocratic leadership style.

3. *Ngono, ya ngono, nanging ajo ngono.* Wadyono recalls that people in south central Java have this expression which in Indonesian is roughly equivalent to '*begitu, ya begitu, tapi jangan begitu*'. In the context of Indonesian political culture the phrase can mean 'It's O.K, sure, to be critical or suggest alternatives, but it's better not to be frank or confrontational about it.' This can make political action difficult, as an exasperated Wadyono points out, 'How can you say in one breath 'go ahead and do it', but in the next breath say 'you'd better not do it in this way'. It's extremely vague and subjective.'

Applied to Indonesian political processes, Wadyono says it is unlikely that the MPR (*Majelis Permusyawaratan Rakyat*, People's Consultative Assembly) would ever be able to exercise its supervisory role over the presidency because they are reluctant to say what they think to their superiors.

In defending Suharto, political commentators are quick to point to the sensitivity of the President to criticism. Recently the President replied to his critics on the question of criticism, in a way that reveals certain cultural values that currently dominate Javanese politics. He said he did not disagree with criticism, as long as it is worthwhile, constructive, provides a solution, and is made in a polite manner. 'What we need' Pak Harto said, 'is criticism that takes account of our culture and our personality. How should criticism be made in a Pancasila way?' Suharto's answer (1993) is significant. People who say that democracy in Indonesia is tired (*loyo*) don't understand the process of mutual deliberation and consensus, which enables people to work through differences of opinion. Several times in his reported speech Suharto came back to the issue of the 'right' way to express criticism under Pancasila Democracy, which must follow 'the correct norms of polite behaviour.'

Views about Pancasila Democracy
> If one thinks about it, what Pancasila Democracy means [is that] whatever comes from above, we accept. It seems like Pak Harto intimidates those who don't agree. (Interview with Susmono in Semarang on 21 October 1992; biography in Lucas (1991:279).

There is considerable ambiguity in the mind of this generation of ex-activists over the question of Pancasila Democracy. Some feel that Pancasila Democracy is acceptable because it unites an ethnically diverse country, and because without Pancasila Democracy 'we would return to civil war like Africa'. Recent events in the former Soviet Union, leave many with a sense of apprehension. PSI leader Moelyono, for example, quoted from memory a recent article he had read (in English): 'Freedom in Russia is like a deadly snake loose from a basket going around biting people' and thought this could also happen in Indonesia. (Taped interview on 30 October 1992) There seems to be no alternative at the moment for Indonesia, yet under this system of democracy people are not protected by the law. Social justice is not easy to achieve in Indonesia these days, because it can be bought, unlike in Malaysia which has a more effective legal system:

> That's what we hope for: protection of the law for the people. In Indonesia it is like everything is decided by policy. In fact policy can be 'stretched' in different ways, and can be used to justify the mistakes and blunders of officials. Government policy in Indonesia can be wrong. That's what makes it difficult. (Interview with Moelyono on 30 October 1992)

Karyaputra says he told his old leftists friends long before the Soviet Union was dissolved that they should stop talking about socialism and people's democracy in Indonesia. As a result of the destruction of the left by the attempted coup of 1965 and its aftermath:

> We have to talk about democracy.... With the experience of military power we have to oppose it with democracy, not Pancasila Democracy but democracy for all groups in society. Pancasila Democracy is Army democracy.
> ...Each group is better represented by parties yes, but it will be a different system to the 1950s. Before the parties were faced with a communist party whose goal was to build socialism and which threatened their interests. Now the times are different. It's impossible to build socialism only by abolishing private ownership.... In Indonesia there will be a [new] progressive political party. We can't put socialism forward according to the Soviet model. That's impossible. Because it is threatening to other people. The progressive party grouping will have to struggle for the working community, [such as] working conditions, wages of workers, and will have to have the right attitude to farmers, a more humanitarian attitude to workers. This will not fundamentally change people's property rights.... Although there are progressive elements in existing political parties, I don't see any of them becoming the kind of progressive party I'm talking about, they have all

been created by the government, so they are not likely to be dynamic or progressive, and will not be used, because they [have to] defend Suharto's power, with whatever means they can. (Interview on 5 November 1992)

Ex-diplomat Suryono Darusman puts his views in a different way:
There is democracy and there is Pancasila Democracy. Those are two different things, entirely different things. Pancasila Democracy is not democracy. It's one man rule. Let's be frank. It's one man rule. He [the President] takes the decisions. He sort of listens to people, he listens to advisers but takes his own decisions disregarding the input. (Interview in Jakarta on 12 November 1992)

Although the issue of political freedom is one which bothers all informants in this study, on the question of economic conditions, most give President Suharto the credit for the improved situation. In regard to food for example:

When Bung Karno went overseas, the price of rice went up, there were queues, and then there was no rice. Every time Bung Karno went overseas this happened. This is Pak Harto's strength. Bung Karno would talk a lot but didn't follow up his words with actions. Bung Karno would say don't talk to hungry people about politics. Don't give hungry people speeches, give them food, he said. It's Pak Harto who has done this. Bung Karno was messed about by politicians. Pak Harto is the only one who has filled Indonesian stomachs. There are no queues for rice when he returns from overseas. But their personalities are far apart...there is a mountain in Kalimantan called Mt Suharto... (Interview with Wahyono Sunarto in Jakarta on 13 November 1992)

Agendas for the Future
Kacang ora ninggal lanjaran ('the peanuts stay attached to the plant') or *De apel valt niet ver van de boom* ('the apple doesn't fall far from the tree')
(Interview with Ali Warsitohardjo in Jakarta on 27 July 1992)

In discussing immediate concerns and possibilities for political change in the future it is instructive to hear the views of the ex-activists themselves and also of several of their children.[11] The ten informants in this study have between them a total of fifty children and over eighty grandchildren, but I was only able to talk at any length with two.

My impression of the children of this generation is that what their fathers were and did has left its mark, as is indicated by the Dutch and Javanese aphorisms which were quoted when I asked the about their childrens' involvement in politics. While the children of the ex-activists were described by their parents as having an interest in politics, most worked in the private sector rather than for the government, and few were involved in any political activities, such as membership of a political party or social or religious organisation. Only a handful were financially well off, and only one was rich. Only two grandchildren of the ten ex-activists could in any sense be

---

11. I thank Herb Feith for suggesting that I ask the children of ex-revolutionary activists the same kind of questions, what their major political concerns were and in what areas of Indonesian political life they would like to see changes.

considered to have political careers, while the daughter of another is an activist in Muhammadiyah educational and community development.

Karyaputra's younger son was born several months before he was arrested (in 1966) and recalls he was constantly asking his mother and older siblings who and where his father was. The reply, until he had nearly finished primarily school when his father returned from Buru in 1977 was 'your father works far from here' or 'he is studying overseas'. Now he says he tries to see the whole event in political terms, asking himself the question 'why was my father imprisoned?' rather than feeling guilty or revengeful about his father's imprisonment, as he observed was the case with the majority of children of political prisoners. Active in the late 1980s in land and environmental issues, he was dismissed from his university along with ten other students for collecting signatures for a petition to the parliament protesting against the closure of the weekly paper *Monitor* and the detention of its editor. (Interview in Yogyakarta on 4 December 1992)

Another 'second generation' activist is Marzuki Darusman. A member of the 'vocal' group in parliament none of whom were re-nominated, Marzuki Darusman, as deputy secretary for Golkar's politics and security section, was well known for his public statements, including an interview last year in the glossy men's magazine *Matra*, in which he said that he wanted to become president, and that two presidential terms were enough (*Tempo* 3 October 1992). Perhaps as compensation for no longer being a member of parliament, Marzuki retains his optimism that the system is slowly moving forward, citing as examples the recent opinion of the Attorney General that the Indonesian High Court is willing to hear a challenge to government legislation (something that the High Court has never done). (Interview with Marzuki Darusman in Jakarta on 13 November 1992). He also notes the plan of the parliament to revoke the Supersemar legislation referring to the legal basis of Suharto's power, the so-called Decision No.6 (TAP 6), as a sign that the parliament as an institution will gradually become more independent of the executive.

Apart from these two examples, most children of former activists during the Revolution have jobs in the private sector. A few work in village administration, and although they are sympathisers with the political views and ideals of their parents (as the two aphorisms often quoted by informants suggest), they are not active in politics. In some cases this is to protect their jobs, but it seems that the majority are just not interested in political careers. In the words of one:

> None of my children have my political aspirations. Why? Because politics is unstable. The political struggle is different now from before, before we were taking everything over; now we have to build things up. You have to have skills and knowledge now. (Interview with Wahyono Sunarto in Jakarta on 26 July 1992)

Grass roots leadership of village level neighbourhood or citizens' groups does not attract the 'second generation' either.

Each of the informants in this study have things they would like to see changed. All want to see more democracy, which would mean a stronger parliament, a greater role for the press, and a change in government policy on agrarian matters. Most want to tinker with the system not change it radically. Only Karyaputra's son sees radical political change happening in the next 10-20 years but only after a transfer of power to Suharto's successor has occurred.

Mustapha Tjokrodihardjo, who believes that Pancasila Democracy meets the needs of Indonesia at present, feels that people should not be moved off their land for recreational projects such as golf courses, or even for private retail development:

> I myself can feel how people are moved off their land for big department stores. If people have to move for public housing which they can pay off, or if the land is used for public offices, that's acceptable, but for stores, that is in the interests of the rich not for the people. As for luxury houses, why does the government support that? Of course the government needs money from permits and licenses, but in whose interest are these being issued? That has to be decided first. There are enough big stores now. It's not a good policy. What is needed is more public housing. This is basic, so the people will feel peaceful. (Interview with Mustapha in Semarang on 22 October 1992)[12]

The changes other ex-activists would like to see in their remaining years include allowing political parties to campaign at the grass roots level (villagers should not be cut off from the democratic process), abolition of the 'ex-political prisoner' category stamped on government identity cards, the introduction of a district system (direct representation) in national elections, and more reporting of debates in the DPR sessions.

Freedom as a 'deadly snake'?

The ex-activists from the Revolution have not had their hopes for a just and prosperous post-revolution Indonesian society fulfilled. Some are more disillusioned, disappointed or bitter than others, such as Karyaputra who says that the legacy of Revolution has left him feeling like a crippled tree — clearly a reference to the events of 1965. Yet the disillusionment and disappointment has not produced a commitment to radical change amongst these ex-activists. Nor does it put them in a strongly anti-Suharto position. Indeed some are quite defensive of 'Pak Harto', even playing down the issue of the wealth of his family by saying that it does not create any unrest in the street. The ambiguity that is underlying much of what they say comes, I

---

12. Mustapha Tjokrodirdjo was born in 1914 in Tegal where he attended HIS and joined the Indonesia Moeda. After Technical School in Semarang he joined the Tegal municipal public works department. During the Revolution he was a member of the Tegal KNI and head of the Pekalongan Region Struggle Bureau. Throughout the 1950s and 60s Mustapha worked as an architect's draftsman on various construction projects in Semarang. From 1971-1992 he was manager of GRIS, the public hall where the still famous wayang stage group Ngesti Pendawa plays in Semarang.

believe, from a fear of fragmentation (epitomised by Moelyono agreeing with the view that in Russia freedom turned out to be a deadly snake). It seems that this group of ex-revolutionaries are prepared to live with authoritarianism, a parliament whose voice is not heard, elections that are dominated by parties, parties that are controlled by the government, and a Pancasila system which preserves social injustices for the sake of unity, because of the fear of fragmentation. Therein also lies the ambiguity of Indonesia's political future.

References

Darusman, S. (1991) *Recollections of Suryono Darusman: Singapore and the Indonesian Revolution 1945-1950*, ISEAS, Singapore.
Feith, H. (1962) *The Decline of Constitutional Democracy in Indonesia*, Cornell University Press, Ithaca.
Hardoyo (1990) 'Apa yang ingin orang asing ketahui tentang Indonesia?' typescript, Jakarta, 17 October 1990.
Lubis, M. (1977) *Manusia Indonesia*, Idayu, Jakarta, (translated as *The Indonesian Dilemma*, Singapore, Graham Brash, 1983).
Lucas, A. (1991) *One Soul One Struggle: Region and Revolution in Indonesia*, Allen and Unwin, Sydney.
Pramoedya Ananta Toer (1951) *Bukan Pasar Malam*, Balai Pustaka, Jakarta.
Suharto (1993) 'Saya Suka Kritik, asal Bermutu dan Sopan', *Republika*, 21 January 1993.

Part Two

PROSPECTS FOR THE 1990s

12

Democratic Prospects in Indonesia

Harold Crouch

What are the prospects for democratisation in Indonesia? What are the forces pushing in a democratic direction and what are the obstacles? Political scientists have adopted a range of different approaches to the politics of the Third World. Some stress change in the class structure as the driving force for political development; others give weight to the consequences of ethnic loyalties in multi-ethnic polities; the main focus is on the state and political competition in another approach; explanations in terms of political culture continue to have adherents; while others look to the role of external forces.

This paper takes what some might regard as the easy way out. All of these approaches have some validity and are not necessarily in conflict with each other. The problem is not to determine which approach is correct but to assess the weight of competing explanations in particular circumstances.

Structural approach

The prospects of democracy can be strengthened if the social structure is favourable and weakened if it is unfavourable. Two aspects of the social structure will be discussed here — the class structure and the ethnic/regional structure.

Class structure

It is commonly believed that there is a positive correlation between economic development and democratisation. The higher the level of economic development, the better the prospects of democracy (Lipset 1960; Rueschemeyer *et al.* 1992). Thus, rich countries tend to be democracies while almost all poor countries are not. But, although this correlation generally holds at the extremes of the economic development ladder (despite exceptions like Brunei and India), there does not appear to be a strong correlation between degrees of wealth and degrees of democracy among countries in the middle-income category, a category to which Indonesia now belongs. Indonesia, however, with a per capita income of only US$560, is at the bottom of the World Bank's middle-income range so, to the extent that the correlation holds, we should not expect pressures toward democratisation to be especially strong.

The relevance of economic development to political development, however, is not limited to the simple relationship between per capita income and the political system. Of far more importance is the effect of economic growth, especially industrialisation and agricultural modernisation, on the class structure. Economic growth results in an expansion of classes — the business class, the middle classes and the working class — which are assumed to make more demands on the government and to be interested in expanding political participation (at least their own participation if not that of the whole community), while the peasantry, which is assumed to be less interested in participation, declines, if not absolutely at least relatively. The result is that the government is faced with growing demands from society which become increasingly difficult to suppress. Eventually, so the argument runs, the government becomes more responsive to pressures from society and extends opportunities for political participation. The emergence of a balance between social classes creates a social environment conducive to democratisation. It is through this process, it is claimed, that economic development eventually produced pressures toward democratisation in the northeast Asian NICs, leading to the overthrow of authoritarian rule in South Korea and democratic concessions in Taiwan. Similar pressures have been felt at a lower level of development in Thailand.

Is this process taking place in Indonesia? There is no question that Indonesia has undergone rapid economic development which has brought about substantial changes in its class structure. The business, middle and working classes have expanded but structural change still has a long way to go before the Indonesian class structure resembles that of South Korea or Taiwan or even Thailand.

The experience of the West suggests that the new business class (bourgeoisie) produced by the process of capitalist industrialisation plays a crucial role in breaking the power of the autocratic/authoritarian state and thus paving the way for democratisation. 'No bourgeois, no democracy', as Barrington Moore put it (1966:418). In Indonesia, however, the business class has yet to build a strong independent political base for itself. Following the expulsion of Dutch and some other foreign capital in the late 1950s and early 1960s, business-state relations were patrimonial in character. The state enterprises which had replaced foreign capital became sources of wealth for politicians and bureaucrats while private business was in the hands of Chinese merchants who allied themselves with *pribumi* patrons occupying positions in the state. Under the New Order, the most important of these patrons were military officers. But, as Robison has argued, the rapid economic growth and industrialisation of the New Order era resulted in the transformation of client enterprises engaged in trading and 'fixing' into huge industrial, commercial and financial conglomerates whose importance for the economy as a whole is so great that their interests must be heeded by the government (Robison 1986). Robison expected that the growing economic strength of the bourgeoisie would make them less reliant on patronage and encourage them to press for increased predictability, rationality and regularity in administration. Similarly, MacIntyre has shown that business at the middle level does not necessarily rely on patronage links but in some cases has formed organisations to pursue common interests collectively (MacIntyre 1990).

Although patronage links still play a big part in business success, it seems that business is increasingly making general policy demands on the government (as opposed to individual requests for favours) and that the government is responding to these demands. But, while this nascent bourgeoisie is prepared to apply pressure on the government in pursuit of policies which serve its own economic interest, there is little to suggest that it is interested in pushing towards broader democratic transformation. A major obstacle is the fact that most members of the big business class are Chinese who see no benefit in risking their favourable economic position in order to achieve political reform which might well be used to their disadvantage by others. As members of a small ethnic minority, they would be unable to mobilise wide political support while it is quite possible that popular resentment could be mobilised against them. Big *pribumi* business, on the other hand, is still very closely tied to the regime and has no interest in challenging its patrons while middle-level *pribumi* business, which might have an interest in a more open political system, is not strong enough to take the lead.

The middle class — professionals, small businesspeople, white-collar employees etc — is also often regarded as a force interested in democratisation. But although it has grown considerably during the past decade, the middle class in Indonesia is still very small. The 1980 census showed that only 3.2% of the work force was employed in professional and administrative occupations while another 3.2% had clerical jobs. Although 12.9% were placed in the sales category, which is considered lower-middle class in many countries, most sales workers in Indonesia were engaged in the informal sector and did not exhibit a middle-class style of life. If ownership of a car is taken as an indicator of the attainment of a middle-class life-style, the proportion of private cars to households was only 2.1% although up to 8.9% of families had motorcycles (Crouch 1984:77). By 1990 the professional and administrative occupations had risen to 3.9% and the clerical category to 4.9% while the ambiguous sales group rose to 14.3% (Biro Pusat Statistik 1992:375). The proportion of cars to households almost doubled to 4.1% while the proportion of motorcycles to households more than doubled to

21.1% (Biro Pusat Statistik 1992:15; *FEER* 1992:6).

Despite the steady growth of the white-collar, educated middle class, it was still very small compared to the middle classes in countries which had experienced sustained economic growth and industrialisation such as South Korea and Taiwan. Moreover, in Indonesia a substantial, although declining, part of those in middle-class employment worked for the government and its agencies and were therefore less inclined to be in the forefront of challenges to the government while those in the private sector were often Chinese. Although the 'independent' middle class is growing, it is still small compared to more developed countries.

The working class is also often identified by political theorists as a class with an interest in democratisation (Rueschemeyer *et al.* 1992) but the Indonesian working class remains small and uninfluential. Although the percentage of the work-force employed in the production, transport and labouring categories had risen from 18.8% in 1980 to 22.1% in 1990 (Biro Pusat Statistik:1982:147, 1992:375), employment in manufacturing, which rose in the same period from 9.1% to 11.6% (Manning 1992:29), was still relatively low. Most workers were employed in small establishments and were not unionised while the government-sponsored national trade union organisation, SPSI, gave no indication of being interested in democratisation. As long as there is a large reserve of unemployed and underemployed labour, the political strength of the working class will remain very limited.

The largest occupational category continued to be that of agricultural workers, although for the first time the percentage fell to below half in the 1990 census. In 1990 49.9% of the work force was employed in agriculture, compared to 54.7% in 1980 (Biro Pusat Statistik 1982:147, 1992:375). If political theorists are correct in regarding the peasantry as the class least likely to press for democratisation, the large size of the agricultural population will make it easier for the government to ignore the demands of urban classes.

Despite the rapid economic growth and industrialisation since the late 1960s, the Indonesian class structure in the 1990s did not provide a solid foundation for a democratic political system. Of the three classes that might be expected to have an interest in democratisation, two seem to have little democratising impact. Although the business class applied political pressure to achieve its own business goals, it was compromised as a democratising force by its ethnic composition and its continuing ties of patronage to the regime, while the working class was almost completely uninfluential. It is only parts of the middle class that have exercised significant pressure towards democratisation but the impact of such pressure has been limited because of the middle class's composition and small size. If democratisation is to take place in the future, the explanation will lie less in the weight of middle class pressure than in opportunities arising from developments at the political level — which are to be discussed later.

Ethnic/regional structure

It is often believed that it is very difficult to practise democracy in multi-ethnic societies and there are plenty of examples of democracy foundering in the face of ethnic conflict (Horowitz 1985:681-84). In Indonesia itself, the decline of constitutional democracy was in no small part due to the inability of the democratic government to deal with ethnic-regional revolts.

But does multi-ethnicity and regionalism always constitute a barrier to democracy? Clearly, when ethnic antagonisms are so strong that violent conflict between members of ethnic groups is commonplace, democracy is hardly viable. But the degree of ethnic antagonism can vary. When ethnic antagonisms are only moderate and produce political rivalries without boiling over into violent conflict, it could be argued that they can contribute to the kind of balance between political forces that favours democracy or at least limits authoritarianism (Soedjatmoko 1967). It could be argued that democracy in India and the Philippines, for example, is facilitated — despite their low ranking in per capita income terms — by ethnic compositions which make it difficult for any single ethnic group to predominate and therefore encourage the formation of multi-ethnic alliances.

What is the effect of multi-ethnic and regional loyalties in Indonesia? According to this line of thinking, an ethnic balance favourable for democracy requires that there be many ethnic groups with no single group constituting a majority. Both the Philippines, where the largest linguistic group makes up less than a quarter of the population, and India, where the largest group forms about two-fifths of the population, meet these requirements. In Indonesia the largest ethnic group, the Javanese, making up 45% of the population, is in a stronger position but is significantly divided along religious lines. In Indonesia, however, the regions have much less autonomous political strength than in the Philippines or India. In Indonesia the regional elites are essentially military and bureaucratic and therefore tied to the centre while in the Philippines and India the regional elites have strong local roots. In the Philippines the regional elites are drawn largely from the big landlord class while in India regional elites often have strong commercial or agrarian bases. While Filipino landlords and Indian businessmen and landlords demand representative institutions through which the political parties that they control can participate, the interests of military and bureaucratic regional elites in Indonesia are better served by their links with the centre than through elected representative institutions.

*****

In Indonesia, therefore, neither the class structure nor the ethnic/regional structure is particularly favourable for democratisation. The classes which are often believed to have an interest in democratisation either do not have such an interest or are quite weak in making their demands while the interests of regional elites are not served by democratisation. While pressure toward democratisation from part of the middle class is an important, indeed indispensable, factor in the democratisation process, it is unlikely to bear fruit unless political circumstances are especially favourable.

Politics approach

In recent years political scientists have tended to play down the significance of socio-economic structures and place more emphasis on political factors in explaining political developments. In analysing transitions to democracy the focus has been on the performance of political institutions and rivalries within political elites (Skocpol 1985; O'Donnell & Schmitter 1986; Diamond 1989). Even when the socio-economic structure is not especially favourable for democratisation, it is suggested, favourable political circumstances might make progress toward democracy possible.

This approach sees the key to change less in pressures arising from society (although these may also be important) than in disunity and lack of cohesiveness in the authoritarian elite. O'Donnell and Schmitter argue that 'no transition can be forced purely by opponents against a regime which maintains the cohesion, capacity, and disposition to apply repression'. According to them, 'there is no transition whose beginning is not the consequence — direct or indirect — of important divisions within the authoritarian regime itself, principally along the fluctuating cleavage between hard-liners and soft-liners' (O'Donnell and Schmitter 1986:21,19). These assumptions have long been accepted by many observers of the Indonesian military who have therefore been trying for many years to detect lines of cleavage within ABRI — whether hard-liners versus soft-liners, Javanese versus non-Javanese (Gregory 1981), Diponegoro versus the other divisions (Anderson 1978), 'centrists' versus 'militants' (Feith 1968), *Angkatan 45* versus *Angkatan Magelang* (Anderson 1978), 'professional' versus 'political' and 'financial' officers (Crouch 1978), 'pragmatic' versus 'principled' officers (Jenkins 1984), or whatever. As Don Emmerson has recently pointed out, the expectation that such divisions would eventually lead to the collapse of the regime turned out to be misplaced (Emmerson 1992). Only one voice, that of Ulf Sundhaussen, was consistently raised to emphasise the fundamental unity of ABRI although even he seemed to be wavering at one point (Sundhaussen 1981).

The maturing of the Suharto regime during the 1980s has, however, seen a new type of division within the elite. During the New Order's first fifteen years the distinction between the military and the government was blurred. The military, headed by General Suharto, was in effect the government or at least the dominant element in it. But the identity between military and government began to be undermined with the rise of Magelang generation officers to the key commands in ABRI in the early 1980s and by 1988 the gap had become obvious when General Moerdani was dismissed as Commander of ABRI shortly before the MPR session which 'elected' Lt. Gen. Sudharmono as vice-president in the face of military protests. The government is now quite distinct from the military and, although many members of the cabinet have military backgrounds, they owe their positions to appointment by President Suharto, not to military backing. The military, of course, remains as a major force within the regime but its leaders are not in a position to dictate to the President.

The division between the government on one hand and the military leadership on the other has been the crucial condition for the *keterbukaan* (openness) of the past few years (Budiman 1992). The military, as guardians of security, have adopted a liberal stance not because they are committed to democratic ideals but in order to put pressure on the government.[1] Thus, in the last two elections the military has refrained from giving the all-out support to Golkar that it had always given in the past, student and other demonstrations have been tolerated, the Petition of 50 group and other retired military dissidents have been allowed to raise their public profiles, and the press has been given a remarkably free hand to raise critical issues such as the business activities of the President's children.

In response, the President has been forced to look beyond the ranks of the military for political support. Reversing his earlier attitude to political Islam, which was regarded as the main threat to the regime until the mid-1980s, Suharto is now wooing the Muslim community. Muslim courts have been given wider powers, Islamic classes have to be provided in Christian schools, girls can wear the *jilbab* at school, the Suharto family has invested in a Muslim bank, a major Islamic festival was held, a new mass organisation for Islamic 'intellectuals' has been established and the Suharto family went on the *haj*. While Golkar hesitated, the Muslim-oriented PPP (*Partai Persatuan Pembangunan*, Unity Development Party) became the first party to propose the re-election of Suharto in 1993.

It would be completely wrong, of course, to imagine that Suharto has abandoned his military base in favour of the Muslim community. The President still has his supporters in the military. On the other hand, it would be no less wrong to imagine that all Muslim leaders and organisations have been won over to the President's side. In these new circumstances the President is continuing to do what he has always done, that is balance rival groups against each other; but now the key rival groups are no longer limited to military factions but include forces with bases in society.

The point, for the purposes of our discussion of the prospects of democracy, is that rivalry in the elite has spilt over into society. The military leaders have been cultivating the pro-democracy forces which they had previously suppressed while the President has been appealing to the Muslim organisations which had previously been most alienated by his policies. In the new atmosphere even peasant demonstrations and workers' strikes have been

---

1. It could be argued that the key figure behind *keterbukaan* is General Benny Moerdani whose previous record hardly suggests a deep commitment to democratic principles.

permitted.

But can 'openness' arising from the consequences of elite rivalry outlast that elite rivalry? If Suharto had selected a vice-presidential candidate who was unacceptable to the military, it could have been expected that government-military rivalry would continue, perhaps at a higher level of intensity. But this scenario was avoided when Suharto agreed to appoint the military's candidate, General Try Sutrisno, who is now well positioned to become Suharto's successor. It is thus not impossible, that, when Suharto finally passes from the scene, the military will be able to regain its dominance and attempt to return to the political style of the 1970s. Re-established as the dominant force in the government, it is unlikely that the new military leaders would have much time for the *keterbukaan* that they are using at present as a weapon to undermine Suharto.

But this is not the only plausible scenario. Developments in Thailand suggest a more optimistic alternative (Crouch 1988:170-72). In Thailand a previously more-or-less cohesive military had been badly split at the time of the student uprising in 1973 but had managed to come back to power in coups in 1976 and 1977. Although it regained power, the military continued to be sharply divided within itself with the result that rival factions sought civilian allies to bolster their positions. This gave considerable room for manoeuvre to the political parties which gradually built up their organisations and independent bases of support. If the military had been able to overcome its factional rivalries at an early stage it would have been able to prevent the strengthening of the parties. But continuing factional conflict inhibited the military from asserting itself while the parties in parliament grew in influence until, in 1989, the military prime minister was replaced by a party leader. While circumstances in Thailand of course differ from those in Indonesia in important respects, the point is that continuing rivalry within the military elite provided the opportunity for civilian parties to build up their own organisational strength so that they were eventually able to form the government.

It is not impossible to imagine continuing rivalries within the military in a post-Suharto Indonesia. One group might try to win over Golkar's support while others might follow Suharto's present strategy of wooing Islam and another group could align itself with the nationalist ideology of the PDI (*Partai Demokrasi Indonesia*, Indonesian Democratic Party). Such manoeuvring would strengthen the bargaining position of the parties and give them scope for organising stronger bases of political support. One important difference with Thailand, of course, lies in the Political Parties Law which limits the number of legal parties to three and prohibits party organisation in the rural areas.

The range of possibilities is therefore wide. In contrast to the structural approach which makes firm (if sometimes inaccurate) predictions about political change on the basis of change in underlying socio-economic structures, the political approach is less confident about what lies ahead because of what O'Donnell and Schmitter call the 'extraordinary uncertainties' of political transitions. Too much depends on the behaviour of political leaders — the assessments of the situation that they make, the strategies that they adopt, the bargains they strike with rivals and completely fortuitous events like the death or illness of key figures. Prediction has to be replaced by the listing of sharply contrasting possible scenarios.

Cultural approach

In recent years several influential political scientists have called for renewed emphasis on cultural and psychological factors in order to explain political developments in the Third World (Huntington 1987:28; Weiner 1987:60; Pye 1985). Much has been written by social scientists about both the durability of traditional culture which is believed to inhibit the development of attitudes favourable for democracy, and modernisation and cultural change which are thought to breed attitudes supportive of democratisation. It is also necessary to take account of popular perceptions arising from historical experience.

To the extent that the Javanese 'Idea of Power' continues to predominate in Indonesia, the prospects of democratisation must be seen as slight. All the evidence suggests that President Suharto's own political outlook largely conforms to traditional Javanese conceptions. Suharto's attitude to Western democracy can probably be understood in part by his commitment to maintaining 'a single, pervasive source of Power and authority' and his 'traditional anxiety about a dispersion of Power'. Like Sukarno and many others, he shared in 'the psychological malaise experienced by the Javanese under the system of multi-party democracy in the early 1950s' (Anderson 1972:22-24) and no doubt prefers the ordered, harmonious and hierarchical structures of *Demokrasi Pancasila* to the democratisation championed by the regime's critics.

But the important question relates to the extent that these ideas are shared by other members of the present elite and by the society in general. First, 55% of Indonesians are not Javanese anyway although their own traditional cultures, of course, are not necessarily more receptive to democratic ideas than are the Javanese. Second, in any case Javanese political behaviour and attitudes in the past have not always conformed to the harmonious Javanese ideal (e.g. the Revolution, the competition of the democratic era, the mobilizational aspects of Guided Democracy, the confrontative policies of the PKI, the anti-Sukarno movement). And third, the expansion of education and the rise of the middle class have created a new constituency whose commitment to traditional culture, while not necessarily abandoned, is at least combined with new attitudes and patterns of behaviour influenced by contact with the 'modern world'. Traditional attitudes towards those in authority have been undermined, especially among members of the younger generation, who are increasingly attracted to the values of the 'world culture' (Feith 1980).

Thus, democratic ideas have spread in Indonesia despite the continuing influence of traditional Javanese and non-Javanese cultures. But, although pro-democratic sentiments are commonplace within the intelligentsia and sections of the urban middle class, there is little to suggest that the democratic culture has acquired deep roots in society. Traditional attitudes are still an obstacle.

The attractiveness of democratic ideas, however, is diluted in the perception of many Indonesians by the lessons they draw from historical experience. First, the general perception of the liberal democracy era continues to be negative, not only because of its lack of congruence with Javanese tradition, but because of what many regard as its 'objective' inadequacies. The fact is that governments in the 1950s were weak, short-lived and often pre-occupied with immediate political survival. The elections of 1955 not only failed to produce strong government but aggravated religious and ethnic tensions. And, in the end, the democratic system proved unable to support a government strong enough to deal with the regional rebellions. Even those who have become alienated from the New Order are not necessarily yearning for a return to 'liberal democracy'.

Historical experience has also underlined the fragility of national unity and social stability. Older Indonesians have experienced the privations of the Japanese occupation, the upheaval of the Revolution, the era of regional rebellions, the rising social tensions of Guided Democracy and the slaughter of 1965-66. These experiences have made them especially appreciative of the political and social stability that has characterised Indonesia since the establishment of the New Order. Even those who are critical of the Suharto regime and military domination hesitate to adopt political strategies which might upset that stability. There is a strong fear that a breakdown in political order would result in the unleashing of racial, religious and ethnic passions and a return to the conflicts of the past. Many Indonesians prefer to go along with the existing order rather than risk the consequences of the upheaval which might accompany its overthrow while most supporters of democratisation want the process to be gradual.

An examination of the likely consequences of Indonesian political culture for democratisation thus leads to ambiguous conclusions. Traditional culture represents an obstacle but traditional culture has never been the sole determinant of political behaviour. Political culture is changing but historical experiences within living memory tend to make people wary of drastic change. While cultural perspectives need not constitute an insuperable barrier to democratisation, they make it likely that the process will be slow.

International approach

To what extent can external forces influence the pace of political change in Indonesia? The dependency approach that was so influential in the 1970s saw external pressure in an entirely negative light. The Western capitalist states were only interested in the Third World as fields for economic exploitation and needed pro-Western governments to look after Western capitalist interests. Thus the United States and its allies favoured strong authoritarian regimes and paid no more than lip service to democratic ideals. Moreover, the West needed Third World allies and friends in its struggle with the Soviet Union. According to this view, the Suharto regime suited Western interests perfectly. Far from pushing Suharto in the direction of political reform, they provided the military and economic aid that he needed to consolidate his regime.

The world of the 1990s has changed drastically. The end of the Cold War has meant that the United States no longer places overwhelming priority on a regime's international allegiance. If a Third World state does not want American support, it can no longer find automatic support elsewhere. The bargaining position of authoritarian rulers is therefore a lot weaker and they are now much more vulnerable to Western pressures in regard to human rights and democracy. But Third World states are not completely without bargaining resources as the West and Japan still have economic interests to preserve in the Third World. Indeed the growing commercial competition between the US, Western Europe and Japan make it unlikely that political pressure on Third World governments will be very onerous.

In any case, it would be naive to believe, except in very unusual circumstances like the case of South Africa, that outside pressure can lead to fundamental political change. And while it might be possible for external pressure to bring about the downfall of an authoritarian regime, it cannot guarantee that the new regime will be democratic. As political theorists have been telling us for many years, democracy is unlikely to work effectively unless socio-economic conditions, political culture and political circumstances are appropriate.

Conclusion

The thrust of this analysis leads to a rather pessimistic conclusion about the prospects of democracy in Indonesia in the 1990s. Neither the social structure nor political culture generates strong pressures towards democratisation. Although economic development has brought about substantial change in the social structure, these changes have not gone far enough to provide a solid foundation for democratisation while the ethnic structure also fails to foster a balance of regional forces which might support democracy. From the cultural perspective, the predominant elite political culture is antagonistic to democracy although the new culture of the educated middle class is more favourable.

It seems that it is only at the political level that circumstances offer much prospect of democratisation. As long as the elite remains divided and their rivalries involve mobilising non-elite support, it is possible that the system will become more open and liberal. The longer this situation continues, the more reforms will become institutionalised and the more the elite will become accustomed to competitive politics. But it remains to be seen how far the authoritarian foundations of the present system will be permanently undermined and a solid basis laid for democracy. Any form of democracy or semi-democracy is likely to be very fragile until economic growth creates a more supportive social structure and the democratic elements in Indonesia's political culture are spread more widely.

References

Anderson, B.R.O'G. (1972) The Idea of Power in Javanese Culture, in C. Holt (ed) *Culture and Politics in Indonesia*, Cornell University Press, Ithaca, NY.
_____ (1978) 'The Last Days of Indonesia's Suharto?', *Southeast Asia Chronicle*, 63, 1978.
Biro Pusat Statistik (1982) *Population of Indonesia*, Series S/1. Jakarta.
_____ (1992) *Population of Indonesia*, Series S/2. Jakarta.
Budiman, A. (1992) Indonesian Politics in the 1990s, in H. Crouch & H. Hill (eds), *Indonesia Assessment 1992*, Department of Political and Social Change, Australian National University, Canberra.
Crouch, H. (1978) *The Army and Politics in Indonesia*, Cornell University Press, Ithaca.
_____ (1984) *Domestic Political Structures and Regional Economic Co-operation*, Institute of Southeast Asian Studies, Singapore.
_____ (1988) 'Indonesia: the rise or fall of Suharto's generals', *Third World Quarterly*, 10.1, January, 1988.
Diamond, L. (1989) Introduction: Persistence, Erosion, Breakdown and Renewal, in L. Diamond, J.J. Linz & S.M. Lipset (eds) *Democracy in Developing Countries*, Volume 3: Asia, Lynne Rienner Publishers, Boulder, Colorado.
Emmerson, D. (1992) 'The Rabbit and the Crocodile: Expecting the End of the New Order in Indonesia, 1966-1991' (unpublished ms).
Far Eastern Economic Review (1992) *Asia Yearbook*, Hong Kong, 1992.
Feith, H. (1968) 'Suharto's Search for a Format', *Australia's Neighbours*, 56-57, May-June, 1968.
_____ (1980) Legitimacy Questions and the Suharto Polity, in J.J. Fox *et al.* (eds) *Indonesia: Australian Perspectives*, Research School of Pacific Studies, Australian National University, Canberra.
Gregory, A. (1981) The Influences of Ethnicity in the Evolution of the Indonesian Miliary Elite, in D.C. Ellinwood & C. Enloe (eds) *Ethnicity and the Military in Asia*, Transaction Books, New Brunswick.
Horowitz, D.l. (1985) *Ethnic Groups in Conflict*, University of California Press, Berkeley.
Huntington, S. P. (1987) The Goals of Development, in M. Weiner & S.P. Huntington (eds), *Understanding Political Development*, Little, Brown and Company, Boston.

Jenkins, D. (1984) *Suharto and His Generals*, Cornell Modern Indonesia Project, Cornell University, Ithaca.

Liddle, R.W. (1992) 'Regime in Crisis? Presidential Succession, the East Timor Massacre, and Prospects for Democratization in Indonesia', Paper presented at the 44th Annual Meeting of the Association for Asian Studies, Washington, D.C., April 2-5, 1992.

Lipset, S.M. (1960) *Political Man*, Doubleday, Garden City.

MacIntyre, A. (1990) *Business and Politics in Indonesia*, Allen & Unwin, North Sydney.

Manning, C. (1992) 'Survey of Recent Developments', *Bulletin of Indonesian Economic Studies*, 28.1, April, 1992.

Moore, B. (1966) *Social Origins of Dictatorship and Democracy*, Allen Lane The Penguin Press, Harmondsworth.

O'Donnell, G. & P.C. Schmitter (1986) *Transitions from Authoritarian Rule: Tentative Conclusions about Uncertain Democracies*, The Johns Hopkins Press, Baltimore.

Pye, L.W. (1985) *Asian Power and Politics: The Cultural Dimensions of Authority*, The Belknap Press of Harvard University Press, Cambridge, Massachusetts.

Robison, R. (1986) *Indonesia: The Rise of Capital*, Allen & Unwin, North Sydney.

Rueschemeyer, D., E.H. Stephens & J.D. Stephens (1992) *Capitalist Development and Democracy*, Polity Press, Cambridge.

Skocpol, T. (1985) Bringing the State Back In: Strategies of Analysis in Current Research, in P.B. Evans, D. Rueschemeyer & T. Skocpol (eds) *Bringing the State Back In*, Cambridge University Press, Cambridge.

Soedjatmoko (1967) 'Indonesia: Problems and Opportunities', *Australian Outlook*, 21.3, December, 1967.

Sundhaussen, U. (1981) 'Regime Crisis in Indonesia: Facts, Fiction, Predictions', *Asian Survey*, XXI.8, August, 1981.

Weiner, M. (1987) Political Change: Asia, Africa and the Middle East, in M. Weiner & S.P. Huntington (eds), *Understanding Political Development*, Little, Brown and Company, Boston.

13

Rewinding 'Back to the Future': the Left and Constitutional Democracy

Ben Anderson

We have perhaps been too long accustomed to thinking of the Aidit-led PKI of 1951-65 as 'normal' or 'modal', partly because of its huge growth over a brief fourteen year period, and partly because it seemed in many ways — organisationally and rhetorically — 'parallel' to other post-World War II communist parties in many places around the globe. It is possible too that this assumption of 'normalcy' may have narrowed the perspective in which we have looked at the communists' participation in the constitutionalist regime of 1950-59, and the Guided Democracy regime that succeeded it. There may therefore be some small advantage in rethinking that normalcy. Perhaps our consideration of that period should look backward as well as forward, to compare the 1950s not only with the 1990s but also with the early years of the nationalist movement.

The international context

Aidit was still a teenager when the Pacific War broke out and Japanese armies occupied the Netherlands East Indies. He was 22 when Nazi Germany and militarist Japan collapsed, 24 when the Cold War emerged in earnest, 26 when Mao took power in Peking, 27 when the Korean War broke out, 28 when he won leadership of the PKI, and 30 when Stalin died. Between his 22nd and 26th year, communist regimes were established throughout Eastern Europe, including Albania and Yugoslavia, as well as in China, Vietnam and North Korea. Between 1947 and 1954, armed communist parties had appeared to have come within hailing distance of power in the neighbouring Philippines, Malaya and Burma. Furthermore, European colonialism was collapsing in most of Asia, if not yet in Africa. Heady times for a young Marxist, times in which Manichean conceptions could flourish, and in which there were plenty of plausible *pratanda* (harbingers/portents) for an imminent, rosy future for communism in a global context. One was within the *arus sejarah*, the fast-forward flow of History.

Those early years of the late 1940s and early 1950s had a partial earlier echo in the aftermath of World War I, in which the great polyglot, polyethnic empires of the Ottomans, Romanovs, Habsburgs and Hohenzollerns had collapsed, and Lenin's Bolshevik regime took power and successfully defended it in a prolonged, bloody civil war. These events did not fail to resonate powerfully in the Indies during what Takashi Shiraishi rightly calls 'An Age in Motion'. Haji Misbach:

> The present age can rightly be called the *jaman balik boeono* [age of the world-turned-upside-down] — for what used to be above is now certainly under. It is said that in the country of Oostenrijk which used to be headed by a *Radja*, there has now been a *balik boeono*. It is now headed by a Republic, and many *ambtenaar* [civil servants] have been killed by the Republic. A former *ambtenaar* has only to show his nose for his throat to be cut, and so on. So, Brothers, remember! This land belongs to none other than ourselves.

Ruth McVey's account of the brave but suicidal communist uprisings of 1926-27 shows how they were accompanied by dreams of Russian aeroplanes and Kemalist battleships coming to the assistance of the insurrectionaries.

But there were also key differences between the two apocalyptic eras at the international level. The Bolshevik Revolution was quite unexpected and therefore it was conducted in many ways by a series of intelligent improvisations. The French Revolution could not provide much more than a rhetorical ground base. Youngsters, such as those who organised themselves into the *Perserikatan Komunist di India/Partij der Kommunisten in Indië* were eager to learn how Lenin had done it, but colonial regimes and complications in communication made it difficult to find out, and there were contending views in Moscow as to what had been crucial to success. Hence, in the Indies too, enthusiastic improvisation was usually the order of the day. Among the unexpected outcomes were the communist rebellions in two of the most Islamic provinces of the Old Colony — Banten and Sumatra's Westkust.

By the 1930s, however, the consolidation of the USSR, the seepage of Great Russian nationalism into its foreign and domestic politics, the entrenchment of Stalin's apparat, and its control over the Comintern, were making possible a 'modular' communism, based on a brutally imposed, singular, organisational and ideological model. By then calculated opportunisms had taken the place of the earlier improvisations.

Hence in the apocalyptic world of the late 1940s and early 1950s, young communists like Aidit were accustomed to a degree of standardisation — in organisational, ideological, ethical, cultural and other spheres — unimaginable in the 1920s. It was precisely the absence of such standardisation that offered an attractive explanation of the failure of the 1926-27 rebellions, as well as of the political catastrophe of the Madiun Affair of 1948. Following a visibly successful model in the wider world promised to associate young Indonesian radicals with the new forward flow of History. Not that the 'following' process was in the least bit easy. But one can not understand the roles of the PKI in the 1950s without the power of the standard model, and the *arus*, being kept in mind.

The legacy of the Revolution
Here I think the key points to be borne in mind are as follows:
Culture
The communist leaders of the 1910s and 1920s grew to maturity in the mestizo culture of the Ethical Period. Alimin was a protege of the Ur-Ethicus Dr. Hazeu, Muso of the liberal theosophist van Hinloopen Labberton, Semaun of the radical Sneevliet, and Tan Malaka of the cultivated Resident of West Sumatra Le Febvre. All spoke Dutch, and some other European languages like German and French. All spent some time in capitalist Europe as well as Communist Russia. They encouraged party work among the *peranakan* Chinese and showed no signs of anti-Chinese racism (indeed in his autobiography Tan Malaka repeatedly expressed gratitude for the help he got from young Chinese both in Indonesia and in warlord China itself). All sat in colonial jails along with Dutch radicals like Bergsma and Baars. After all, why not? Were they not 'Communists in the Indies'?

Aidit's generation had a very different formation. They were teenagers in the repressive Indies of De Jonge and Tjarda, with the Ethical Policy long since discredited, the Vaderlandsche Club on the rapid rise, and racial polarisation sharply increased. Probably only a minority were fluent in Dutch, let alone any other foreign language; even fewer were personally acquainted with Europeans. None travelled to or lived in Europe. They came to early maturity under the violent, but also violently attractive, Japanese military regime of 1942-45. (Perhaps this is why in 1963-64 I often heard PKI demonstrators singing anti-Western songs sponsored by the Japanese, even though the Japanese had executed most of the then Communist Party leaders). Above all, they participated, as Rex Mortimer so aptly pointed out (1974), in the *pemuda* culture of the Revolution, alongside tens of thousands of other *pemuda* associated with different political parties and the *badan perdjuangan* [armed resistance groups].

This Revolution was a profound national one, in a way that the uprisings of 1926-27 had not centrally been. In its worst moments, fearful of treason, it targeted for vengeance white people, Indos, Chinese, Ambonese, and Menadonese, regardless of their actual political loyalties or behaviour. There are good reasons to believe that the young communists shunned these extremities, but they resented the 'European airs' of older aristocratic communist returnees from Holland, such as Raden Mas Setiadjit, Raden Mas Abdulmadjid Djojoadiningrat and Raden Mas Maruto Darusman. Later they removed the elderly *peranakan* communist Tan Ling Djie from power, and instituted a policy of excluding *peranakan* from the official party membership rosters. The Party would be a *pribumi* Communist Party. After 1950 Party leaders would start to travel rather extensively, but always in official capacities, as it were, representing 'Indonesia' in overseas fora. Did any of them have any real non-Indonesian personal friends? Could they have imagined, or approved of, radically leftwing Indonesian novels entitled *Anak Semua Bangsa* and *Bumi Manusia*?

But their formation also made them much more 'like' many of their competitors than perhaps was the case in the previous generation. Tan Malaka, Semaun, Muso, Darsono — these all seem to us striking personalities, standing out against their social backgrounds, in a way that Aidit, Njoto, Lukman and Sudisman do not.

Political experience

In the colonial 1910s and 1920s, there were — in contrast to British Burma or the American Philippines — no remotely plausible elections or serious legislators. The young PKI was thus led by people who were much more like 'activists' than professional politicians. Tan Malaka loved the SR schools he set up, Semaun was a trade union official, Muso (for a time) an underground subversive. And they were ceaselessly on the move, harried by the PID and the *pribumi* police. Their world was a world of *vergaderingen*, congresses, strikes, pamphleteerings, conspiracies. Not, of course, of guerrilla warfare.

But Aidit and his colleagues were in most ways professional politicians. Although they subsequently claimed to have been underground conspirators during the later Japanese Occupation, these claims are not strong. Certainly any such activity would have been very brief and without real results. They became politicians largely because of the peculiar character of the Revolution. It erupted, largely from below, and with a high degree of spontaneity, in the vacuum of power between the fall of the Japanese empire and the return of the British and Dutch colonists in force. It had a markedly decentralised character — and not only because of the dispersed archipelagic nature of the country. The official army (TKR-TRI-TNI) was gradually assembled from below in an essentially 'electoral' process, and it was parallelled, if not matched, by dozens of non-official armed mass organisations. At no point was it united politically or organised coherently enough to assume the leadership of the Republic. No single political party came close to assuming dominant leadership either, and all Revolutionary cabinets were complex coalitions. Perhaps this dispersal of power explains why, to an astonishing degree (if one looks around the 1940s world), the revolutionary regime was a 'constitutional democracy', with seven very different ministries in a mere four years (quite like the Constitutional Democracy of the 1950s, in fact). While extra-parliamentary forces, including President Sukarno and Vice-President Hatta, as well as various armed groups, played important roles, the KNIP with its Badan Pekerdja remained a central political institution.

What was Aidit doing during the Revolution? The Party became a legal institution from the very start, alongside a plethora of other parties, and he soon made his mark as the leader of the PKI 'fraction' in the KNIP, i.e., as very able parliamentarian. Many of his colleagues of the 1950s played similar roles. Even people like Sudisman (Pesindo) and Sakirman (Lasjkar Rakjat) did, so far as I can tell, little fighting, but were the political specialists of these organisations, in which role they participated in parliamentary affairs, and the myriad congresses and conferences, internal and inter-organisational, that marked the inner life of the Republic. Since the Dutch rather quickly took control over the coastal-urban areas and plantations where communist-influenced unions had once sprung up, Communists with training in union organisation, such as Njono, had little room in which to exercise their talents. Hence it was that, after 1949, it did not take much to encourage Aidit and his colleagues to continue on this parliamentary track. This track also meant disbanding embryo guerrilla groups in the Merapi-Merbabu Complex, and subordinating 'activist' elements in the plantations, wharves, factories and railway stations.

Madiun

The Madiun Affair was costly to the communists in many different respects. In the immediate sense, the major loss was of any substantial presence in the Army. Communist-influenced units were destroyed or disbanded, and many left-leaning officers were dismissed, imprisoned or killed. The Army leadership emerged from the Affair with an abiding suspicion of, and hostility towards, the Party, a hostility only accentuated after 1950 by the Army's close relations with the Pentagon, and, eventually, control of the advanced sectors of the economy after the nationalisations of Dutch enterprises in 1957. Their loss of influence in the Army also effectively ruled out any 'Bolshevik' dreams that the Party leaders might ever have had, and made 'parliamentarism' all the more attractive.

In the second place, Aidit and his associates recognised that the Party had been drastically outmanoeuvred in 1948. In a formal sense the Affair had begun when Sumarsono, a Surabayan Pesindo leader of middle rank, spurred by the 'Wild West' in Surakarta, took control of the town of Madiun, declaring a 'revolutionary' local government. The central government, directed by Sukarno, Hatta and Col. Nasution, seized on this opportunity to denounce this local affair, on national radio, as the beginning of a treacherous, national-level uprising by the communists. Taken by surprise, the Party, formally led by an elderly Muso recently returned from the Soviet Union, fell into the government's trap and denounced Sukarno and Hatta as Japanese-era quislings. Jogjakarta proceeded to order the crushing of the Party and its allies as *traitors* to the national cause. Many party leaders died in the brief period of fighting, and others were executed at the beginning of the second Dutch 'Police Action' of mid December 1948. Communists, who had been a part of almost all Republican ministries thus far, and who had always read (back) the revolt of 1926-27 as the highpoint of colonial-era national resistance, were now for the first time effectively branded as un-national or anti-national. The communists of the 1950s felt that they had to work overtime to overcome this anti-national reputation — and a key condition for doing so was to show that they could cooperate closely with non-party 'strong-nationalist' personalities and organisations, typically in a subordinate capacity. While there were many other reasons for the Party's vehement hostility to the Dutch, the British, and the Americans during the 1950s, recuperating from Madiun was a certainly central stimulus.

A final residue of Madiun was the eruption, really for the first time in Indonesia's (modern) history, of violence at the village level — in Java — between Muslims and communists: something that had not occurred at all in the 1920s even when Muslim and communist leaders had quarrelled. Just why the violence occurred has never been properly studied, and I do not pretend to know the answers. The '*aliran*' explanation is frequently adduced and there is no doubt about the long existence of *abangan-santri* tensions. It is also probable that, just as for communists, the 1930s and 1940s saw a process of standardisation among Muslims. The huge increase in Western-style Muslim organisations that began with Muhammadiyah, the spread of print-capitalist literacy, and the inroads of a self-conscious, ideological modernism, surely all played their parts. But it is nonetheless rather striking that, in the 'wild' days of 1945-46, when central authority broke down in many regions, social revolutions took place, and there were plenty of opportunities for '*aliran*' violence to surge up from below, very little actually occurred.

For our purposes, however, the importance of Madiun was its effect on the communists and their constituencies in the 1950s. Amir Sjarifuddin may not have liked Hatta and Sukiman very much, but they met all the time and did deals with one another in a 'normal' political way. They were all part of the *pergerakan* [the Movement] culture of the colonial period. But the younger communists who survived Madiun, and were not in the *pergerakan* club, had a visceral hatred for these two more or less Muslim leaders which had less to do with their Islamic-ness than their putative direction of the killings of 1948. These feelings were cordially reciprocated. This hatred was fanned by the politics of Constitutional Democracy, as we shall observe.

A final 'outcome' of Madiun involved the United States. Up until 1948, the Republican leaders had, on the whole, been united in support of whatever form of 'neutralist' foreign policy seemed feasible. I stress feasible. The Soviet Union lay a half-globe away from Indonesia and had no effective means of exercising power in Southeast Asia. America, however, had won the Pacific War and emerged as the dominant world power. It was powerfully entrenched in East and Southeast Asia, and had enormous influence in imperial Europe. Nothing is more striking than the caution with which the leftwing-led governments of the Republic between 1945 and 1948 attempted to deal with the Americans, and the trust in US emissary Frank Graham evidenced by Amir Sjarifuddin till his fall from power in January 1948. Up until then, there was no strong evidence of American intentions to meddle in the *internal* politics of the Republic. But for reasons that need not detain us here, in the spring of 1948, as the Cold War deepened, as Mao's armies proceeded triumphantly across China, and as political polarisation increased through Southeast Asia, the Americans began to intervene domestically, in particular giving their support to leading Muslim politicians — something that had never happened before. Thus the US came to be associated with the repressions linked to the Madiun Affair. Out of Madiun came the alignments of the 1950s that pitted Muslims, the military leadership and America against the PKI and its *abangan*, nationalist allies.

Constitutional Democracy
The context

The context in which constitutional democracy emerged in the aftermath of the Round Table Conference was, I have argued elsewhere, the absence of real alternatives. The Republic came to the Conference with only a moderately strong hand to play. It had little practical influence in East Indonesia which had been under Dutch control since late 1946. It had no Air Force and almost no Navy — both essential for establishing centralised control of the whole country. Its military was decentralised, provincially-rooted and full of internal fissures. There was no more possibility of establishing an authoritarian regime in 1949 than there had been in 1945.

This fragility was a central factor in the remarkable comeback of the PKI in the early and middle 1950s. Even during the Madiun Affair the Party had not, as such, been made illegal, and during the Second Dutch Action many middle and lower-level cadres were released from detention and joined the struggle in various capacities. Hence, provided the state remained weak, there were good possibilities for reviving and expanding the Party — legally — both in areas of Western Indonesia where it had roots from the 1920s, and in an Eastern Indonesia where it never had opportunities to expand before. The Party leaders recognised the critical importance of its legality, and of the constitutional regime as its guarantee.

At the same time the Party leaders, culturally strongly nationalist, also recognised that a weak state was threatened by regionalism and secessionist sentiments, as well as by external intervention. They found themselves therefore nudged into the uncomfortable position of supporting not only the Sukarno who had denounced Muso as a traitor, but a centralising military leadership which was strongly anti-communist and linked to the Americans. The Party did what it could by encouraging inter-service rivalry and pressing Sukarno to get the infant Navy and Air Force trained and equipped by the USSR. But the contradictions were never effectively solved, and reached climactic proportions during the PRRI-Permesta rebellion and the transition to Guided Democracy.

The short-term logic of this situation suggested that the PKI should try to maximise its influence within the powerful existing constraints (the most important of these was its lack of any military power, and its commitment to maintenance of the vast Republic's territorial integrity). Hence the curious situation that in practice the Party was a determined supporter of the constitutional regime, while for other reasons it was never in a position to 'say so' unequivocally.

It could not say so because its ideological idioms were formally revolutionary and anti-parliamentary, and its 'model' even more so. Aidit and his associates were perfectly aware that no Communist Party had ever come to national-level power (in the exclusive Stalinist sense) by parliamentary means. Yet they also observed parliamentary communists governing sub-national states in India, and many municipalities and districts in Italy and France, without being in much danger of imprisonment or execution. Is it possible, then, that in their heart of hearts, some of the PKI leaders did not think seriously about a future along such Indian, French, and Italian lines?

One might think so from the way in which the Party threw itself into the national election campaign of 1955 and the provincial elections of 1957. (Hard to imagine Tan Malaka, Alimin, and Darsono in such a situation). There is no doubt that the huge expansion of the Party's membership — which also substantially diluted its militancy — was motored by these legislative elections. The professional politicians directing the Party thus found electoralism very well adapted to their skills and experience.

Electoralism

The electoralism of 1954-57 is very revealing of the Party's proclivities and problems. Like the other three 'Big Parties' to emerge from the 1955 elections, the PKI found that electoral success depended, in the short run at least, on tapping into traditional patronage networks and village level rivalries. It was simpler (if one could manage it) to win over a village headman, and use his local, traditional authority to bring in village voters, than to expend costly time and energy cultivating ordinary villagers one on one. It was also simpler to join other parties in battening on local quarrels, *aliran* antipathies and, in Java, vivid memories of Madiun and the social revolutions. Electoralism thus pushed the PKI towards often conservative rural leaderships and towards *aliran*ism in a way that would have struck the men of 1920 as peculiar. These tactics certainly won the party substantial representation in legislatures at different levels, and after the Decentralisation Act of 1957, promised to open up access, *à l'italienne*, to provincial executive positions. But these successes, as they multiplied, also made possible 'constitutional careers' for many Party cadres, who would have strong personal reasons to invest in the existing system.

Electoralism also focussed the Party's hierarchy and energies in a specific direction. If the Party's main task was winning elections then a certain priority had to be given to specialists in such matters, i.e. party politicians and propagandists, with less attention to specialists in other spheres such as trade unions, peasant leagues, and women's organisations — in effect the spectrum of *ormas* (mass organisations). (This logic worked for all parties.

When the prospect of elections disappeared under Guided Democracy, core parties atrophied while the *ormas* developed rapidly and spectacularly across the board). One can thus estimate that even if the Party leaders — at the front of their minds — may have regarded their participation in electoral politics under a constitutional regime as 'tactical', the real consequences of electoralism were, as Don Hindley (1966) noted long ago, to domesticate the Party and to adapt it organisationally to parliamentary politics.

The logic of electoralism pointed in still another direction which should not be overlooked. The voting patterns in 1955 and 1957, shaped by both the Party and its competitors, showed that a truly hegemonic party was out of the question. If elections had been held in 1960, it is possible that the PKI would have become the largest single party, *but it would still have been miles away from a majority.* Any government in which it could expect to participate would have to be a coalition government — as in 1945-48. And such a government would also have to have a distinctly *verzuiling* character to survive in strength. But here too a contradiction would inevitably emerge, especially in a poverty-stricken, post-revolutionary agrarian society. Coalition politics of the *verzuiling* type require tight vertical control by party leaderships over party membership and party followings. But could such control and support be maintained given the typically conservative outcomes of *verzuiling* politics? The Party would always find it difficult to resist the pressures from below which would expand, within limits, its electoral base but also undermine the stability of *verzuiling* coalitions.

There is a last irony in the PKI's electoral successes during the 1950s. One element in those successes was to make many progressive Indonesians increasingly believe that the Party was the only credible mass-based representative of the Left, something not at all self-evident in the early 1950s. A post-1955 drift in the PKI's direction was particularly evident among intellectuals — note the rapid rise of Lekra from that time. This movement in turn pushed the inner politics of the other parties in a rightward direction. The PSI's embarrassing performance in the elections directly contributed to Sumitro Djojohadikusumo's near toppling of Sjahrir, and more energetic PSI efforts to cultivate clandestine relations with the military. In the PNI, Hardi and Hadisubeno came to the fore. Masyumi leaders like Natsir and Sjafruddin abandoned electoral politics altogether for a foolish PRRI insurrection. Extra-electoral anti-Chinese agitation, largely absent in 1950-55, was another sinister consequence of the communists' parliamentary advances.

Arus sejarah

It was, however, not merely the local tactical skills of the PKI leaders that counted. The 'pull' towards, and away from, the PKI also derived from its real and imagined external linkages — more the latter in fact than the former. For the Party leaders, these linkages were a rather mixed blessing. They were fully aware that Indonesia lay firmly in the American sphere of influence, and that the practical help that they could get from a remote

Soviet Union, and a close, but poverty-stricken, and militarily weak China, was quite small. But for electoral purposes, and for the rapid building of a mass party, the image of the PKI as associated with a powerful, world-wide movement opposed to the international status quo — Western economic and military domination — was very attractive. On the other hand, precisely the image of this external support alarmed the Party's enemies, and threatened its strictly nationalist credentials. Perhaps still more important was the sense, deep inside the party itself, that its own domestic trajectory was — had to be — 'rhythmically' bound to the *arus* of the world-wide movement.

We have, thanks to the writings of Ruth McVey in particular, some idea of the problems thereby involved. The leadership was sensitive to contradictory external expectations, and did what it could to accommodate them. It knew very well that the Chinese communists were deeply sceptical about the Party's 'domesticated' parliamentary-style politics — which seemed close to the cul-de-sac practice of the PCI and PCF, and the thinking of the CPSU — and that the only 'successful' Asian communist parties owed their achievements to armed struggle. It attempted to compensate for this aberrance by an increasingly Maoist rhetoric, by the urging of a national foreign policy which would align Indonesia with China, North Korea, and Vietnam, and eventually by the fateful, extra-parliamentary *aksi sepihak* [unilateral action] campaign of 1964. It is quite probable that the *kulturkampf* of 1964-65 should be understood in the same perspective.

Little of all this redounded to the Party's long-term advantage. Talking revolution while practicing parliamentary-style coalition politics increased domestic polarisation, and encouraged unfulfillable expectations among the Party's own following. It became increasingly vulnerable to an apocalyptic political reaction against which it had no effective means of defending itself. One can best see the logic here if one tries to imagine the massacres of 1965-66 occurring at any point in post-war France or Italy.

The conjuncture of the 1990s
Residues

The party was, for all intents and purposes, destroyed between late 1965 and 1968 — at the height of Mao's and Brezhnev's power. No external allies or associates proved capable in any way of protecting the Party or mitigating its decimation. No imperialist power was visibly responsible for its fate. Over the subsequent quarter of a century the PKI has shown not the slightest sign of re-emergence. No doubt the ferocity of Suharto's *matanza* in the later 1960s, and the vigilance of a huge security apparatus built up since then, account in part for this lack of life. But at least as important were the betrayals of many senior party cadres during the nightmare years, the success with which the New Order regime blamed the 30 September 1965 abortive coup on Party leaders, and a widespread feeling among the Party's following that the leadership's policies had brought them to the abyss.

Yet one might, under other circumstances, have expected the Party eventually to reappear, as it had done after the disasters of 1926-27 and 1948. But the circumstances of the late 1980s and the early 1990s — the collapse of the USSR, Teng Hsiao-pingism and the CPR-US alliance, the disastrous condition of Indochina, the impending fall of the Castro regime, the isolation and weakness of that in Pyongyang — rule out any of the global hopes and sense of *arus sejarah* that had earlier helped revive a stricken party. Nowhere in the contemporary world is a Marxist party on a 'rising curve'.

On the other hand, one can not easily imagine the real disappearance of two basic residues of the Aidit era. In its last heyday, the Party claimed a membership of 3 millions, with another 17 million or so in its associated *ormas*. Even if we believe that a million (one twentieth) of these human beings died in 1965-68, and that old age and disease have carried off perhaps another two or three million, we are nonetheless left with millions of people still alive who had some association with the Party, and millions more, mainly the children of the late 1960s, who remember and still feel vividly the tragic consequences of massacre, imprisonment, torture, and social ostracism. We have very little idea of how these people, especially the young, interpret what they have experienced and inherited. Second, while repression, undreamed of oil and natural gas wealth, and vast infusions, over a quarter of a century, of foreign capital in state and private shapes, have in many ways transformed Indonesian society and the Indonesian social structure, it would be rash to suppose that some old social problems have not persisted and that new ones have not emerged. The older ones, such as unemployment, unequal division of wealth, and landless labour, are quite evident. The newer ones are perhaps more striking. Two are of particular interest: 1) The creation of a much larger, and more repressed, stratum of wage-labourers than ever before existed in Indonesia. 2) Intractable regional-cum-security difficulties. In interesting contrast with the past, regional dissatisfaction today has very strong centrifugal, even secessionist features. In the 1950s, only the RMS wanted to leave the Republic, but today, in varying degrees of strength, insurrectionary movements in East Timor, Irian Jaya, and Aceh seek to free themselves fully and finally from Jakarta's grip. They are operating in an international environment in which secession has more legitimacy than at any time since World War II; and they appear to have more political support much further 'down' the social pyramid than any of their predecessors. How will these dissatisfactions find lasting political form, and under what types of leadership?

The other side of the coin is the memory of the PKI's aging enemies. One has to be, I reckon, at least 40 years old to have any substantial direct recollection of the Party in its final heyday: a substantial *minority* of contemporary Indonesians. How successfully have these enmities been transmitted across generations?

Culture

One of the most interesting features of the New Order regime has been its powerful and sustained endeavour to change the culture, including the political culture, that had been constructed, more or less continuously, since the early days of the *pergerakan*. Let me just mention the more salient aspects of this campaign (in some ways nicely symbolised by the orthographic change to *ejaan baru*). First and foremost was a change in public language as drastic as anything outside early revolutionary China, Vietnam, or Cuba. I am not thinking only of the ban on explicitly Marxist discourse, but the suppression of Sukarnoism, and the political languages of the constitutional era. In place of *marhaen, gembong, ormas, buruh, trias politica, pentjoleng, tionghoa, kedaulatan rakjat, aliran,* and a hundred others have come *siskamling, mantan, kotor lingkungan, repelita, cina, akselerasi modernisasi, rawan, kesinambungan, rekayasa,* SARA[1], as well as a numbing accumulation of techno-bureaucratic, and Indonesianised American social science terminologies. The big question is whether this vocabulary, and the discourses underlying it, have established hegemonic roots, especially among the young.

Second has been the fate of History. We all remember the late Nugroho Notosusanto's corrupt manipulations of the official national history project of the 1970s. But on the whole the New Order has preferred to work by suppression rather than by refiguring. For example, I know of no serious attempt to link the New Order systematically or logically with the colonial-era movement. (It is also striking that only in 1992, seventeen years after the occupation of Portuguese East Timor, did the government get around to commissioning history books for young Timorese which would —but how?— incorporate East Timor's long history into the much briefer one of Indonesia). In place of History a peculiarly shallow, ahistorical 'Javanese tradition' has been presented, but even then rather halfheartedly. (This policy has been inadvertently assisted by the huge decline in popular capacity to decipher the Javanese orthography in which 95% of Javanese historical records and literary works are encased). But can History really be so profoundly erased? The experience of erasing regimes in other parts of the 20th century does not suggest that the New Order will ultimately be successful.

Third is the occlusion of artistic activity, not only in the field of literature, but also drama, poetry, film, and so forth. No one would deny that the New Order regime is profoundly philistine. It is very hard to imagine President

---

1. Old Order: *Marhaen*: Sukarno's name for Indonesia's toiling classes. *Gembong*: ringleader. *Ormas*: party-aligned mass organisation. *Buruh*: worker. *Trias politica*: the separation of powers. *Pentjoleng*: embezzler. *Tionghoa*: Chinese. *Kedaulatan rakjat*: popular sovereignty. *Aliran*: political-religious 'streams'.
New Order: *Siskamling*: neighbourhood security system. *Mantan*: 'former' (especially for state officials). *Kotor lingkungan*: politically polluted. *Repelita*: Five Year Plan. *Cina*: Chink. *Akselerasi modernisasi*: accelerated modernisation. *Rawan*: insecure. *Kesinambungan*: continuity. *Rekayasa*: political and social engineering. SARA: [the prohibition on raising issues related to] ethnicity, religion, race and class.

Suharto ever reading a novel or going voluntarily to a play. But how successfully has this philistine drabness been imposed? Jim Siegel has frequently stressed the remarkable absence of any substantial Indonesian samizdat over the part 25 years. Does the determined boringness of *Kompas* — the New Order newspaper par excellence — contribute to its authority and huge readership? Is *Tempo*'s mannered knowingness exactly what is required of a non-oppositional opposition? Should we take off our hats in recognising that not a single substantial novel about New Order Indonesia has ever been published? Or, if one makes an exception for Putu Wijaya's powerful *Nyali*, that it did not need to be banned, simply let go unnoticed?

The other side of the coin is best represented by the case of Pramoedya, whose works are banned in Indonesia, required highschool and college reading in conservative Malaysia (luckily the New Order has not had the imagination shrewdly to follow suit), and so successfully published in the rich West that a Nobel Prize some day is not out of the question. The importance of Pramoedya is not simply that, with the possible exception of Amir Hamzah, he is the one writer of genius that modern Indonesia has produced, or that his work can not be permanently erased. His other significance lies in his relation to Indonesia's history in every sense. The 1930s and 1940s are incomparably there for retrieval in *Tjerita dari Blora*, *Subuh*, and *Pertjikan Revolusi*, the 1950s in *Tjerita dari Djakarta* and *Korupsi*. The Buru tetralogy, along with *Sang Pemula*, are in themselves remarkable attempts at the imaginative recuperation of the *pergerakan*. But Pramoedya has also been attempting, since the late 1950s, to excavate a huge literary archive, stretching back through Kartini into the late 19th century, which, even when he started his labours, was deep in organised dust.

All of this labour is awaiting its appointed time. When that time comes, and it is probably not far away, it will be interesting to see how its reappearance is handled by the humanists who have for so long collaborated in its suppression.

Fourth is the radical political restructuring that, aside from suppressing the Left, created Golkar, and generated the toothless PDI and PPP. We do not yet have many good studies of any of these apparatuses, or of the deeper conceptions that underlay their construction. Formally the party system of the New Order was said to aim at the supersession of the *aliran* politics which had 'poisoned' the 'Old Order' and Constitutional Democracy. Yet both PPP and PDI, despite their emollient names, are clearly predicated on *aliran* thinking. Was there an original intent permanently to discredit such thinking — by holding visibly impotent *aliran* parties in constant view, by forcibly merging historically antagonistic Muslim streams within the PPP and marhaenist and Christian streams in the PDI, and by imposing mercenary and mediocre leaders on both?

If so, is the party-system, such as it now stands, well implanted? Again, no-one really knows. This ignorance prevails in all directions. It is possible that the New Order has succeeded in one key respect — in marginalising the peculiar *aliran* politics of 1947-65 (which, if I am right, did not exist in the 1920s). But this marginalisation is more likely to prove partial. For example, it seems inconceivable that a democratised Indonesia would not have a large Muslim party with a strong popular base. Or perhaps multiple Muslim parties but not necessarily divided along the old Masyumi-NU, urban-rural lines. Whether anything like the old PNI could be reborn seems much more uncertain; and the long-term viability of Golkar, which had never had a plausible identity or anything better than mediocrities in its leadership, is very dubious. Where there have been partially spontaneous expressions of popular politics, the lines drawn have been inter-ethnic, and inter-religious more than anything else, and it is anyone's guess how these tendencies might become institutionally channelled, if at all. In one sense, this shapelessness may open up '1990s' possibilities for younger people on the Left.

Leadership

One of the typical sociological consequences of entrenched authoritarian regimes dominated by a single, long-lasting personality is leadership atrophy. Suharto, for very obvious reasons, has made sure that he has had no impressive personal rivals, but he has also had the resources to suborn or coopt a good part of the potential leadership of the generation of people in their 40s and 50s.

In some cases the absence of believable leadership is obviously worrying. One crucial step towards a normalisation of Indonesian political life — and one crucial to shaping the future of the Left — has to be the ending of the Left's legally pariah status, especially as regards the whole poisonous *kotor lingkungan* racket. The time for such change may be ripening, even for the military. Wismoyo's AMN class, graduated in 1963, was then too young to play any significant role in the bloody crushing of the Left in 1965-66. The 'enemies' they have faced in their maturity have not been leftists. But the normalisation I have in mind (which would require major legal and administrative changes) would seem to require courageous and determined political leadership.

Afterword

When the first democratisation process began in Indonesia, around 1910, it was up against a powerful autocratic state, led by Dutchmen, but heavily manned by Indonesian bureaucrats. As Takashi Shiraishi shows so beautifully in his *An Age in Motion*, the early *pergerakan* — shouldn't we revive this marvellous word? — lived by improvisation, experimentation, and inclusionary discourse. Leaders quarrelled with each other in the way that politicians always do, but they felt that they were part of a single emancipatory *arus*. Not simply an internal Indies *arus*, but a world *arus* that encompassed Turkey and Oostenrijk, India and the infant Soviet Union. Perhaps this is why that era produced leaders of a quality and quantity we have not seen since: Sang Pemula, Douwes Dekker, Tjipto, Semaun, Suwardi Surjaningrat, Marco, Misbach, Tjokro, Sutomo, Sukarno, Tan Malaka, Hatta,

Natsir, Sjafruddin, Amir Sjarifuddin, Sartono, Sjahrir, Daud Beureueh, Yamin, Roem, Djuanda, Salim, Wachid Hasjim, Wilopo, Sarmidi, and so many others. Wouldn't we all love to have had the chance to chat with them? (Can you think of a single one of NEI's tens of thousands of Melayu bureaucrats of whom this might be said?)

It didn't generally occur to them to kill or torture each other until the fateful year of 1948. The emancipatory project had by then met the Cold War. When Constitutional Democracy was set in formal place at the beginning of the 1950s, Indonesia had begun to become a place where one could imagine it was patriotic to collaborate more closely with the CIA or with the emissaries of Moscow than with one's own president or prime minister. Some cancerous residues of this era are certainly still with us.

It is the great merit of Pramoedya's Buru tetralogy to re-create so vividly, in the era of post-communism, the Indonesia of pre-communism, in every sense of these terms. We perhaps all need reminding of the turbulent, quarrelsome, vitality of the Age in Motion, with its prostitutes, *ulama, pokrol bambu*, journalists, socialists, *jago, priyayi*, Eurasian gangsters, actresses, Frenchmen, Chinese utopians, spies, dispossessed peasants, printers, *raja mogok*, traders and so on (but without social scientists, generals, *sekwilda*, and consultants).

We do not exactly feel today that we are in an Age in Motion, but we are in an era where there is a stronger sense of a single *arus* than at any time in the last half century. It could be a propitious time for *pergerakan*-style experiments, quarrels, improvisations, and camaraderie in the face of what, after more than a quarter of a century, we should get used to calling the 'Old Order'.

References

Mortimer, Rex (1974) *Indonesian Communism under Sukarno*, Cornell University Press, Ithaca.

Hindley, Donald (1966) *The Communist Party of Indonesia, 1951-1963*, University of California Press, Berkeley and Los Angeles.

14

The Impact of neo-Modernism on Indonesian Islamic thought: the Emergence of a new Pluralism[1]

Greg Barton

The changing map of Indonesian Islam
In the fifties and sixties Indonesian Islamic thought could crudely, but reasonably accurately, be described in terms of the two major *aliran*, or streams, of Traditionalism and Modernism, but by the 1980s such terms were no more than inadequate, and vaguely passé, starting points in describing Indonesian Islamic thought. Of course there were always differences in character and outlook within the Muslim community that were not adequately explained by the simple Traditionalist/Modernist model but during the last thirty years the trend has been for Islam to become even more diverse. Muhammadiyah, for example, can still be described as being a Modernist organisation, but that appellation is not nearly as informative as it once was. Today Muhammadiyah, the organisation, is itself a rather loose fitting wrapping for a whole host of related but different *aliran* (religious-ideological streams). Many senior members in Muhammadiyah may not have greatly changed in their ideological orientation from the heady days of Masyumi, the 1950s Modernist political party, some of them have become somewhat more conservative and even reactionary, whilst amongst the

---

[1]. Sources for the this paper consist mainly of interviews that I have conducted on various occasions over the past four years, in the course of my doctoral research on the emergence of neo-Modernism in Indonesian Islamic thought, with the Islamic thinkers referred to in the paper. This paper in places draws upon a paper written for the 3rd Biennial East-West Philosophy Conference held at the University of Queensland, Brisbane, Australia, 9-11 July 1992.

organisation's younger members neo-Modernist ideas have clearly influenced many whose orientation towards progressive thought marks them out as belonging to a clearly different aliran from that of their fathers.

The diversity is not merely the product of simple generational change either, for individuals of the same generation such as Amein Rais and Kuntowijoyo stand at opposite extremities of the spectrum of thought found within Muhammadiyah. This story is repeated throughout the majority of long established Islamic organisations including the peak student organisation *Himpunan Mahasiswa Islam*, which, even though it is in many respects true to its essentially Modernist origins, can no longer adequately be described as being a Modernist organisation. When the Traditionalist side of the *umat* (Muslim community) is examined the changes of the past two decades are even more apparent. Whilst clearly not all, perhaps not even a majority, of Nahdlatul Ulama's 35 million affiliates support the profound changes introduced by Abdurrahman Wahid, many millions clearly do. Many within Nahdlatul Ulama (NU), particularly amongst the many young people whose educational experience includes both *pesantren* and university, support Abdurrahman not just because of his personal charisma or political brilliance but also because of his progressive liberal thought, a rich compound of Traditionalism and Modernism, classicism and modernity. To speak of NU as representing a single *aliran* now makes very little sense. A point has now been reached where the philosophical/ideological distance between individuals within a given Islamic organisation is often far greater than the distance between them and some of their colleagues outside the organisation.

There was of course a good deal of diversity in the 1950s and 60s, both within organisations as well as between them. Not every member of Muhammadiyah, for example, supported the political ideology of Masyumi, and even within Masyumi itself there were considerable differences of opinion. Similarly, the vision that Wahid Hasjim had for NU was not that which was later implemented by Idham Chalid. Nevertheless the diversity and complexity of Islamic thought in those decades was of one order, whilst that of the present decade is of another order altogether. The crude *aliran* model of Islamic ideological cartography which once did workman-like duty is now clearly inadequate, made obsolete by a sea change in Indonesian Islamic thought. This change is of great importance. It is not merely a matter of importance to academic map makers of Indonesian society; it both indicates, and contributes to, the growing concern for democratic reform.

To a great extent this change in Indonesian Islam has come about because of the flowering of new thought since the 1970s. This new thought has taken many forms but the most significant development is a new school of thought (it is sufficiently coherent and complete to be called a school of thought in its own right) whose seminal thinkers include Djohan Effendi, Nurcholish Madjid, the late Ahmad Wahib and Abdurrahman Wahid (Barton 1991). This school has been described in various ways but the term that best sums up this kind of thought is neo-Modernism, a term coined by the late Pakistani-

American Islamic intellectual, Fazlur Rahman, to describe to what he saw as being the next stage of evolution in Islamic Modernist thought (Rahman 1979; Bahasoan 1985; Ali and Effendy 1986). This school of neo-Modernist Islam has been a major force in the reshaping of the terrain of Islamic thought in Indonesia, and largely because of the various kinds of new thought that fanned out in the wake of neo-Modernism's avant garde, the cartography of Islamic thought in the 1990s is profoundly different from that of the 1950s and 1960s. One outcome of this process of change is that the commitment to pluralism and to the core values of democracy amongst Islamic intellectuals, and amongst the significant number of Muslims who look to these intellectuals for inspiration and guidance, is greater now than it has ever been before.

Islamic neo-Modernism

Perhaps neo-Modernism's greatest contribution to current Islamic thought is that it has provided a new conceptual apparatus, one both more profound and more intellectually consistent than the somewhat clumsy and awkward device fashioned by earlier Modernism. At the core of its intellectual concerns is the concept of contextualised *ijtihad* (*ijtihad* being personal interpretation of the scriptures), a commitment to combining rational inquiry and classical Islamic scholarship, a sincere openness and a rejection of dogmatism based upon an appreciation of pluralism (out of which, as we shall see later, comes a conviction that there should be a separation of 'church and state' allied with which is a concern for the democratisation of society). This commitment to contextualised *ijtihad* lays the foundations for the continued evolution of Islamic thought.

Neo-Modernism and Fazlur Rahman's paradigm of Islamic reform movements

While not all Indonesian Islamic intellectuals who fit into the movement broadly defined by Fazlur Rahman as neo-Modernism choose to identify themselves by his terminology, it is nevertheless worth retaining the term in discussing current developments in Indonesian Islamic thought for a number of reasons. One important reason for continuing to use Rahman's terminology is that, as was mentioned above, few suitable equivalents exist. Bahtiar Effendy has coined the term 'substantialist', which he uses in opposition to 'scripturalist', as a catch-all for all 'progressive, liberal' thinkers including all who accept the label neo-Modernist and some, such as Dawam Rahardjo, who do not (Liddle 1993:2); but this term creates as many problems as it solves. Another reason is that Rahman's paradigm, or model, of Islamic reform movements is very instructive; it provides a way of seeing developments in Indonesia not just in the context of the Islamic world at large but also in the context of history. Fazlur Rahman views the past two centuries as a period of change in the Islamic world in which four broad but distinct movements towards renewal or revival have emerged, with each new movement being a reaction both to earlier movements and to a changed environment. The first phase, or movement, of Islamic reformism Rahman calls simply Islamic Revivalism, after the manner of conventional practice. Likewise he follows convention in referring to the next phase as Islamic Modernism. Rahman's innovation is to recognise that since Modernism two further distinct movements have occurred. The first of these two new movements he refers to as neo-Revivalism, being like the revivalism of the Wahhabis and Sanusis in its concern for reform and renewal but being also very much a product of the era of Islamic Modernism. To a certain extent neo-Revivalism can be said to have grown out of a degenerative phase of Modernism. Certainly in Indonesia it is clear that many of the individuals concerned with the cause of Modernism in the 1950s and earlier had by the 1970s become sufficiently embittered and reactionary to have moved away from their earlier Modernist position towards something approaching Revivalism, or as Rahman styles it, neo-Revivalism. The final movement described by Rahman represents a reworking of Islamic Modernism, being a profound reapplication of Modernism's insights and interpretive methodology coupled with a fresh appreciation of classical Islamic learning. Because this movement, like Modernism, is essentially concerned with reinterpretation, or *ijtihad*, of the Qur'an and the Sunnah and is marked by a thorough going concern for rationalism, Rahman refers to it as neo-Modernism.

Rahman's paradigm is of considerable value in the Indonesian context in describing the process of mutation of Modernism and its final evolution into a fresh new movement of thought. As such the model has met with a good deal of acceptance, particularly amongst younger thinkers. Nevertheless it has also aroused a fair degree of controversy. Seminal thinkers aside, not all like-minded liberal, progressive Muslim intellectuals in Indonesia would classify themselves as neo-Modernist but this does not deny its efficacy. One of the chief virtues of Rahman's paradigm is that it provides a means of clearly delineating this intellectual movement and distinguishing it from both Traditionalism and Islamic Modernism whilst also alluding to its origins in the ideas of the earlier Modernist movement.

As has already been indicated, the new depth and thoroughness evident in the approach of these Indonesian scholars to *ijtihad* is, to a large extent, due to their combining classical Islamic scholarship with modern, or western, analytical methods. It is noteworthy that all the figures mentioned above have had the benefit of having both a classical or traditional Islamic education, revolving around the study of the Qur'an and classical Arabic texts, and a modern western style education. In this resect the example of Abdurrahman Wahid graphically illustrates the unique nature of this new Modernist, or neo-Modernist, movement for he represents in his person the resolution of half a century of antagonism between Modernists and Traditionalists in Indonesia. As the chairman since December 1984 of Nahdlatul Ulama, the leading Traditionalist Islamic organisation in Indonesia with perhaps as many as 35 million followers, and as the grandson of NU's founder Hasjim Ashari, and son of Wahid Hasjim, a greatly respected leader of NU, he has impeccable Traditionalist credentials. Yet his extensive reading of all manner of literature, western, Middle Eastern and Asian, his writing on a diverse range of matters, and his wide range of thought defy the limitations of the term Traditionalist. In a very real sense these thinkers represent the first generation of Indonesian intellectuals to have enjoyed such an education, for traditional Muslims in the past have generally not had access to a western style eduction, and precious few Modernists have had real command of either literary Arabic or the classical texts. Arising directly out of this new attitude and approach to *ijtihad* in particular, and learning in general, is a non-exclusivistic embracing of pluralism in society. And linked with this acceptance of, even welcoming of, pluralism is the strongly held conviction that party-political activity in the name of Islam is both counter productive for the *umat*, and, inasmuch as such activity gives rise to sectarianism, is unhealthy for society at large.

By the mid 1970s Abdurrahman and his colleagues were expressing the conviction that the interests of the *umat*, and of broader society, would be better served by the *umat* turning away from party-political activity and embracing the non-sectarian state philosophy of Pancasila, fifteen years before it became popular, or even acceptable, to express such thoughts.

The impact of neo-Modernism on Indonesian society

Neo-Modernism has been instrumental in the creation of a new intellectual/political position in Indonesian Islamic thought. 'Instrumental' because neo-Modernism has been a significant contributor to change but it is not by any means the sole agent of change. Inasmuch as new schools of thought gradually lead to broader change neo-Modernism is the most significant new school of thought. Many of the other positions or schools of thought could be said to be offshoots of neo-Modernism or, speaking in broad terms, subsets within neo-Modernism. The words 'intellectual/political position' express the fact that while neo-Modernism, because of its commitment to pluralism and its concern that sectarianism does not emerge once again to threaten the harmony of Indonesian society, eschews party-political activity, it is nevertheless concerned with matters of political ideology and philosophy. Finally the words 'Islamic thought' are used because neo-Modernism is directly influential/significant in the realm of thought and only indirectly (though importantly) with social and organisational change.

In response to the charge that he, or Paramadina as an organisation, is simply concerned with, or at least only influential within, elite circles, Nurcholish Madjid (1992:18; 1980) has said that whilst his focus is indeed on urban middle class society, there is nevertheless a 'trickle down effect' of ideas and attitudes, and that ultimately these ideas can be very powerful agents for social change. That this should be the case should not come at all as a surprise, for many, if not most, of the important social changes in Islamic society, beginning with the time of the prophet Mohammad, have come about as a result of the influence of key ideas, or constellations of ideas.

Whilst the influence of Nurcholish is often said to be confined to elite circles, few doubt the influence of Abdurrahman. Abdurrahman's thought however is little examined by outside commentators, leaving the clear impression that he is important primarily because of his connections, his grass roots networking and his political acumen, not because of his ideas. Yet it may be that at the end of the day his thought will be considered to have been his most important contribution. Further evidence of this kind of scholarly myopia here is the treatment given to Djohan Effendi. Whilst Djohan is considered to be a very important figure by his peers and by the scores of young intellectuals who are his intellectual beneficiaries, few outside observers pay any attention to his writing. This is graphically illustrated by Howard Federspiel's latest book on Islamic intellectuals in Indonesia (1991), in which Djohan is conspicuously absent.

Neo-Modernism and pluralism

Perhaps neo-Modernism's single biggest contribution to change in broader Indonesian society has been in the area of pluralism. The fact that neo-Modernism advocates pluralism and encourages Indonesians to take a pluralistic, inclusivistic stance towards others, is not an accident (Effendi 1986). It is not merely the product of the personalities involved, nor is it simply a matter of political expediency (or even common sense). Rather it is a direct outcome of a philosophical position which in itself is a product of the coming together of Islamic learning and western thought in an era of relative political stability. More specifically the source of neo-Modernism's concern with pluralism is to be found within its approach to *ijtihad*. Neo-Modernism stresses, even more than earlier Modernism did, that *ijtihad* must be an ongoing process because absolute knowledge of truth can never be achieved (Effendi 1983). Consequently neo-Modernism encourages a process of dialectal inquiry both vertically downwards through the course of the history of Islamic thought and that of humankind more generally and horizontally across the spectrum of contemporary thought, both Islamic and non-Islamic. Allied with this approach to *ijtihad* is a conviction that God intends human beings to think and behave rationally, employing their intellects to the task of improving the common lot of humanity. This is based on the Qur'anic injunctions that believers should exercise both *iman*, or faith and *akal*, or reasoning, throughout every facet of their daily existence (based on the understanding that human beings are composite beings, part material, part spiritual), and that they should constantly and energetically pursue knowledge, as one *hadith* has it: 'even unto China' (i.e. the furthermost, and most foreign, parts of the earth). All of this, it should be added, is set against the backdrop of an understanding and conviction in Islamic thought, seen especially clearly in neo-Modernism, that the Qur'an and the *Sunnah* teach that every faith and belief system has a right to exist.

Neo-Modernism and democracy

That pluralism is an elemental component of democracy is self evident. This is not to say that the broad adoption of a pluralist attitude by members of a society will necessarily of itself produce democracy, but it is impossible to imagine any genuinely sustainable form of democracy without it. There are a number of ways in which neo-Modernism has contributed to the cause of democracy in Indonesia. In general it has had a considerable influence through raising awareness of, and appreciation for, a pluralist position. In terms of direct action in the engendering of democracy it is significant that Abdurrahman, Djohan and Nurcholish, the first generation of neo-Modernist thinkers, are actively committed to the process of democratisation within Indonesian society (Liddle 1991).

Nurcholish, for example, has been consistently vocal in maintaining that Indonesia needs a strong opposition party. Recently he caused a considerable stir by suggesting this, recalling his vocal support in the 1977 election campaign for the PPP not because he was personally committed to PPP's platform but because, as he put it: 'we have to pump up the flat tyres' — in other words opposition parties ought to be helped attain a position of reasonable strength for the sake of having an opposition.

Djohan and Abdurrahman have also been directly active in the cause of democracy. Djohan writes frequently for the print media, generally seeking to engender an appreciation of democratic values through his articles, often in a very direct fashion. He joined with Abdurrahman in setting up *Forum Demokrasi*, in the wake of the disturbance that followed the 'Monitor Affair'. Whilst it is true that *Forum Demokrasi* is a very small organisation, it appears to have made a considerable impact and certainly gains excellent media coverage.

If *Forum Demokrasi* is small then NU is the reverse. It would be foolish to suggest that Abdurrahman Wahid has been completely successful in instilling an appreciation for democracy in the minds of all 35 million or so of NU's affiliates, but he has undoubtedly influenced many, and in the process achieved much in preparing the ground for democratic reform.

References

Bahasoan, Awad (1985) 'The Islamic Reform Movement: An Interpretation and Criticism', *Prisma* No.35, March 1985, pp.131-160.

Ali, Fachry and Bahtiar Effendy (eds) (1986) *Merambah Jalan Baru Islam/Rekonstruksi Pemikiran Islam Masa Orde Baru*, Mizan, Bandung.

Barton, G. (1991) The International Context of the Emergence of Islamic Neo Modernism in Indonesia, in M.C. Ricklefs (ed) *Islam in the Indonesian Social Context*, Annual Indonesian Lecture Series #15, CSEAS Monash University, Melbourne.

Effendi, Djohan (1983) 'The Contextual Understanding of the Holy Qur'an',

Iqbal Society For The Development of Religious Thought, Jakarta, December 1983.

_____ (1986) 'Towards a Theology of Harmony', Iqbal Society For The Development of Religious Thought, Jakarta.

Federspiel, H.M. (1991) *Muslim Intellectuals and National Development in Indonesia*, Nova Science Publisher, Inc., New York.

Liddle, R.W. (1991) 'Changing Political Culture: Three Indonesian Cases', (working paper) presented at the Conference on Modern Indonesian Culture: Asking the Right Questions, Flinders University, Adelaide, South Australia, September 1991.

_____ (1993) '*Media Dakwah* Scripturalism: One Form of Islamic Political Thought and Action in New Order Indonesia', unpublished conference paper.

Madjid, Nurcholish (1992) 'Tidak Usah Munafik!/Nurcholish Madjid, Pluralisme Agama, HMI, dan Keluarga Bahagia', (interview by Mohammad Sobary) *Matra*, No.77, December 1992

Rahman, Fazlur (1979) Islam: Past Influence and Present Challenge, in *Islam: Challenges and Opportunities*, Edinburgh University Press, Edinburgh. pp.315-330.

15

Islam, Politics and Democracy in the 1950s and 1990s

Abdurrahman Wahid

Indonesian national politics in two different decades could be distinguished by one main characteristic. In the earlier period, Pancasila was treated as a political compromise and was used to support different political ideologies. In the later period Pancasila becomes the only ideology, politically or otherwise. The MPR decided in 1978 to spell out ways of properly understanding and implementing Pancasila (the P4 program) and definitely stamped out any other 'confessional' interpretation, leaving only the single formal interpretation as the 'ideology of the state and society in Indonesia'.

Islam, then, ceases at present to be the political ideology of the Muslims in Indonesia, as it was in the 1950s and 1960s. Similar to the fate of Socialism and Communism, Islam has now to subordinate itself to the 'national ideology' of Pancasila, and to be satisfied with merely becoming a 'political orientation'. The Unity Development Party (PPP) is seen as 'Islamic' at present because of its Islamic political orientation, not because of that religion's dominant position as an ideology. Even Nationalism ceases to be an ideology by itself, but only an 'insight' (*wawasan*) or spirit (*semangat*). This condition of 'non-affinity' to other political ideologies made it necessary to establish Pancasila as a formal ideology. It has been reborn as a state ideology in the current New Order era.

The relegation of Islam, as well as other ideologies of the 1950s, to the position of a 'political orientation' was part of a process of de-confessionalising Indonesian politics, which took place progressively from the early 1970s to its total completion in the last seven years though the enactment of Laws no.3 and 8 of 1985 on political and social organisations. The de-confessionalisation of politics reaches its full and logical consequence in the designating of those who are seen as deviating from Pancasila's formal interpretation by the state as subversives or extremists. This process of de-confessionalisation of politics also bears on such 'neutral convictions' as liberalism, which in the view of many ideologues is not really an ideology at all. This bureaucratisation of ideology results, also, in the bureaucratisation of politics. The acknowledged political groups are those only which conform to the types of activity, orientation and objectives acceptable to the government. Groups whose activities, orientation and objectives are unacceptable to the government run the risk of being categorised as subversive or extremist.

The result is the emergence of groups openly deviating from the 'proper political course', for example, the Legal Aid Institute (*Lembaga Bantuan Hukum* — LBH) and of other groups which conceal their ideological affinity under the guise of developing their own political orientation of the 'Pancasila ideology', for example the emergence of the so-called ex-PSI technocrats etc. Old rivalries, based on ideological differences in the Old Order, resurface in the New Order as rivalries between 'political orientations'. Even those groups outside the formally acceptable ones, for example many non-governmental organisations (NGOs), could still feel the reverberations of this kind of rivalry, as denoted by allegations that they are PSI-influenced NGOs. Ideology-based affinity is replaced by an orientation-based one. Accordingly, the politics of ideology (*politik ideologis*) has developed into the politics of orientation (*politik orientasi*). Nevertheless the reversal of the situation — from Pancasila supporting political ideologies in the Old Order to political orientations supporting Pancasila as an ideology in the New Order — results in Indonesian politics still having a confessional nature at present. However strong they are, the core group of political organisations and social associations cannot always provide the backbone of actors and personnel needed in a central position in Indonesia's political life. This fact is especially evident in the groups comprising Golkar, the current 'government party'. The groups of administrators, professionals, intellectuals etc, which controlled Golkar from the outset, will have to cater soon to different political orientations. Hence the need to accommodate different political orientations at the same time, resulting in the emergence of a new kind of Islamic political approach. Instead of presenting Islam as the alternative to Pancasila, as was done in the Constituent Assembly in 1957-59, religion is touted as representing the genuine interests of the majority of Indonesians, and consequently, it is argued, it should be given priority by the state.

Thus Islam relates to politics in different ways in the two periods, 1950s and 1990s. The main ingredient of 'political Islam' is still the same, i.e. the interests of those formal Islamic groups as the 'legitimate representatives' of the majority of Indonesia's population. Those interests, in due course, emerge in the demands that Islam's representation in the formal organs of the state should be 'balanced' with the proportion of the majority nature of the Muslim population.

The basic reason behind this demand is the argument that Islam never recognises a total separation between religion and politics, and that the state should reflect in itself the norms of the majority. Hence the 'imperative' of 'Islamic representation', however informal, in formal governmental agencies and state organs to ensure that the state would not allow the enactment of regulations and laws contrary to Islamic teachings, and the accompanying demand, advanced incessantly by Muslim thinkers and intellectuals, as well as by activists of different Islamic organisations and groups, for the 'Islamisation of the law'. This, of course, was the very point of contention between Islamic and other parties from the 1930s to the deadlock of the Constituent Assembly in 1959. The deadlock had been temporarily solved by dropping the 'Jakarta Charter' passages in the draft 1945 Constitution's Preamble on 17 August 1945, to enable the newly proclaimed state to function. The said Charter specifically stipulated the 'obligation of adherents of Islam to implement Islamic Law (*Syari'ah*)', which implies also the obligation to enact Islamic Law as the law of the land. So, basically the nominal demand of those 'legal-formalists' among Muslim political activists has not changed during all those years; it merely submerges when the time is not appropriate for the making of such a demand.

This brings us to the main question of what the basic agenda of Islamic movements in Indonesia should be, if such a demand is not to be raised. What form of 'social persuasion' can be used to safeguard the implementation of Islamic teachings by its adherents? How can Muslims uphold the *Syari'ah*, the all embracing way of life for them, if not through the functioning of state organs? This is a difficult question, though society in general has provided an answer to it historically, through the implementation of the *Syari'ah* as the social ethics of the Muslims in Indonesia during more than three centuries of Dutch colonial rule and Japanese occupation. This social ethics framework provides the right answer, according to those Muslim activists who do not see the feasibility of imposing the *Syari'ah* as a complete code of law to be enacted as the national law.

This main disagreement between the 'legal-formalist' and 'non-legalist' Muslim activists in Indonesia now relates to their different approaches to politics, although we have to admit that the division between the two is not always neat. For the 'legal-formalist' activists, political organisation of an Islamic nature is necessary, in the form of a formal and independent entity such as an Islamic political party, or, if that is not possible, in the form of an Islamic caucus within existing political groups and the bureaucracy. The main ingredient of this approach is the ever present need to have a political entity to strive for the second group of Muslim activists who think in other terms. The political approach is valid only in a non-pluralistic society, where Islamic teachings operate as the only law of the land, as in Saudi Arabia, Iran and Afghanistan. In a highly pluralistic society such as Indonesia, another approach would certainly be more beneficial to the majority and minority alike, namely the moral, educational and persuasive approach to

Islamic teachings. While the first, legal-formalistic, 'imperative' could be described as the political approach to the role of Islam in society, the other approach could be categorised as the cultural one.

Of course, the division of Muslim activists into the two camps is not adequately satisfying for serious research, since it does not take into account, for example, those entering politics on behalf of Islam opportunistically and without the intention of establishing the *Syari'ah* as the law of the land. But such a generalisation is needed given the very intricate complexity of Islamic movements in modern Indonesia.

Beside the political and merely cultural approaches, we could discern, from developments in the last decade, a third approach among Muslim activists in the current Indonesian situation. This approach rejects the 'imperative' of a political role, if that denotes a legal-formalistic 'mission' to Islamise Indonesia's current national law. It does not repudiate political participation designed to achieve the realisation of political objectives dear to the principles of Islam, such as justice, the rule of law and equality before the law.

As such this approach — to concretise the basic principles of Islam in the social life of Indonesia — can not be confined to the political field of activity alone, since the said principles involve endeavours to establish a new society in all its dimensions. This approach necessitates the development of 'Islamic elements' commensurate with both the principles of Islam and the needs of the time in Indonesia, as a part of the new 'national constructs' of Indonesian society. Instead of being satisfied by merely developing Muslims with 'good religious conduct', as espoused by the cultural approach, which is basically concerned with Muslims as individuals, the third approach sees the need for a social framework for Islam in the development of a new Indonesian society. Social institutions have to be built to reflect Islam's concerns for liberty, social justice and rule of law. Although cultural in its tendency of persuasive and educative ways instead of stressing the importance of legal Islamic norms, this approach differs from the cultural approach. We could call it a socio-cultural approach to Islam in Indonesia. Working within the framework of 'social experiments' such as community development, technology transfer and restoration of the natural environment, this third approach provides us with a good example of how Muslim activists could participate in democratisation of the society as a whole, without resorting to any formal political identity. Through NGOs, 'social organisations' such as religious organisations, movements to 'promote Islamic propagation' (*dakwah*), this socio-cultural approach in essence forms a cluster of activities which will contribute to the democratisation of Indonesia in the long run.

In their turn, these three approaches, political, cultural and socio-cultural, provide also the vehicles for the internal dynamics of Islamic movements, and as such they also form the dynamics of social change taking place in Indonesia at present, by providing different perspectives of Islam's relationship with democracy in modern Indonesia. These approaches highlight the different nature of that relationship. Whereas in the 1950s there was political struggle to establish a democratic Indonesia, albeit with a sectarian adjective of 'Islamic democracy', the current situation shows the emergence of a more varied endeavour not exclusively subordinated to a concept of 'political representation' for the Muslim population. Whereas the 1950s gave the stage only to political endeavours, the 1990s provide the opportunity for Muslim activists to make use of a wide variety of efforts to democratise Indonesian society in all its aspects, within the framework of achieving a national identity shared by all Indonesians in the future.

16

Pancasila Discourse in Suharto's late New Order[1]

Douglas E. Ramage

Contention over Pancasila as the value basis of Indonesian politics is as acute today as at any time in the history of Indonesia. Interviews with politicians, bureaucrats, religious and social leaders, intellectuals, scholars, and military officers demonstrate that questions regarding the political implications of Pancasila as the philosophical basis of the Indonesian state are far from resolved.[2] The discourse over what kind of nation Indonesia should be, or more precisely, what kind of political system Indonesia should have, often revolves around different meanings and political functions Indonesians give to Pancasila. Dissatisfaction towards the government today is rarely directed at the Pancasila itself. This is quite different from the long history of outright resistance to Pancasila, sometimes from Islamic organisations, that had been part of the political landscape of Indonesia since 1945. Indonesians are no longer disputing **whether** Pancasila should be the basis of the state. Over the past decade the permanence of Pancasila as the formal, textual value basis of the state has become uncontested. The current debate is over Pancasila's meaning and its implications for the political structure and the participation of

---

1. This article is a highly condensed version of the author's Ph.D. dissertation (Ideological Discourse in the Indonesian New Order: State Ideology and the Beliefs of an Elite, 1985-1993, University of South Carolina, Columbia, South Carolina, USA, 1993).

2. Most information in this article is based on interviews conducted in Indonesia between November 1991 and October 1993. Over 150 interviews with a wide range of Indonesian political, government, military, religious and intellectual figures were conducted.

citizens in the political process.

The lively and vibrant discourse concerning the use and meaning of Pancasila has significant implications for our understanding of contemporary Indonesian politics. The purpose of this paper is to outline the limits of this discourse, taking into account the following perspectives, or 'voices', in the discourse: Nahdlatul Ulama under the leadership of Abdurrahman Wahid; Islamic activists and scholars associated with ICMI; and the Armed Forces (ABRI), including its use of a concept known as 'integralism'. Some of these voices, particularly those of Wahid and leading members of ABRI, also express concern over various 'threats' to Pancasila. An examination of what these perceived threats are will illustrate the ways in which some groups of Indonesians perceive the value basis of the state.

Finally, this paper will examine ways in which a range of political actors, including critics of the New Order, have appropriated Pancasila to challenge the regime's authority and legitimise their participation in politics.

Abdurrahman Wahid and Nahdlatul Ulama

The voice of Abdurrahman Wahid's Nahdlatul Ulama is an appropriate starting point for a study of contemporary Pancasila debate. Discourse by Abdurrahman Wahid about the 'state' is often expressed with reference to Pancasila. This was most prominently illustrated by the Pancasila Message issued by NU at the 1 March 1992 Rapat Akbar.

A few caveats are necessary concerning Wahid's role in recent political discourse. First, Wahid's voice is perhaps the loudest single voice in contemporary discourse about Pancasila. Wahid's contributions to national debate emanate both from his position as chief representative of NU and, since 1991, from his role as the leader of Forum Demokrasi. Second, Abdurrahman Wahid deserves particular attention because the content of what he says has contributed to setting the terms and major issues of political debate in the past several years. Wahid's arguments about Islam, politics, democracy and Pancasila are a distinct, identifiable part of contemporary ideological and political debate. Importantly, what Wahid says has had the effect of prompting reactions — sometimes defensive — from other political actors.

It must also be recognised that Abdurrahman Wahid alone is not NU. With millions of members and numerous prominent *kiai*, there is no way that one person could reflect the political and ideological aspirations of so many. Indeed, many of Wahid's critics note that 'Wahid represents himself, not NU.' However, Wahid has been twice elected to head NU and, more than any other single NU figure, he does dominate his organisation's outlook and thoughts in public debate.

In order to understand Wahid's use and interpretation of Pancasila in the 1990s, we need to recognise that he makes it clear that NU withdrew from politics in 1983 in order to participate more effectively in politics. According to Wahid, NU saw that continued participation in the New Order political structure would eventually render the organisation politically impotent. In fact, Wahid argues that NU's freedom of 'political' movement has been heightened **outside** the formal structure of New Order politics which, in turn, has allowed NU more effectively to participate 'in' politics over the last decade (Interviews, 18 June & 24 June 1992). The most obvious example of this strategy, and of NU's appropriation of Pancasila to serve its own political needs, and to inoculate it against accusations of anti-Pancasila behaviour revolves around the politics of NU's Rapat Akbar held in Jakarta on 1 March 1992.

The Rapat Akbar, 1 March 1992

On 1 March 1992 Nahdlatul Ulama commemorated its anniversary by holding the Rapat Akbar at the Senayan Sports Stadium in Jakarta. Between 150,000 and 200,000 people attended the rally.[3] The ostensible purpose of the rally was to celebrate the organisation's anniversary by publicly reiterating NU's loyalty to Pancasila.

Several things are curious in this. Why would the nation's largest mass-based Islamic organisation commemorate its anniversary by pledging loyalty to the state ideology? After all, NU had already taken a major decision — in 1983-84 at Sitobundo — to accept Pancasila as its formal ideological basis.

At the Rapat Akbar NU issued a powerful and passionate endorsement of Pancasila, the Constitution, and democracy.[4] Why did Abdurrahman Wahid feel the need to stress once again NU's support for Pancasila at a time when this was not an obvious political issue? There are several reasons. First, Wahid was searching for a way to avoid endorsing President Suharto for a fifth five-year term in office. Wahid argued that because NU was no longer a 'political' organisation a specific endorsement of the President was inappropriate. He argued that NU could avoid an explicit political endorsement if it limited itself to public reiteration of loyalty to Pancasila.

Second, Wahid perceived a rising tide of sectarianism and fundamentalism in Indonesia and was anxious to depict, at the Rapat Akbar, a pluralistic, non-sectarian Islam. In particular, he was deeply distressed by the formation of the new government-sponsored Islamic organisation, ICMI. He was anxious to demonstrate in the Rapat Akbar that the *umat*

---

3. See 'Rapat Akbar NU Aman, Tertib, Lancar', *Kompas*, 2 March 1992 and 'Only 150,000 Come to NU Gathering,' *Jakarta Post*, 2 March 1992 and other Indonesian dailies from 2 March.

4. See 'NU: RI Yang Berdasar Pancasila dan UUD 1945, Bentuk Final Negara Kami', *Suara Karya*, 2 March 1992 and 'Nilai Pancasila Belum Sepenuhnya Diamalkan', *Suara Pembaruan*, 1 March 1992:1.

was still united behind him and supportive of an inclusive, democratic Islam. ICMI, Wahid believes, legitimises Islamic separatism and degrades Muslim tolerance for non-Muslim Indonesians. Wahid wished to show that NU supported a nascent democratisation process and would not be coopted in the manner of Muslim intellectuals who had recently thrown their weight behind the government-backed ICMI.

Underscoring these concerns was Wahid's belief that the New Order formula for de-linking religion and other 'primordial' affinities from mass politics was under grave threat (Interviews, Wahid, 18 & 25 June and 15 October 1992). There was also an internal NU purpose to the Rapat Akbar. Wahid sought to demonstrate that his control and support of NU could be objectively demonstrated by a rally which he initially planned would bring together up to two million NU members (*Matra*, March 1992:13).

Wahid's use of Pancasila to advance the political objectives outlined above made it very difficult, in turn, for the government to de-legitimise and thereby prohibit NU's Rapat Akbar.

The NU case represents a genuinely distinctive view of what a Pancasila State should mean politically. Abdurrahman Wahid's NU appears to be saying that in order to realise a state based on the five generally decent and humane values expressed in the Pancasila, and for such values to have real meaning for Indonesia, then Pancasila must not be appropriated to legitimise and strengthen the current system of politics. This is fundamentally different from the nature of the debate about the meaning of Pancasila in earlier decades. The NU message regarding the implementation of Pancasila as enunciated by Wahid is complex and multilayered, involving concerns about Islam, democratisation, human rights, and the role of the Armed Forces in politics (Interviews, Abdurrahman Wahid, 18 June, 24 June, and 15 October 1992).

It is essential to recognise that Wahid's desire is for a 'deconfessionalised' polity in which religion is not the organising principle for political behaviour. This grows out of a shared desire with the New Order to avoid repeating the political conflict of the 1950s and 60s which was manifested along religious, regional and ethnic lines. Wahid (and NU under his leadership) is supportive of Pancasila as an inclusive ideology — it is the political compromise which holds the nation together. For Wahid, NU, and many others, Pancasila's essence is tolerance and mutual respect between Indonesia's diverse religious, regional, and ethnic groups. Thus for NU, Pancasila is both a means of advancing its own political agenda and protecting itself against government perceptions of anti-regime behaviour and of ensuring that Indonesia is a tolerant and 'deconfessionalised' polity.

Abdurrahman Wahid's reiteration of NU loyalty and adherence to Pancasila at the Rapat Akbar should also be understood in the context of Wahid's response to what he perceives as threats to Pancasila. It is clear that the growing accommodation between the government of President Suharto and elements of the Islamic movement are seen by Wahid as jeopardising the New Order's conception of a non-Islamic polity. Many ABRI officers also share Wahid's concern over the reemergence of 'Islamic' politics. Much of both Wahid and ABRI's worry is focused on ICMI, the government sponsored Islamic Intellectuals Association (addressed more fully below).

A fear among democrats, and those seeking a political future in which the military role in Indonesian politics is reduced, is that nationalists and religious and ethnic minorities will see ABRI as their protection against Islam. Abdurrahman Wahid argues that his is the 'most narrow path' — he argues that he is trying to look to a political future of greater democratisation, less military influence, and no Islamic fundamentalism. Yet Wahid fears that democratisation may provide Indonesians with the opportunity to choose Islam, which, in turn, may play into the hands of Islamic radicals. According to Wahid, the democratic option may then be exercised only once — and then a fundamentally undemocratic state may emerge from a democratic process. It may be that in the interests of a 'deconfessionalised' state — where Islam continues to have no formal link to government and political organisation — many Indonesians, and perhaps Wahid as well, may opt for an ABRI-dominated, less democratic state, that at least protects religious, ethnic and regional minority rights — in the spirit of Pancasila's tolerance — and in the interest of national unity. Pancasila then, for Abdurrahman Wahid and NU, may be more accurately seen as an ongoing expression of political tolerance necessary for a civil society rather than as an ideology of democracy. Pancasila as a political compromise for a non-Islamic state is for Wahid and perhaps NU in general, a precondition for democracy in the 1990s.

ICMI and its implications for Pancasila discourse

The establishment of ICMI in December 1990 constitutes one of the most important political events of recent years. ICMI's creation has had a profound impact on political and ideological discourse in the 1990s. This section is not intended as a complete discussion of ICMI and its meaning for contemporary Indonesian politics but rather as a brief examination of the implications of ICMI participation in the Pancasila discourse.

ICMI's appearance on the Indonesian political scene has had profound implications regarding debate and discourse about Indonesia's politics and Pancasila. The comment by a leading Islamic scholar associated with ICMI that 'the scariest thing is to be accused of being an enemy of Pancasila' (Interview, Amien Rais, 7 October 1992) is testimony to the Suharto regime's success in setting the guidelines of what is permissible in the Pancasila State. It is a losing strategy to oppose Pancasila, to criticise it, or call for its replacement with an ideological alternative.

Perhaps the most revealing comment on the implications of ICMI for political discourse came from a leading member of ICMI: 'It's the only way to be free in Indonesia today.' (Interview, M. Imaduddin Abdul Rahim, 16 April 1993) For Muslims who have been searching for a legitimate political role compatible with the New Order's strict proscription of 'confessional' ('Islamic') politics, ICMI may represent the opportunity they have been searching for. Certainly, continued contestation of Pancasila by Islamic activists would never have allowed the creation of ICMI. The legitimate, unmolested right to contribute to political discourse and to speak out on national development and all manner of politics appears, in the eyes of ICMI activists, to far outweigh the 'price' of being coopted by Suharto. Yet ICMI activists are fully conscious that they have been used to bolster the political position of the President. For this they offer no apologies. They calculate, however, that they can equally take advantage of Suharto's perceived need for them to advance their own political interests, particularly to promote their conceptions of an Islamic society (Interviews with ICMI activists, November 1992, March and April 1993).

In the three years of its existence, several major achievements of ICMI can be identified. First, as suggested above, ICMI has legitimised the participation of Muslim activists in national discourse more so than any other development in New Order history. Leading ICMI figures themselves speak of their new ability to break the monopolisation of political discourse, especially by representatives of the historic *aliran*s in Indonesian Islam.[5]

ICMI has also successfully institutionalised itself in a very prominent fashion. ICMI itself has grown rapidly with branches throughout Indonesia and even overseas. *Republika* has become the daily voice of ICMI. The creation of an Islamic bank, Bank Muamalat, in 1992, is indicative of ICMI influence according to a leading ICMI intellectual. Finally, the reduction in the number of non-Muslims in the new cabinet is also seen as attainment of one of ICMI's objectives. This, according to one leading ICMI figure, contributes to eliminating feelings of 'insecurity' among Muslims who felt 'trauma' and bitterness at being locked out of meaningful participation in the early New Order (Interview, Soetjipto Wirosardjono, 2 April 1993). Therefore, some ICMI members argue that proportional Muslim representation in cabinet and in the MPR is a 'good thing' as it does indeed begin to show concretely that Muslims are not a threat and should participate fully in government (Interviews with prominent members of ICMI, November 1992 and March-April 1993).

---

5. This achievement must be strongly qualified as 'Islam' never left the discourse. For example, Nurcholish Madjid's call for Islamic rethinking and the complete abandonment of desire for an Islamic state in the early 1970s, as well as Abdurrahman Wahid's dramatic infusion of pluralism and democratic issues into discourse about Islam, politics and the state, indicates that political Islam was **never** de-legitimised.

What then has happened? If the creation of ICMI is indicative of a new, more accommodative era in state-Islam relations, is it not a 'good thing' that some Muslims no longer feel they stand in opposition to Pancasila? Is it really the case that fears about ICMI are exaggerations? Are the many moves by Suharto to accommodate Islam a genuinely healthy development which contributes towards the final positive resolution of an 'Islam versus Pancasila' dichotomy in Indonesian ideological discourse? What then are the implications for the development of institutions like ICMI that, suggests Nurcholish Madjid, are the natural consequence of cultural and educational trends extant in Indonesian society (Interview, 25 June 1992)? Why then is ICMI so controversial and relevant to discourse about Pancasila? What makes it so provocative both within the Islamic movement, towards ABRI, and among other intellectuals?

Possible answers to these questions are suggested in several ways. For Abdurrahman Wahid it is the 'process' more than anything else that disturbs him. He argues that the government has given opportunity through ICMI for the expression of intolerant, and ultimately anti-Pancasilaist, Islamic political views. This process, Wahid contends, is a contravention of the New Order's own Pancasila path: the path of de-linking religion from politics so that a repetition of history — violence and destructive politics based on *aliran* affiliations — is forever avoided. Wahid and other intellectuals argue that ICMI activists' promotion of an 'Islamic society' camouflages a revived desire for, in effect, an Islamic state which would contravene the political compromise to avoid a formal link between Islam to the state, expressed in Pancasila and established at the founding of the Republic.

ABRI, on the other hand, is infuriated at the entry into political discourse of an ICMI strategy of democratisation (or Islamisation) through demilitarisation, under the banner of Islam and protected by Minister Habibie and the President. Nearly all ABRI ideological thinking is challenged by such a formula for political change.[6]

ICMI as part of the 'Pancasila-isation' of Islam?

Is it possible that the concerns of many opponents of ICMI are misplaced? Has President Suharto managed simultaneously to accommodate the legitimate symbolic aspirations of Muslims in a positive fashion (through the establishment of ICMI, by making the *haj*, creating an Islamic bank, and passing legislation favourable to Islamic courts and education) while, in essence, 'capturing' Muslim politicians in an organisation indebted to the New Order? Similarly, has the President managed adeptly to eliminate the outstanding Muslim concerns about the

---

6. ABRI views are based on the author's interviews with sixteen active and retired officers from all branch services in 1992-93.

over-representation of non-Muslims in the cabinet and MPR while avoiding replacing them with Muslim intellectuals that may still harbor reservations about the Pancasila State the New Order has built? In 1991 and 1992 Suharto reminded ICMI in addresses to its national congresses that 'ideological alternatives' to Pancasila must never be allowed to reappear in Indonesia. The President also warned ICMI to guard against revival of 'sectarianism and primordialism.'[7]

President Suharto's concessions have disarmed his critics on the Islamic right. But has Suharto allowed the Islamisation of the government? No. Not in the sense that Muslims who advocate a formalisation of links between Islam and the government have made any significant short-term political gains.

The most important point that can be made thus far is that political discourse in contemporary Indonesia, is heavily influenced by the ICMI phenomenon. Contention over the meaning of Pancasila is clearly still an acute element in national political and ideological discourse.

The Armed Forces

ABRI as an institution is deeply imbued with a comprehensive ideological notion of itself and of the nation. This ideological vision is in part negatively defined. That is, Indonesia as a Pancasila State is often defined by ABRI's perceptions of threats to the state, which are synonymous with perceived threats to Pancasila. These threats are communism, an Islamic state, and 'liberalism'. Since the 1950s the perception that liberal democracy was not appropriate for Indonesia has become a central tenet of ABRI ideology. This is clearly reflected in ABRI's integral role in the conceptualisation of the depoliticisation strategies formulated and implemented by the New Order.

The purpose here is to focus on how and why ABRI is participating in contemporary national discourse, particularly with reference to Pancasila. There are several areas of consideration. First, the ideological imperative for ABRI to maintain its legitimacy is a key factor in ABRI participation in the Pancasila discourse. A concept known as 'integralism', a largely military-supported ideological argument with roots in the Independence Investigating Committee debates of 1945 is a significant component of ABRI's perspective. Senior officers would often volunteer a definition of Pancasila as an 'integralistic ideology' — usually indicating a commitment to a concept of the state aand society as an organic totality in which the primary emphasis is not in terms of individual rights, but in terms of social obligations. In interviews officers would frequently draw on 'integralistic thinking' to explain most fully the permanence and Indo-

---

7. See 'Presiden Soeharto pada ICMI: Dijaga, Agar Tak Muncul Sistem Alternatif Terhadap Pancasila', *Pelita*, 8 December 1992:1 and 'Presiden Soeharto: Munculnya Sektarianisme dan Primordialisme Harus Dicegah', *Kompas*, 6 December 1991.

nesian-ness of *dwifungsi* and its relationship to Pancasila (Interviews: Brig. Gen. Abdul Kadir Besar, 25 August 1992, Vice Admiral Sunardi, 10 November 1992, Air Vice Marshall Teddy Rusdy, 11 November 1992, Lt. Gen. Harsudiono Hartas, 28 April 1993).

Second, ABRI's participation in Pancasila discourse is often linked to its institutional ideological threat perceptions and efforts to define the boundaries of permissible political behaviour in the Pancasila Democracy. Two major areas of focus are ABRI's relationship with 'Islam', especially with political manifestations of Islam, notably ICMI and Abdurrahman Wahid and NU, and ABRI's interaction with the democratisation movement in Indonesia and its use of Pancasila in that debate.

Senior ABRI leaders frequently dominate public discourse about Pancasila through speeches and warnings of threats to the ideology. For example, then Defence Minister Moerdani vowed to 'crush any attempts to replace the Pancasila state ideology with *religious or ethnic* ideologies.'[8] Former Army Chief of Staff (and Minister of Defence since March 1993) General Edy Sudrajat and former Social and Political Affairs chief Lt. Gen. Harsudiono Hartas both specifically identified proponents of liberal democracy and western human rights as threats to Pancasila and national unity. Lt. Gen. Hartas also warned against the reemergence of threats from the 'extreme right', the usual official term for Islamic fundamentalism.[9] Also in a reference to continued Islamic threats to the state, Lt. Gen. Hartas recently warned of a rising tide of religious intolerance and specifically noted that he perceived ICMI as a manifestation of an anti-Pancasila threat to the state (Interview, 28 April 1993).

ABRI's contemporary Pancasila discourse can be summarised by recognising what is new in its participation in debate concerning Pancasila and what remains the same in the post-*asas tunggal* period. First, 'integralistic' thinking has become a more frequent referent for ABRI leaders. Pancasila is often interpreted by ABRI leaders as an 'integralistic ideology' in which the military's socio-political functions are legitimised not only on the basis of *Sapta Marga, dwifungsi* or even the Constitution, but on the deeply embedded political culture and national personality of Indonesia. And ABRI views Pancasila as the ideological expression of this indigenous political culture.

Second, ICMI's appearance on the national political stage is cause for concern among many in ABRI. It is identified as potentially incompatible

---

8. 'Moerdani Vows to Crush Attempts to Replace Pancasila', *Jakarta Post*, 11 September 1991:2.

9. See 'Edy Wants People Alert Against Opportunists,' *Jakarta Post*, 26 December 1991:2; 'Ancaman Disintegrasi Sudah Mulai Muncul', *Republika*, 22 February 1993:10; An example of general ABRI explanation of threats to Pancasila is in *Angkatan Bersenjata*'s 'Demokrasi Liberal Tidak Cocok Dengan Kita', 12 January 1993. See also in 'Kassospol ABRI: Pemasyarakatan Demokrasi Pancasila Makan Waktu', *Kompas*, 26 February 1993.

with the religious tolerance implied in Pancasila Democracy. Although many ABRI leaders express an appreciation for a better relationship between Islam and the government and recognition of Suharto's strategy to coopt remaining Muslim intellectuals and politicians in a government-controlled and thereby 'safe' organisation, there is concern that the process of cooptation has 'gone too far'. The presence of Habibie as the General Chairman of ICMI, as well as the prominent activities of other well-known Islamic intellectuals and activists in ICMI, clearly irritates ABRI. A perception of ICMI as supportive of a strategy of democratisation (or Islamisation) through demilitarisation under the protection of Minister Habibie both weakens ICMI's ability to institutionalise itself (because of the generation of fairly widespread ABRI opposition to this strategy) and raises another issue to further problematise the Suharto-ABRI relationship (Interviews with senior ABRI leaders, November 1992, April and May 1993).

Although Many ABRI officers view NU as the most legitimate mass Islamic organisation, Abdurrahman Wahid's leadership of Forum Demokrasi also troubles ABRI. Entrenched ABRI suspicions of liberalism and liberal democracy tends to neutralise the nationalist credentials that Wahid believes keep him in good standing with ABRI. There is, however, significant overlap in the desire of both Wahid and ABRI to maintain the process of ensuring that politics in Indonesia does not return to religiously-based political mobilisation.

New elements and factors that influence ABRI's Pancasila discourse therefore include the following: 'integralism' and the desire to ground ABRI's socio-political permanence firmly in Pancasila as an integralistic ideology; suspicions about ICMI (even though ABRI does appreciate and recognise major changes in the Pancasila discourse since *asas-tunggal* and that all Islamic organisations accept Pancasila); and a complicated relationship with NU led by Abdurrahman Wahid both because of their shared visions of a 'deconfessionalised' state and clashing visions of liberal democracy.

A number of elements of ABRI's Pancasila discourse have not changed, however. These include ABRI's institutional obsession with enforcing avoidance of issues which could inflame communal tensions (SARA). The desire to avoid SARA issues is shared by Abdurrahman Wahid, secular nationalists, intellectuals (including many in ICMI), and religious minorities. Additionally, ABRI's commitment to maintenance of Indonesia as a unified state is intimately linked to Pancasila and its own *dwifungsi*. Finally, there is the persistence of ideological threat perceptions from Islam. Although not expressed by ABRI officers, other Indonesians, notably Muslim intellectuals (including both Wahid and many in ICMI) worry that ABRI has not completely abandoned previously exaggerated suspicions of Islam. Some members of the elite worry that ABRI may again seek to depict an 'Islamic threat' in order to continue justification of

ABRI's role as the protector of Pancasila and the state from threats on the 'extreme right'.

Conclusion

This study was undertaken with the broad purpose of analysing the meaning that discourse about Pancasila has for our understanding of contemporary Indonesian politics. 'Pancasila' means different things for various members of the political, military, and Islamic and other intellectual elites. Yet for almost all of them it remains a potent ideological referent for fundamental issues of national life.

For President Suharto and his New Order government, Pancasila has always been the ultimate ideology of legitimacy. It is tied to the New Order's promise to rectify the ideological, political, and the economic mistakes of the Old Order. It has also been used as a potent means of proscribing political behaviour in the Pancasila State. Pancasila has represented an effective means of delineating the permissible boundaries of political discourse and behaviour for twenty-five years. It also represents the positive expression of constructive, ideals deemed necessary for nation-building: tolerance, respect for diversity, social and economic justice and a democratic political system compatible with indigenous political culture. The degree to which these ideals have yet been fulfilled is a matter of intense debate.

The Indonesian Armed Forces are doctrinally linked to Pancasila as the defenders of the national ideology. The historic role of ABRI as the only national institution with both political and security functions is justified as the implementation of Pancasila as an 'integralistic' ideology in which ABRI's political role is considered an inseparable, integral element of the Pancasila State. Along with President Suharto, ABRI has also used Pancasila to differentiate between acceptable political behaviour and conduct judged incompatible with the military interpretation of Pancasila.

Abdurrahman Wahid, personally the most powerful Islamic leader and head of the largest mass-based Muslim organisation, appeals for a democratic society whose necessary *precondition* is adherence to Pancasila as the guarantor of a non-Islamic and non-military dominated polity. Yet he argues that some of the government's short-term political needs have contributed to a 'reconfessionalisation' of Indonesian politics which will undermine the tolerance stipulated by Pancasila. Although undesirable, the implication of Wahid's views is that continued military domination of Indonesian politics is preferable to an Islamic state which may emerge through an ostensibly democratic process.

Islamic intellectuals associated with ICMI are only marginally concerned with Pancasila *per se*; many of them regard it as a non-issue. However, the single most important aspect of Pancasila for this ICMI voice is that the national ideology is no longer seen as inimical or contrary to Islam. This represents a dramatic change in Islamic discourse on Pancasila.

However, a desire of some Muslim activists associated with ICMI to create an 'Islamic society', rather than an Islamic state, is viewed by some non-Muslims, Wahid, numerous intellectuals and ABRI as potentially incompatible with Pancasila. Therefore, the ICMI voice is deeply relevant to national Pancasila discourse. In order to strive for an Islamic society in which politics and government policy imbued with 'Islamic values,' mainstream Muslim activists have dropped their previous opposition to the New Order and to Pancasila, and have endorsed Suharto's continuance in office.

Finally, many intellectuals and officials interviewed see Pancasila as the ideological guarantor of minority, non-Muslim rights. They fear that a possible future democratically elected Islamic-majority government may limit the rights of non-Muslims. Therefore, Indonesians interested in democratisation without political Islamisation face a dilemma of seeking greater democratisation, which for many involves a reduced military role in politics (a goal shared with some in ICMI), while avoiding a democratically elected political structure that prioritizes 'majority' Muslim interests.

There is a consensus, however, among most of the persons interviewed for this project that Pancasila principles are a decent and sufficient value basis for the state. There is no overt rejection of Pancasila in the 1990s. However, it is clear that debate over the meaning of Pancasila and its implications for politics is an acute element of Indonesian political discourse in the 1990s.

17

Gender Interests and Indonesian Democracy

Susan Blackburn

The central question posed in this paper is whether the existence or otherwise of democracy in Indonesia makes any difference to that half of the population who are women. Public political discourse in Indonesia has rarely involved reference to gender, despite (or more probably because of) the fact that Indonesian women have had very little role in this sphere, either when Indonesia experienced parliamentary democracy in the 1950s or since then. That women are almost invisible in politics does not mean, however, that they are not affected by the state and its policies. Different regimes serve gender interests and affect the construction of gender in different ways. The shift from a military-dominated regime to one controlled by civilians must in itself have important consequences for gender interests in Indonesia.

In studying the impact on women produced by changes in a country's political regime, a useful approach has been suggested by Maxine Molyneux (1986). Taking Nicaragua as her case study, she considers the hypothesis that women's interests are not served by socialist revolutions. She observes, first of all, that women *as women* cannot be said to have interests in common because of their diversity in terms of class, ethnicity, religion and so on. The fact that women do not constitute a homogeneous category, however, should not override the *gender interests* which women (or men) in any particular society may develop by virtue of their shared gender attributes, arising from the social construction of gender in that society.

Molyneux distinguishes between 'strategic' and 'practical' gender interests. The former arise from an analysis of women's subordination in society, resulting in 'the formulation of an alternative, more satisfactory set of arrangements to those that exist' (Molyneux 1986:284). Such arrangements may encompass the abolition of the sexual division of labour, freedom of choice over childbearing, and the establishment of political equality. These are the kinds of demands commonly associated with feminism. Practical gender interests, on the other hand, 'arise from the concrete conditions of women's positioning by virtue of their gender within the division of labour' (Molyneux 1986:284). Women frequently express demands which do not entail questioning the basic gender construction in society but which arise from their difficulties in performing the functions which are required of them, such as providing their children with food and health care. These practical gender interests are likely to vary according to the class or other attributes of the group of women involved, and with their situation at any particular time and place. Clearly there are elements of subjectivity and objectivity in this differentiation of interests: whereas it is possible to regard the demands expressed by all kinds of women's organisations as a reliable gauge of women's practical gender interests, relatively few such organisations in any society engage in feminist analysis of strategic gender interests. Moreover, as Alvarez (1991:26) points out, one woman's strategic interests may threaten another's practical gender interests: a movement for fair wages and conditions for domestic servants may be opposed by middle class female employers.

Taking Molyneux' distinction between practical and strategic gender interests as its methodological starting point, this paper analyses the impact of democracy on Indonesia. Just as Molyneux studies how women's gender interests fared under the Sandinistas in Nicaragua compared with the previous regime, I compare the fate of women's practical and strategic gender interests under Parliamentary Democracy in Indonesia in the 1950s with their experience under the New Order, and speculate as to the effects of democratisation in the 1990s.

Women and democracy in Indonesia, 1950-1959

Following the national struggle for independence, women's organisations in Indonesia were active and vocal in their pursuit of what they saw as women's interests. Although there were variations between such organisations according to their membership among women of different classes, regions, ethnic and religious groupings, at this time when Indonesian society was struggling to recover from the onslaughts of war and civil strife, women were in general agreement about their urgent needs: shelter, food, clothing and basic health and education were required by most families for whom women saw themselves responsible. Across the archipelago women were engaged in social welfare work, trying to meet these needs (See Woodsmall 1960 and Vreede-de Stuers 1960).

At this time the resources of government were so limited that there was little differentiation between state and civil society: women worked both as paid civil servants and as volunteers to provide basic requirements. The nationalist fervour of the Revolution years carried over into the ready mobilisation of many women in national rehabilitation and reconstruction. Women's organisations of all descriptions worked with the government to provide kindergartens, schools, mother and child health clinics, orphanages, hostels, banks and cooperatives. The pioneering quality of women in these years comes through in the autobiography of Sujatin Kartowijono, the leader of one of the largest women's organisations, Perwari. On a visit to North Sumatra in 1954 as part of her work in the adult literacy campaign, for instance, she describes the courage of a literacy worker who frequently conducted her classes for villagers in the evening. Too poor to afford even a lamp, she quite often encountered tigers in the jungle on her way home (1983:117).

Whose practical gender interests are best served by any regime depends largely on how well organised and articulate social groups are in pressing for their wishes to be fulfilled. This in turn depends on the scope permitted by the state for such organisation, the strength of social sanctions against it, and the resources available to any group. In the 1950s, it was the latter two determinants which most applied, since the democratic form of the state provided extensive freedom of expression and organisation. Most women's organisations were formed among, and were led by, urban, better educated women. But rural and working class women also received attention, principally from Gerwani, whose activities spurred on other organisations into greater attempts to mobilise poorer women (See Hindley 1966, Ch.17; Wieringa 1988).

As a result of the combined efforts of state and civil society, during the period of Parliamentary Democracy considerable improvements were made in areas that women's organisations regarded as priorities, such as mother and child health care, and literacy (Woodsmall 1960). Although these benefits were unevenly spread in terms of regions and the urban/rural divide, they were a promising start. By the end of the decade, however, serious questions were being raised by women about the economic problems which the government failed to resolve, leading to inflation in the prices of daily necessities which women, as keepers of the household budget, were responsible for buying. The record of parliamentary democracy in meeting women's practical gender interests, then, was a mixed one, critically affected by the economy as much as by the form of the polity.

What about women's strategic gender interests? Was women's subordination alleviated in the 1950s, were forms of discrimination against them removed, were fundamental structures of society transformed so as to change the sexual division of labour with its inherent devaluing of women's work? Few women's organisations in the 1950s tackled these questions, yet most were aware and appreciative of many gains made during the 1950s, largely as a result of women's involvement in the nationalist struggle. Women had in fact gained the vote at the tail end of Dutch colonial rule, and this right was also enshrined in the 1945 and 1950 Constitutions of the independent Republic. Governments proceeded to ratify United Nations conventions on political equality for women, and discrimination on the basis of sex was outlawed in some legislation, e.g. equal pay for equal work was introduced into the civil service, which also offered paid maternity leave. There was widespread praise for the government's commitment to political equality, and pride amongst women's organisations in their practice of new responsibilities as democratic citizens, notably the high rate of women's turnout to vote in the general elections of 1955.

The main legislative omission which troubled women's organisations was the failure of successive governments to agree on a national marriage law, which constituted a long-standing demand of the Indonesian women's movement, dating back to 1928. The majority of Indonesians, being Muslims, married under customary or Islamic law supervised by local Islamic or customary law courts, which offered no certainty for women as to their rights within or outside of marriage. In this case women's and men's strategic gender interests clearly conflicted, since many women were in effect asking that the domination of men in Islamic marriages should be restricted: they wanted to provide greater equality between men and women in all matters pertaining to marriage, including consent to marriage, divorce and polygamy. Despite disagreements between Muslim and non-Muslim women's organisations on the issue of the marriage law, it was obvious from the statements of Muslim women leaders that they too wanted a marriage law which would provide reliable nation-wide legal enforcement of the rights of women in marriage according to their reading of the spirit of Islam, which entailed considerable restrictions on men's traditional freedoms.[1] Nor was marriage legislation just a matter of concern to wealthier women, although clearly the burning issue of polygamy affected them far more than poor women: child marriage, arbitrary divorce by husbands and difficulties for women in initiating divorce were suffered by Muslim women across the board.

Not surprisingly, governments and parliaments dominated by men did not give this matter high priority. Since the issue was yet another one which divided parties and threatened cabinet stability, governments during the period of Parliamentary Democracy clearly did not think it worth the trouble of tackling it, even if it would have provided satisfaction to half the population. That half, having no observable political power, could be overlooked. Year after year, governments postponed resolving the question.

By the end of the Parliamentary Democracy period it was becoming clear that legislative gains for women did not always translate into equality in practice. The right to vote did not ensure women equal numbers in

---

1. Reading the 1959 marriage bill debates in the DPR is instructive in this respect. When the government failed to introduce marriage legislation, a woman member of the DPR introduced a private bill, which produced heated debate but no final outcome. On this occasion women members of Islamic parties made it clear that they welcomed an Islamic marriage law which would limit men's 'abuse' of the right to polygamy and divorce.

parliament or cabinet, for the same reasons that women have been excluded from public positions in other democracies.[2] Although during the late 1940s Republican governments incorporated two influential nationalist women into their cabinets[3], there were no such appointments in the 1950s.

Parties were reluctant to promote women candidates and, as in other countries, the whole social and economic system continued to militate against women putting themselves forward in public life: home responsibilities, social disapproval, lack of resources and women's socialization to regard politics as men's business combined to discourage them (See Randall 1987, Ch.3). Similarly, although women were appointed in growing numbers to the bureaucracy, they remained at the lower levels. As in most democracies, governments thought it enough that women were offered formal access to power: they did not think it their business to tackle systematically the obstacles that prevent women everywhere from taking up those opportunities. A number of women's organisations, however, made it their business and tried to encourage parties and women to draw women into public life.[4]

Of more concern to the majority of women, discrimination in the workforce was not seriously tackled by governments during the period of Parliamentary Democracy. Although labour legislation regulated such things as hours of work and maternity leave, laws were regularly flouted, women in most workplaces continued to be paid less than men for the same work and the workforce continued to be divided according to gender, relegating women to a narrower and more lowly range of jobs. Although many trusted that the expansion of educational opportunities for women would bring change in these respects, despite the rapid growth of schooling for girls, its content and method did not seem to be geared to breaking down the traditional division of labour between the sexes in Indonesia. Nor was it enough to trust that trade unions would conduct the fight against employment discrimination on behalf of women: trade unions in Indonesia were both weak and male-dominated.

---

2. In the DPR between 1950 and 1955 there were only 9 women members of parliament out of a total of 236, giving a percentage of 3.8; following the 1955 elections there were 17 women in a DPR of 272, making 6.9% (Hardjito Notopuro, 1979:143) In the Constituent Assembly after the 1955 elections there were 25 women amongst a total of 488 (Woodsmall, 1960:223). It is interesting that the lack of women is taken so much for granted that most commentators on Indonesian elections do not bother to mention it. Thus in a recent article Ben Anderson (1992:57) could write that the 1955 elections in Indonesia 'did not produce a representative body that was radically out of kilter with the constituency it represented'.

3. Maria Ulfah Santoso (Minister of Social Welfare 1945-7) and S.K. Trimurti (Minister of Labour 1947-9).

4. Women's sections of political parties were quite active in this respect. In Nahdlatul Ulama, for instance, it was the women's wing, Muslimat, which pressured the party to stand female candidates in the 1955 election (*Sejarah Muslimat Nahdlatul Ulama*, 1979:64). For a vivid picture of the activities of the non-partisan but very political women's organisation, Perwari, see Sujatin Kartowijono (1983).

Another important realm of women's strategic interests which the government failed to tackle was that of access to contraception. Although there were few reliable forms of birth control available in the 1950s, the government did not adopt a family planning program which would have made contraception well-known and affordable to women. However, as with other areas of women's interests, it was important that the authorities did not obstruct the spread of contraceptive knowledge, which was another of the tasks taken on voluntarily by some women's organisations (See Vreede-de Stuers 1960:146).

The great difficulty in drawing conclusions about the extent to which democracy in Indonesia served women's gender interests in the 1950s is that we are discussing a few short years when the Indonesian state was struggling to establish itself and had few resources at its disposal. Democracy itself was brand-new, and people were just beginning to explore its possibilities. Apart from the major disappointment of the marriage legislation, from the point of view of most women these were years of hope and promise. Women's organisations threw themselves into the tasks of meeting the needs of families and generally revelled in their new-found freedom to organise, train for leadership roles, and voice their views. The proliferation of organisations stimulated rivalry to win new members, encouraging more and more women to formulate their interests vis-a-vis the new Republic. Although the emphasis tended to be more on responsibilities than rights, women's organisations served to raise the awareness of their members about common concerns and powers. Some women's organisations demonstrated quite militantly on behalf of the strategic gender interests of women.

By the late 1950s many women were clearly wondering whether the government could control the economy in a way that would enable the basic material requirements of their families to be met. Compared with the previous decade of turmoil, however, even the disorder of the fifties must have seemed an improvement. From the point of view of women's gender interests, it was too soon to conclude that democracy had failed: rather, considerable progress had been made and there was no reason to believe it would not continue, given the growth of women's organisations able to act as a pressure group on governments.

The New Order

The present regime in Indonesia is not a democratic one. It imposes considerable restrictions on people's freedom of organisation and expression, and on the significance of elections in terms of candidacy, voting rights and control of the executive by elected representatives. Since its inception, the New Order has been dominated by military personnel and bureaucrats, two groups which are virtually male preserves.

Now that the possibility of democratic change is being openly discussed in Indonesia, the question should be asked whether, regardless of the regime's nature, the New Order has served women's gender interests any worse or better than did parliamentary democracy. A strong case can be made out for the present regime as regards women's practical gender interests, because of the emphasis placed by the government on development. In many areas close to the hearts of Indonesian women, the New Order has produced great improvements. Universal primary education has almost been achieved, and girls' access to secondary education is approaching that of boys. Infant and maternal mortality rates have declined dramatically since the 1960s. Following the Green Revolution, nutrition levels have risen (UNICEF 1992:72, 74, 78, 84).

In all these areas of endeavour, the New Order has harnessed women's organisations strongly behind its policies. A feature of the New Order has been its corporatisation of society: it has created new organisations like the PKK (*Pembinaan Kesejahteraan Keluarga* — Family Welfare Guidance) which drafts women at all levels into providing voluntary work for its family welfare program, and it has fostered the growth of the so-called 'wives' organisations', whereby the wives of government employees are organised into social welfare activities. The main umbrella body for women's organisations, Kowani, has come under government control, ensuring the full coordination of women's efforts on behalf of development according to the government guidelines (See Douglas 1980; Wieringa 1992).

There have been criticisms of the government's achievements. It can be pointed out that in some areas of development affecting women closely, progress has been slower than other ASEAN countries: infant and maternal mortality rates in Indonesia are higher, and births attended by health personnel and access to safe water and sanitation lower (UNDP 1992:130, 134, 150). For most Indonesian women, however, the comparisons are more likely to be made with their own past rather than with neighbouring countries, and it is the undeniable improvement which counts.

A number of critics have claimed that it is middle class women who have gained most from the New Order and that development policies have either neglected or actually damaged the interests of poor women. The picture is not quite so clear-cut. True, middle class women have had best access to services like health and education, which tend to be concentrated in urban areas, and they have benefited disproportionately from the expansion of white-collar employment under the New Order. On the other hand, their freedom to organise themselves as they wish has been much restricted and they have been recruited into organisations which are run along lines which exactly parallel the hierarchies of their husbands' workplaces: leadership positions are assumed by the wives of the top-ranking men. There are signs of middle-class women chafing under these arrangements.

Considerable evidence has been provided by researchers of the ways in which economic development under the New Order has damaged the interests of poor women. As workers, they have been displaced by technological changes in agriculture and manufacturing, and young women have been recruited into factories under grossly exploitative terms and conditions.

Compared with male workers, they seem to have fared worse, and lack even the weak unions of the past through which to voice their grievances, since labour has until recently been very strictly controlled by the authorities (See Mayling Oey 1985:18-46; White 1990:121-35; 'Hak-Hak Perempuan...' 1991). Since restrictions have been partially lifted, cities like Jakarta have seen an unprecedented wave of strikes by factory workers, primarily young women ('Special Report...' 1991:1-9). Following the policy of 'floating mass', the rural population lacks any effective political organisation, so rural women no longer have the kind of avenues for expression which groups like Gerwani (outlawed since 1966) offered in the past (See Wieringa 1992).

The justifiable grievances of poor women should not, however, lead us to ignore the gains made by women across the board in relation to education, life expectancy and so on. Undeniably, compared with Indonesia of the 1950s the standard of living of the vast majority of Indonesians has improved, largely as a result of successful economic management by the New Order regime and its deployment of the greatly increased resources provided by the oil boom. Concerned as they still are first and foremost with the material well-being of their families, most Indonesian women have good reason to be grateful to the New Order, democracy or no democracy. While many millions of poor women are still faced with the daily struggle for survival, millions more have advanced beyond that threshold and most can be sure that they and their children will be fed and get basic education.

Precisely because the issue of sheer survival no longer consumes most Indonesian women's lives as it did in the past, strategic gender interests begin to loom rather larger for Indonesian women. Here too, the New Order has provided some impressive gains. One of its main achievements has been the passing of a Marriage Law in 1974, the first such piece of national legislation covering all marriages in the history of Indonesia. It could be argued that it was only because Indonesia was *not* democratic that the law was passed. For the first time Indonesia had a government with the will and the power to push through this legislation, no doubt in part because of the strong support of the President's wife: a very different matter from the previous president's lack of enthusiasm for any law which might limit his freedom within marriage. Admittedly, the opposition inside and outside the parliament from Muslim groups to the original form of the legislation was such that extensive amendments were required, yet the government was strong and determined enough to negotiate a generally accepted compromise. While the outcome did not completely satisfy the women's organisations which had long campaigned for a Marriage Law, they were relieved at last to have legislation which went far to equalise the rights and responsibilities of men and women in marriage.

Another notable strategic gain for women in recent decades has been the provision by the government of information about birth control and access to cheap or free contraceptive technology (Warwick 1986). The family planning program has been one of the New Order's chief ways of 'integrating women into development' and women's organisations have been extensively mobilised behind the program. Inevitably there have been criticisms of the pressure applied by the government to limit family size and to promote certain forms of contraception over others, but the fact remains that for the first time in Indonesian history women have access to cheap, reliable means of controlling the number of children they will bear. This is an important step forward for women in determining their own lives.

What troubles most critics about the New Order's attitude towards women is the very restricted role which it allocates them. Although the government is anxious to mobilise women behind its development efforts, it envisages women as playing a part in Indonesian society which is even narrower than most women are accustomed to. The view of women propagated through the PKK, for instance, is one of responsibility towards the family and support for their menfolk. There is little conception of women having any public role, although a more recent version of the stereotype speaks of women's 'dual role', as family carers and income earners. Since men are not regarded as playing two roles, one can only assume that women are intended to bear a double burden.[5] Ironically, the New Order attempt to define women as belonging to a 'private' sphere outside politics comes at a time when the state has never been more active in intervening in family life, notably in its attempt to control births.

An analysis of elementary school textbooks in Indonesia has shown the Education Department to be propagating a domesticated, middle-class image of women as mothers who stay at home to look after the house and children while men go out to earn a living for the family (Logsdon 1985). A number of studies have shown media support also for this image of women which is far from the reality of most women's lives. Although it is impossible for most women to conform to this image, its promotion must militate against efforts by women to enter public life. Nor are such stereotypes of merely academic interest. As Gaynor Dawson (1992) has shown in her study of the government's transmigration program, they are the basis for the government's vastly unequal allocation of resources and power to men and women, while women continue to bear an arduous and unacknowledged workload.

Its restricted construction of gender has limited the effectiveness of the New Order's efforts to 'integrate women into development', a strategy to which it became converted during the International Decade of Women. The assumption underlying the government's policies in this respect has been that women need to be encouraged to do more for national development, largely in their role as mothers and keepers of family morality. Such an approach can scarcely accommodate the fact that most Indonesian women work very long hours and, far from needing to learn how to contribute more, need

---

5. On the concept of 'dual roles' see Mayling Oey-Gardiner and Kartini Sjahrir (1991:107) and Kartini Sjahrir (1985:17). For general discussion of the New Order's restricted stereotype of women, see Norma Sullivan (1991) and Gaynor Dawson (1992).

rather to be relieved of burdens such as fetching fuel and drinking water (See e.g. Hull 1979; Darwin 1992). Because the government sees 'Women in Development' in terms of special projects to be implemented by the PKK, the strategy is necessarily a 'top-down' one which sees women as in need of enlightenment and as an adjunct to national programs.

Not surprisingly, women have had even less political prominence under the New Order than during the period of Parliamentary Democracy. For many years they had no representation in government, and gained a place in the ministry only through the creation in 1983 of a position of Minister for Women's Affairs, which commands virtually no power or resources. Women comprise one of the many 'functional groups' represented in the government party, Golkar, but only women who conform with government requirements are appointed. A few women appear in the ranks of the two opposition parties, but because of the limitations on their activities, poor women, like poor men, have no avenues of political representation whatever (See Douglas 1980). Representation of women is low at all levels of public political life and within the higher ranks of the civil service also. Fundamentally, the philosophy of the New Order is opposed to the notion that women might have interests of their own to represent in politics: the government prefers to make up its own mind about the needs of women, conceived as a homogeneous group. This outlook offers little hope for women's groups which wish to lay claims outside the narrow scope offered by the activities of organisations like the PKK and Dharma Wanita.

In the first decade or so of the New Order, when its control was particularly heavy-handed, it was extremely difficult for women's organisations to operate outside the government's ambit. As a result, discussion of women's strategic gender interests was almost non-existent. The veteran leader S.K. Trimurti commented in 1972 that although a number of women's organisations were very 'busy', political awareness among women was lower than it was during the colonial period (Trimurti 1972:6). With rather more freedom in recent years, some women have become more outspoken in their demands. The growth of the middle class under the New Order, too, has produced a group of well educated women who, like their male counterparts, now talk in terms of rights rather than responsibilities as favoured by the government. For instance Mely Tan, pointing to the very small proportion of women in government and public service positions, has written recently:

> It is...clear that if we really and consistently want to raise the role and status of women in society and thus in development, it will need many more women in decision-making positions. In other words, women need *empowerment* [sic], that is a position which gives them the ability to wield power. (Mely G. Tan (ed) 1991:xiv)

The verdict on the New Order's record regarding women's gender interests must be that although a number of their practical and strategic gender interests have been fulfilled, the regime seems to be ideologically opposed to important strategic gender interests of women as far as combating their subordination is concerned, and it shows little concern about discrimination against poor women.

Women and the democratic transition

The New Order is now undergoing a slow process of political change, apparently in the direction of greater democratic freedoms. What gender interests are at stake for women in this transition period?

First of all, they have something to lose. Indonesian women have made numerous gains since independence, in terms of social development and legislation in favour of greater equality. Turbulence leading to economic recession would not benefit them or their families. A return to military rule would constitute a set-back, narrowing the options for women to those of the first decade of the New Order.

In itself democratisation cannot guarantee to fulfil women's gender interests. As far as women are concerned, democracies around the world offer a range of outcomes, from the subjugated position of most poor women in India to the advances made by women in almost every sphere, including the political, in Norway. The construction of gender is associated with social values which are slow to change, and it is unusual for democratic governments to act as agents of radical change. What democratic states have shown is that improvement in the gender situation of women depends on a combination of commitment from governments and pressure from strong autonomous women's organisations. Democratic processes provide the opportunity for women to organise themselves, but they do not ensure either the success of those organisations or the readiness of governments to comply with their demands.[6]

With democratisation, Indonesian women can hope to organise themselves more effectively to represent their full range of gender interests, both practical and strategic. Already signs of this are emerging: in addition to the large 'establishment' women's organisations beloved of the New Order, in the past few years a number of smaller groups have been formed to work with and for rural and industrial female workers and domestic servants, and to push for a number of women's 'strategic' gender interests such as access to land, opposition to rape, sexual harassment and domestic violence. For the first time these latter concerns are receiving publicity in Indonesia, and since they affect most women, some may even be endorsed by larger women's organisations, although this will be difficult in view of the heavy pressure which such women have been under to avoid any issues which imply division in Indonesian society.[7]

---

6. In recent years some excellent research has been published concerning women and democratic polities, including Phillips (1991), Alvarez (1991), Jaquette (ed) (1989), and E. Haavio-Mannila *et al.* (eds) (1985). For a review essay of some of the literature, see Nelson (1992:491-5).

7. The new organisations include Kalayanamitra, Solidaritas Perempuan, Yayasan Perempuan Mardika, Forum Diskusi Perempuan Yogyakarta and Yasanti. For some discussion of the new trend, see Soendari S. (1991:17-20).

As much as anything, women's organisations are essential for building women's public confidence. It is hard for women to participate in organisations, given all their family responsibilities, but experience has shown that it is vital in the awareness-raising process. Women are so unaccustomed to public life that their own organisations are crucial in building leadership skills, increasing their access to information about public affairs, exchanging views which can lead to a shift in perceptions and agendas, and generally producing empowerment, which is essential for the advancement of marginal groups in society. The kind of 'top-down' women's organisations promoted by the New Order, however, have less hope of empowering women than truly autonomous groups.

Finally, the transition period offers opportunities to women. As Jaquette says, commenting on the role of social movements, including the women's movement, in the shift away from military dictatorships in Latin America,

> Transitions are political 'openings': there is a general willingness to rethink the bases of social consensus and revise the rules of the game. This gives social movements an extraordinary opportunity to raise new issues and influence popular expectations.(1989:13)

For Indonesian women, their role in this transition period will be important in determining gender policies and practice in the next regime. Indonesian women benefited politically in the years immediately following independence from the earlier close association between the nationalist movement and the women's movement, especially during the Revolution. However, that moment of opportunity was brief, because the nationalist women had subordinated their own concerns to those of the male leaders, many of whom had not experienced any serious change in their attitudes to women. Women's organisations now face an uphill task: they must work to transform general attitudes towards women while at the same time trying to influence the main players in the transition, the political parties and the Islamic groups, with whom they have much in common in terms of wanting to enlarge the democratic space in Indonesia so as to politicise their constituencies and articulate their concerns to higher authorities. Since the parties have lacked credibility, they will also need to expand their social bases, which may offer opportunities to women.

There is no guarantee that a return to democracy will benefit women. At the very least, however, democratisation will enable women to form their own organisations independent of government control and thus work out their own agendas. Although those agendas are likely to be as diverse as Indonesian women themselves are, they have something new to offer Indonesian politics, which has up to now marginalised half its constituency.

References

Hak-Hak Perempuan dalam Hubungan Kerja, in *Demokrasi Masih Terbenam: Catatan Keadaan Hak-Hak Asasi Manusia di Indonesia 1991*, Yayasan Lembaga Bantuan Hukum Indonesia, Jakarta, 1991.
'Special Report: Labour Rights and Wrongs', *Inside Indonesia*, no.27 (June 1991) pp.1-9
Alvarez, S. (1991) *Engendering Democracy in Brazil: Women's Movements in Transition Politics*, Princeton University Press, Princeton.
Anderson, B. (1992) 'Thailand, the Philippines and Indonesia: What Price Democracy?' *ABC Radio 24 Hours*, August 1992.
Dawson, Gaynor (1992) *Development Planning for Women in the Indonesian Transmigration Program*, Centre for Development Studies, Monash University, Clayton.
Douglas, S.A. (1980) Women in Indonesian Politics: The Myth of Functional Interest, in S.A. Chipp and J.J. Green (eds) *Asian Women in Transition*, Pennsylvania State University Press, University Park
Haavio-Mannila, E. *et al.* (eds) (1985) *Unfinished Democracy: Women in Nordic Politics*, Pergamon Press, Oxford
Hardjito Notopuro, (1979) *Peranan Wanita Dalam Masa Pembangunan di Indonesia*, Ghalia Indonesia, Jakarta
Hindley, D. (1966) *The Communist Party of Indonesia, 1951-1963*, University of California Press, Berkeley
Hull, V. (1979) *A Woman's Place...Social Class Variations in Women's Work Patterns in a Javanese Village*, Population Studies Center, Gadjah Mada University, Yogyakarta.
Jaquette, J.S. (ed) (1989) *The Women's Movement in Latin America: Feminism and the Transition to Democracy*, Unwin Hyman, Boston
Logsdon, M. (1985) Gender Roles in Elementary School Texts, in M.J. Goodman (ed) *Women in Asia and the Pacific*, University of Hawaii Press, Honolulu.
Molyneux, M. (1986) Mobilization Without Emancipation? Women's Interests, State, and Revolution, in R.R. Fagen, C.D. Deere and J.L. Coraggio (eds) *Transition and Development: Problems of Third World Socialism*, New York Monthly Review Press, New York.
Nelson, B.J. (1992) 'The Role of Sex and Gender in Comparative Analysis: Individuals, Institutions and Regimes', *American Journal of Political Science*, Vol.86 no.2 (June 1992)
Oey-Gardiner, Mayling and Kartini Sjahrir, (1991) 'Commentary from an Indonesian Perspective', *Asian Studies Review*, July 1991
Oey, Mayling (1985) 'Changing Work Patterns of Women in Indonesia during the 1970s: Causes and Consequences', *Prisma*, no.37, 1985. pp.18-46
Phillips, A. (1991) *Engendering Democracy*, Polity Press, Cambridge.
Randall, V. (1987) *Women and Politics: An International Perspective*,

Macmillan, Houndmills, 2nd edition
Sejarah Muslimat Nahdlatul Ulama, PP Muslimat NU, Jakarta, 1979.
Sjahrir, Kartini (1985) 'Women: Some Anthropological Notes', *Prisma* No.37 1985.
Soendari S. (1991) 'Potret Pergerakan Perempuan Indonesia: Berjuang Melawan Kediktaturan Orde Baru' *Progres* Vol.1 no.3, 1991. pp.17-20
Sujatin Kartowijono, (1983) *Mencari Makna Hidupku*, Sinar Harapan, Jakarta.
Sullivan, N. (1991) Gender and Politics in Indonesia, in M. Stivens (ed) *Why Gender Matters in Southeast Asian Politics*, Monash University, Centre of Southeast Asian Studies, Clayton.
Tan, Mely G. (ed) (1991) *Perempuan Indonesia: Pemimpin Masa Depan?*, Pustaka Sinar Harapan, Jakarta.
UNDP (1992) *The Human Development Report 1992*, Oxford University Press, New York.
UNICEF (1992) *The State of the World's Children, 1992*, Oxford University Press, Oxford.
Vreede-de Stuers, C. (1960) *The Indonesian Woman*, Mouton and Co., 's-Gravenhage.
Warwick, D.P. (1986) 'The Indonesian Family Planning Program: Government Influence and Client Choice', *Population and Development Review*, Vol.12 no.3 (September 1986). pp.453-490
White, M.C. (1990) 'Improving the Welfare of Women Factory Workers: Lessons from Indonesia', *International Labour Review* Vol.129 no.1, 1990. pp.121-135
Wieringa, S. (1992) 'Ibu and the Beast: Gender Interests in Two Indonesian Women's Organizations', *Feminist Review* No.41 (Summer, 1992) pp.98-112
_____ (1988) Aborted Feminism in Indonesia: A History of Indonesian Socialist Feminism, in S. Wieringa (ed) *Women's Struggles and Strategies*, Gower, Aldershot.
Woodsmall, R. (1960) *Women and the New East*, The Middle East Institute, Washington.

18

Free from what? Responsible to whom? The Problem of Democracy and the Indonesian Press

Paul Tickell

Commentaries on the Indonesian press, by Indonesians (e.g. Oey 1971) and non-Indonesians (e.g. Smith 1983), give the general impression that, from the Liberal Democracy period through Guided Democracy into the New Order, there has been an almost inexorable movement away from press and other freedoms towards more authoritarian and restrictive patterns of the press in particular and politics in general. The Indonesian press today is consequently a different and arguably more restricted creature than the press of the liberal democracy period and exists in a radically different legislative/legal, social, political and cultural environment.

While the liberal democracy years were not a period of complete press freedom, a number of factors do appear to have worked to create an atmosphere of relative liberalism and press liberty. The impermanence of governments, and the shifting alliances that constituted these governments, generally appear to have restrained repressive tendencies (Smith 1983:51). The weakness and fractured nature of the Indonesian military — that extra-party political force that, under martial law in the Guided Democracy period, was to provide much of the apparatus for press-state relations that persist to the present — also meant one less repressive element. A general, but admittedly imperfect, ideological commitment to the ideals of democracy, pluralism and (press) freedom also gave the Indonesian Fourth Estate of the early 1950s a political legitimacy and autonomy that would subsequently be challenged and modified under Guided Democracy and the New Order. And in many ways the move away from a relatively free press and the political ideology and consensus that permitted such freedoms, towards a press constrained both by formal devices of legislation and government regulation and by extra-legal constraints, is now an undeniable and demonstrable reality in Indonesia.

Yet this move from freedom to restriction, from political and press pluralism to state corporatism, *asas tunggal* and authoritarianism, says little about how or whether the Indonesian press was or is democratic. The relationship between concepts of press freedom (viz, the absence of state intervention in and censorship of the press) and democracy are never simple, even more so in a multi-ethnic, polyglot and geographically diffuse country such as Indonesia.

At the very least this conflation of press freedom with democracy runs the risk, for those with a political preference for liberal democracy, of sentimentalising Indonesia's period of liberal democracy and depicting it as a golden age of Indonesian press freedom and press democracy. The point which I will argue below is that in terms of 'freedom' this was undeniably the case, but in terms of 'democracy', the issues are far less clear cut. Alternatively for those who view (perhaps with some justification) liberal democracy in Indonesia as an unmitigated national political disaster, the shift away from liberal press freedoms to a more corporatist, institutionalised, regulated and controlled press becomes the acceptable, indeed necessary, price to be paid for national unity and, national development.

Both the permissive, libertarian and the corporatist, restrictive approaches to the problem of the press and democracy in Indonesia work with a number of givens that remained largely unquestioned. Liberal democratic press theory and practice is frequently rejected in Indonesia as alien and inapplicable to Indonesia's unique situation. Judgements based on its underlying value system, like those of fundamental individual human rights, are rejected as Eurocentric. Similarly critics of Indonesia's current 'press system' see little more than repression and political opportunism on the part of the current regime (*Indonesian Human Rights Forum* 1991:5-11).

In liberal democratic discourse the problem of press freedom is frequently expressed in terms of the interests of a repressive state clashing with the interests of a free, open and democratic press. Frequently in either explicit or implicit terms, this 'contest' between the press and the state comes to be expressed in terms of the good press leading the fight against the bad regime, with the press extolling and struggling for the right to know and the state being seen as an agent of control and restriction. In such characterisations the press is depicted as the guardian of freedom, and as a representative and legitimate voice of public opinion and civil society. However, the relationship between the press and the state is frequently more complex than this antagonistic, polarised and essentially political contest-model would suggest. While autonomy from the state expressed in terms of a lack of censorship, a flow of information, an absence of official or unofficial harassment of journalists indicate a freedom of the press, they do not guarantee democracy of or in the press.

The centrality of this autonomy to conventional arguments of press democracy is based on a number of assumptions about the state, its legitimacy, the law and rights and responsibilities of citizens within the state. These arguments in turn may not be directly or completely applicable to the Indonesian context. Frequently English language commentary based on the experience and practice of the common law anglophone world with its division of authority between executive, legislative and courts, assumes that this experience and practice, the relationship between the semi-autonomous components of what is in many ways a curiously uncentred concept of the state, are applicable beyond its dominant legal and cultural community. Projecting this experience on to the West as a singular whole, where civil law with its more centred and theorised conception of the state is dominant, is fraught with danger. To project this experience and assume its validity to the non-West is even more problematic. Where Western conceptions of democracy see the checks, balances and autonomy of various components of the state (the executive, judiciary, legislature and less directly, the press) as necessary guards against despotism, corporate/corporatising states (like Indonesia) see these formal separations of power as an impediment to the achievement of wider collective goals.

In contemporary Western societies the viability of a 'libertarian' press is made possible either by an unspoken, but widely accepted political and social consensus, or by the effective marginalising of social and political forces that may threaten that consensus. An indicator of this process may be the domination of politics by parties of the centre, the acceptance of a kind of non-confrontational pluralism, where real power and authority still remains vested in an elite group. If we look at Indonesia in the 1950s — especially the period of liberal parliamentary democracy — such preconditions did not exist. There was no working political consensus and while there was pluralism, in many ways it was a destructive pluralism — perhaps even representing the 'extreme conditions' where 'a quarrelling civil society can bludgeon itself to death.' (Keane 1991:149) While there was also a sense that national political authority was vested in an elite, this elite was a fractured and fractious, non-homogenous group, squabbling over the spoils of Indonesian power.

A press-state relationship based exclusively on the idea of 'contest' provides only a partial explanation of the situation of the Indonesian press, so partial, in fact, as to be inadequate for anything but a cliched and superficial understanding. Additionally it is only through consideration of a number of particular historical, political, legal, cultural and linguistic factors that we can begin to arrive at a multifaceted understanding of the diverse and often contradictory relationships between the Indonesian press and the Indonesian state, and be able to evaluate the democratic or other potentials of the Indonesian press from the 1950s to the present.

The cultural and historic conditions surrounding the emergence of print media in Indonesia suggest a degree of consonance, rather than contest between the press and Indonesian state. Close links — personal and organisational — between the nationalist movement, nationalist politics and the Indonesian press almost continuously from the first or second decades of this century to the present appear to have been the norm, rather than the exception. In many ways the Indonesian language press appears as the intellectual vanguard of Indonesian nationalism. These clear and unambiguous links between the 'mainstream' Indonesian press,[1] the nationalist movement and the anti-colonial struggle predispose this press towards pluralism and democracy, but a pluralism bounded within the limits of that political and ideological construct that is Indonesia. Within these limits this tendency towards pluralism emerges out of the close links, and more importantly in contemporary Indonesia, public identification between newspapers and political parties and in turn reflects the spectrum of political opinion and ideological diversity that has characterised Indonesian nationalist thought.

If pluralism is seen as a mark of democracy, the Indonesian press in the liberal democracy period was distinctly plural, allowed a free rein and may therefore be seen as 'democratic'. In the period until 1958, there were relatively few instances of government censorship,[2] even though, until 1953 at least, much of the specific repressive colonial legal apparatus relating directly to the press as well as other more general forms of state legal control remained valid under Indonesian law. The transition to Guided Democracy saw the consolidation of a number of political, but more importantly extra-parliamentary groups — in particular an increasingly powerful and consistent role by the Indonesian Army. In a practical, administrative sense, this saw an escalation of restrictions on the press. Largely under the aegis of martial law, a system of permits was established that in one form or another have characterised the mechanisms of press control in Indonesia since then (Oey 1971:110-132). While press pluralism did not disappear, and links with political parties remained a particular characteristic of the Indonesian press, there were a number of cases of press censorship — both of the Leftist and right-wing press, which gave the impression, if not indicating the reality, of a narrowing of press options.

The range of acceptable opinions and the style of public rhetoric during the period was also increasingly limited to Sukarnoist sloganeering. As Oey Hong Lee has noted (1971:144), there was some room to move in this increasingly tight verbal straight-jacket, but options were increasingly limited. The logical conclusion of this restriction on the range of opinions

---

1. By 'mainstream' Indonesian press, I mean the Indonesian language medium press largely run by and sold to ethnic Indonesians. This is in contrast to the colonial Dutch language press and the Sino-Malay/Indonesian dialect press.

2. See Oey (1971:51) for details of censorship moves taken against the newspapers affiliated with the Indonesian Communist Party in 1951.

and public rhetoric — and with it a lessening of political and journalistic pluralism — was reached in the 1980s when demands that Pancasila become the *asas tunggal* (sole foundation) of all public bodies and organisations in Indonesia became a legal reality.

In the 1990s the mechanisms of control over the Indonesian press remain largely as they were. Indeed they may be regarded as direct descendants of those established in the 1960s under Sukarno's Old Order. The Basic Press Law of 1966, for example, was amended in 1982, purged of its leftist wording, but with basic substantive relationships between the press and the state remaining the same. *Surat Izin Terbit* (SIT or Publication Permits) and *Surat Izin Cetak* (SIC or Printing Permits) have been abolished, but newspapers are now required to obtain a *Surat Izin Usaha Penerbitan Pers* (a SIUPP — a permit to run a press publication business). Although the SIUPP is ostensibly not a device to muzzle the press (Djajamihardja 1987:44) the withdrawal of SIUPP have been effectively used in recent times to silence the press.[3] It seems as if the New Order has merely refined Old Order mechanisms of control, rather than substantially changing them.

Institutional and formal controls on the press cannot be ignored and obviously influence the role the press can play in wider democratic processes. Such controls and restrictions are, however, not the only factors that determine 'democracy' of and in the Indonesian press. If they are not an absolute guide to democracy of the press, important questions of how we evaluate this democracy must be raised. What criteria are applicable and useful in the Indonesian context? What are the specific characteristics of the Indonesian press that determine its democratic potential?

This paper will suggest two criteria useful in the evaluation of democracy in the press: participation and representation. As a mass medium that is both capital intensive and a consumer product, participation can be understood in two ways. It can be seen in terms of the production and ownership of the press, where a broad spectrum of ownership across a wide political spectrum will be seen as conducive to pluralism, if not democracy. Participation can also be seen in terms of consumption — in terms of readership, where consumption of newspapers across class, ethnicity, gender and geography is seen as yet another mark of a plural democracy. This notion of broad consumption leads on to the problem of representation and to the posing of the questions: What social, political and cultural values are represented in the press? What alternative or contrary values are excluded?

If we look at the Indonesian press from the early 1950s to the present, just how participatory and how representative (or representative of precisely what?) was it? In one sense, the links already noted with Indonesian nationalism and national culture suggest that the Indonesian press represented

---

3. For a recent example of how the withdrawal of a SIUPP has been used to silence a publication, see Andrew Rosser's (1992) discussion of the *Monitor* Affair.

a broad section of the Indonesian population. The links between the press and political parties with their (more or less) developed grass-roots organisational structures suggest that the impact of the press could have been greater than merely being an urban, capital-city phenomenon.

A number of other factors, however, may be put forward to suggest that the Indonesian press in the 1950s was a narrow phenomenon, restricted in its capacity to represent the diversity of political, social and cultural aspirations of the Indonesian population, and highly restricted in terms of participation — especially participation in the form of consumption. It may be suggested that in terms of its language medium (i.e. almost exclusively Indonesian language) the Indonesian press of the 1950s was linguistically alienated and remote from that vast majority of the Indonesian population, most of whom at that time certainly could not read Indonesian. In another sense the press and its conceptual universe, its dominant ideas, were culturally remote from the experience and needs of the majority of the population. The concept of 'news' is historically and culturally very specific. The need or desire to know what is *new* appears to be relatively unimportant to non-urban, 'traditional' societies.

Lack of participation is mirrored in circulation figures for Indonesian newspapers. While such figures can never be a perfect index, what figures for the early 1960s (Oey 1971:150) and early 1980s (*Persuratkabaran* 1986:136-40) suggest is that although absolute circulation figures have risen over this period (from 1.49 million newspapers nationally in 1964 to 2.65 million in 1982 — with the national population rising from 97 million to 154 million over the same period), newspaper reading was and remains a restricted practice in Indonesia with Jakarta producing (and to a large degree consuming) the largest part of Indonesia's newspaper production. In 1964, over 40% of newspapers were Jakarta-based (Oey 1971:150). In 1982 this had declined to 37.85% of circulation (*Persuratkabaran* 1986:136). Both in terms of absolute circulation figures and the geographic distribution of newspaper readership, this leads to the unremarkable discovery that relatively few Indonesians read newspapers and those who do, tend to live in cities and in particular in the national capital, Jakarta. While there has been both a considerable expansion of circulation from independence to the present, and a greater geographic distribution of the press, the press as a *mass* medium still barely touches the lives of the mass of the Indonesian population. It may therefore be argued that in terms of participation the contemporary Indonesian press, although more restricted by formal controls than in the liberal democracy period, is now in one sense at least more democratic. Access to the press measured by readership is now greater than at any time in the past. In terms of representation of cultural, political and social aspirations, it could also be argued that wider and more geographically diverse circulation points to greater representation. Whether in response to economic imperatives (viz, potential markets) or changing consciousness, the Indonesian print media is now characterised by an increased specialisation and segmentation. The New Order period has seen a burgeoning of specialist publications ranging from women's magazines, teenage and children's publications, through to gardening magazines.

Through its language medium and its cultural orientation, the Indonesian press still clearly remains one of the prime forms of Indonesian national cultural expression. As such it still clearly represents the cultural, social and political aspirations of those in Indonesia who possess and have the greatest investment in Indonesian national 'cultural capital'. In spite of a broadening of this group since independence, they remain a numerical, cultural and linguistic minority.

These limitations in representation can be seen more clearly if we briefly explore what has been excluded or has disappeared from the world of the Indonesian press over time. Aside from the obvious exclusion of the communist left after 1966, the increasing cultural hegemony of 'metropolitan superculture' can be seen in the marginalisation and subsequently virtual elimination of the 'regional language' press. In effect from Indonesian independence onwards, to publish a newspaper in Indonesia has come to mean to publish an Indonesian-language newspaper. The 'de-Sinification' of the Indonesian press is another example of exclusion. In colonial times, the Sino-Malay/Java-Malay 'dialect' press and the ethnic Chinese played a substantial and pioneering role in the non-European press. In the post-independence period, the 'low Malay' dialect associated with the Indonesian Chinese (and the Chinese of Java in particular) has been expunged as a written reality. In its place the officially standardised (and therefore 'controlled') version of the Indonesian language has become *de rigeur* as the language of the press.

This paper has attempted to show that democracy of/in the press is not merely a matter of contest between the State and the Press. While freedom of the press can be measured in terms of absence of censorship, restrictive regulations and the like, its democracy cannot. As Indonesian press commentators frequently point out, Indonesia is not a liberal democracy and has no pretensions of being one. More contentiously these commentators will also suggest that the institutions of Western liberal democracy are not well suited to the kind of political and social reality Indonesian elites have been constructing from the 1950s to the present. Although viewing with a degree of scepticism the assertion of absolute Indonesian difference that such a political and social construction implies, it has been suggested in the discussion above that the relationship between the State, the Press and readers in conventional liberal definitions of press freedom (and by extension, 'democracy') are either idealised fictions, inappropriate to the specifics of the Indonesian context or have been overtaken by economic, political and cultural change, in both Indonesia and the West.

To sum up, the press represents particular economic, political, social and cultural interest groups, which may or may not be in contest with the State or other elements of civil society, but which can never claim to speak for all groups in society. In the Indonesian context of a multilingual, multiethnic, geographically and culturally diverse nation, the position of the press, and who and what it may claim to represent, are complicated even further. As the herald of an Indonesian national culture, by virtue of its political, linguistic and historical linkages, the Indonesian press is able to lay claim to a powerful legitimacy within the political and cultural boundaries of the Indonesian nation that its circulation and mass impact have never justified. While it may be suggested on one level that the expansion of readership, the increasing immediacy and relevance of Indonesian language and culture from the 1950s to the present, suggest a widening appeal, and therefore greater participation and democratisation of the Indonesian press (in the face of a formalisation and systemising of state imposed restrictions), it may also be suggested that this assumes the legitimacy of the metanarrative of the Indonesian nation. It is this national metanarrative that determines the boundaries of discourse, of what is permissible and not permissible, what is included and excluded. Notions of cultural permissibility, inclusion and legitimacy have a profound effect on democracy and freedom. Whether it be the clear examples of the impermissibility of East Timorese and West Papuan national imaginings, which the Indonesian metanarrative sees as 'separatism', or the general subordination of 'regional' cultures and languages, it is the dominant narrative of Indonesian nation-ness/nationhood/- nationality that largely, though not exclusively, determines the limits of democracy in the Indonesian press. In an age of global communications, of apparently new political and environmental order(s), whether this metanarrative will retain its power remains open to question and with it the possibility of a new and different plural, decentred democracy in the Indonesian press.

References

'Background Report: Freedom of the Press', *Indonesian Human Rights Forum* No.2. 1991.

Djajamihardja, Hidayat (1987) Reporting Indonesia: An Indonesian Journalist's Perspective, in P. Tickell (ed) 'The Indonesian Press: its past, its people, its problems', Centre of Southeast Asian Studies, Monash University.

Keane, J. (1991) *The Media and Democracy*, Polity Press, Cambridge.

Oey Hong Lee (1971) *The Indonesian Government and Press during Guided Democracy*, IDC. Zug.

Rosser, A.J. (1992) *Political Openness and Social Forces in New Order Indonesia: The Monitor Affair*. B.A. (Hons) thesis, Flinders University of South Australia, Adelaide.

Smith, E.C. (1983) *Pembreidelan Pers di Indonesia*, Grafiti Pers, Jakarta.

19

Challenging State Corporatism on the Labour Front: Working Class Politics in the 1990s

Vedi R. Hadiz[1]

> The respective positions of the bourgeoisie and the working class show that capitalism creates democratic pressures in spite of capitalists, not because of them. Democracy was the outcome of the contradictory nature of capitalist development, which, of necessity, created subordinate classes, particularly the working class, with the capacity for self-organisation.
>
> Rueschemeyer, Stephens and Stephens (1992:271-72)

A considerable literature exists on the different facets of the export-oriented industrialisation strategy successfully pursued by the East Asian NICs. Many observers have argued that this industrialisation strategy has been based on the maintenance of a cheap and politically docile labour force. Such writers, perhaps most notably Deyo, have described industrialisation in these economies as characterised by the political exclusion of labour (Deyo 1987:199). Except for South Korea, it is generally agreed that the labour regimes developed in each of these countries have effectively curtailed the growth of labour militancy and maintained industrial order.

Following in the footsteps of such well-established NICs, Indonesia since the mid-1980s has taken up the strategy of export-led industrialisation, which by that time had become an important part of the new orthodoxy in

---

[1]. The author would like to thank Ian Chalmers and Laksmi Pamuntjak for their comments and editorial help with earlier versions of this paper.

development thinking. In Indonesia's case, it was of course the drastic fall of international oil prices in the early 1980s that forced the reorientation of industrialisation policies that Indonesia has followed, more or less consistently, for nearly a decade.

In accordance with the principles of economic rationality which inform this current world-wide orthodoxy, Indonesia now gives much emphasis to the development of the labour intensive, low-wage, light manufacturing sector, considered crucial in the current campaign to raise non-oil export revenues. An important feature of development in Indonesia in the last decade has been the steady rise in the number of those employed in this sector. Hence, the presence of an industrial proletariat in similar kinds of industries that have underpinned the early success of the NICs, is increasingly visible. Hull estimates that the number of workers in the manufacturing sector has risen from 4.7 million in 1980 to 5.8 million in 1985 to 8.2 million in 1990, out of a total working class of 25 million people (Hull 1992:3). Also reminiscent of the NICs experience is the political docility of the Indonesian industrial working force which has also often been presented as a major favourable point in encouraging investment in Indonesia.

This paper will discuss issues related to the emergence of an industrial working class in Indonesia and its political expression. It will be argued that a new working class politics is emerging which poses a challenge to the established system of labour control. A major question here is whether the outcome of this challenge will be a reform of the formal structuring of state-capital-labour relations in which the interests of labour are better accommodated, or a reimposition of the authoritarian reins in which labour will be violently suppressed.

The emergence of a new working class politics

The contemporary regime of labour control in Indonesia was imposed quite a long time before the advent of export-led industrialisation in the mid-1980s. Indeed, some elements might be traced to labour policies as far back as the 1950s. These elements were incorporated into the basic framework for labour control which was firmly established in the early and mid-1970s. It was the product of an overriding objective to ensure the state's capacity to maintain social and political stability, believed to be the major pre-requisite of any kind of successful economic development (Murtopo 1972:82-87). In the case of labour, state planners maintained that the main threat to stability and order was any kind of resurgence in the influence of left-wing elements, which had been dominant in labour politics in the 1950s and early 1960s. The framework of labour control established in the early 1970s had thus little to do with any specific requirements of the largely import substitution industrialisation strategy pursued at the time.

The New Order framework of labour control, for the most part, proved effective in restricting independent labour organisation and ensuring workers' acquiescence in the existing scheme of things, except for the occurrence of periodic outbursts of industrial action in the late 1970s and early 1980s. Independent labour organisation was hindered by the effective imposition of the All-Indonesia Workers Federation (FBSI - *Federasi Buruh Seluruh Indonesia*) as the sole organisation of worker representation in 1973, followed by its even more centralised mid-1980s successor, the All-Indonesia Workers Union (SPSI - *Serikat Pekerja Seluruh Indonesia*). Another basic right that workers have largely had to do without is the right to strike. The introduction of the concept of Pancasila Industrial Relations (HIP - *Hubungan Industrial Pancasila*) provided the ideological legitimacy for pervasive state intervention in the maintenance of industrial peace by condemning all strike activity on the grounds that it transgressed the principle of harmonious, family like, state-capital-labour relations. As the President himself put it, '[I]n the Pancasila environment there is no place for confrontation' (Murtopo 1975:15).

However, as Indonesia treads further down the path of industrialisation based on low wage, light manufacturing, cracks seem to be emerging in the overall system of labour control which seemed to have worked so well in the past. Many observers have been struck by the distinctive rise in working class militancy and activism in Indonesia in the early 1990s (Schwarz 1990:14-16; Lane 1991:71-73, Hadiz 1992). One indicator of this is the rise in the number of strikes. Near the end of 1991, Minister of Manpower Cosmas Batubara noted that cases of strikes had risen to 85 by September of that year, from only 19 for the whole of 1989 (Batubara 1991:4). Manning notes that while strikes averaged only 46 cases between 1986 and 1990, 114 cases were documented for the whole of 1991, 96% of which occurred in manufacturing (Manning, forthcoming). Near the end of 1992, 177 cases of strikes were officially documented for the year (*Kompas* 18 November 1992). Originally confined for the most part to the industrial centres around Jakarta, they have spread more recently to other urban centres. The wave of labour unrest is significant given the fact that the successful domestication of labour seemed to have been accepted as one of the prominent features of the New Order. The wave of strikes is even more notable when one considers how mass action of the size that is sometimes involved — 14,000 workers in a single factory in one case (Lane 1991:71) — is in such stark contrast to the image of stability that has been successfully projected by the New Order. Another important development is that the current wave of strikes has been accompanied by the establishment and proliferation of new, independent, alternative labour-based organisations at the grass-roots level, which have successfully avoided the constraints imposed on direct organising. The presence of such organisations constitutes an increasingly serious problem to the formal arrangements of state-capital-labour relations which have been institutionalised over more than twenty years.

The New Order government, at least for the moment, is displaying a somewhat uncharacteristic inability to respond decisively to this increasingly serious challenge to state corporatism on the labour front. It is a question whether the challenge can be sustained so as to force a more fundamental redefinition of state-capital-labour relations. At this point there are contradictory signs: some may be interpreted as signalling moves toward a softening of state labour policies which many labour activists hope to achieve. However, alternative labour organisations are still weak, as is labour as a class, and the state is sufficiently strong to make a more or less violent clampdown on labour activism a possibility in the near future.

How this question is resolved has considerable implications for the prospects for democratisation in Indonesia. Those who argue that some kind of accommodation with the interests of labour is necessary for any kind of democracy could perhaps take heart from the fact that the liberal democracies that we now know are, to a large degree, the historical product of compromise between capital and labour, in which the interests of both are accommodated to some extent (Rueschemeyer, Stephens and Stephens 1992:269-302). The link between labour struggles and broader democratic struggles has not been lost on many labour activists in Indonesia.

The evolving regime of labour control

As already mentioned, many of the features of the New Order's control of labour have developed out of industrial relations practices that go back to at least the early 1950s. One of the more important legacies of the 1950s is the steady tightening of the controls on the right to strike. As early as 1951, an emergency law was produced by the Sukiman government that, while still upholding the right to strike, imposed restrictions on the exercise of that right. It carefully regulated the handling of disputes and in reality established a system of compulsory arbitration to determine wages, hours and working conditions in place of a free system of collective bargaining (Hawkins 1963a:264). One facet of this law, inherited by the New Order and incorporated into its system of labour control, is represented by the institution of regional and central disputes committees (respectively, P4D - *Panitia Penyelesaian Perselisihan Perburuhan Daerah* and P4P - *Panitia Penyelesaian Perselisihan Perburuhan Pusat*). These played an important role in the maintenance of industrial order in 1950s Indonesia, and still continue to do so.

In 1957 the 1951 emergency law was replaced by a new labour law, which — aside from changing the composition of the P4D and P4P to include worker representatives and employers, in addition to bureaucrats — stipulated more rigorous conditions and procedures for the taking of legal industrial action by workers (Hawkins 1963b:131-33). The non-fulfilment of these procedures and conditions — e.g. reporting the intent to strike in advance, allowing time for sufficient arbitration, etc. — continue to be the basis for resisting direct industrial action in the New Order.

The seizure of Dutch companies in 1957, initially led by workers and unions, ironically was to result in further developments which would prove unfavourable to militant unionism. The nationalised businesses were placed under the control of the military, putting it in direct opposition to the more militant and radical unions represented especially in the PKI-affiliated SOBSI (All-Indonesia Central Workers Organisation - *Sentral Organisasi Buruh Seluruh Indonesia*).

The military thus came increasingly to be involved in the management of labour relations after 1957. To counterbalance the influence of SOBSI over labour, the military set up the BKS-BUMIL (Body for the Cooperation of the Military and Labour - *Badan Kerja Sama Buruh dan Militer*), whose duties included advising the military on matters pertaining to the labour field, ensuring that workers did their duty in the firms taken over from the Dutch, and seeing that plants were kept in good running condition. Though the importance of the BKS-BUMIL gradually receded, the Army continued to play a major role in labour relations and succeeded in preventing strikes by keeping tight controls over the radical unions (Hawkins 1963a:268). Direct military involvement in labour affairs was also represented by the establishment of the Army-sponsored association of employees of state industries, SOKSI (Union of Indonesian Socialist Karyawan Organisations - *Serikat Organisasi Karyawan Sosialis Indonesia*) in 1962, which was clearly designed as a further effort to undermine the influence of the communist SOBSI. Even the idea of creating an FBSI-like single corporatist labour organisation dates from the early 1960s with the Army's abortive attempt to form an Organisation of Indonesian Worker Associations (OPPI).

Attempts at developing ideas of harmonious, state-labour-capital relations were also occurring in the early 1960s, the most notable being represented by the *Dewan Perusahaan* (Enterprise Councils). According to this scheme, carefully screened labour representatives were included in enterprise councils designed to give labour a voice in the setting of enterprise policy, while maintaining management authority (Hawkins 1963a:269-70).

All these features of labour control were to be developed to a much more sophisticated level under the New Order. The right to strike was severely undermined when, in 1974, the idea of Pancasila Industrial Relations (HIP) was introduced as a concept of state-capital-labour relations based on family principles, with the state acting as benevolent father (Murtopo 1975:13-31). The main concern was to dispel any lingering influence that notions of class conflict might have on industrial relations in Indonesia, and the result was to regard any form of overt confrontation between labour and capital as contradicting the harmonious relations prescribed in the concept of HIP. In the same vein, advocates of HIP would contrast the 'partnership' relations of labour and capital in Indonesia with the 'confrontational' relations that exist in the 'liberal' West (Sudono 1977:177-89; Murtopo 1975:13-15).

The subordination of labour organisations to the state reached a new high point with the establishment of the FBSI in 1973, followed by its further centralisation in the form of the SPSI in 1985. If the right to strike has been restricted through the imposition of HIP, the right to organise has been hindered with the imposition of the FBSI/SPSI. As one of the various corporatist institutions of representation that were established in the early 1970s for different sections of society, such as the peasantry and youth (Murtopo 1975:9), the FBSI also represented the culmination of renewed efforts to create a single national worker organisation.

The more hierarchical, military-like structure of the SPSI[2], eliminated the sector-based individual unions (*Serikat Buruh Lapangan Pekerjaan* - SBLP) that had made up the FBSI federation, and which had been the base for the maintenance of some limited, local-level, grassroots activism that made labour disturbances possible in the late 1970s and early 1980s. Furthermore, Agus Sudono, who had a strong trade union background and extensive contacts with international labour organisations, was replaced by Imam Soedarwo, who had neither.

These changes were introduced under the auspices of Sudomo, the former security chief who was Minister of Manpower between 1983 and 1988. It is reasonable to conclude that his instalment as minister and the changes he introduced to the FBSI/SPSI were designed both to ensure that labour unruliness did not interfere with the economic reorientation process which Indonesia was beginning at the time, particularly because a new emphasis on low wage industries was involved.

That a former security chief came to be responsible for managing labour affairs in the crucial 1983-88 period is perhaps an apt symbol of the extent to which military involvement in the settlement of labour disputes has become a more ubiquitous feature under the New Order's system of labour control. This is evidenced both by the increasing number of military officers serving in state institutions that deal with labour and in the increasing importance of local Koramil (military sub-district commands) as sites for the 'adjudication' of labour disputes. It was during this period that military involvement in quelling strikes was legitimised in a 1986 Minister of Manpower Decision.[3]

Cracks in the system: recent challenges to the regime of labour control

To the surprise of most observers, labour militancy has recently been on the rise in Indonesia. Given that stringent control over labour has been exercised successfully in the past, the recent emergence of working class militancy is indeed rather difficult to explain. A perplexing question is how such a development has been possible in the absence of any kind of significant independent trade union.

It is possible to explain this rise of labour militancy as a more or less direct by-product of moves toward democratisation, indicated by the so-called *keterbukaan* (openness) debate of 1989-1991. From this point of view it

---

2. Note the replacement of '*Buruh*' in FBSI with the more politically passive '*Pekerja*' in SPSI, which brings to mind comparisons with Leclerc's observations on the introduction of the word '*Karyawan*' in the early 1960s. See Leclerc (1972).

3. This ruling was repealed in January 1994, shortly before going to press (eds).

would be possible to point to the annulment, in August 1990, of a 1963 Presidential Decision that barred strikes in certain institutions and projects, as the 'catalyst' for the wave of the recent strike actions in Indonesia, signifying as it were, the 'genuineness' of *keterbukaan*. From this point of view, workers merely 'reacted' to an opportunity that was provided by a particular decision, made to meet the particular exigencies of politics at the time.

Thus, one interpretation of the rise of working class action in the early 1990s would be to relate it to the establishment in September 1990 of 'Setiakawan', the first organisation to announce itself as an alternative union to the SPSI. Its formation was certainly inspired by the annulment of the 1963 decision, and was thus a clear by-product of the brief period in which '*keterbukaan*' was taken more or less seriously. However, as important as Setiakawan was, particularly in the early part of its life, in attracting attention to the labour cause in Indonesia, abroad, and in the local press, it is doubtful whether one should attribute the wave of strike action that has occurred in the last few years to its establishment. Since its formation Setiakawan has often been incapacitated by internal conflict (*Tempo* 28 September 1991:40-41), and its claim to be the sole challenger to the SPSI's monopoly position has in turn been challenged by some of its own disaffected members who formed the Indonesian Prosperous Workers Union (SBSI) (*Tempo* 2 May 1992:24). Furthermore, the fact that strike actions are continuing independently of Setiakawan's leading role seems to suggest that other forces are at work.

A strictly labour market-based argument might suggest the incompatibility of the development of a significant labour movement with the conditions of marked excess labour supply that exist in Indonesia. While labour market conditions constitute a very real countervailing factor to the successful political organisation of labour in the longer term, the development of labour militancy cannot be easily dismissed as the product of the actions of a group of misguided activists. If that were true it would seem unlikely that it could have grown to the extent that it has. Although labour organisers and activists have certainly played an important role, the rise of working class action can only be properly understood in relation to wider processes of social and political development.

Perhaps the fundamental problem for the government lies in the fact that the existing regime of labour control, constructed as it was out of the conditions and requirements of the 1970s, no longer seems adequate to accommodate changes which have occurred in Indonesia on the labour front over 25 years of development under the New Order. This has more to do with the broad, gradual formation of an industrial working class and its political expression, than a simple process of a group of labour activists 'reacting' to an opportunity provided by a particular change in government policy.

As mentioned earlier, the number of people involved in light manufacturing has been growing steadily over the last decade, and can be expected to continue to grow with the current emphasis on labour-intensive exports. By now a new generation of workers, raised or perhaps even born in urban or semi-urban areas, especially in Java, has come of age. For a small but growing number of such workers, life in the city and the factories is not temporary, as it was for their predecessors. For them, the factory, or at least the city, is the only source of livelihood, and the major source of living experience. The village can no longer offer them the refuge or place of retreat that it had in the past (Hadiz 1992, Farid 1992). It is not being suggested here that ties with the village have been totally severed; they have not and it would take a longer, sustained period of industrialisation for this to happen. Nevertheless, it is quite clear that the newer generation of workers has become much more urbanised.

The implication is that workers will feel that they have a more permanent stake in struggles to improve their work and living conditions in the factories and cities. This changing 'world view', supported by the higher level of education that the Indonesian labour force in general now possesses (Jones, 1989) makes higher levels of political organisation among such workers more possible than in the past. It is no longer very uncommon for factory workers to be high school graduates. How this 'world view' is changing is revealed quite startlingly in the words of the workers themselves. Thoughtful and relatively sophisticated writings on the general conditions of work and factory life, on state-capital-labour relations, and on ways of overcoming their political subordination, have been produced by the pens of individual workers in recent years. These are a fascinating source for the study of contemporary working class culture. Moreover, these scattered pieces probably constitute the most persuasive evidence for the importance of experiences in contemporary urban working class life to the recent rise in industrial action.

Recent events show that the SPSI's monopoly of worker organisation and education has been challenged by the setting up of small, informal groups — they may be discussion groups, educational groups, *koperasi simpan-pinjam* or even *kelompok arisan* — outside of the SPSI framework. Such groups become the means by which workers exchange experiences and ideas, and start to gain an understanding of their social milieu. Although some leaders have arisen from among the workers themselves, such groups are commonly run in partnership with activists of small labour-oriented NGOs, whose members might consist of veteran labour, as well as current and former student activists. It is through interaction within groups and organisations such as these, combined with the conditions to be found in factory life — that the slow process of developing a worker identity, seems to be taking place.

It is important to note the role that current and former student activists play in these groups and organisations. Why and how such activists have come to labour organising involves the history of the student movement in the

New Order, in particular, the history of student politics in the 1980s. However, this is not the place for a discussion of such a topic. Suffice it to say that the growth of labour militancy has occurred concurrently with the marginalisation of students from official, legitimate political life. Politically and socially aware students have become, in consequence, increasingly radicalised. These student activists have probably found it easier to work together with the small but growing number of urbanised and better educated young workers employed in the factories of today's sprawling new industrial estates than they would have with workers of preceding generations. Thus, largely invisible to most eyes, such groups and organisations in which students and workers combine have been the focus for the emergence of much of the contemporary labour militancy.

State responses: redefining State-labour-capital relations or reimposing the authoritarian reins?

The recent wave of strikes that have rocked the urban industrial estates, particularly of Java, has been taken seriously by state authorities. No effective way has been found of meeting this challenge to industrial order and the formal structuring of state-capital-labour relations. The question, then, is whether the challenge will eventually be met by renewed and even more severe repressive policies or whether a more sophisticated corporatist strategy, more accommodating to the demands and interests of workers, can be the outcome.

To some extent the visible rise in labour militancy has strengthened the hand of those in the state apparatus favouring limited reforms in labour relations. Such a strategy was advocated, for example, by the former Minister of Manpower Cosmas Batubara. Publicly critical of the inadequacies of the SPSI (*Kompas* 4 May 1992), he called for reforms aimed at enhancing the legitimacy of this state-backed organisation. He took pains to salvage Indonesia's badly tarnished overseas reputation in the field of labour relations (*Jakarta Post* 20 July 1992). His main achievement was to get himself elected to the prestigious position of president of the annual conference of the International Labour Organisation in June 1991 (*Kompas* 5 May 1991).

In spite of Batubara's efforts, the SPSI is still unrecognised by the International Confederation of Free Trade Unions because of Indonesia's non-compliance with international labour standards. Furthermore, to the distress of Indonesian economic policy-makers, the AFL-CIO continues to recommend to the United States Congress the removal of Indonesia from the American GSP (Generalised System of Preferences) list. The importance of improving Indonesia's image in the area of labour relations was underscored by Batubara:

> If we want to take part in globalisation we have to respect international labour standards, such as the right to organise, the right to bargain. If we do not follow international labour standards, our commodities will be

blocked. (Batubara 1992:67).

It is quite clear that Batubara's ideas about reforms in the area of labour relations, including improving the image and performance of the SPSI, were aimed at eroding the attractiveness of the alternative independent labour-oriented organisations which are considered to have caused much of the trouble on the labour front. Hence, his comments about 'making the SPSI work the way it should'. With his blessing, the SPSI structure was again revamped in 1990 to accommodate some sector-based units within the organisation, in response to pressures to revive the old SBLPs. However, his reluctance to transgress the boundaries and the language of HIP reflected the limitations of his vision (Batubara 1992:62-74).[4] His criticism of the SPSI did not lead him to agree to the need for an alternative labour union (*Jakarta Post* 8 July 1992). The SPSI was still to be the only recognised labour union, thus ensuring the renegade status of any alternative organisation that workers might set up independently (Forum Solidaritas Buruh 1992; *Jakarta Post* 7 May 1992).

However, Batubara recognised that maintaining industrial peace would, in part, entail fulfilling some of the easier-to-meet demands of workers, while more important changes in the future were promised more cautiously. In a clear attempt to placate them, he ordered the raising of the minimum wage in some industrial sectors and talked vaguely about the aim of having it meet minimum physical needs of workers in the near future (*Kompas* 15 June 1992 & 16 October 1992). At the moment it meets only 60% of their needs, according to official calculations. He also chastised employers for their intransigence in dealing with worker demands and made the point that they have been partly responsible for the emergence of some of the more serious cases of industrial dispute. Specifically, Batubara warned businessmen of the detrimental effects of maintaining unrealistically low wages (*Kompas* 27 January 1992). Keeping wages too low, he said, would cause instability, disrupt the economy, and make Indonesia unattractive to foreign investors (*Kompas* 17 December 1992).

Batubara's initiatives seemed to attract the support of the President who later made his own statements in favour of workers, while being fairly critical of the stance taken by employers. For example, he urged employers to refrain from interfering in the process of the formation of factory-level SPSI branches, something which had been common practice in the past. Although all of this may be said to have more of a symbolic than real impact on labour reform, it is important to note how much the official rhetoric since 1992 has diverged from that of the mid-1980s, when there was never a question of whether to present troublesome workers with a carrot or a stick.

---

4. In this interview, which appeared in *Prisma* no.3 1992, Batubara even repeats the culturalist defence of labour policies in Indonesia, asking why foreigners cannot understand that, to Indonesians, asking the local military command to help settle a labour dispute was quite the normal thing to do.

It should not be concluded from this that Batubara's downplaying of the use of the stick, so to speak, was based on strictly altruistic motives. An important difference between Batubara and Sudomo is that the former's institutional base did not encompass the state's repressive apparatus, which was the case with ex-security chief Sudomo, later Coordinating Minister for Politics and Security. Thus, it was in Batubara's own political interests to promote an approach for the handling of labour tensions that did not overly rely on the use of coercive measures, but which enhanced the position of his Ministry and that of the SPSI, institutions that, unlike the security apparatus, were under his formal jurisdiction.

It would be a grievous error, however, to suggest that what is popularly known as the 'security approach' to the handling of labour tensions has been abandoned. Throughout Batubara's tenure as minister, Sudomo still had a say in labour matters and at times was known openly to contradict Ministry of Manpower statements, particularly about the use of force to keep workers in line. Today, security forces continue to be involved in the 'adjudication' of labour matters, a practice which still draws the most vehement domestic and foreign criticism of labour policies in Indonesia (e.g. Nurbaeti n.d.).

While this may be a matter of combining the carrot and stick approaches, developments in 1991 and 1992 may also reflect the confusion about how best to deal with the unexpected rise in working class action. This confusion was quite evident at the local level. In contradiction to developments at the national level, several provincial committees representing labour, capital and the state, were reported to have called for a postponement in the implementation of new minimum wage stipulations, which were set in response to the rise in worker discontent (*Kompas* 20 April 1992). The participation of local SPSI branches in this endeavour was promptly criticised by members of the national leadership of that organisation. Furthermore, reviving memories of the Sudomo period, the regent of Bekasi attempted to impose a ban on strikes in his area of jurisdiction, despite the fact that few national level officials would still categorically deny workers the right to strike (*Kompas* 15 May 1992). A similar move was attempted by the Regent of Tangerang, another major site for industrial estates in the areas surrounding Jakarta.

Thus, developments of the last two years seem to suggest an uncharacteristic inability on the part of state authorities to find an effective policy to contain a growing source of threat to public order. Though state authorities now seem to emphasise policies of appeasement, the option of resorting to violent measures to curb the further development of militant labour has not been ruled out.

The working class in the democratisation debate

Twenty five years of capitalist development under New Order rule has brought about the growth of classes associated with the maturation of capitalism: a capital-owning class, professional and salaried urban middle classes, and an industrial working class. Important studies of the development of the capital-owning class have been produced in recent years (Robison 1986; Shin 1989; MacIntyre 1991), and inevitably, much more attention will be given to studies of the middle classes in the future (an early, notable, effort is Young and Tanter, 1990). Unsurprisingly, it is the working class which has been the most under-studied.

Much contemporary discussion of Indonesian politics, at various levels, is inspired by the belief in the reformist role that an enlightened bourgeoisie or middle class will play: it is often argued that they will eventually develop the right cast of mind to demand democratic reforms and a loosening of authoritarian reins. Related to this view is the idea that the liberalisation of the Indonesian economy will result in the enhanced ability of 'society' (a term, revealingly, often used to refer only to the capital owning and/or middle classes) to counter-balance the power of the state.[5]

Capitalism has indeed unleashed forces that are changing the nature of Indonesian politics and society. Emerging social forces are exerting pressures on the state, and they are not forces which can be easily controlled and circumvented. One force that capitalism has ushered in is an industrial working class. Although this class is still quite small and weak, further industrialisation will ensure its growth and maturation. While conditions for the objective development of the working class are ripening, it still remains to be seen whether workers are able to develop the level of political organisation necessary to exert sufficient pressure for the reorganisation of the existing framework of state-capital-labour relations in a manner more accommodating to the interests of labour. At the very least, this would involve the lifting of current restrictions on the right to organise. Recent developments show that the rise in working class pressure has not been successful in eliciting more than piecemeal reforms.

Because reforms have been both too piecemeal and too slow, it is highly likely that working class discontent will grow and that current forms of experimentation with independent labour organising in the fringes of the

---

5. On the other hand, it may be argued just as strongly that the bourgeoisie has emerged within a framework of state power and is dependent to a considerable extent on that power. The degree of that dependence is often underestimated and the potential for development toward a liberal democratic type of political regime, often assumed to suit the interest of any increasingly self-confident bourgeoisie, is exaggerated.

It may not be a mere coincidence that the discussion on democratisation in Indonesia, essentially carried out by middle class agents in academia (with real links to either the state bureaucracy or enterprises run by the bourgeoisie), is often limited to the role of such institutions as parliament, political parties, and the armed forces that are also recognised by the state to have a place within the proper realm of politics. In general, the politics that go on outside of this delimited space is left unnoticed. Thus, any intelligent commentary on labour and politics in Indonesia becomes implausible: the absence of officially legitimated labour-oriented institutions, which in the first place is the result of New Order policies, becomes a reason to assume that there are no politics of labour at all. Hence, the officially enforced divorce of labour from politics, also becomes a reason to divorce labour from academic discourse.

system will continue. The wave of strikes that has troubled industry in recent years is also likely to continue. And the possibility remains that the state will finally resort to stark violence and coercion to clamp down on all of this once and for all.

References

Batubara, Cosmas (1991) 'Kebijaksanaan Penyelesaian Perburuhan', paper presented during panel discussion on labour disputes organised by the Indonesian Legal Aid Foundation (YLBHI), Jakarta, 15 October 1991.
_____ (1992) Interview in *Prisma* no.3, pp.62-74.
Deyo, F. (1987) State and Labour: Modes of Political Exclusion in East Asian Development, in F. Deyo (ed) *The Political Economy of the Asian Industrialism*, Cornell University Press, Ithaca.
Farid, Hilmar (1992) 'Covering Strikes: Indonesian Workers and 'Their' Media'. Paper contributed to Second Indian Ocean Region Trade Union Conference, Perth, 4-12 December 1992.
Forum Solidaritas Untuk Buruh (1992) 'Hak Buruh Untuk Berorganisasi Masih Dikekang' (Leaflet).
Hadiz, V. (1992) The Political Significance of Recent Working Class Action in Indonesia, in D. Bourchier (ed) *Indonesia's Emerging Proletariat: Workers and their Struggles*, Winter Lecture Series, Centre of Southeast Asian Studies, Monash University (forthcoming)
Hawkins, E.D. (1963a) Labour in Transition, in R. McVey (ed) *Indonesia*, Yale University, New Haven. pp. 265-267.
_____ (1963b) Indonesia, in W. Galenson (ed) *Labor in Developing Economies*, University of California Press, Berkeley, pp. 71-137.
Hull, T. (1992) Workers in the Shadows: A Statistical Wayang, in D. Bourchier (ed) *Indonesia's Emerging Proletariat: Workers and their Struggles*, Winter Lecture Series, Centre of Southeast Asian Studies, Monash University (forthcoming).
Jones, G. (1989) 'Indonesia: Overview of Educational Trends and Growth and Changing Structure of the Labour Force.' Paper for Conference on Indonesia's New Order: Past, Present and Future', Australian National University, 4-8 December.
Lane, M. (1991) *'Openness', Political Discontent and Succession in Indonesia: Political Developments in Indonesia, 1989-91*. Centre for the Study of Australia-Asia Relations, Griffith University.
Leclerc, J. (1972) 'An Ideological Problem of Indonesian Trade Unionism in the Sixties: 'Karyawan' versus 'Buruh'', *Review of Indonesian and Malayan Affairs*, Vol. 6 No.1, 1972.
MacIntyre, A. (1991) *Business and Politics in Indonesia*, Allen and Unwin, Sydney.
Manning C. (forthcoming) 'Structural Change and Industrial Relations in a

Labour Surplus Economy: The Case of Indonesia'.

Murtopo, A. (1972) *Akselerasi dan Modernisasi Pembangunan 25 Tahun*. Yayasan Proklamasi/Centre for Strategic and International Studies, Jakarta.

_____ (1975) *Buruh dan Tani dalam Pembangunan*, Centre for Strategic and International Studies, Jakarta.

Nurbaeti, Ati (1986) 'Penataan Perburuhan dalam Struktur Politik Orde Baru: Kasus Buruh Industri Tekstil di PT ITM, Kec. Tangerang, Kab. Tangerang', Sarjana Thesis, Faculty of Social and Political Science, University of Indonesia.

_____ (n.d.) 'Potret Keterlibatan Aparat Keamanan dalam Konflik Buruh-Majikan'. n.d.

Robison, R. (1986) *Indonesia: The Rise of Capital*, Allen and Unwin, Sydney.

Rueschemeyer, D., E.H. Stephens, and J.D. Stephens (1992) *Capitalist Development and Democracy*, Polity Press, Cambridge.

Schwarz, A. (1990) 'Pressures of Work', *Far Eastern Economic Review*, 20 June 1990

Shin, Yoon-Hwan (1989) 'Demystifying the Capitalist State: Political Patronage, Bureaucratic Interests and Capitalists-in-Formation in Soeharto's Indonesia', PhD Thesis, Yale University.

Sudono, Agus (1977) *Gerakan Buruh Indonesia; Kumpulan Pidato/ Ceramah/Sambutan*, FBSI in cooperation with AAFLI, Jakarta.

Tanter, R. and K. Young (1990) *The Politics of Middle Class Indonesia*, Centre of Southeast Asian Studies, Monash University.

20

Regionalism and Decentralisation

Audrey R. Kahin

The size and geographic, ethnic, and cultural diversity of the Indonesian archipelago would have seemed to demand a form of government allowing for considerable devolution of power from the centre. Yet neither under the Dutch nor in the subsequent nearly half century of independence has anything more than lip-service been paid to such devolution. This is understandable in view of the legacy bequeathed by the colonial Netherlands Indies state — a strong, centralised administration, albeit with a shell of largely powerless regional representative bodies. But from the revolutionary years, the Indonesian Republic also inherited a number of relatively strong local governments that had had to carry on the anti-Dutch struggle in their own areas largely independent of guidance and directives from the centre. Any chances of the new Indonesia evolving as a federal system rested not only on this revolutionary experience, but also on the fact that Vice-President Hatta, who had been prime minister of the Republic in the later stages of the independence revolution, was a strong advocate of autonomy for the regions. Indeed, the need for a considerable devolution of power was widely recognised at least in principle by the independent Indonesian government, and throughout the early 1950s decentralisation remained one of its official goals.

However, the Jakarta government also confronted restrictions left behind by its Dutch predecessor. First, although the administration the Dutch had built up during the late colonial period did indeed involve 'a limited devolution of authority from the central government of the Indies to lower regions,' (Legge 1961:7) this was within the framework of a strong centralised state. The sinews of the state were provided by an administrative corps of Dutch and indigenous, mainly Javanese, civil servants, the *pamong praja,* which constituted, as John Legge has described it, 'a highly developed pyramid of command with its apex in the Ministry of Home Affairs in Djakarta and with authority passed down through a descending scale of levels to the base of society.' (Legge 1961:14-15)[1] In dealing with the massive problems facing Indonesia after ten years of war and revolution, the Republic understandably turned to this core of indigenous civil servants, who, however discredited by their ties to the former colonial power, formed one of the few networks that spread across the archipelago[2] and provided the possibility of welding Indonesia into a functioning entity.

At the same time, the Republic was pushed away from implementing greater autonomy for the regions by memories of Dutch manipulation of the concept of federalism during the independence struggle, when in the late 1940s the Netherlands administration began moves to create a Federal State of Indonesia, establishing a total of fifteen federal units mostly in the territories outside Java, as counterweights to the Indonesian Republic. Dutch efforts were directed at undermining adherence to the goal of independence by raising fears in the outer islands of the 'Javanese imperialism' that they warned would be instituted by the independent Republic. Through these Dutch attempts to shore up their power, federalism was discredited to such an extent that in the early years of the newly independent state the concept was no longer politically viable and advocacy of such a system was frequently viewed as tantamount to treason.[3] It was shared opposition to these Dutch tactics that led the United States of Indonesia, established under the Round Table Agreements, to be replaced by the unitary Republic. But in incorporating the federal states into the new unitary state, the Republic did promise to implement considerable decentralisation (Maryanov 1958:2). And it was on this rather ambiguous ground of a promised decentralised unitary state that Indonesia's initial efforts at state development were constructed.

During the early 1950s, as the new government struggled to establish a unitary state and a parliamentary democracy, the strength of regionalist and occasionally even separatist tendencies began to exert pressure on the central government, so that it became imperative that measures be taken to relieve the discontent.

By 1956 memories of the Dutch misuse of the federal system had largely

---

1. The precise location of this base level in the administrative structure varied in different parts of the archipelago — in directly ruled areas being either at the district (*kecamatan*) or sometimes at the village (*desa*) level, while under indirect rule, it stopped at the level of the 'self-governing' state. (Ibid:22-24)

2. The traditional aristocracies formed parallel structures in a few scattered indirectly ruled outer island areas, but they were unable to play important national roles because of their essentially localistic nature. On these aristocracies, see Magenda (1989).

3. These feelings were exacerbated in the early months after the transfer of sovereignty by the roles played in opposition movements to the Republic by the ex-KNIL captain, Raymond 'Turk' Westerling in West Java and his ties with West Kalimantan's major supporter of federalism, Sultan Hamid of Pontianak. See Feith (1962:61-63). On the subsequent Andi Aziz affair in South Sulawesi and the separatist movement in the Moluccas, see Feith 1962:65-71.

been overtaken by dismay at the subsequent political and economic disarray which led to both the unitary state and parliamentary democracy being equally discredited. There was widespread regional resentment at the preponderance of the country's foreign exchange being channelled to Java, while nearly three-fourths of this income was being earned from the natural resources of the other islands. In the political field these economic grievances were matched by anger at the corruption on the Jakarta scene and resentment at the shifting of much local authority to the centre, exacerbated by Jakarta's insistence on appointing civilian provincial heads rather than their being elected by the people they served.

In the early years of Indonesian independence it was at the provincial level that the centre's exercise of authority came up against local demands for greater representation in decision making regarding the powers of both the *kepala daerah* and the local representative council. Under the original regional Law No. 22 of 1948 and the subsequent laws passed in 1950 setting up the provinces on Java and Sumatra, it was specifically provided that the autonomous regions:

> ...must, as an absolute condition have a democratic organisation in which power must be in the hands of the people of the region....The highest instruments of authority must be held by a Regional Representative Council the organisation of which must be determined by election.
> (Maryanov 1958:70)

But no elections were held for the regional councils, which either came into existence on an ad hoc and provisional basis or were appointed by the central government. The lack of elected regional bodies constituted one of the major grievances of the regions during the early 1950s.

Of the loci of provincial authority, the position of the *kepala daerah* was pivotal, for he stood at the margin of central and regional authority and could perceive his role either primarily to represent the people of the region or as that of an administrator responsible for carrying out the policies determined at the centre. In the early years of independence, Jakarta made sure that the provincial head performed the latter function. Jakarta assumed the right to appoint provincial heads, and the appointments were usually made from the *pamong praja*, and frequently not from the regions to which they were appointed.

In retrospect, what especially distinguished the potency of the regional dissidence in the mid-1950s from that of any subsequent period, however, was not its strength or justification but rather the fact that it preceded the imposition of a centralised army structure on Indonesia. In these early years of independence there was considerable identity of interests between the civilian opponents of the centre in the dissatisfied regions and their military counterparts, many of whom were still stationed in their home areas where they had fought in the anti-Dutch struggle. In confronting the central government, the civil-miliary alliance in the regions thus possessed significant power and posed a real threat to Jakarta's dominance. At the same time, in the regions as in the centre, the memory of Republican leadership of the Revolution was still sufficiently strong, Sukarno and Hatta still commanded enough widespread allegiance, and the ideals of the nationalist movement over the preceding decades were still potent enough to offset tendencies toward secession in even the most disaffected regions. With such a balance between centripetal and centrifugal tendencies, Indonesia's political situation seemed ripe for some form of decentralised or even federal government where regional aspirations were recognised. When in 1956 the Constituent Assembly, whose members had been chosen in popular elections the previous December, began its deliberations on a permanent constitution to replace the existing one, it seemed likely that the new instrument would have provision for some real measures of regional autonomy.

A new decentralisation Law, No.1/1957, was passed which strengthened the provisions of the laws already on the books. As Feith described the law, it 'greatly increased the power of elected legislative councils in the provinces, regencies, and municipalities and provided for the gradual elimination of *pamong pradja* from territorial jurisdiction,' (1962:552) and it incorporated one major change of emphasis from the previous laws governing relations between the regions and the centre. The earlier laws enumerated the fields in which the regions had authority, and all residual powers were left with the central government. In the new law, it was proposed that matters within the purview of the central government would include foreign affairs, defence, currency etc. (Maryanov 1958:56-57) with residual responsibilities in effect left with the regions. These provisions, however, were never implemented.

That no real devolution of power ever actually took place can in large part be traced to the course and defeat of the regional rebellions. Although in the immediate aftermath of the proclamation of the regional councils in Sumatra and Sulawesi in December 1956 and March 1957, an attempt was begun to put the new decentralisation law into effect, this effort was stymied by the policies pursued by the rebel leaders. The rebels' decision to challenge the Sukarno government directly rather than use their leverage to bargain with and gain concessions from Jakarta, gave the centre justification and support in moving militarily against the regional dissidents. So, not only did the rebels fail in their goal of gaining greater autonomy from Jakarta, they were also discredited by their open confrontation of the central government, by their formation of a competing government, and by their reliance on and ties to foreign powers. Forced to confront what had become a threat to the very existence of the Indonesian state, Jakarta had the excuse to impose martial law and strengthen and centralise its military structure, and ultimately impose through force a centralised unitary state.

Sorting out cause and effect between the actions of the rebels and Sukarno's moves toward Guided Democracy is not easy. They acted on each other in tandem, with Guided Democracy raising fears and spectres in the regions, while the increasingly defiant actions of the regional leaders speeded the march toward the centre's monopolisation of power.

But it was not merely the regional rebellions that gave the initial impetus to the development of a centralised state imposed through an increasingly unified and hierarchical military structure. The increasing frenzy of the campaign for West Irian added a further cause and slogan for pursuit of unity in confronting a national problem and a hostile outside world.[4] In the wake of the defeat of the regional rebellions, a martial law structure had been set in place in a way which enabled a strong military government to impose conformity on the archipelago. Early in the period of the regional councils, in March 1957, a State of War and Siege had been proclaimed, which strengthened the powers of the central military command over the conduct of the country's affairs (Feith 1962:547-48; Lev 1966:59-70). Military control over the economy was greatly expanded with the take-over of Dutch enterprises at the end of 1957. The fact that it was in large part the centre's military establishment that assumed the responsibility for running the confiscated enterprises, provided an economic base that it, as well as the central government, would be able to use to amass the rewards necessary for winning loyalty and cooperation from the restless regions. But had the regional councils been willing to stop short of open warfare they themselves might have been in a position to develop and retain a substantial portion of these new resources which would have provided them with the economic base for building up truly significant autonomy in much of the archipelago within a reasonably loose federal structure.

During the spring of 1959, as a direct result of the regional challenge, Sukarno initiated moves to concentrate executive powers in the hands of the President and his hand-picked advisory councils. On July 5, 1959, he issued a decree dissolving the Constituent Assembly and reintroducing the 1945 Constitution, making Presidential Decrees legitimate sources of power on a par with laws, and severely restricting the power of parliament.[5] It also revoked the provisions of Law No. 1 of 1957 allowing for the election of the governor, who now was to be again appointed by the central government (MacAndrews 1986:38). At the end of 1959, on December 16, Emergency Martial Law was declared, placing the entire area of Indonesia in a state of war, and combining supreme executive and legislative power in the hands of the Supreme Commander of the Armed Forces, the President.

The competition for power between the President and the military ended with the October 1965 coup and the purge which followed it. The advent of President Suharto and the domination of the military over the government meant that the centre eventually was able to develop the force necessary to destroy any real opposition potential in the regions and undercut any threats posed by movements for regional autonomy. The first steps were taken in

---

4. Thus, Soedjatmoko reported that at the end of 1956, Sukarno said to him: 'We need Irian, because we need to have a common enemy in order to unite the country.... With the Irian issue I can reunite the Army and the youth.' Interview with GK, Spring 1959.

5. On the return to the 1945 Constitution, see Lev (1966:277-79) and A.H. Nasution 1984:305-6)

1969 when there was a major structural reorganisation of the Armed Forces, centralising control within the Department of Defence and Security and creating a new system of regional commands that ensured greater subordination to the centre. Through the Army's territorial structure, which corresponded to the various levels of the civilian bureaucracy, the regime was able to exert political pressure at every level of society, enabling the Army not only to exercise its military functions but also to monitor and largely control political and social developments.[6] The concept of the Army's dual function, or *dwifungsi*, originally developed by General Nasution in the 1950s, was much expanded under Suharto's New Order. This doctrine asserted not only the Army's right but its duty to participate as a 'social-political force' throughout the society with its commanding role legitimised in the civilian as well as military arena.

To prevent the warlordism of the 1950s from re-emerging in the regions, Army headquarters saw to it that throughout the 1970s no territorial command outside Java was held by a native son, and that Javanese dominated all top echelons of the Army hierarchy.[7] The discovery of massive oil and natural gas resources particularly in Sumatra and Kalimantan, and the willingness of foreign governments to pump huge amounts of support to the Suharto regime through the IGGI and the World Bank, also provided the central government with the powers and rewards it could exploit to ensure loyalty throughout the archipelago.

I just wish to touch briefly on the present situation. Any possibilities for either a federal structure or institution of any real degree of regional autonomy seem to have disappeared over the last 20 years. This is not only because the military has succeeded in centralising its control to an extent never dreamed of in the 1950s or early 1960s, but also because the administrative authority of the central government permeates the society to an extent that would have seemed impossible in earlier decades. Initially the law passed in 1974 on the 'Principles of Regional Government Administration' laid the groundwork for tightening central control over regional administrations (Amal 1990). Then, during the 1980s, this central control was institutionalised right down to the village level through the local administration law (Law No. 5) of 1979, which aimed to standardise village administrative structure throughout Indonesia. The law established a uniform function and name (*desa*) for the lowest unit of the administration, and specified its internal organisation, functioning and prerogatives, patterning the whole structure on the Javanese model of village government.[8] The

---

6. For a table of the parallel military and civilian bureaucracies and their interaction, see Jenkins (1984:46).

7. See Current Data (1978:161) and (1980:157), which show that Javanese constituted between 74 and 80% of the listed military office holders during this period.

8. For the law's implementation in the province of Riau, see Kato (1989) and for some of its implications in West Sumatra, see Ambler (1988).

implementation of this law has led to a massive increase in the number of villages particularly outside Java. (While between 1974 and 1986 the number of villages on Java increased from 22,638 to 25,849, those outside Java jumped from 27,463 to 42,100) (Kato 1989:90 Table 1). The smaller standardised village unit has given the central government much greater control, particularly as the village head, previously elected, was replaced under this law by a civil servant appointed by the governor, and election procedures for other village officials are controlled from higher up the administrative hierarchy (MacAndrews 1986:39).[9]

With the need to abolish traditional village structures in order to introduce the standardised *desa*, many sources of revenue prescribed under local custom and law became inoperative. As a result, according to Kato (1989:108) 'The desa, especially outside Java, are now more or less completely dependent on government funds, above all desa development subsidies, for their revenues.' And integration of the village within the state structure has been increased by the fact that all village officials, like their counterparts higher up the administrative hierarchy, are expected to become members of the Golkar (Kato 1989:108-9; MacAndrews 1986:41).

The chain of authority from the central government, then, now stretches down to the lowest levels of the administration. Over the past decade, however, there have been indications that at least some elements in the central government have come to realise both the social and the economic disadvantages of the degree of centralisation that the Jakarta government has imposed upon the archipelago. The local administration law has led to growing friction and inefficiency in several regions outside Java (see e.g. Ambler 1988:73-76), and in fiscal matters, the disadvantages of overcentralisation also became clear in the mid-1980s. According to Anne Booth:

> With the fall in oil revenues, in money terms, in 1984/5 and the decline expected to continue in the balance of the *Repelita IV* period [1984/85-1988/89], there is a pressing need, already widely recognised by the government planners, both to increase non-oil government revenues and to reduce the degree of regional fiscal dependency on the centre....These objectives can only be achieved by encouraging both provinces and sub-provincial levels of government to increase their revenue effort. (Booth 1986:96)

Furthermore, the need for more regional economic development, particularly in the private sector, has come up against the inability of either the political or physical infrastructure in many parts of the archipelago to provide effective support for such development. And in view of the undeveloped physical and administrative infrastructure, most foreign firms

---

9. According to MacAndrews, the official appointed to the position of village head 'represents the government in the administration of the village. However, a new position, that of *kepala desa* was created. He is elected by the villagers and takes an active part in village affairs although he lacks the traditional authority of the *lurah*.' Ibid.

are reluctant to locate in the outer areas.

Even if, despite the problem of inadequate infrastructure, private firms are willing to locate in areas outside Java, the regions involved are unable to ensure that their people share in the rewards brought by these new enterprises. In Aceh, East Kalimantan, and Riau, for example, the location of large industries in the region has led to the emergence of 'enclave' centres, cut off from the surrounding society and not benefiting but in fact detracting from the well-being of that society.[10] In order for the introduction of private capital investments into the regions to lead to more equity for the local people, the regional governments need to be in a position to exert independent pressure on the outside entrepreneurs. But for the regional governments to play such a role demands their having the power and authority to negotiate terms on behalf of their regions in attracting foreign investment — a far cry from the present situation.

As noted above, there have been indications that elements in the central government recognise the need for some decentralisation in the interests of Indonesia's overall development. It seems unlikely, however, that in the near term this recognition will lead to any reversal of the trends of the past 30 years away from any real devolution of power to the regions. Moves toward granting such a devolution are almost sure to be still contested in the interests of what is perceived as, or rationalised as, greater political stability.

At the same time, chances of any widespread and potent general demands for greater autonomy coming from the regions themselves would seem to be precluded by a number of factors: 1) the efficiency of the central government's control mechanisms; 2) cooptation of so many local elements that could otherwise have provided focus and leadership for disaffection;[11] 3) growing lack of ethnic homogeneity in some of the more uneasy regions, in part because of transmigration programs;[12] and 4) the displacement of any regional authorities which previously exercised power in accord with local traditions and institutions, by an all-embracing hierarchical bureaucratic structure of government. This has led to a situation where local organisations and leaders look upwards and outwards for their rewards and futures rather than to the people of their own regions.

Nevertheless, the government is beginning to face a similar problem to that

---

10. This situation is most stark in Aceh. See Dawood and Sjafrizal 1989:122. For an excellent treatment of the effects of these enclaves on the surrounding society in Aceh and how they have fuelled the dissension there, see Kell (1992:10-16,34-39).

11. A notable example of this cooptation are the ulama in Aceh, see Kell (1992:25)

12. The most quoted case in this connection is that of Irian Jaya. Between 1964 and 1986, 100,048 transmigrants had been settled in Irian Jaya. The target number of transmigrants for Repelita IV was originally 138,000 families (or about 700,000 people), but by 1986 the government had had to rethink the plans and had scaled down its target. The probable number for this period was expected to be about a quarter of the original target. For a sympathetic treatment of the government's program see Manning and Rumbiak (1989:97-104).

of the 1950s in that, by choosing to keep all the levers of power in the centre's hands, it is both undermining the future potential of development of the archipelago and creating further seeds of regional dissatisfaction. Although some of Jakarta's more realistic economic planners can see the need for local bodies to have more freedom to develop their regional economies, such a loosening of control cannot be realised without the central government being willing to grant the local authorities a more powerful voice in the way their regions are governed. In the eyes of Jakarta, the risks of such a course, would seem to far exceed the benefits, and any moves toward administrative or economic decentralisation are likely to be within the context of strong central control.

The possibility of compromise on these issues appears remote, for the present governmental structure as it has developed over the past few decades lacks the flexibility to respond to legitimate regional grievances except through force. Given the strength and all-embracing character of the Suharto regime's control throughout Indonesia it is difficult to believe that any regional disaffection resulting from government policies insensitive to local traditions and needs will lead to anything more than sporadic outbursts of violence in isolated areas, at least for several years to come.

References

Amal, Ichlasul (1990) 'Otonomi Tingkat Dua,' *Editor* September 1, 1990.

Ambler, J.S. (1988) 'Historical Perspectives on Sawah Cultivation and the Political and Economic Context for Irrigation in West Sumatra,' *Indonesia* 46 (October 1988)

Booth, A. (1986) Efforts to Decentralise Fiscal Policy: Problems of Taxable Capacity, Tax Effort and Revenue Sharing, in C. MacAndrews (ed) *Central Government and Local Development in Indonesia*, Oxford University Press, Singapore.

'Current Data on the Indonesian Military Elite' (1980) prepared by the editors of *Indonesia* No. 29 (April 1980)

'Current Data on the Indonesian Military Elite' (1978) prepared by the editors of *Indonesia* No. 26 (October 1978)

Dawood, D. and Sjafrizal (1989) Aceh. The LNG Boom and Enclave Development, in H. Hill (ed) *Unity and Diversity: Regional Economic Development in Indonesia since 1970*, Oxford University Press, Singapore.

Feith, H. (1962) *Decline of Constitutional Democracy in Indonesia*, Cornell University Press: Ithaca.

Jenkins, D. (1984) *Suharto and His Generals*, Cornell Modern Indonesia Project, Ithaca.

Kato, Tsuyoshi (1989) 'Different Fields, Similar Locusts: Adat communities and the Village Law of 1979 in Indonesia', *Indonesia* 47 (April 1989)

Kell, T. (1992) *The Roots of Acehnese Rebellion, 1989-1992*, MA dissertation, Centre for South-East Asian Studies, University of Hull.

Legge, J.D. (1961) *Central Authority and Regional Autonomy in Indonesia: A Study in Local Administration 1950-1960*, Cornell University Press, Ithaca.

Lev, D.S. (1966) *The Transition to Guided Democracy: Indonesian Politics, 1957-1959*, Cornell Modern Indonesia Project, Ithaca.

MacAndrews, C. (1986) The Structure of Government in Indonesia, in C. MacAndrews (ed) *Central Government and Local Development in Indonesia*, Oxford University Press, Singapore.

Magenda, B. (1989) *The Surviving Aristocracy in Indonesia: Politics in Three Provinces of the Outer Islands*, PhD. dissertation, Cornell University.

Manning, C. and Michael Rumbiak (1989) Irian Jaya: Economic Change, Migrants, and Indigenous Welfare, in H. Hill (ed) *Unity and Diversity: Regional Economic Development in Indonesia since 1970*, Oxford University Press, Singapore.

Maryanov, G.S. (1958) *Decentralisation in Indonesia as a Political Problem*, Cornell Modern Indonesia Project, Ithaca.

Nasution, A.H. (1984) *Memenuhi Panggilan Tugas, Jilid 4: Masa Pancaroba Kedua* Gunung Agung, Jakarta.

21

The Dilemmas of Decentralisation and Democratisation

Ichlasul Amal

The dilemma of decentralisation and democratisation is one which confronts Indonesia in common with many other countries. One important reason for this is that almost all developing countries have faced the problem of nation building and development. While nation building requires a degree of centralisation, development requires community participation and supervision. The way in which local interests can increase their political strength locally is to work through national institutions to alter the territorial distribution of power. National decision-makers meanwhile seek to use local elites to control lower levels of government, whether it be for progressive or regressive redistribution. The development of decentralisation in Indonesia reflects these tendencies which manifest themselves in the emergence of regionalism on the one hand and, on the other, bureaucratisation which provides the central government with virtually unlimited authority to interfere in and supervise almost all development policies and local politics in the regions.

Starting from the colonial inheritance within the structure and bureaucracy of the independent Republic this paper tries to explain the New Order's changing political formats, its policy on decentralisation and their relation to the degree and the future course of democracy in Indonesia.

The historical background of the dilemmas

Formally, Indonesia became a united territory in the first decade of this century after the Dutch colonial government succeeded in ending the Aceh war in 1904. Thereafter, all of the occupied territory outside of Java, except for several districts in Sumatra, were incorporated in the Netherlands East

Indies (NEI). Most of the newly acquired areas, however, continued under a government system known as 'indirect rule'. This system, basically, appeared to allow a measure of decentralisation in the administration of the outlying areas, in that the areas under the rule of certain sovereigns (i.e. small kingdoms, especially in eastern Indonesia) were allowed to retain their traditional feudal government systems and to continue their trade system as long as they did not interfere with the trade activities imposed by the colonial government. The primary requirement of local sovereigns under this indirect rule system was their unconditional loyalty to the colonial government in Jakarta.

The decentralisation experience of the colonial period had its legacy in the period immediately after World War II. The small, traditional, feudal kingdoms which were under the indirect rule of the colonial government were inclined to oppose absorption into a unitary Republic of Indonesia because it brought into question their continued existence and threatened the autonomy of local traditions and cultures. On the other hand, the central administration viewed efforts to encourage the aspirations for decentralisation as providing an opportunity to centrifugal forces, that could potentially endanger the unity of the Indonesian nation. In spite of its policies of indirect rule, the colonial government had never administered a genuinely decentralised system, and because of that, the Indonesian government did not inherit the institutions or techniques for decentralised government. On the contrary, the traditional system of the colonial civil service, and its very centralistic bureaucratic spirit, became rooted in the Indonesian government which replaced the colonial Dutch administration.

Regionalism and decentralisation in the 1950s

In the early days of the newly united nation the dominant parties (especially Masyumi and PNI) apparently depended heavily on bureaucratic organs inherited from the colonial administration, such as the territorial civil service (*pamong praja*). The civil service became an instrument for, as well as the object of, a struggle for power between parties. An increasingly strong conflict emerged between Masyumi (the party whose basis of primary support lay outside Java), which did not receive much support from the civil service corps, and the PNI, whose leadership had cultural affinities with Javanese aristocrats and which developed a close relationship with the civil service.

After the elections of 1955 the politics of decentralisation and democratisation flared up with the enactment of law No.1/1957, which concerned regional autonomy. This act, inspired by parties representing regional interests, aimed to paralyse the centralising tendency of the civil service corps, which was considered to be an instrument of the central administration in the districts, and to replace it with political parties. According to this law, the position of *bupati* (district head) was to become an elected position and would thus belong to the parties and no longer be held by the civil service corps. However, the era of glory for the political parties known as the 'liberal democracy' period ended with the Presidential Decree that announced a return to the 1945 Constitution and the introduction of Guided Democracy, and the parliamentary system with party supremacy was replaced by a presidential system in which President Sukarno, supported by the military, became the central figure of politics.

The struggle for a more decentralised system of government in the 1950s, therefore, was intricately intertwined with party politics and regional feeling both of which encouraged and enhanced regional movements in many areas — in western Sumatra and northern Sulawesi as well as in Aceh and south Sulawesi. In western Sumatra and northern Sulawesi the PRRI and the Permesta movements were attempting to change the balance of political forces at the centre, thus reflecting the interests of Masyumi and the PSI, two political parties whose influence had declined after the 1955 elections. In the case of Darul Islam in Aceh and South Sulawesi the goal was not to topple the Jakarta government but to secure greater recognition of these regions themselves. In such a political condition, efforts to decentralise the political system were mainly aimed at satisfying regional feeling and appeasing political dissatisfaction rather than creating an efficient territorial administration.

Decentralisation and regionalism in the New Order

The New Order government that replaced Sukarno's Guided Democracy after the abortive coup of 1965 was a military dominated regime which faced three immediate problems: to strengthen its position as against Sukarno's supporters in the military forces, political parties and government bureaucracy, to decide on a political format for the New Order, and to engineer a recovery from the economic decay inherited from the previous regime. Efforts to overcome these problems led it to a situation of increasing centralisation and bureaucratisation (Feith 1968; Crouch 1978:221-72; Sundhaussen 1989).

The first problem was more or less resolved when, in 1968, Suharto was elected as full president by the MPRS (*Majelis Permusyawaratan Rakyat Sementara*, Provisional People's Consultative Assembly). However, the cost was the increasing domination of the military in politics. The Special Operations Command for the Restoration of Security and Order (KOPKAMTIB) was a very powerful and effective instrument in the hands of the President to suppress all political rivals of the President and the New Order groups. The second problem related to the quest of legitimacy for President Suharto. The MPRS decision of 1966 stated that the government should hold elections in 1968. After fierce public debates on an election bill (a debate, amongst other things, about whether it should establish a district or proportional system), the government finally chose a proportional system modified to limit the number of parties and to allow parties to propose candidates for parliament representing (though only nominally) regions. In

1969, anticipating the general election that would be held in 1971. The government decided to turn the 'functional groups' organisation Golkar into, in effect, a government party side by side with other political parties. Golkar was backboned by two essential elements of the New Order government, i.e. the military and government bureaucracy. It was predictable, therefore, that it should achieve a landslide victory winning 62.8 percent of the votes. This victory not only enhanced President Suharto's legitimacy but also it had involved civil servants directly in politics. The economic rehabilitation which was worked out through foreign aid and investment, and through the oil boom of the early 1970s aimed to resolve the third problem, and achieved some impressive results. Within a few years the spiralling inflation had been curbed successfully. But, this economic miracle brought also a negative political consequence: that the central government gained control over almost all fields of life. Politics as the commander was replaced by economics as the commander, and mass mobilisation on party foundations was slowly pushed aside by a dominating bureaucratic network which controlled all aspects of life and by policies which were technocratic and elitist. If the source of development funds comes from the 'sky' (foreign loans and oil revenue) and not from extraction from the society's economic activities and resources then it is not surprising that development management should be determined entirely at the top level of government.

The political infrastructure that was formed during the New Order was thus one that required a high degree of centralisation. The technocrats and the military, the two primary forces which emerged from the political competition of 1965 and which held the main reins of government policy, formed an association of political forces which were complementary and mutually sustaining. Neither, however, had grassroots support. Such political infrastructure created the impression that the central government would never give an opportunity to the public to take its own independent initiative because all such policies would benefit political parties that had more emotional ties to the community and this would loosen the political reins that the central government or bureaucracy held over the community. This impression was strengthened by the launching of a number of development projects that were formally intended to raise community initiative and participation or, in other words, projects that were formally decentralised, but in actuality, still concentrated the power in the centre. This issue of decentralisation apparently was limited only to the distribution of funds to the regions and, indeed, never touched the problem of 'power sharing' as the requirement for a democratic development process in the regions — either between the central and regional governments or between the bureaucracy and the community.

Following the 1971 election victory, the government moved to reduce further the capacity of parties to play independent roles. One initiative was a measure to pressure the nine non-government parties to group themselves into two blocks. In 1973 the Unity Development Party (PPP) was formed from the four existing Islamic parties and the Indonesian Democratic Party (PDI) from the other five parties. Thereafter, the parties in the legislative bodies largely functioned as legitimators of government decisions.

Prior to this party reorganisation, the government also encouraged public discussion of the concept of a 'floating mass'. Popularised by leaders of Golkar and the Army this idea was geared to the government's 'modernisation and development' goal. The bulk of the population, it was argued, especially the villagers, should 'float' in relation to political parties. Therefore, party branches below the *kabupaten* (district) level should be closed down. Villagers' political preferences should be expressed only through elections every five years. Between elections they should not be disturbed by politics or agitation.

The 'floating mass' idea ensured that hierarchical command of the New Order government would reach into the village without party interference. It also removed the basis of the parties' political support at the village level.

People's resentment was largely channelled through student demonstrations, and this proved the ineffectiveness of parties as articulators of political demands as well as the capacity of the government to neutralise challenges by cooptation and suppression. The government, however, remained committed to a democratic veneer which would legitimate its dominant position. The 1977, 1982 and 1987 elections were intended to preserve this democratic fiction and the results were in most respects similar to the election of 1971. And though, constitutionally, the DPR, the national parliament, had the power to supervise government policy, its composition, dominated by Golkar and military representatives, prevented any significant confrontation with the government. Critics of the situation have described the DPR in terms of the four D's: *datang* (attend), *duduk* (sit-down), *diam* (be silent) and *duit* (collect money/honoraria).

At the lower levels, both province and district or municipality, the political position of the DPRD (*Dewan Perwakilan Rakyat Daerah*, Regional People's Representative Council) vis-a-vis the local executive was even more peripheral. According to the Law No.5/1974, which became the foundation of the New Order's regional government system and supposedly the foundation of widespread and responsible 'regional autonomy', DPRDs are part of the provincial and district local government system. Provincial and district governments are headed, respectively, by a governor or *bupati/walikota*. As the heads of local governments these represent local interests but at the same time they represent the authority of the President (central government) in their own territorial jurisdictions. Each DPRD, therefore, though it is chaired by a person elected from its own members, is indirectly under the supervision of the governor or *bupati*. This is even more true if the membership of the DPRD is dominated by Golkar and the appointed military members, which is almost always the case.

The law No.5/1974 granted a degree of decentralisation, but, as can be seen from the regulations concerning the nomination of the local government head, the budget system, the power relation between the DPRD and government bureaucracy and the reduction of DPRD authority in general, it was extremely limited. Actually, there were two meanings of decentralisation: administrative decentralisation and political decentralisation. Administrative decentralisation was generally termed 'deconcentration' and had the notion of delegation of a portion of the authority for program implementation to the lower levels. Local officials operated only on the plans and budgets that had been determined by the central authorities. Meanwhile, political decentralisation or devolution meant that a portion of the decision-making authority and control of revenue sources was delegated to regional or local governments. The element of decentralisation of the Law No.5/1974 fell into the first meaning (administrative decentralisation), and much of the regional governments' power and authority was limited by the designation of the Department of the Interior as determiner of what could and could not be executed by the regional administrations. In practice, the government's decentralisation policies were limited by an administrative system which gave more opportunities and power to the central government organs (Morfit 1986:57-58).

As far as the Law No.5/1974 is concerned, it is certain that the political environment for decentralisation and regional autonomy created by the law prevented the emergence of any genuine regional initiative in politics as well as in the local government administrative system. Yet, the New Order government was not only able to control the regions better, but was also able to inspire greater loyalty in comparison with previous governments. During the New Order period, the only major secessionist revolts against state authority were the *Gerakan Aceh Merdeka* (Independent Aceh Movement) in northern Sumatra, the East-Timorese movement and the smaller *Gerakan Papua Merdeka* in Irian Jaya. The former was a really separatist movement which, contrary to the Darul Islam movement of the 1950s, proclaimed Aceh as an independent state separated from Indonesia. The last two were also separatist movements but the underlying background was completely different, especially as East Timor 'did not belong to the Indonesian nation as it came to be "imagined" during the anti Dutch colonial struggle' (Thompson 1992:18). *Gerakan Aceh Merdeka* was a problem of horizontal or territorial integration, while the movements in East Timor and in Irian Jaya were responses to vertical or political integration (Sjamsuddin 1989:70-90). Regardless of the political background of the movements, the military, in accordance with its claim to be the guardian of national unity and stability harshly suppressed those regional movements.

In general, in the New Order period, regional demands have been absorbed and neutralised by the bureaucratic authority of the government. At times of succession of a governorship, regional feeling has expressed itself in the demand that the governor should be a *putera daerah* (native son). For provinces where the degree of ethnicity and cohesiveness were very high, such a demand has been a common pattern since the 1950s, but as far as appointments were concerned the government has retained control and either the ethnic background of appointees was Javanese, or military officers were appointed. Though the cry for *putera daerah* continued to be heard it was accepted that appointments should be in harmony with the interests of the centre.

There is thus a tendency for greater centralisation in the government process and it is the New Order government which, by bringing effective state power to bear throughout Indonesia, makes it possible for the new form of regional feeling and identity to fit comfortably within a united Indonesia.

Prospects for decentralisation and democratisation

Lacking the power to suppress rebellion, and lacking the authority to govern, are common criticisms of democracy among many power holders and government officials in Indonesia today. They use the 1950s liberal democracy as the example and proof of the inability of the system to govern the country. According to them, it failed to create political stability and succumbed to internal division created by the parties' ideological competition and struggles for power. And above all it has been officially considered as the main cause of the social and political fragmentation which came close to disrupting the unity of the country. Thanks to the successful massive program of propagating the state ideology, Pancasila and State Policy Guidelines (GBHN, *Garis Besar Haluan Negara*), such an impression has been adopted not only by government officials but also by political elites in the centre as well as in the regions.

If that perception has been dominant among the Indonesian populace, evaluation and prediction of democracy in Indonesia should be based on this local political condition. However, the present era of globalisation, which leaves no country immune to rapid economic change and political development, has brought also new ideas and political attitudes. Almost all cabinet ministers, including the President himself, followed by high-ranking bureaucrats, on many occasions express their support for *keterbukaan* (openness) in the implementation of government programs. In fact, there are many government policies that indicate that this concern is genuine. Government control and censorship of the press, public speeches and even demonstrations have been loosened; discussion on democracy and democratisation itself, especially among intellectuals and academics, is frequently promoted by elements of the government bureaucracy; the Armed Forces confined themselves to a non-partisan role during the 1992 election campaign and, most importantly, public debates have been allowed about the limitation of presidential incumbency (whether it should be limited to two terms or have no limitation at all, but depend entirely on the decision of the MPR) and about the national leadership succession. Even some regional feelings may now be expressed openly. This could be seen in the nomination process conducted by the DPRDs for the appointment of new governors in the provinces of West Sumatra, Southeast Sulawesi, Maluku and East Timor in which the central government seems to have given greater scope for manoeuvre to local political forces in choosing their own candidates. Though the final decision remains in the hands of the president, the process is quite different from the former pattern in which the candidate for governor was 'dropped' from the centre. These are only a few indications of the government's concerns about *keterbukaan*, the implications of which have encouraged people to think about the future of democracy in Indonesia.

One may detect here two streams of thinking: the optimists and pessimists. The optimists believe that those indications of *keterbukaan* will snowball and affect many political institutions such as the DPR, the political parties and Golkar and the political behaviour of the bureaucracy in general. This process, in turn, will bring the political public to demand essential changes in the power structure, from a monolithic to a pluralistic system which means that there will be something of a devolution of power to the lower levels and increasing numbers of countervailing forces within the society.

The pessimists, on the other hand, claim that the present *keterbukaan* is no more than a political mirage. The loosening of government control and censorship indicates the existence of intra-elite conflicts in the centre. The conflicts cover a wide range of political issues, such as religion, the civil-military relationship, conglomeration in economic activities and business clientelism, attitudes to ethnic minority business prominence, leadership competition within the Army and the struggle for power to become the next president and vice-president.

Aside from the predictions of optimists and pessimists, decentralisation as one important element of the present *keterbukaan* might be a useful way of considering the future problem of Indonesian democracy. It has been pointed out earlier that the established system of governance contains limited decentralisation. Although President Suharto and the Interior Minister have several times raised the issue of decentralisation within the local government system, the whole idea so far is nothing but deconcentration or bureaucratic decentralisation. The main aim of this policy — unlike political decentralisation which is designed to reflect the unique characteristics, problems and needs of different regions and localities — is to contain the forces of localism and enforce uniformity in decision-making across the country. Deconcentration seems, for the time being, to be an appropriate system since it is especially useful in combining the historical centralistic trend and the decentralising requirements of development. It is also an efficient political instrument to combine a strong central government for the sake of nation-building and a substantial delegation of authority to regions because of the culturally and geographically heterogenous nature of Indonesia. Building real structural foundations for democracy, i.e. decentralisation, needs extra political effort and experiment and the political risk is great. It could incite unhealthy regional competition and even stimulate regional rebellion. As well the elites must fear the return of the intense ideological and social conflict which disrupted the experience of democracy.

Such an understanding leads to a conclusion that the present elites do not want to put their reputation on the line or to make a substantial political change which they think will jeopardise their future political careers. The future of democracy in Indonesia, therefore, will be facing a state of inertia and be stalemated in the position that has been widely accepted up to the present time. The official name of this kind of democracy is Pancasila Democracy.

References

Crouch, H. (1978) *The Army and Politics in Indonesia*, Cornell University Press, Ithaca and London.

Feith, H. (1962) *The Decline of Constitutional Democracy in Indonesia*, Cornell University Press, Ithaca, New York.

_____ (1968) 'Suharto's Search for a Political Format', *Indonesia*, No.6 (October), 1968

Legge, J.D. (1961) *Central Authority and Regional Autonomy in Indonesia: A Study in Local Administration 1950-1965*, Cornell University Press, Ithaca, New York.

Liddle, R.W. (1977) *Cultural and Class Politics in New Order Indonesia*, Research Notes and Discussion Series No.2, ISEAS, Singapore.

Morfit, M. (1986) Strengthening the Capacities of Local Government: Policies and Constraint, in C. MacAndrews (ed) *Central Government and Local Development in Indonesia*, Oxford University Press, Singapore.

Sjamsuddin, Nazaruddin (1989) *Integrasi Politik di Indonesia*, Gramedia, Jakarta.

Smith, B.C. (1985) *Decentralisation, The Territorial Dimension of the State*, George Allen Unwin, London.

Sundhaussen, U. (1989) Indonesia: Past and Present Encounters with Democracy, in L. Diamond, J.J. Linz, and S.M. Lipset (eds) *Democracy in Developing Countries*, Volume 3: Asia, Lynne Riener, Boulder, Colorado.

Thompson, M.R. (1983) 'State and Regime Legitimacy in Southeast Asia' Unpublished Paper, April 1992

Ward, K.E. (1970) *The Foundation of the Partai Muslimin Indonesia*, Modern Indonesia Project, Cornell University Press, Ithaca, New York.

22

Ethnicity in Indonesian Politics

Burhan D. Magenda

Recent events in Yugoslavia and the former Soviet Union have revived a new interest in the study of 'ethnic identity' and, in particular, in the relationship between the state and particular ethnic groups, and in how economic development has strengthened the power of the state vis a vis society. Where the state is identified with particular ethnic groups the problem has been seen as one of 'internal colonialism'.

In relating the processes of state-building and of growing ethnic consciousness in modern societies, recent studies have overcome the shortcomings of earlier ones such as those of Geertz and Wallerstein. The basic premise of both Geertz and Wallerstein was that ethnic identity was a temporary phenomenon. Once national integration and unity had been achieved under the institutions of the modern nation-state such 'primordial sentiments' would automatically disappear, to be replaced by a new loyalty to the civil society. The persistence of ethnic identity in modern states can be seen as the common denominator of the increasing interest of present day social scientists in 'ethnic problems'.

It is the opinion of Enloe (1980) that state-building could be used by some ethnic groups to gain state power over other ethnic groups within the nation-state, supported by particular policies in various fields of government. While her description was mostly drawn from Malaysia's example her analysis could be used as an approach to explaining more generally the complex relationship between state building and the role of ethnicity in Third World countries.

While one cannot deny the inherent disparity of class interests in a world dominated by states, it is fair to say that in most Third World countries the political mobilisation of such interests, especially of the lower classes, has been difficult to achieve. Recent studies have shown that ethnic identity and ethnic consciousness can become potent tools for political mobilisation better known as 'cultural mobilisation'. Modern governments have offered other incentives to displace those of class mobilisation, and if there is no such mobilisation, simple repression is quite common. Hence, the trend toward what O'Donnell (1973) called 'the bureaucratic authoritarian state' or what Feith (1982) called 'repressive developmentalist regimes', in which the processes of economic development and state-building go hand in hand with the suppression of class interests and organised political groups. In states where ethnic structures are more complex, cultural mobilisation based on ethnic identity might be used by the state to prevent mobilisation on the basis of class interests, thereby channelling the forces created by economic development in ways that guarantee, or at least strengthen, the power of the state.

It is in this theoretical analysis that Indonesia forms a unique object of study. The concept of 'internal colonialism' (Hechter 1975; Casanova 1976) cannot be applied to Indonesia because the structures of ethnic groups in Indonesia are more complex than in Mexico or in Celtic communities, where the relationship of ethnic groups is always dichotomous. Moreover, despite their position of dominance, the Javanese constitute merely the largest of many minority Indonesian ethnic groups, placing them in a unique position to play the role of unifying the ethnic polities — unlike the situation in other countries such as those described by Casanova, Hechter, or in this case, Enloe as well.

The persistence of a strong nationalist ideology can be seen as the constraint which any argument for cultural mobilisation in Indonesia has to take into consideration. Studies on Indonesia in general, have taken nationalism so much for granted that the 'ethnic problems' are rarely touched upon, except in anthropological studies. Benedict Anderson (1983) has drawn attention to the strengthening of the state qua state as reflected, in particular, in the expansion of civil bureaucracy from 250,000 persons in 1940 to 2,500,000 persons in 1968. Similarly Richard Robison (1986) has emphasised the rise of indigenous capitalists under the protection of the state. In these two studies — among others — the role of ethnic groups have been inadequately addressed. The main argument of this paper is to show how a certain class within an ethnic group — the Javanese *priyayi* — has dominated the state apparatus and has formed a complex array of alliances with other groups of Indonesia's 'primordial sentiments', including ethnic accommodation.

Parliamentary Democracy

One important element in studying ethnic groups in Indonesia has been the prominent role that has been played by the elite of any particular ethnic group, namely its aristocracy, especially in the small ethnic groups of the Outer Islands. Even in a homogenous Javanese society, the descendants of *priyayi*, and especially *bupati*s, have continued to play important roles in civilian and military bureaucracies. Therefore, 'ethnic sentiments' were best expressed by the aristocracy of particular ethnic groups.

In his classic study of the Indonesian Revolution, Kahin (1952) has described how the Dutch exploited the local aristocracies in supporting their federal scheme, especially in the Outer Islands. It was the local aristocratic delegates that supported the federal system at the Malino Conference in July, 1946. In some areas, this pro-federal attitude had led to the destruction of aristocratic power by Republican forces, as in the social revolution in East Sumatra and Aceh. But in other areas of the Outer Islands where the Dutch had consolidated their military power, particularly in the eastern part of Indonesia, aristocratic rule was well maintained until 1958. Indonesia of the 1950s could therefore be divided into two areas. Java and many parts of the Outer Islands constituted one system where competition for ethnic leadership was intense between the Republican *pejuang* and the discredited aristocracy (with the main exception of the Sultan Hamengkubuwono IX of Yogyakarta). In most other areas, local aristocracies remained.

Feith's dichotomy between 'administrators' and 'solidarity makers' may look clear enough in Jakarta but less so in the regions where the intensity of inter ethnic conflict had forced many local aristocracies to join political parties and to play the roles of 'solidarity makers' in order to survive. Therefore, Feith's contention that 'the administrators' saw maintenance of support as a secondary matter was not the case in many regions. Many local aristocrats joined the PIR (Greater Indonesian Party) and the PNI precisely because these two parties dominated the Department of Internal Affairs in the early 1950s. Many local aristocrats from the Outer Islands played important roles in the national politics of the 1950s. Important examples were Prof. Hazairin, Minister of Interior from the PIR in the first Ali cabinet, and Ide Anak Agung Gde Agung, Minister of Foreign Affairs in the Burhanuddin Harahap cabinet. The establishment of so many parties in the 1950s had been able to accommodate ethnic groups of the Outer Islands in national politics to the extent that there were demands for 'purification' of national politics from 'the cooperators'.

Feith was right, however, when he acknowledged that there was little development of regional autonomy in the 1949-1957 period. It was a period marked by many 'regional' movements and rebellions, as in South Kalimantan, Aceh, South Sulawesi, West Java and the Moluccas. There were two types of movement against the Central Government and, sometimes interchangeably, against the domination of Javanese officials. The first were the rebellions, mainly backed by Islamic landowners and merchants, in Aceh, South Kalimantan, West Java and South Sulawesi. The real reasons for these were numerous but eventually they took 'the Islamic banner'. They were led by guerilla leaders and because of that local troops found it difficult to fight them. The Central Government then sent troops from divisions in Java which enabled the rebels to arouse anti-Javanese feelings among the local population.

The second type of movement was mobilised by local aristocrats in the

Outer Islands in their competition with the Javanese officials, in both military and civilian bureaucracies. Many local aristocrats in the Outer Islands were considered to be 'cooperators' in the Dutch-created federation and were not considered for high positions such as that of Governor. Those who were on the Republican side were seen as not having enough experience and credentials for the job. The overall effect was the appointment by the Central Government of administrators from outside the regions, most of whom were Javanese and Minangkabau, creating the demand for the appointment of 'native sons' (*putera daerah*). Examples were the removal of Colonel Gatot Subroto by Colonel Warouw as *Panglima* of Wirabuana in Sulawesi after the October 17th 1952 Affair and the demonstrations against Governors Murdjadi in Banjarmasin and Sudiro in Makassar.

Another problem related to the lack of regional autonomy was the resistance of various *Panglima* to the financial and political power of the Central Government, leading to the PRRI/Permesta rebellion. Law No. 1/1957 made provision for greatly extended powers of local government, and planned to abolish the *Pamong Praja* corps but the Army gave strong support for its continued existence, leading to the replacement of the Law No. 1/1957 by Presidential Decree No. 6/1959 which returned to the central government the power to appoint regional heads. Hence, the survival of the *Pamong Praja* corps which consisted mainly of people with *priyayi* backgrounds.

The Central Government solved the ethnic and regional problems of the late 1950s with the creation of many new *kabupaten* (districts) and provinces. It fulfilled the demand for greater autonomy from many ethnic groups in the Outer Islands such as in Kalimantan, Nusatenggara, Sulawesi and Sumatra. Many small ethnic groups such as the Gayos, the Niase, the Torajanese, the Tolakis and the Sangirese, were guaranteed their own *kabupaten*. These local governments were mainly staffed by local people as the first graduates from university started to enter the bureaucratic ladder. Most of them were the children of the local aristocrats who constituted more than 70 percent of student population of the Interior Department's college, the APDM (the Academy for Local Government). Hence, by the early 1960s, the local aristocrats had allied themselves with the *Pamong Praja* officials of the Central Government and survived the attacks from the Republican *pejuang* and Islamic landowners and merchants. With the consolidation of the Army in 1959, there was another ally in the corps of Army officers.

The New Order

During the New Order, the creation of a 'bureaucratic polity' has strengthened the power of the *priyayi*-based state. The model *priyayi* was supposed to be superior in character. He was to be a *ksatria* (knight), free from selfish motives in his service to the state, and he was follow a certain spiritual training such as the period of *lara* (pain) and *nyuwita* (apprenticeship). The weakening of political parties has led to the strengthening of the bureaucratic state, under the leadership of *priyayi* officers and officials.

It should be noted that, from the beginning, the Army cadets, like their colleagues in civilian bureaucracy, have been recruited from most ethnic groups in Indonesia . However, the strict examination entrance has benefited mostly students from high schools in Java. Moreover, with the quotas for old strategic Kodams in Java being higher than Kodams in Outer Islands, the end result has been the high percentages of officers from the island of Java. Despite this fact, the Armed Forces hierarchy has recently attempted to balance the ethnic backgrounds of its high commands by giving 'ethnic dividends' to officers of non-Javanese origin. However these officers from the Military Academy, have been socialised politically by the suppression of regional (often Islamic) rebellions and the revolts of the Javanese masses under the PKI leadership in 1964-1966. The end result has been to consolidate the mainstream of *priyayi* traditional doctrine: to lead the masses in traditional ways (that is by their own aristocrats); to ensure the power of the Centre; to suspect Islamic and communist ideologies, partly because of their alien nature, and partly because of their appeal to the masses.

The *priyayi*'s main ally has been the aristocracies of many ethnic groups, especially from the Outer Islands. There have been various ways of achieving such an alliance. Ideologically, both groups are unfriendly to the Islamic groups (which had tried to abolish them in the 1950s), although since 1980s there have been some rapprochement with Islam through the cooperation of Islamic graduates. Hence, the 'bureaucratisation' of Islamic politics since the 1980s.

The main avenue for the alliance has been the political process itself, including the leadership of the government-backed organisation, Golkar, and the power of appointment to such positions as those of *Bupati*, Governor and members of parliament. In most instances, the native sons appointed to those positions were from aristocratic backgrounds, and lately, from Islamic groups.

Hence, it can be concluded that the coalition between the *priyayi* and the aristocrats of many non-Javanese ethnic groups has been consolidated during the period of New Order government in Indonesia. There has emerged something of a middle class among many ethnic groups especially with the increasing urbanisation during the 1970s and the 1980s. However, the ethnic associations in big cities have been led by state employees and are quite different from the anti-*swapraja* movements of the 1950s (under landowners and merchants). It is in this context that one might observe the difficulty of creating a more democratic polity in Indonesia, given the fact that patrimonial leadership has dominated in most of the ethnic groups in Indonesia making reform from above the only feasible way of achieving a gradual democratisation.

References

Anderson, B.R.O'G. (1983) 'Old State, New Society: Indonesia's New Order in Comparative Historical Perspective', *Journal of Asian Studies*, May 1983.

Casanova, F.A. (1976) *New Horizons for the Third World*, Public Affairs Press, Washington.

Enloe, C.H. (1980) *Ethnic Soldiers: State Security in Divided Societies*, Harmondsworth, Penguin, Middlesex.

Feith, H. (1982) 'Repressive-Developmentalist Regimes in Asia', *Alternatives*, (Spring 1982).

Hechter, M. (1975) *Internal colonialism : the Celtic fringe in British national development, 1536-1966*, University of California Press, Berkeley.

Kahin, G.McT., (1952) *Nationalism and Revolution in Indonesia*, Cornell University Press, Ithaca, NY. (Reprinted 1970)

O'Donnell, G. (1973) *Modernization and Bureaucratic-Authoritarianism*, Institute of International Studies, Berkeley.

Robison, R. (1986) *Indonesia: The Rise of Capital*, Allen and Unwin, Sydney.

23

From Lower to Middle Class: Political Activities before and after 1988

Arief Budiman

In 1988, General Benny Moerdani, Commander-in-Chief of the Indonesian Armed Forces, was replaced. Until then he had been the most powerful man in the Indonesian military.

This replacement came quite suddenly, because at that time the MPR was ready to re-elect General Suharto for his fifth term in office. Under normal circumstances Moerdani would have been expected to retain his position until the MPR meeting was over. However, this did not happen and it was obvious that President Suharto did not wish to have Moerdani remain in this top military position during the re-election process.

During the MPR session, several interesting things occurred. J. Naro, the head of the predominantly Muslim PPP was suddenly nominated by his party to run for vice-president. In the New Order political tradition, this was very unusual. Although it did not violate the Constitution, it was unthinkable that somebody would dare to contest President Suharto's will to appoint General Sudharmono as his vice-president. Suharto was quite unhappy about this and in his subsequent autobiography he accused Naro of ignoring the spirit of Pancasila by putting himself forward as a candidate even though he knew he could not win.

It was understood at the time that Naro's action could only have occurred if he had received strong backing by a powerful political group that dared to challenge Suharto. It was assumed that a faction of the military, associated with General Benny Moerdani, was the group responsible.

After this, an interesting 'incident' occurred in the 1988 MPR session. A high military officer, Brigadier General Ibrahim Saleh, suddenly came forward during the plenary session and expressed his disappointment that Sudharmono had been elected vice-president. He was grabbed by other military generals and was taken back to his seat before he could finish saying what he wanted to say.[1] This incident was later reported fully on the front pages of the Indonesian newspapers, which was rather unusual for the tightly controlled Indonesian press.

These events were read by many political observers as reflecting a profound conflict between Suharto and some faction of the military. As usual, this conflict was not expressed openly, but the above indicators point strongly to the existence of a conflict.

Many observers agree that this conflict has continued to the present. It has become an important factor in explaining the political processes after 1988. The democratic space that has been created after 1988 can be explained by this factor and it is worth examining events before and after that date.

Political activities challenging the state before 1988

The many political activities contesting State power before 1988 fall broadly into two groups: those organised by lower classes, and those representing elite or middle class activity.

Lower class political activities

Political movements based on lower class action emerged as socio-economic protests. Among these, we can mention racial/anti-chinese riots in Solo, Semarang, Ujungpandang and Aceh (1980 and 1981), the Imron case (plane hijacking, 1981), the Lapangan Banteng incident (the violent attack against Golkar constituents during the 1982 election campaign), and the Tanjung Priok case (the 1984 demonstration by Muslim people against state economic policies that favoured the Chinese which ended up with the shooting of demonstrators by the military, resulting in many dead and injured).[2] As can be seen, many of these movements were quite violent and were based on religion (Islam) or race (anti-Chinese sentiment).

The government dealt toughly with these movements. Military action was taken and people from both sides were killed.

Middle class political movements

The middle class movements manifested themselves mostly in critical writings, through artistic expression, or through the formation of loyal opposition groups.

---

1. Saleh was later dismissed as member of the MPR, as a punishment. However, this punishment was considered very mild, considering his 'sin' — namely challenging the President's will.

2. I do not include separatist movements in Aceh, Irian Jaya and East Timor. These movements are also lower class based. They are not aimed at democratising the State, however, but at liberating their respective lands in order to become free nations. These movements require separate discussion.

Critical writings appeared again and again in the media. The government was quick to warn publishers by phone. If this did not work, more serious measures were taken. Between 1980 and 1988, several media were banned temporarily or permanently: *Tempo* and *Pelita* in 1982 (temporarily), *Sinar Harapan* in 1986 (permanently, but the government allowed another daily, *Suara Pembaruan*, to be published in its place), and *Prioritas* in 1987 (permanently). Critical comments were also expressed in art, for instance by the poet Rendra who was forbidden to read his poems in public.

The formation of the Petition of Fifty group in 1980, was another example of a middle class movement challenging the State. The Petition of Fifty was more direct and open in criticising the government, while keeping within the bounds of the existing legal system.

However, the government still took strong measures against this group. It banned the civil rights of the Petition of Fifty's members. They were not allowed to leave the country, they could not get bank loans, and newspapers were warned against publishing their political opinions.

*****

Before 1988, then, there were many sporadic socio-political movements challenging the State, ranging from ones using violence, to those which may be described as loyal-opposition groups, and which could express critical ideas expressed in the media or in art. Compared to the post-1988 movements, many of the pre-1988 movements displayed a greater degree of violence. Many were carried out by lower class people, under the Muslim banner, coloured by anti-Chinese attitudes, attacking the State. The post-1988 movements are more middle class based and less violent. In consequence they were more easily controlled by the State.

Political activities after 1988

After 1988, there emerged many political activities by 'opposition' groups that would have been unthinkable before. These included student demonstrations, labour strikes, open exposures in the media of the President's family businesses, more daring campaigns by the PDI during the 1992 elections and the public re-emergence of the Petition of Fifty.[3] The election result whereby Golkar lost 17 seats and PDI gained 16 seats, was also perhaps a sign that people had become more forthright in expressing opposition to Golkar, the government party.

---

3. In 1993, the Petition of Fifty group was not only reported in the press, but they are also able to criticise the State openly (albeit still in very mild terms). Some important members such as Ali Sadikin have been invited again to official state ceremonies. General Nasution was even invited to the palace and had the chance to meet the President.

Lower Class Based Movements

The most important lower class based movement after 1988 was the Lampung incident. In this case, a group of peasants, most of them transmigrants, were gunned down by the military. These peasants, defending their land, were organised under the Muslim banner. They killed one soldier. In retaliation, these peasants were attacked by the military and many of them were killed. This was the only violent incident recorded after 1968.

However, the most frequent lower class based political movements after 1988 have been labour strikes. The number of labour strikes keeps increasing. There were 19 labour strikes in 1989, 61 in 1990, and 110 in 1991. The largest strike was in August 1991, when 12,000 workers marched in the streets of Tangerang (Etty 1992).

In 1990, the union *Serikat Buruh Merdeka Setia Kawan* was established, challenging the government's policy of allowing only one union to exist. The only union endorsed by the government was the SPSI (*Serikat Pekerja Seluruh Indonesia*). Thus, the new union was considered illegal, but no concrete measures were taken against it.

In 1992, during the general election, people rallied in the streets to support non-government parties. Political parties that criticised the government, especially the PDI, received open support from the masses. The result of the election was also quite impressive from the point of view of those who wanted to change the political status quo. Nationally, Golkar lost 17 seats. Of these seats, 16 went to PDI, and one went to PPP, the other non-government party allowed by law.

Post-1988 political activism has not been characterised by violence. There was only one violent movement, still using the Muslim banner.[4] Labour strikes, which have characterised post-1988 political activity by the lower class, have been quite peaceful.

Middle class based movements

The most important political event after 1988 was the founding of ICMI (Indonesian Muslim Intellectuals' Association) in 1990. Supported strongly by President Suharto and the Minister of Research and Technology B.J. Habibie, this organisation has grown rapidly and has become very influential. Many of its members became members of parliament and some became cabinet ministers. A daily newspaper, *Republika*, was founded, an Islamic bank, *Bank Muamalat*, was established, and CIDES, a Muslim body for intellectuals and academicians, started to operate. Very quickly, this middle class Muslim organisation has taken over the dynamic of the Islamic movement in Indonesia.

Before the establishment of ICMI, the case of the tabloid *Monitor*

---

4. Muslim political movements in recent years have been channelled through ICMI, the Indonesian Muslim Intellectuals' Association, which was established in 1990. Since then, the Muslim struggle has been taken into the hands of the Muslim middle class, linked in turn with a powerful faction of the State.

exploded. This magazine, owned by a Catholic press conglomerate, was accused of insulting the Prophet Mohammad. There were demonstrations in several big cities organised by Muslim youth organisations and university students. This tabloid was then closed down by the government, and the chief editor was put in jail.

Another important phenomenon after 1988 has been the increasing number of student demonstrations. Starting in Yogyakarta with a small group, it spread out to other cities including Jakarta. Student demonstrations against the Kedung Ombo dam in Central Java were a notable case. Later, student demonstrations against the visit of the Interior Minister, General Rudini, to the campus of the Bandung Institute of Technology ended in the arrest of some of the student leaders. The last 'radical' student demonstration occurred during the 1993 MPR session re-electing President Suharto for his sixth term of office. The students demanded that Suharto resign. However, the most notable thing was not the demonstration itself, but the fact that none of these students was arrested.

The re-emergence of the Petition of Fifty has to be noted also as one of the most significant political events after 1988. From its pariah status, this group has suddenly become an important political asset to be embraced by the State.

In 1991, a group of intellectuals in Jakarta established *Forum Demokrasi*, headed by the progressive Muslim leader Abdurrahman Wahid. Moving very cautiously, while maintaining its critical stance against the government, this organisation has barely been able to survive in the face of various pressures and obstacles set up by the government. Its fate contrasts sharply with ICMI in this respect.

Last but not least, the 12 November 1991 Dili incident has to be mentioned. The aftermath of this incident has been very important to the domestic political process in Indonesia. For the first time, as a result of the effective campaign by many human rights groups in western Europe and the USA, Indonesia has been under strong pressure to democratise its political system.

In mid 1993, the US government put strong pressure on the Indonesian government to liberalise its labour policies, threatening economic measures which would hit the Indonesian economy quite heavily. Human rights issues have also been raised by the new Democratic administration, resulting in the termination of some military assistance to Indonesia from the US.

*****

It is obvious that, after 1988, the Muslim struggle has changed drastically. From a lower class based movement, it has been transformed into a middle class one. From a movement based outside the State, the Muslim struggle has become a struggle from within the State. It involves less violence, and has become more sophisticated in its political techniques.

The lower class based movements have now been taken over by the industrial workers. Strikes occur more frequently. Some NGOs and student groups have assisted them. Compared to the incidents before 1988, these lower class based political activities have become less violent.

Another important aspect is the presence of more intensive intervention from abroad, but especially by the US, to force the Indonesian government to liberalise and democratise its political system. Human rights have been one of the most important issues.

Discussion and conclusion

1. In 1988, the conflict between President Suharto and a faction of the military emerged into the public arena. No open confrontation has yet occurred, but various political events since then can be better explained if we keep this factor in mind.

2. Prior to 1988, the State elite was relatively unified. Political openness in this period is better called political liberalisation. In this process, the State takes the initiative in providing the democratic space. It is thus the expression of a State confident of its own strength. Elsewhere, I have called this type of 'democracy' *loan democracy* (Budiman 1992). The State is strong, and it allows people to criticise. However, when the State thinks that the criticism has gone too far, this 'democracy' will be stopped. The people are not strong enough to resist.

In this situation, there is little possibility of people taking advantage of factionalism within the political elite. In defending their interests they are therefore quite weak. This was expressed in the weak struggle of the middle class before 1988. At the lower level, common people have to use violence to defend their interests. This reflected the character of 'democracy' in New Order Indonesia before 1988.

3. After 1988, democratic struggle has taken a different form. The middle class seems to have gained more power. This is made possible due to the conflict among the State elites. Some middle class factions have aligned themselves with some factions of the State elites. ICMI is one of the most notable cases. The re-emergence of the Petition of Fifty group is also the result of this type of 'palace politics', which has intensified during the 1993 MPR session.

That conflict has also created more 'democratic' space for some grassroots organisations, such as NGOs, student movements, and labour unions. This 'democratic' process is then strengthened by the foreign human rights campaigns. The Indonesian government has been quite vulnerable to pressure from abroad, especially from the wealthy industrial countries on which Indonesia has been dependent economically.

The process of democratisation after 1988 has thus been the result of a combination of internal and external factors.

4. What can we say about the democratisation process in the near future? It is difficult to talk in black-and-white terms. It is true that the State has been

weakened by the conflicts among the elites which control it. Both the lower and the middle classes are becoming more organised. However, it is still easy to see that the State is still much stronger than the people.

A strong civil society in the Hegelian sense is still in the slow process of being born.

References

Budiman, Arief (1992) Indonesian Politics in the 1990s, in Harold Crouch and Hal Hill (eds) 'Indonesia Assessment 1992: Political Perspectives on the 1990s', Canberra: Department of Political and Social Change, Research School of Pacific Studies, Australian National University.

Etty, Tom (1992): 'Some Problems in the Field of Labor,' Paper presented to the Eighth INGI Conference in Odawara, Japan, 21-23 March 1992.

24

Party and Parliamentary Politics 1987-1993

Michael R.J. Vatikiotis

A paper on party and parliamentary politics in Indonesia raises puzzling questions, since to my knowledge, neither political parties nor a parliament exist in the commonly defined sense in contemporary Indonesia. That is not to say that there is absolutely no trace of either of these intrinsically Western political institutions; nor can we rule out a more familiar manifestation at some point in the future — although this is at best doubtful.

There is a tradition of parliamentary party politics in Indonesia, one comprehensively described by Herb Feith (1962), but for over thirty years it has been emasculated, first by Sukarno's Guided Democracy, and then by the New Order's almost obsessive concerns for order, unity and therefore uniformity. Under the New Order, political parties have either been banned or fused into nebulous 'functional groups'. Parliament (DPR) has become a component of the New Order's all embracing concept of Pancasila Democracy, elected once every five years, but with no power to table legislation, only the duty to pass it.

The roots of Indonesia's democratic imperfections are deep and enduring. Given the diversity of indigenous political cultures in the region it can be argued that democratic pluralism along recognisably Western lines is not necessarily the inevitable destination of Indonesia's development.

It is fashionable nowadays to support predictions of enhanced political pluralism in Southeast Asia by reference to the rise of its middle classes. The image of mobile phone-toting pro-democracy demonstrators in Bangkok last May — though much exaggerated — did much to popularise this notion, which first saw the light of day in this region after the fall of Ferdinand Marcos of the Philippines in 1986. If the same analysts had witnessed the demonstrations that tore through the streets of Jakarta in early 1966, they might well have said the same things. Here too there were students; intellectuals and professionals, breathless with calls for democracy. The difference was that, instead of facing the tanks, the students were riding on them; intellectuals embraced the military because of the relief they brought to the suffocating ideological rigours of Sukarnoism. They were tired of politics, which Sukarno had insisted should command the ongoing Indonesian revolution.

As nascent professionals some of these student activists of the 1966 generation, reflecting on the period, have told me they longed for stability, for a chance to exercise their talents and skills in a normalised environment free of ideological divides. Some now admit they were too willing to trade political freedom for the chance to prosper. Some were less willing, but were later induced to toe the line as much by the economic shelter the new regime offered as by its repressive undertones. For those of non-indigenous or non-Muslim origin, the imposition of order offered a chance to bottle up the centrifugal ethnic and religious tendencies in Indonesian society — another way of ensuring they would prosper.

Reversing Sukarno's 'politics as commander' dogma, therefore, economic development took precedence over political development. The new slogan was 'economics first, politics later'. In other words, the middle classes of Indonesia in the mid-1960s would have confounded today's bourgeois theorists by volunteering to qualify democracy along the lines Lee Kuan Yew was talking about recently in Manila.[1]

This preference for order and security over participation affects contemporary perceptions of that early period of Constitutional Democracy in the 1950s. Even after twenty five years of political sterility very many Indonesian intellectuals view the Constitutional Democracy period as one of interminable political chaos. At the time the parliamentary system was favoured not so much because of a genuine belief in the merits of the system but, as Feith and later Mahasin have pointed out (Feith 1963; Mahasin 1984), as a legitimising vehicle at a period when liberal democracy enjoyed international acclaim. I believe this theme of Democracy and its attendant institutions, perceived in a symbolic legitimising, rather than a fundamental sense, continues to govern the development of modern political institutions.

Against this background, I would like to sketch out the trends in the late 1980s and early 1990s — specifically the 1987-1992 period — as they affected the New Order's political institutions.

The 1988 session of the MPR inaugurated a stormy political cycle for the New Order. Suharto's choice of vice-president for the period 1988-92

---

1. Speaking at the Philippine Business Conference on Democracy and Development held in Manila on 18-20 November, Senior Minister Lee Kuan Yew from Singapore said: 'I believe that what a country needs to develop is discipline more than democracy. The exuberance of democracy leads to undisciplined and disorderly conditions which are inimical to development.'

angered the Armed Forces (ABRI). By choosing Sudharmono, one of the architects of the New Order's bureaucratic and legal frameworks and the powerful chairman of Golkar, Suharto was placing a man who had done much to undermine the military's financial and political power for over a decade technically just a heartbeat away from the presidency.

The MPR session itself broke new ground in Indonesian politics. ABRI's attempts to head Sudharmono off at the pass by engineering an alternative candidate at the last moment, interrupted the carefully choreographed MPR process. It seemed to those of us covering the session that the MPR members were being goaded into playing a role beyond their intended bit parts. In fact, the whole show was very much in the Army's hands, and in the end they lost. Suharto stood his ground despite personal appeals by a group of senior officers, and Sudharmono was duly 'elected' vice-president.

Sudharmono's concurrent role as vice-president and Golkar chairman (until November 1988) set the stage for an ABRI-Golkar struggle which appeared at first to herald a more independent role for the party, but which as we shall see ultimately weakened it. In an effort to undermine Sudharmono, ABRI launched a campaign to regain some of the ground they had lost to his group within the party. Over the past decade, Sudharmono had used his powerful position as State secretary to weaken ABRI's grip over provincial level Golkar chairmanships. At the centre, he had placed civilian cadres in key Golkar positions, and deliberately fostered a clique of progressive politicians willing to question ABRI's role in politics.

Outwardly, the trend was promising. After years of serving essentially as ABRI's political arm, Golkar politicians began to aspire to a more independent role. Sudharmono brought in some of the student leaders of the mid-seventies, men whose experiences had imbued in them resentment of ABRI's political role. However, their power base was weak. Golkar had no grass-roots strength without ABRI, which channelled support for the party through its territorial command system. Suharto's refusal to allow Sudharmono to develop Golkar's fund raising potential by collecting membership dues at the grass-roots level was one alternative denied them. Another obstacle was the weakness of the civilian bureaucracy as an institution; its esprit de corps was undermined by the relative importance of military appointments.

This left the DPR as the only arena in which Sudharmono's nascent civilian clique could play politics. For a while, they were quite effective. The new DPR convened on 1 October 1987 and looked encouragingly fresh. Sudharmono placed his men well in the Golkar faction, which participated more actively in parliamentary commissions, and even dared to question

ABRI or government prerogatives.² In response, ABRI increased the size of its parliamentary faction from 75 to 100 and moved 28 former ABRI faction MPs into the Golkar faction to balance the forces (*FEER*, 15 October 1987:17). The following year, ABRI mounted a spirited campaign to deprive Sudharmono of support at the provincial level by coaxing active officers to contest Golkar positions.

The scramble for control over Golkar created the illusion of enhanced civilian political influence in the party, a development seen as encouraging by those watching for signs of incipient democratisation under the New Order. It was, however, just an illusion.

Sudharmono's defeat as Golkar chairman in November 1988, left Golkar rudderless and divided. ABRI controlled between 67-70% of the provincial chairmanships but Sudharmono's men remained entrenched at the party's Slipi headquarters. The situation benefited Suharto, who by all accounts was uneasy with Sudharmono's over-zealous development of the party. The party's new chairman, Wahono, a close aide of Suharto's during the 1965-66 period, was seen as safely unambitious. A reorganisation of the council overseeing Golkar put Suharto in a better position to control the party. Neither a Golkar totally dependent on ABRI, nor a Golkar totally independent of ABRI, suited the President, who might justifiably fear its use as a power base.

Meanwhile, the more progressive image Golkar acquired under the stewardship of Sudharmono's clique impressed outsiders and some Indonesian intellectuals who had begun to despair of ever seeing political pluralism develop under the New Order. There was talk of Golkar achieving more independence from ABRI and the executive and of an incipient separation of powers. It was against this backdrop that the term '*keterbukaan*', or 'openness' appeared in the Indonesian political vocabulary in 1989. Was this just another illusion?

Many of the political actors at the time believed there was more to it than that. Going over the notes of the many interviews I had with leading Golkar civilian leaders in the 1968-91 period, men like Sarwono Kusumaatmadja, Rachmat Witoelar, and Marzuki Darusman, I am struck by their optimism about the chances of playing a less marginal role in New Order politics. Some of them hoped this would lead to a reduced emphasis on the military in politics. Briefly, their view was that, responding to internal and external pressures for more openness and participation in government, Golkar was in an ideal position to act as a constructive but at the same time responsible agent of political development. What better vehicle for the country's faltering steps towards a more open democracy than an institution cast as pro-

---

2. Specifically, the Golkar faction in the DPR was active, together with progressive members of the ABRI faction, in the defence of small landowners against developers. Golkar MPs also showed a surprising willingness to criticise aspects of the draft law on soldiership when it came before the DPR in late 1987.

government?

In hindsight, even this moderate approach may have proved unpalatable to Suharto. Whilst he spoke of more a open system in his annual independence speech of August 1990, and came back to theme in 1991, Suharto was unwilling to entertain substantive changes to the political process. By striking off the names of the more vocal Golkar MPs from the list of candidates for the 1992 elections, it was clear that their energies had not convinced the executive.

To explain the failure of Golkar's liberal leaders of this period to expand and consolidate their participation in government, I think we have to understand Suharto's view of the system he presided over. In his ghost-written autobiography, Suharto (1989:260) talks about elections as a necessary function of Indonesia's democracy, but he dwells on the importance of the election running smoothly and almost overlooks the significance of the results. The results are not significant; the votes don't have to be rigged, because the differences between parties are stylised and minimal. There is virtually nothing to differ about. For Suharto it is important for the people to be granted an act of choice, not actually to choose. The appearances are everything.

Suharto has used Golkar as an incubator for fresh political blood, but at the same time he has restrained the party from developing any degree of independence from the executive. Golkar is funded exclusively by three foundations, or *yayasans*, controlled by Suharto and members of his family. As well as controlling party funds, Suharto maintains overall control by sitting at the head of the Presidium that governs the party, the *dewan pembina* or guidance council. Sudharmono developed the party into an efficient vote-winning organisation, but was allowed to go no further.

What about the other two political parties? There was excitement over the performance of the PDI in the 1987 elections when it gained votes at the expense of Golkar in urban areas, and out-performed the supposedly Islamically-inclined Unity Development Party (PPP). But soon after the elections, the party returned to the dormant state it was expected to assume in the inter-election period, compounded by an internal power struggle. That the two 'opposition' parties stuck closely to their scripts for most of the 1988-92 period was something of a disappointment to liberal-minded observers, bent on detecting substance in the new climate of 'openness'. But it demonstrated the intrinsic strength of the New Order's political framework, even when the squabbling over succession had become a fixture of the political scene.

The 1992 election results showed significant falls in Golkar support in Central Java, where the PDI scored well. There was some evidence that the Roman Catholic church helped boost the PDI vote in the Yogyakarta area. Remarkably enough, senior Golkar officials were pleased. The civilian liberals managing this election were almost happy to see Golkar with a reduced majority, as one of them put it, so that Golkar would look more credible as a political party.³

However, Suharto had other plans. The power equation had begun to change, leaving both Golkar and ABRI slightly off centre. At the end of 1990, Suharto surprised everybody by appearing to give the Muslim majority what it had always been denied under the New Order, a political voice. The establishment of ICMI (Indonesian Muslim Intellectuals Association) in December 1990 has generally been interpreted as a shrewd move by Suharto to tap new areas of support in the run up to the presidential election in March 1993. Ignored, or worse still proscribed, for almost twenty years, Muslim intellectuals had been forced to sit on the sidelines of politics, though as I have argued elsewhere this exclusion from the formal political arena did not mean they were not influential (1993:129). In fact, the strictures imposed on Islamic discourse had, over the years, forced Muslim thinkers to adapt rather successfully. Unable to promote fundamental religious dogma, and encouraged to train in the west rather than the Islamic east, the younger generation of Islamic scholars found themselves well-equipped to deal with the social and economic problems facing the Muslim community.

While the Christian community watched nervously, Suharto cultivated a new Islamic tone, established an Islamic bank, went on the *haj*, hosted an Islamic festival, and so on. But there are two points to note. Firstly, he did not channel this new Islamic energy into any formal political institution like the PPP. Secondly, the Nahdlatul Ulama, the largest mass-based Muslim organisation opted to abstain from ICMI which was dominated instead by members of the more urban-oriented Muhammadiyah.

Much has been said about the political opportunities and problems this created for NU, and its controversial executive chairman Abdurrahman Wahid. What has been less noted is that NU's exclusion from ICMI arguably divided the Muslims even as they found the opportunity to coalesce under a sanctioned umbrella organisation for the first time in over twenty years. And why did Suharto select Professor Habibie to lead ICMI — why not a man with better Islamic credentials? Was he perhaps more interested in the symbolism of Islamic political resurgence than in actually allowing it to happen?

We must assume, I think, that Suharto's innate suspicion of single group dominance — driven both by political pragmatism and Javanese syncretic instincts — probably prevented him from allowing ICMI to develop the political clout others feared it might have. As with Golkar, the general model was to shape a political mould, but build in flaws to weaken the finished vessel. Thus, ICMI granted Muslims the chance to organise but, significantly, deprived them of a credible Muslim leader.

This summary of political currents in the late 1980s and early 1990s

---

3. Interview with senior Golkar official, Jakarta 10 June 1992.

reveals the pressures for political change in the direction of more democratic pluralism, but it also demonstrates Suharto's skill at resisting these pressures. Despite all the talk, the energy spent on enhancing the role of the parties and the DPR, the situation by late 1992 was little different from that of late 1987.

The New Order's resilience has confounded many of its students over the years. There are those who have persistently questioned its legitimacy, those who have charted its imperfections, and detected the not insignificant pressures for change. Much of the confusion stems, perhaps from misdiagnosis. The health of the New Order has been measured against generalised social and institutional norms. Accordingly, development has generated prosperity, and prosperity is in turn generating demands for political participation. Therefore the best prescription for renewal is the development of political institutions that will accommodate these economically inspired social urges. As Tanter and Young (1990:12) pointed out: 'Many now look [to the middle classes in Indonesia] as the source of new energies and initiatives which will carry Indonesian politics beyond the New Order.'

But if we look at the real essence of the New Order, which I would argue has always been the individual leadership rather than the system fashioned around it, the symptoms of change are harder to detect. Respect for Suharto's authority remains firm, if only because of the lack of obvious alternatives. The power of that authority to coopt and manipulate institutions — even those subject to intense social and political pressures — appears undiminished and unquestioned. Indonesia, for all its complexity, remains bound to an astonishingly simple culture of power which values leadership above other aspects of government. Therefore it is hard for political parties to play much of a role beyond that of symbolic, legitimising props — for now.

References

Feith, H. (1962) *The Decline of Constitutional Democracy in Indonesia.* Ithaca, Cornell University Press.
Soeharto (1989) *Soeharto: My Thoughts, Words and Deeds*, PT Citra Lamtoro Gung Persada, Jakarta.
Tanter, R. and Young, K. (eds) (1990) *The Politics of Middle Class Indonesia*, Centre of Southeast Asian Studies, Monash University, Clayton.
Vatikiotis, M.R.J. (1993) *Indonesian Politics Under Suharto* London, Routledge.

25

Interpretation of the Current Scene

Soetjipto Wirosardjono

During the past five years or so, dramatic changes have taken place in the Indonesian political scene. An initial mood of change and progress has been translated into initiatives, strategies and actions. This mood of change comes not only from among contending political factions but can be seen also within the top levels of power which have displayed a significant degree of sensitivity to aspirations for reform and change coming from below. Because of Indonesia's unique political culture, and the response of the national media to its political imperatives, these initiatives, strategies and actions were not explicitly reported. One has to read between the lines in order to grasp the essential political, social and cultural dynamics currently taking place.

Let me begin with one of the core political actors. As chairman of the dominant political organisation, Golkar, Sudharmono achieved success in three areas: in the areas of development, elections and in the organisational consolidation of Golkar. I will focus on the third of these and consider its meaning, its substance and its impact on subsequent national political development.

During Sudharmono's tenure, senior Golkar officials spoke openly about the need to make the organisation more independent and self-reliant. Its membership was made more active and card-carrying members were encouraged with a view to establishing a sound base for cadre formation. Some Golkar functionaries were beginning to talk about building a strong layer of civil society to speed up the process of Indonesia's modernisation. Ultimately Golkar should be able to respond independently to demands for change and direct the emphasis, pace and shape of national development. The establishment of strict internal rules and procedures were among the emphases of the organisation's consolidation agenda. Rules securing the autonomy of Golkar cadres could enable a gradual detachment from the former dependence on bureaucratic (mainly *pamong praja*) support and from dependence on ABRI. '*Kemandirian*' (self-reliance) became one of Golkar's watchwords.

Sudharmono's initial success resulted not only in Golkar's landslide victory in the 1987 elections, but also in bringing Sudharmono himself to the office of vice-president, albeit with a certain amount of controversy. When Wahono, previously Governor of East Java, replaced Sudharmono as Golkar chairman, he inherited a consolidated organisation with an energetic rank and file. Wahono, however, has had to rehabilitate and enhance Golkar's relations with the *tiga jalur* (the 'three channels') comprising Golkar's sister organisations, and its coalition partners, the *pamong praja* and ABRI which had been affected by the strategy of self-reliance laid down during Sudharmono's tenure.

Meanwhile, national attention focussed on the implications of Golkar's success in the 1987 elections and the structural consolidation forged during the Sudharmono era. The PPP welcomed Sudharmono's subsequent appointment as vice-president, especially after their attempt to nominate their party chairman, John Naro, ended in stalemate. The PPP managed to re-establish itself in the post election period with little government involvement in the choice of its office bearers. The PPP's vote had declined so badly, however, that it could not recover its initial strength.

ABRI also set its sights on consolidating its position in the post 1987 election period. The bottom line for ABRI after the 1987 election was to revitalise *dwifungsi*, the 'dual function' doctrine according to which the Armed Forces should not only be active in the defence and security of the country but also function as the stabilising and dynamising element in the socio-political arena. In the five years since the 1987 elections ABRI has therefore been attempting to strengthen its socio-political role. ABRI's leadership has frequently expressed concern about possible reactions to Golkar's 'over-representation' in the MPR and DPR. A better balance of representation among existing political organisations in the DPR and in Provincial and District Councils would provide a more democratic system which could eventually improve the existing mechanisms controlling executive power. Sometimes tentative figures were quoted as constituting the 'desired' level of representation so as to give leeway to political parties and other social and political forces to exercise effective leverage.

The ABRI faction in the House of Representatives has nevertheless been strengthened by the insistence of Armed Forces headquarters that it comprise only active (non-retired) ABRI officers. Retired Armed Forces officers, meanwhile, were encouraged to join the civilian wing, mostly in Golkar. In fact, some young and promising officers were released and given early 'voluntary' retirement and directed by their commanders to contest the positions of chairman and vice chairman in the Golkar regional and district chapters and branches, particularly in the strategic regions and municipalities.

In order to gain sufficient representation in the list of election candidates, social and political organisations were mobilised under the banner of *'Keluarga Besar ABRI'* (The Big ABRI Family). This was effected through the use of Golkar's three channel forum (*forum tiga jalur*), its *Dewan Penasihat* (Advisory Council) as well as its *Dewan Pembina Daerah* (Regional Management Councils) which are responsible for processing its list of candidates. ABRI's efforts to consolidate *dwifungsi* through Golkar ran counter to Sudharmono's strategy of building up Golkar's self-reliance, and this has had some repercussions. Many of the plans set in motion under Sudharmono to steer Golkar toward greater self-reliance have now been put at risk. Some of them have been deliberately set aside or simply disregarded.

After these efforts, the Keluarga Besar ABRI was reported to account for about 40% of the seats reserved for the Golkar faction in the house of representatives, in addition to the 100 seats specially reserved for active military officers appointed by the President on the recommendation of Armed Forces Headquarters. In the last election, the PDI gained some advantage from the strategic position of the Armed Forces within Golkar. Having won a 'healthy' victory in 1987, the parties were allowed a greater degree of manoeuvre in the 1992 campaign. The PDI was able to exploit the 'oppressed and deprived' sentiments of the *wong cilik*, the 'outcast', the unfavoured and the unemployed. Some retired military officers and young businessmen, artists and Sukarnoists, including Sukarno's children, openly joined this political party to add 'strength and courage' during and after the election campaign. As a result, the PDI improved its position over that of the preceding election.

ABRI's reform and consolidation agenda over the past five years, and the position it has taken in the election of speakers of Provincial Councils which choose the regional representatives to the MPR, has enabled it to gain seats in both the MPR and DPR.

This unorthodox means of mobilising support may be expected to arouse opposition from those who may not share the same sentiments, or look at the national issues in the same way, as do the strategists within ABRI. It is a question of how the politics of consensus-seeking can operate in such delicate circumstances, given the balance of leverage among contending interests and the excessive degree of power-building in the state and among political institutions. How can these developments be directed for the national interest? What procedures can be adopted in order to arrive at an acceptable consensus about the direction and course of change? If present initiatives and strategies have come from ABRI, reciprocal political moves by other parties in the national discourse may be in order.

For those familiar with political processes in Indonesia, an effort to counter these limitations by subtle or not so subtle means has been practised in the past and can be expected to be practised again. Take for example the choice of the functional representatives in the MPR. In practice this has been the prerogative of the head of state. The qualifications of persons selected as functional representatives in the MPR suggest that, to some degree, the choice has been exercised so as to secure a balance among the participating parties in the assembly. The choice for the posts of office bearers in the MPR and DPR, the factional leaders of the *Badan Pekerja* (Working Groups) and commission chairs can be seen as an attempt to limit the possible excessive leverage of any one group. Remember that present practice prescribes the making of decisions by deliberation and consensus rather than through the taking of a vote. No voting should be necessary if a consensus can be reached by common consent and by the voluntary endorsement of a negotiated compromise. Thus, the recent election of office bearers in the MPR and DPR, the appointment of members and officers of the *Badan Pekerja*, and the choice of chairs and secretaries of the party should be read as the political response to the delicate strategy laid down earlier by ABRI as one of the participants in the national political discourse.

What then are the areas of consensus? It is difficult to predict at the outset what can be reached during a deliberation. Since most of the decisions will be taken by way of consensus, and therefore by compromise, one can interpret a decision as the ultimate and final outcome of the consensus. On the other hand, it may represent merely a stage of progress, an indication of what could be achieved through the mechanism, given the existing balance of leverage.

One might gain an idea of the areas of possible consensus by noting what all parties agree in rejecting. On the mood for change and progress my own reading is that all emphasise the need to retain national unity and to preserve all the achievements that have been attained so far, tangible or otherwise. No one would wish to return to square one. ABRI more often emphasises its view that stability and national unity must be placed above all other considerations, and must be defended at all costs. And nobody wants to pursue change or progress through violent means. All parties, in fact, believe deep in their hearts that Pancasila and the 1945 Constitution will remain the uniting platform. They may differ about its interpretation, about how it is to be implemented and about the means of enforcing it, but there are no visible signs of a desire to alter the common platform, the *asas tunggal* and the Constitution. All are pledged to adhere to the Constitution. Unconstitutional change would be rejected by all contending parties.

In the political field the reform agenda which has been much discussed is that of openness (*keterbukaan*), democratisation and respect for human rights. This agenda has been expressed in different ways and with different emphases. In my view the success of this agenda will be determined more by social and cultural dynamics than through constitutional or legal means. Whether by design or by default, the emergence of a growing middle class will eventually bring about a civic society which will determine the pace of social and cultural change. There have already been visible efforts on the part of concerned citizens, including politicians, to bring about this civic society. There has also been pressure for more autonomy to be given to local government, particularly at the district and municipal levels. The concession of greater authority and responsibility to the second tier of government, *Otonomi Daerah Tingkat II*, will eventually bring about a greater political responsibility and accountability.

In the area of economic growth and social welfare, there are emerging opportunities, but also dangers faced by the current stage of Indonesian development. Everybody wants further economic growth and a more equitable distribution of the fruits of development, a broader base of employment opportunities, a respectable level of income and the eradication of absolute poverty. What has been achieved is a stable provision of basic needs, particularly in the area of food supply, (thanks to Indonesian self-sufficiency in rice) and the control of inflation. Indonesia is capable of focussing investment planning in the areas of resource utilisation, industrialisation and the promotion of the service sectors. Shortage of capital has been met by a policy of further investment liberalisation, deregulation and international trade policy designed to promote the export of goods and services. But the latent threat is posed by the remaining fraction of the Indonesian population still living below the poverty line. This constitutes the major challenge to Indonesia's current economic development. At the microeconomic level, economic inefficiency, controversial monopolies and unwelcome rent-seeking business activities still linger as areas to be attended to delicately in the years to come.

If B.J. Habibie's description of the direction of Indonesia's economic trajectory may be used as a yardstick of reform in the economic field, there are two areas of concern to be noticed. One is the need for Indonesia's economy to participate in high-tech ventures, to enhance the level of added value in Indonesia's production and export. The second is the need to promote human resource development by substantial investment in education and training, designed to cater for the labour requirements of enhanced technological application in business and industry.

Who is to share the burden of these elements of the reform agenda of the 1990s? A stereotyped answer would be that every Indonesian must share the duty and the responsibility. A political response, however, will not be as trivial. The question will be who has the power to introduce change and progress, or who will emerge as victor in this delicate national political discourse.

26

A New Political Context: the Urbanisation of the Rural

Kenneth R. Young

The rural masses of Indonesia, especially the villagers of Java, have always represented the major repository of hopes and disappointments for a mass, participatory politics in post-Independence Indonesia. It was the vast twenty-million-strong membership of PKI-affiliated organisations in the early 1960s that gave the communist party such a formidable presence in the Old Order. Even today the independent religious schools of the rural hinterland still remain the most significant institutions that exist outside direct government influence. If there is to be any movement beyond a minimalist reading of democracy — competition between elites as a brake on arbitrary rule, legitimacy through representation drawn from carefully managed constituencies — then the rural population of Indonesia will have to be brought into the political process.

This line of reasoning might lead on to a consideration of issues and organisation, of evaluation of the lessons of the 1950s and so on, were it not for one very striking development which significantly complicates both comparisons between the two periods, and assumptions about the degree of social, political and cultural continuity between then and now. The mass democratic politics of the 1950s were the politics of a poorly educated, recently liberated, post-colonial agrarian society. To oversimplify somewhat, the Indonesian polity of the 1950s, viewed from Jakarta, consisted of a commercial and administrative urban centre (supplemented in the regions and outer islands by smaller replicas of itself) surrounded by a populous rural mass living in dispersed 'self-sufficient' (see Breman 1982) village communities. In the 1990s, levels of education are dramatically higher, and today's political agendas could scarcely have been anticipated in the 1950s. Indonesia is no longer an agrarian society in any simple sense, and that kind of sharp rural/urban contrast is both misleading and inaccurate.

The dissolution of a tidy rural/urban distinction in Indonesia has many political implications. I will briefly review some of the measurable material changes that have led to what I will argue is, by comparison with the 1950s, a significantly different political context. However, the main point I will try to make is about a more qualitative, and less easily measured, shift in the way of life and the outlooks of large parts of the Indonesian population still viewed as 'rural', whose material and symbolic environment has been substantially 'urbanised'. The possibilities for democratisation are not all that promising, but I prefer to base my speculation about that subject on a more accurate characterisation of the situation outside the major cities. Exploration of these issues also allows me to develop a case that the *aliran* politics of the 1950s will not re-emerge. Comparisons of the 1950s and the 1990s are more useful if we recognise the extent and full significance of change in rural areas.

These points receive a measure of support from the preliminary research results of a collaborative study of a spontaneous frontier settlement adjacent to a large mine site in East Kalimantan, and from a number of other current research projects with which I am involved in urban and peri-urban Java. In the Kalimantan study, the population is small — around three thousand — and not especially cohesive. Looking for the major lines of co-operation and division within this settlement we carefully assessed the role of religion and of distinctions based on class, ethnicity and gender. Occupational rank was important, but the most salient division within the community was not one that we expected — a self-imposed bifurcation of the residents into *orang kampung* and *orang kota* (idiomatically, a distinction between 'country folks' and 'city slickers'). I don't want to make too much of this, but the way they identified themselves resonated with related cases I know of, but whose more general significance I had not previously recognised. The 'city slickers', by the way, were mostly from villages or small provincial towns. Their criteria for self-identification as *orang kota* were based not on origins, but on knowledge — knowledge of a cultural code of urban living, knowing how to get on in the modern industrial world, being streetwise. The case on its own proves very little. It did, however, alert me to aspects of the shifts in the orientation towards modernity that I have observed in both urban and rural Indonesia that help me explain my difficulty in contemplating the recrudescence of *aliran*.

The urbanisation of the rural

At the heart of my argument is a claim that rural Indonesia has changed so much that the politics of the Old Order will not re-emerge even if developments in the (urban) political centre lead again to a degree of political openness. If rural people are to participate more actively in the political process in the future, then the forms of political participation are highly likely to be different in the way they are organised and more surely in their political idioms from those of the 1950s.

The changes in the rural political context in the past two and a half decades affect many aspects of life and lived experience. Many of them are observable and some are readily measurable — changes in communications, transportation, education, work, consumption, social welfare, housing, infrastructure, public utilities, markets and so on. These material changes are fairly obvious, and their importance I trust is no less manifest. However, in order to give emphasis to my central point, I want to step past them for the moment to move directly to the more elusive changes in the way of life and the outlooks of rural people brought about with these material transformations. In particular I want to look at the way they have fostered new orientations and new symbolic grounds for proto-political orientations which are enmeshed with the 'politics of identity[1]' which were so central to the political contests of the Old Order. This symbolic field, I believe, has greatly altered, and with it the discourses and even the modes of organisation that are appropriate to the conditions of the 1990s. These now deserve fresh analysis.

In Indonesia in the 1950s the distinction between rural and urban politics was important. This was not just because of important differences in local and regional issues and in the configuration of class and other social divisions between city and country, but because, in wide regions of Indonesia, such local issues were only weakly displaced by the politics of Jakarta, and national issues were often mediated through local referents which gave them characteristically local meanings. There was a sense then in which the real, concrete, immediate and emotionally-charged stuff of politics was predominantly focussed around local issues. The politics of the centre, and of the nation, was more of a remote backdrop; the substance of politics was to be found locally. Taking as given the rural-urban distinction of the 1950s, my concern is to question its continued utility in the 1990s.

The most useful term for the changes I want to refer to is the 'urbanisation of the rural'. By this I mean that the social, economic and political concerns that absorb people living in cities and which find expression in a variety of 'urban' discourses are shared by a wide and increasing proportion of people who live outside the major cities. It follows that a tidy rural/urban distinction is no longer appropriate for the analysis of Indonesian politics, society and culture. At the core of these discourses are shared understandings about the nature of modernity, the type of society modern Indonesia is becoming, and the personal qualities of individuals who participate in this emerging society. These understandings are often implicit, but have a strong normative

---

1. For a discussion of this field in relation to arguments about modernity, modernism and post-modernism and the politics of identity see Lasch and Friedman 1992.

influence on those who recognise its code, allowing them to signify (or reject) membership of a consciously 'modern' sub-culture. Although those who internalise this discourse may be themselves socially marginal, it is usually assumed to be the discourse of the upwardly mobile, and, more nebulously, the powerful.

The 'urbanisation of the rural' is most characteristic of Java and of other densely populated parts of the 'outer islands'. There still is some point in drawing socio-cultural boundaries to mark off some populations which are only partly caught up in the process of cultural 'urbanisation'. My point is that the place to draw the boundary is no longer at the city limits, if it ever was.

The boundaries of the 'urban'

Indeed, many difficulties are avoided once we cease trying to understand the dispersal of urban culture primarily in spatial terms. The 'urban' discourses are clearly not used by everyone living in cities; on the other hand their currency is not restricted by class, ethnicity or gender, even if they may be most characteristic of the middle classes. Indeed, one of the characteristics of 'urban Indonesian' culture is the degree to which it has freed itself from association with place (although the cultural-political pull of Jakarta is undeniable). It diverges as well from the 'metropolitan superculture' identified by Hildred Geertz (1963) in the 1950s in a number of key respects, and certainly differs from the regionally distinctive structures of meaning that we associate with the more geographically specific cultures of Indonesia's numerous *suku bangsa*. Contemporary urban Indonesian culture participates in a far more developed international cultural complex than the 1950s urban elite — the bearers of the 'metropolitan superculture' — ever had open to them. Even the more unambiguously 'local' cultures were immobile, and therefore geographically specific, because their members tended to communicate and interact mainly with each other, and were less likely to move outside their culture area than is the case today. In addition, modern urban Indonesian culture is less place-bound because it is also consciously cosmopolitan, deliberately open to a plurality of cultures, and predominantly claimed by people who possess the competence to move between it and other cultural codes.

My reference to 'urbanisation' is almost entirely based on cultural changes and therefore has no need to sort out the difficult issues associated with the demographic/administrative designation of urban *areas* for census and other purposes. Nevertheless it is also clear that the increasing predominance of 'urban' cultures outside the cities is in no small part bound up with powerful trends of urbanisation and industrialisation in Indonesia. This is especially true of Java where 'many rural areas...now have population densities and access to facilities which would be regarded as 'urban' under current definitions' (Hugo *et al.* 1987:332). The population densities, occupational structure, personal mobility, education levels, access to and use of transport and communications and many other aspects of the lives of that majority of the Indonesian population who live in Java[2] are in many respects not qualitatively dissimilar from those of unambiguous city dwellers[3]. The way of life in 'rural' Java offers too many alternatives to allow it to be characterised as if it belonged to the relatively self-contained and locally bounded cultural units that are usually associated with peasant culture.

In any case much of Java, and to a lesser degree parts of Sumatra and South Sulawesi, are experiencing rates of growth in officially defined 'urban' areas which are rapidly outstripping the rate of change in relatively static 'rural' areas. While the issues of rural-urban migration are complex, and important intermediate-size provincial cities are frequently not growing as fast as the major cities (Hugo *et al.* 1987 ch. 3:86f), there is no doubt that the major urban growth poles are expanding at a spectacular pace. Jabotabek — the conurbation of Jakarta, Bogor, Tangerang and Bekasi — will exceed sixteen million by the end of this decade. The capital alone, DKI Jakarta itself, will exceed twelve million. The ten largest cities of Indonesia will have roughly doubled in size between 1980 and the year 2000 (Hugo *et al.* 1987:333). The majority of these cities are on Java — Jakarta (12.01 million by 2000), Bandung (3.37m), Surabaya (3.23m), Bogor (2.25m), Semarang (1.59m), Yogyakarta (0.97m) and Malang (0.95m) — but there are cities of significant size on other islands, especially on Sumatra: Medan (2.56 million by 2000), Palembang (1.75m) and Ujung Pandang (1.75m). These rapidly growing urban centres are mostly linked to major areas of industrial expansion or other major export sectors (as are cities such as Balikpapan and Samarinda in Kalimantan). Many industrial sites are located 'outside' the cities in peri-urban areas, or along major highways (such as the road connecting Jakarta to the steel-making centres around Cilegon in West Java). The workforce for these factories are drawn in from 'rural' villages around the cities and highways so that areas well beyond the administrative boundaries of the cities are changed along with the city itself.

While the effects of these changes are uneven, the simple, and politically significant, fact is that it is no longer sensible, even in a purely descriptive sense, to view Indonesia as a predominantly agrarian society. In the 1950s, the overwhelming majority of Indonesians lived in villages. This is no longer true in the 1990s, and that is highly significant politically. Furthermore, I

---

2. Why draw the line there? Bali; Madura; South, Central and North Sumatra and other contiguous regions in Western Indonesia are linked to this complex as well.

3. Anthony Giddens (1989:553) dramatises the 'conurbations' and 'megalopolis' city-complexes of the northern-eastern seaboard of the United States by informing his readers that 'in this region about forty million people live at a density of over 700 persons per square mile'. (*loc cit*). In 1985, one hundred million people lived on Java with a density of 735 persons per square *kilometre* - i.e. 1,911 persons per square *mile*. (Hugo *et al.* 1987:42, Table 2.2.) In rural *kabupaten* Kediri, where I worked in the mid-1980s, the population density in 1983 was 887/sq.km. Some individual *kecamatan* in Kediri almost exceeded 1,000 persons/sq.km. (Pemda Kediri 1983:6,21).

believe we should recognise that — on Java especially, but beyond Java as well — large sections of the population who live in areas classed statistically as 'rural' lead lives whose significant symbolic, economic and political referents extend well beyond their neighbourhood. While national and other 'outside' influences were not absent in rural areas in the 1950s, the change in degree is not simply quantitative, it is qualitative. Even in purely quantitative terms which are known[4] to underestimate the degree of substantive urbanisation, the movement towards a more urban (and industrial — see Hill 1992) society is impressive. Hugo *et al.* (1987:333) summarise the trends as follows (my emphasis):

> ...There seems little doubt that the 'formal' urban share of Indonesia's population will have risen above 30 per cent at the end of the century while the proportion of the population working in urban areas, having access to urban services and being within easy travelling distance of cities, *will be well over a majority*. This latter phenomenon is analogous to the 'suburbanisation' process found in developed countries.

The discourses of the urban

Thus the sheer weight of demographic change alone shows that the social, cultural and political context of the 1990s is greatly changed from that of the 1950s. These shifts towards the urban involve a great deal more. They signal changing social environments and relationships, and beyond that, novel ways of understanding a changing world. The newly built environments of burgeoning new cities express above all else a manifest logic of modernity in literally palpable ways — through the transformation of space, relationships and the social environment. It manifests the distinctively Indonesian evolution of the logics of capitalism, state formation, bureaucratic rationality, industrialism, and perhaps even democracy (see Arnason 1990:209). Nowhere is this clearer than in Jakarta. Therefore it is unsurprising, perhaps, that the discourses of the urban signify and celebrate participation in Indonesian and global modernity.

There is more at work here, however, than simply the expression of a distinctive environment. The codes used are prescriptive and exclusive in various ways and have more than a casual relationship with the new forms of power that have emerged under the New Order. There is a fascinating interaction at work here — of a scope and complexity far beyond the length

---

4. The definition of 'urban' used by Biro Pusat Statistik and the Census has been refined in successive censuses, 'adopting a much more meaningful, functionally based definition of what constitutes an urban area' (Hugo *et al.* 1987:86). However, the 'urban' population is still underestimated since:

> ...[there] are hundreds of thousands of Indonesians who, although they have their permanent residence in rural areas, spend much of their working lives in cities via the processes of circular migration and commuting. This 'hidden urbanisation' blurs the social and economic meaning of 'rural' and 'urban' in Indonesia. (Hugo *et al.* 1987:86).

of this paper — in which the deliberate manipulations of categories of discourse, of attitudes and values by the State blend with the more spontaneous forms of expression that emerge and circulate beyond the official sphere (See Heryanto 1988). The latter are no less importantly refracted by relations of power and the whole evolving net of self-understandings thrown up by urban society is critically mediated by intellectuals (understood broadly) in widely variable social settings and media of communication. The discourses that become established — because they speak authoritatively or, equally, with authority — have a variety of uses: aesthetic, instrumental and normative.

As well as considering the uses of these discourses we need to ask *who* uses them. All too obviously the most fluent exponents are the new middle classes, not least because they are best equipped to give local meanings and displays of mastery of transnational[5] cultural forms. Thus intellectuals, bureaucrats, business-people, professionals, journalists and the like generate, mediate and serve as models in the competent expression of urban discourses.

However authoritative these exemplars may be, they also stand at too great a social distance from their more marginal fellow urbanites, and even more so from the masses of people who live in the penumbra between the urban and the rural. At this level it is often hard to know whether adoption of a range of fairly rudimentary 'urban' symbols — in language, dress, behaviour and so on — is simply instrumental. Traders who wear jeans, use a certain vocabulary, smoke particular brands of cigarettes and successfully project themselves as being competent in an urban industrial setting attract more customers, it is said. They are more likely to get jobs, particularly the better paid wage jobs (or such, it seems, is the popular wisdom). Such rationales suggest a fairly superficial, instrumental attachment to the shibboleths of urban modernity. However, the evidence of my research and of others I have worked with suggests deeper motivations. I have been consistently impressed, in a variety of rural and urban research settings, with the very high valuation put by many people — and they appear to be most numerous among the younger generations who have grown to maturity in the New Order period — on seeing themselves and being seen by others as 'modern'. This is not to deny ambivalent feelings about modernity[6] among the young, or to claim that they are simply being absorbed at the fringes of an urban bourgeois

---

5. Like Hannerz, I would like to head off any implicit misunderstanding that 'global culture' implies a homogenisation of systems of meaning and expression. Rather, as he remarks, 'it is marked by an organisation of diversity rather than a replication of uniformity' (1990:237).

6. Having witnessed in Jakarta in 1990 the howls of scorn directed at idle 'yuppies' in response to the mordant lyrics of Iwan Fals delivered at a concert of over one hundred thousand rapturous youthful 'rock' fans, I have few doubts that these idioms also serve as vehicles for powerful class and other resentments. They remain, for all that, distinctively Indonesian, and distinctively modern.

culture. The process is selective, the perceived meanings are approved of because they are seen to fit the new urban world of these people and to express their ambivalence about what it offers. They do not tend to become 'modern' in quite the same way that middle class sophisticates do. Rather they simulate the aura of that modernity through its symbols, and fashion it to uses in their own environment. Having said this, however, it seems equally clear that they are determined thereby to remake themselves as 'city people'. In the process they accentuate the distance between themselves and the *orang daerah* or *orang kampung* who have not made the same transition. There are many Indonesians who do not conform to these patterns, but they are probably outnumbered by those who do. The longevity of the New Order is important here.

The majority of the population now live in the urban and the 'urbanised rural' parts of the country. The majority never knew the Old Order directly. Already by the late 1980s, 37% of the population were born after 1976, (66% had been born shortly before or during the New Order).

A new political context

I suggest that these new urbanised discourses, and the patterns of behaviour associated with them, become important when we try to anticipate the forms of political mobilisation that might emerge in certain post-Suharto contexts. These could be scenarios of greater political openness, or simply of the loosening of state controls because of intra-elite contestation over the succession. The new discourses are not overtly political, but they exhibit the range of social imaginaries (Castoriadis 1987) possessed by a large proportion of the population, particularly the younger generation. In other words, they tell us a lot about how these people think of themselves and their social environment, about what they would like to become, and about their perceptions of what Indonesian urban society is and where it is going.

There is a great contrast between, on the one hand, the 1990s world inhabited by city people, and by rural villagers whose lives have been permeated by influences emanating from the cities, and, on the other, the social imaginaries of the rural villages of the 1950s. We have a shorthand for the situation in the Parliamentary and Guided Democracy periods; we refer to the 'politics of *aliran*'. This reference invokes the 'cultural pillarisation' (McVey 1970) which permeated, at least in rural Java, the constituencies of the major political parties, which provided the idiom of the major mechanisms of political patronage (Wertheim 1969), and which cut across and blunted the lines of intensifying class confrontation (Mortimer 1969; Lyon 1970). Our analyses of the political dynamics of the 1950s have a strong dependence on anthropological analyses of the period, particularly the work of the 'Modjokuto' team (Geertz, Jay, Dewey and others). Those studies, and the typologies they produced, laid the foundations of our understandings of the social imaginaries of the 1950s. If we want to anticipate the social and political movements that might emerge in the context of a transitional regime in the 1990s, it is all too tempting to draw upon those powerful studies from the 1950s. To do so would be a serious mistake. In a short paper I can only indicate the broadest reasons for this assertion. Put most simply, life in many Indonesian communities has changed too much for this to be plausible. Only among the rural communities guided by NU *pesantren* are there unbroken lines of continuity, and even those have participated in the general processes of 'modernisation' and social transformation, and, in doing so, are far from untouched by the changes of the New Order period. Politics, conflict, class domination (see Hart 1986) and other aspects of the ferment of the 1950s have not gone away, but the idioms that are used to describe the social and political world are different, and we should expect that the practices and organisational forms of successful mass movements of the 1990s (if there are to be any) will also differ. They must differ, because their success will depend on their ability to articulate popular aspirations in a vastly changed social environment. These arguments need to be elaborated in greater detail than is possible here. However, as a final shorthand, imagine a 1950s party official suddenly licensed to begin recruiting among 1990s high school graduates with urban-centred ambitions. What ideas and aspirations from that earlier period could be readily transposed to the 1990s? What would have to be fashioned afresh to make sense in the new social, political and cultural context? The changes manifest among the urbanised population, be they in the cities or the countryside, suggest that the mass politics of the 1950s, the *aliran* conflicts, will not re-emerge in post-agrarian Indonesia.

References

Arnason, J.P. (1990) 'Nationalism, Globalization and Modernity', *Theory Culture and Society* 7, 2-3 (June 1990: Special Issue on 'Global Culture'): 237-251.

Breman, J. (1982) 'The Village on Java and the Early Colonial State', *Journal of Peasant Studies* 9, 4: 189-240.

Castoriadis, C. (1987) *The Imaginary Institution of Society*, Cambridge University Press, Cambridge.

Geertz, H. (1963) Indonesian Societies and Cultures, in R. McVey (ed) *Indonesia*, Yale, New Haven.

Giddens, A. (1989) *Sociology*, Polity Press, Cambridge.

Hannerz, U. (1990) 'Cosmopolitans and Locals in World Culture', *Theory Culture and Society* 7, 2-3 (June 1990: Special Issue on 'Global Culture'): 237-251.

Hart, G. (1986) *Power, Labor and Livelihood: Processes of Change in Rural Java*, University of California Press, Berkeley, Cal.:

Heryanto, Ariel (1988) 'The Development of 'Development'', *Indonesia* 46 October 1988.

Hill, H. (1992) The Economy 1991/92, in H. Crouch and H. Hill (eds)

Indonesia Assessment 1992: Political Perspectives on the 1990s, ANU Political and Social Change Monograph 17, Canberra.

Hugo, G.J., Hull, T.H., Hull, V.J., Jones G.W. (1987) *The Demographic Dimension in Indonesian Development*, Oxford University Press, Singapore.

Lasch, S. & Friedman, J. (eds) (1992) *Modernity and Identity*, Blackwell, Oxford.

Lyon, M. (1970) *Bases of Conflict in Rural Java* University of California Research Monograph Series, Center for South and Southeast Asia Studies, Berkeley, Cal.

Merton, R.K. (1957) *Social Theory and Social Structure*, Free Press, Glencoe, Il.

McVey, R.T. (1970) Nationalism, Islam and Marxism: the management of ideological conflict in Indonesia, Introduction to Sukarno, 'Nationalism, Islam and Marxism', Cornell Modern Indonesia Project, Ithaca, N.Y.:

Mortimer, R. (1969) 'Class, Social Cleavage and Indonesian Communism', *Indonesia* 8: 1-20.

Pemda Kediri (1983) *Kabupaten Kediri dalam Angka*, Kantor Statistik Kabupaten Kediri, Kediri.

Wertheim. W.F. (1969) 'From Aliran to Class Struggle in the Countryside of Java', *Pacific Viewpoint*, 10:1-17.

Young, K.R. (1990) Local and national influences in the violence of 1965, in R. Cribb (ed) *The Indonesian Killings 1965-66*, Monash Centre of Southeast Asian Studies, Melbourne.

27

Transformation of the Informal Sector: Social and Political Consequences

Hans-Dieter Evers

Most Indonesians still earn their living in the so-called informal sector, though it is, as we will show, declining. Instead a proletariat of wage workers and a middle class of salaried employees is emerging. Based on the experience of industrialising countries, scholars and development planners have pinned their hope on precisely these social strata as promulgators of modernisation and political change.

In my paper I shall present census statistics, my own survey data and ethnographic observations and some ideas on the reasons for, and consequences of, the social and economic transformation of Indonesian society. After recording some salient arguments of the discourse on the informal sector in developing societies, some statistical data on the rise and decline of the informal sector will be presented. The following section of the paper documents and discusses the other side of the coin, namely the rise of wage labour and the development of a labour market during the eighties. After an analysis of the factors that have stimulated these fundamental changes of Indonesian society, some tentative conclusions in relation to the social and political consequences of this change are drawn.

The growth and decline of the informal sector
Interpretations of the informal sector

In the discussions about social and economic change in Indonesia the concept of the so-called 'informal sector' made its appearance with a book by ILO expert Sethuraman and a large survey by LEKNAS-LIPI (Moir

1978) only a few years after the concept was first used in a study on Ghana (Hart 1973). It has meanwhile been accorded official status and has been used both in the GBHN (State Guidelines) and in REPELITA, Indonesia's Five-Year-Plan. The current change of Indonesia's development strategy from a production-oriented to a human resources development-oriented approach will again bring the informal sector into the forefront of discussion in preparation for REPELITA VI, starting in 1994. Nevertheless many influential Indonesian officials still take a negative view of the informal sector and wish to restrain its development.[1]

The concept has found ready acceptance in Indonesia not so much because of its analytical value or empirical relevance but because it fitted in very well with the scholarly tradition of writing on Indonesia. The formal and informal sectors resemble Boeke's dual economy, whereas the informal sector encompasses all the characteristics of an involuted economy as described by Clifford Geertz (1963). In all three cases the 'oriental', 'the involuted' and the 'informal' part of the economy and society are defined as unorganised, under-developed, and stagnant.

Though in recent years a few studies have appeared to challenge this view it is still widely and erroneously held. In this paper I shall therefore stress the dynamic changes that have occurred in the so-called informal sector and the social, economic and political consequences of this process.

Defining the informal sector

If we use a simple definition of the informal sector, we will at least be able to present a time series of informal sector development that enables us to get a rough idea of the direction of its change (see Table 1).

Secondary data analysis, based on Population Census data, has to use available census criteria, in this case self-employment and unwaged family labour to define and to estimate informal sector employment. This type of analysis has its obvious weaknesses. It assigns small unlicensed establishments employing at least one wage labourer to the formal sector, whereas a highly paid and skilled professional will be classified as an informal sector worker.[2] As the number of independent professionals is still relatively small, their number has been ignored. Of greater significance is the question, whether or not all small farmers should be counted as part of the informal sector. As long as they only employ family members and not wage labour on a regular basis they are here included in the informal sector.

---

1. Thus Cosmas Batubara, Minister of Labour between 1988 and 1993 maintained this negative view of the informal sector in several public statements. See Cremer 1992:198.

2. Appropriate corrections can be made on the basis of occupational statistics, though no major shifts in the data occur due to the relatively small numbers of free professionals in Indonesia.

Table 1 **Informal/formal sector definition**

Informal sector	Formal sector
Self employed (own account worker)	Employer
Self employed (assisted by family member)	Employee
Family worker	

Macro trends in informal sector employment

Using the above definition of the informal sector, we can estimate its growth in terms of the proportion of people, gaining an income from informal activities. The estimate in table 2 shows that the informal sector has grown rapidly since 1967, the beginning of the 'New Order' government, but has started to decline during the 1980s.

Table 2 **Estimated employment in the informal sector Indonesia, 1967-1990** (percent of labour force)

Year	1967	1971	1980	1985	1990
% Informal	41.2	61.3	70.0	68.8	63.7

Sources: 1967-75: Sethuraman 1976:128; Moir 1978: 101, 140; Evers 1989:159; Census 1971, 1980, 1990. SUPAS 1985

As the census sampling procedures and the census questions and definitions differ somewhat from year to year these figures have to be treated with caution. They can, however, be taken as rough indicators of a trend in informal sector employment. As the informal sector is negatively correlated with formal sector employment, at least in the definition used currently by the Indonesian Central Bureau of Statistics, the surprising fact arises that obviously a larger proportion of Indonesians worked in the formal, wage earning sector in 1971, than during the past decade from 1980 to 1990.

With growing administrative and economic development the informal sector was able to absorb a growing share of the labour force, keeping formal unemployment at low levels. This trend has now been reversed. The labour absorption capacity of the informal sector will, in the next planning period REPELITA VI, no longer be able to provide employment to a disproportionately large labour force. Our survey data[3] from Central Java point in the same direction (Evers 1991, 1992, Evers and Mehmet 1994).

Though in absolute terms the number of informal sector workers has

---

3. A survey on informal sector trade in Central Java was carried out under the direction of Hans-Dieter Evers and Tajuddin N.E. by a team of the Population Studies Center, Gadjah Mada University in September-October 1992.

increased by 18.4 percent during the 1980s, absorbing an additional 9.5 million workers, its share of the total labour force has decreased from 70 to 63.7 percent.

The growth of wage labour
Economic growth and informal sector employment

The statistical evidence is quite clear: The informal sector has grown during the early period of the New Order government and has then started to decline during the 1980s. If we accept the statistical evidence as true, we are faced with considerable problems in explaining this trend in the light of conventional wisdom about the informal sector. The growth of an informal economy is usually interpreted as a sign of slow economic growth, of low productivity, of increasing poverty, of marginalisation and over-urbanisation. Often the floating mass of informal sector workers is held responsible for political unrest, criminality and insecurity. The Indonesian data point into a different direction.

The informal sector did expand considerably during the period of rapid economic growth between 1967 and 1980. Towards the end of that period it had become larger than during the period of economic decline in the early 60s. If our analysis is correct, informal sector growth is not a sign of macro-economic decline but of social transformation and economic growth — at least up to a turning point, when its importance is reduced. This happened, as we have seen, from the early 1980s onward. During 1980-90 the Indonesian GDP grew by over 7% in real terms. Employment grew by 4% annually, whereas informal sector employment grew only by 3%. The relative importance of the informal sector was reduced and that of the formal sector was enhanced. In other words work in the informal sector receded behind wage labour.

What caused this change and what are its social and economic consequences?

Labour market expansion

After an expansion of production and product markets as expressed in GNP growth we now seem to experience an expansion of the labour market. This means that family labour in household subsistence production has been step by step replaced by wage labour. In addition new jobs are created in services and, since the mid 1980s, increasingly in manufacturing industries. In rural areas the expansion of the labour market was experienced mainly as an increase of non-agricultural off-farm employment (Evers 1991).

It is a matter of debate, whether employment in agriculture actually grew in relative or absolute terms during the 1970s and 1980s. As Chris Manning has argued, 'even in densely populated Java, rapid agricultural growth has been accompanied by increased employment in agriculture' during the green revolution and the oil boom years (Manning 1988:48). Outside agriculture, 'the spin-off in employment creation in rural areas as a consequence of the green revolution has probably been remarkably small and largely in service activities and construction rather than in manufacturing' (Manning 1988:50). This is, however, contradicted by Anne Booth, who shows that growth of agricultural employment was slow at best, and that the years between 1976 and 1982 showed 'an overall decline in the agricultural labour force in Java' (Booth 1988:50). Especially 'wage labour in agriculture has been decreasing since the mid seventies as a consequence of rationalisation and extensification' in Central Java (Hüsken 1989: 321). The overall decline of employment in agriculture has continued and as of now (1994) less than 50% of the Indonesian labour force still work in agriculture.

As 'agricultural employment' here means mainly self-employment and the use of family members, the agricultural informal sector has probably also declined. If this is the case, employment must have come from elsewhere, namely from non-agricultural off-farm employment. As it appears, employment growth in rural Java has been concentrated, until the early 1980s, in small-scale trade and transport, i.e. in the informal sector (Gerke 1991). The relative decline of the informal and the rise of the formal sector during the 1980s and 1990s was apparently due to the further expansion of the labour market, new employment opportunities in the rapidly growing industrial sector, and a vast expansion of the bureaucracy.

The growth of a working class

The employment situation is now changing rapidly, at least in Java. The increase of more formalised work relationships, particularly in the form of wage labour have been observed by field researchers during the 1980s primarily in the relatively highly developed Javanese provinces (Gerke 1992:175, Schweizer 1987:67, 1990) and our field surveys, carried out in 1987-8 and 1992 (Abdullah *et al.* 1989, Effendi 1991, Evers 1991, Evers and Schrader 1994). In some of the outlying regions the labour market appears still to be relatively underdeveloped and people looking for wage labour tend to migrate to other regions rather then seek employment locally.[4]

Though migration of job seekers also occurs on Java, local labour markets have expanded rapidly. In the 1970s researchers drew attention to the growth of the *tebasan* system, where work gangs led by a patron roamed the country side to take over harvesting and other agricultural work, earlier performed by relatives of landowners or members of the village community. This temporary reduction of agricultural wage labour has contributed to the phenomenal rise of the informal sector during this period. Men started to work as circular migrants in the cities while women took up informal sector trade (Evers 1991, 1992, 1993). Meanwhile it has become clear, that the *tebasan* system has not spread further but that the use of local wage labour has again become prevalent. A fairly stable and locally bound class of

---

4. Data collected during field trips 1993/94 to the Natuna Islands (Kepulauan Riau) in the South China Sea and to Timor.

landless agricultural labourers has emerged, who find waged agricultural employment with a limited number of farmers or farm operators (tenants). Most of the rural wage labourers are, however, employed in the non-farm sectors of trade, transport and rural industries.

A rural 'proletariat', to use a by now old-fashioned term, is now emerging in the form of wage labourers with low, but fairly stable incomes. In the words of contemporary institutional economics, we witness the growth of a formal labour market and labour market institutions.

Mobility from the informal to the formal sector is high. According to our 1992 survey data from Central Java, 45.7% of wage labourers in trade, who had previously worked, had moved over from the informal sector. According to our 1993 survey in West Sumatra 12.3% of formal sector workers had previously worked in the informal sector.[5] Whereas the Javanese data concern only the trade sector, the West Sumatra survey covered all occupations and all industries. This explains part of the difference, but part of it is also due to the greater rate of change towards a labour market economy in Java.

From a macro point of view the counter image of the informal sector is wage labour. Statistically speaking, when one sector increases, the other has to decrease proportionately. In Indonesia as a whole, the percentage proportion of informal to formal sector workers changed from 70/30 to 64/36 between 1980 and 1990. Table 3 indicates that this change is particularly strong in urban areas, but the trend is also visible in the rural areas.

What accounts for the decline of the informal sector and the social transformation it indicates? To answer this question, we shall look at several factors which have contributed to the decline of the informal sector and the growth of wage labour.

Formalisation of off-farm employment We have already drawn attention to the growth of off-farm employment. Authors differ on the reason for this development. While White (1986) has claimed that the growth of rural non- or off-farm employment has been stimulated by the green revolution, Manning (1988) and Effendi (1991) have taken the opposite view and stressed macro-economic factors like growing government expenditures following the oil boom of the 1970s to account for rural employment growth. Probably both positions are correct, though the impact may have been differently weighted according to time period, region and social stratum.

---

5. This survey on labour market segmentation (n=506) was carried out in 1993 under the direction of Solvay Gerke and Hans-Dieter Evers by a team of staff members of the Centre for the Study of Development and Socio-Cultural Change (Director: Prof. Aziz Saleh), Andalas University.

Table 3 **The growth of a formal labour market 1980-1990**
(Employers and employees as percentage of total employment)

Year	Employers and employees as percentage of total employment		
	Rural	**Urban**	**Total**
1980	19.22	10.74	29.96
1990	19.69	16.64	36.33

The issue of labour mobility has been less intensively discussed. It remains an open question, into which sectors the move from agricultural employment has occurred.[6] In all probability the strong growth of informal sector employment during the 1960s and 1970s was due to a movement into off-farm employment in the informal sector, especially petty trade. In the course of the formalisation of the informal sector and the growth of wage labour a move from informal to formal sector activities has probably occurred in the way indicated by our survey data discussed above.

An important question remains unanswered: Will females be excluded from this transformation to wage labour?

Up to 80 percent of workers in small scale informal sector trade are women. The rapid growth of petty trade during the 1970s, at least in Java, is due to a disproportionate increase in female employment. The informal sector development has come to a halt now. Was growing female employment a sign of declining household income in rural areas, which forced women to take on off-farm employment and does the current decline in informal sector employment signal increased employment opportunities in an expanding market economy?

In 1971 the proportion of wage labour in the male agricultural labour force in Java had grown to 31%, substantially higher than at the beginning of this century. This can be interpreted as a sign of increasing landlessness, which forced male workers to rely increasingly on wage labour. 'The female data for 1971 were very similar to those of 1905, with the exception of Yogyakarta, indicating that the great majority of female agricultural workers continued to be either wage workers or unpaid family workers' (Booth 1988:49). The rapid change occurred during the 1970s, when female informal sector employment rose considerably from 29% to 36% of the labour force. This rapid growth, which in Java was concentrated in informal sector trade, has now levelled off (Evers 1993, Evers and Mehmet 1994).

Industrialisation After a slow start industrialisation is finally moving ahead.

---

6. According to our 1992 survey in Central Java 20.2% of wage earners in the trade sector had previously worked in agriculture.

Whereas by 1986 the factory workforce of large and medium firms was still 'remarkably small' (Hill 1990:85), it has subsequently grown rapidly without changing the ratio of workers in small and large companies (Hill 1992:31). The change, however, from informal to formal sector employment during the 1980s is most pronounced. According to census figures the proportion of informal sector employment in manufacturing declined by 9% from 1980 to 1985, and by 35% from 1985 to 1990, whereas formal sector employment grew by 8% and 27% respectively (Rice 1992:71).

Government support programs, like KIK (*Kredit Industri Kecil*) have probably provided the means to formalise cottage industries and to create additional employment. The growth of non-oil exports, like textiles, clothing and footwear, which doubled between 1989 and 1991, also indicate employment growth as a result of deregulation policies (Evers 1993b, Hill 1992:31).

On the basis of recent field studies[7] we can only speculate on the direction and shape of this process. Though also women find employment in the growing manufacturing sector, hiring practices are strongly biased towards the employment of young, unmarried women without children. Contrary to all legislation married women are seldom re-employed after they have given birth to their first child. As the return to the informal sector is now getting more difficult due to the above described formalisation process, the social cost of 'modernisation' and formalisation is born by women.

These as well as other data support our thesis on the shift from informal to formal sector work, the growth of industrial wage labour, and the formation of a new class of wage workers. Also the data on rapid bureaucratisation support our claim that formal waged employment is substituting self-employment and informal sector work in rural and urban areas.

Bureaucratisation To be able to push through measures of deregulation and structural adjustment against the opposition of the lower civil service, the Indonesian government has reduced political pressure through the rapid increase of civil service employment. The long-term process of bureaucratisation has been analysed elsewhere (Evers 1987). In the period under discussion here (1970 to 1990) the Indonesian bureaucracy has expanded even further.

---

7. Fieldwork carried out in 1992-93 in textile factories in Yogyakarta and Pekalongan by Susetiawan and Rochman Achwan (doctoral candidates, Sociology of Development Research Centre, University of Bielefeld).

Table 4 **Government employees (thousand and per 1000 population) Indonesia 1920-1990**

Year	Thousand government employees	Government employees per 1000 population
1920	81.5	1.6
1930	111.0	1.8
1940	82.0	1.1
1950	303.5	3.7
1960	393.0	4.1
1970	515.0	4.4
1980	2,047.0	13.9
1990	3,771.2	21.0

Source: Evers (1987), updated

The importance of waged or salaried employment by the government cannot be overestimated. Most urbanised villages (*kelurahan*) are now administered by civil servants. Central and provincial government departments have established branch offices at the sub-district (*kecamatan*) and district (*kabupaten*) level. Primary and secondary schools and the appropriate number of government salaried teachers are found even in remote areas and health services, infrastructure programs and a multitude of government run or sponsored projects employ government servants or create employment through the disbursement of project funds. Government officials are no longer single persons who occasionally may visit a rural area, but a growing class of salaried officials with a distinct life-style and consumption pattern (Gerke 1992:192-86). Police and military personnel, distributed throughout Indonesia in small command posts have to be counted as part of this class.

The recent debate on the growth of an Indonesian middle class and its democratisation potential (Tanter and Young 1990) has generally overlooked the fact that this new middle class is largely made up of government employees and their families.

The growth of a middle class

Average incomes have risen steadily during the past decade, bringing about new patterns of consumption and a new life-style (Gerke 1994). Bicycles have been replaced by motor bikes, television sets and parabola antennas are found in the remotest villages and newly constructed houses are embellished with Greek columns and double or triple roofs and are equipped with modern, factory made furniture. Families enjoy a night out at the Pizza Hut or Kentucky Fried Chicken, shop in a department store instead at the neighbourhood *toko* and enjoy American films at one of the many new cinemas. In short, middle class consumption patterns are visible everywhere and catch the eye more than the occasional Mercedes 300 or the villas of the nouveau riche hidden among the hills surrounding the big cities of Java.

Whereas during the 1970s the middle class was still judged to be 'relatively few in numbers' (Crouch 1984), its size has apparently grown rapidly in recent years. Exact figures are, of course, not available and estimates depend very much on the definition of the term 'middle class'.[8]

The expectation is now frequently voiced that constitutional democracy is going to re-emerge based on the rise of an Indonesian urban middle class (Tanter and Young 1990). The new middle class, united by a particular lifestyle and consumption patterns is, however, dominated by civil servants, as is clear from the following table.

Table 5 **Social composition of the new middle class**[9]
Distribution of middle class occupations in Yogyakarta and Padang

Occupation	Yogyakarta	Padang
Labourer	12.3%	17.1%
Employee	29.2%	21.5%
Govt. officials	58.4%	61.3%
Middle class as % of total	38.5	47.6

n=455 (Yogya 169, Padang 226), wage earners only.

Government employees in turn are politically organised by Golkar, an organisation not necessarily known for its leanings towards liberal democracy. To expect a push towards democratisation from the middle class misreads

---

8. For a definition and for estimates of mobility into the middle class see Evers and Gerke 1994.
9. Members of the 'middle class' earn between Rp5,000 and Rp20,000 per day **and** have completed high school (see Evers and Gerke 1993, 1994). The survey on labour market expansion and segmentation was carried out in 1993-94 in West Sumatra and Yogyakarta by Hans-Dieter Evers and Solvay Gerke in cooperation with the Department of Sociology, Andalas University and the Population Studies Center, Gadjah Mada University.

the social composition and political culture of this growing stratum of Indonesian society, dominated by bureaucrats.

Social transformation and the rise of constitutional democracy

Southeast Asian economies have registered remarkable rates of economic growth. Indonesia has not been an exception, despite the fact that it is neither Confucian nor Westernised. One of the most noteworthy features of high economic growth in Indonesia (and elsewhere in Asia) has been the accompanying political stagnation since 1965. The basic features of the Indonesian New Order government were well established during the first decade and are only now being challenged.

Observers agree that the Indonesian countryside has undergone considerable changes in the past two or three decades after the dramatic and traumatic upheaval before and after 1965. The economic situation in most of rural Indonesia has dramatically changed. The great polarisation between a landowning class and an impoverished peasantry has not materialised as predicted by students of the Green Revolution. Poverty has not disappeared, but it has receded and has been regionally redistributed. Urban areas have grown rapidly partly because of rural-urban migration, but particularly through the extension of an urban way-of-life into the surrounding countryside.

The decline of the informal sector and the growth of wage labour is part and parcel of an expansion of a market economy and market institutions. This has important implications which have been studied for a long time, but whose far-reaching consequences have become apparent again after the demise of communism in Eastern Europe.

The growth of an informal sector is a culturally and politically important phenomenon. A large part of the informal sector is made up of traders (currently more than 10 million people work in the trade sector, about 80% of them in the informal sector). Markets have always been places of gossip and of information and the expansion of markets is connected with an expansion of ideas. Media can be controlled by strong governments but the gossip of the market place defies any kind of government control. The expansion of markets is therefore often seen as a precondition for democratisation (Evers 1993c:364).

On the other hand the informal sector consists primarily of so-called self-employed persons, i.e. of workers who are not proletarians in the original European sense of the term, and who are not subjugated under the direct authority of a landlord, an employer or a bureaucrat. Informal sector traders have nothing to sell but their commodities (to paraphrase Marx's famous dictum). They do not owe allegiance to anyone on economic grounds, and can therefore be easily mobilised for short term political actions, such as demonstrations. They are usually quite willing to sell anything to anybody, among other things also their vote in a general election. The Indonesian power elite has always been afraid of this '*masa apung*' (floating mass) and has therefore gladly accepted the Japanese organising principle of wards (RT) under an elected or appointed head in urban as well as in rural areas, to allow a more effective government control. This control has now partially broken down as shown by mass violence in the slums of Jakarta and in anti-government riots in some rural areas.

During the early 1990s labour unrest has been on the increase, reflecting the growth of industrial wage labour under unfavourable working conditions and earning wages often below the relatively low official minimum wage (currently somewhere between Rp2500 and Rp3500 according to province). It has been estimated, that only a third of the industrial companies adhere to the minimum wage legislation. Though the law allowing employers to call in the military to support them during a labour conflict was revoked in 1993, 'informal' meddling of local military commanders on behalf of employers is still widespread. Another line of conflict, especially in urban areas, is drawn between squatters, often wage labourers, and the government, often acting on behalf of large formal sector companies.

As we have shown, the social stratum of employees and wage labourers is now growing and will eventually look for political representation. Free trade unions would be able to take on this task to a certain extent (as shown by the recent attempts on the part of independent unions to take strike action), but a political party will have to emerge to represent the new working class. In short, the informal sector and its counter image, the proletariat of wage workers, hold key positions in the political process of Indonesia and are likely to be more important players in the process of democratisation than the new, civil service dominated middle class.

References

Abdullah, Irwan, M. Molo and W. Clauss (1989), *Kesempatan Kerja dan Perdagangan di Pedesaan*, Pusat Penelitian Kependudukan, Universitas Gadjah Mada, Yogyakarta.

Booth, A. (1988) *Agricultural Development in Indonesia*, Allen and Unwin, Sydney.

Cremer, G. (1992) *Suchverhalten, Statuserwartungen und offene Arbeitslosigkeit in Entwicklungsökonomien mit rasch expandierendem Bildungssystem*, Eine Untersuchung am Beispiel Indonesiens. Unpublished Habilitation thesis, University of Freiburg i.Br.

Crouch, H., (1984) *Domestic Political Structures and Regional Economic Cooperation*, Singapore: ISEAS

Effendi, Tajuddin Noer (1991) *The Growth of Rural Non-Farm Activities at the Local Level: A Case Study of Causes and Effects in a Subdistrict of Upland Central Java*, Ph.D. dissertation, Flinders University, Adelaide.

Evers, H-D. (1981) 'The Contribution of Urban Subsistence Production to Incomes in Jakarta', *Bulletin of Indonesian Economic Studies XVII*, No.

2: 89-96
_____ (1987) 'The Bureaucratization of Southeast Asia', *Comparative Studies in Society and History* 29,4:66-0-85
_____ (1991) 'Trade as Off-Farm Employment in Central Java', *Sojourn* (Singapore) Vol.6, No.1:1-21
_____ (1992) Large Markets and Small Profits: A Sociological Interpretation of Javanese Petty Trade, in L. Camman (ed) *Traditional Marketing Systems*, Feldafing: DSE, München.
_____ (1993) *Informal Sector Trade in Central Java*, Population Studies Center, Gadjah Mada University, Yogyakarta.
_____ (1993b) *Structural Adjustment Policies and the Social Impact of Market Expansion*, Working Paper No. 187, Sociology of Development Research Centre, University of Bielefeld
_____ (1993c) Perdagangan dan Demokrasi Liberal, in Hotman M. Siahaan dan Tjahjo Purnomo W. (eds) *Sosok Demokrasi Ekonomi Indonesia*, Surabaya Post, Surabaya. pp.361-178
_____ and Solvay Gerke (1993) *Labour Market Segmentation in West Sumatra*, Working Paper No. 197, Sociology of Development Research· Centre, University of Bielefeld
_____ and Solvay Gerke (1994) *Social Mobility and the Transformation of Indonesian Society*, Working Paper, Sociology of Development Research Centre, University of Bielefeld
_____ and H. Schrader (1993) *The Moral Economy of Trade. Ethnicity and the Expansion of Markets*, Routledge, London.
_____ and Ozay Mehmet (1994) 'The Management of Risk: Informal Sector Trade in Indonesia', *World Development*, Vol.22, No.1 (forthcoming)
Geertz, C. (1963) *Agricultural Involution* University of California Press. Berkeley, Cal.
Gerke, S. (1991) *Changes in the Small-Scale Trade Sector in Rural Java*, Working Paper No.146. Sociology of Development Research Centre, Bielefeld.
_____ (1992) *Social Change and Life Planning of Rural Javanese Women*, Bielefeld Studies on the Sociology of Development No.51., Breitenbach Publishers, Saarbrücken and Fort Lauderdale, Fla.
_____ (1994) 'Symbolic Consumption and the Indonesian Middle Class', Paper, Workshop on Postmodern Scholarship in Southeast Asia, ISEAS, Singapore 25 February 1994
Hart, J.K. (1973) 'Informal Income Urban Employment in Ghana', *Journal of Modern African Studies*, Vol. 11.
Hill, H. (1990) 'Indonesia's Industrial Transformation', *BIES* 26,2:79-120; 26,3:75-109
_____ (1992) 'Survey of Recent Developments', *BIES* 28,2:1-45
Hüsken, F. (1989) Cycles of Commercialization and Accumulation in a Central Javanese Village, in G. Hart *et al.* (eds) *Agrarian Transformations: Local Processes and the State in Southeast Asia*, University of

California Press, Berkeley.
Manning, C. (1988) 'Rural Employment Creation in Java: Lessons from the Green Revolution and the Oil Boom', *Population and Development Review* 14, 1: 47-80
Moir, H. (1978) *The Informal Sector of Jakarta*. LEKNAS-LIPI, Jakarta.
Rice, R.C. (1992) *The Informal Sector Employment in Indonesia: Some Issues and Suggestions for Improvement*, Information System for Employment Development and Manpower Planning, Report Series A, No.11. DEPNAKER/UNDP/ILO, Jakarta.
Schweizer, T. (1987) 'Agrarian Transformation? Rice Production in a Javanese Village', *BIES* 23,2:38-70
Schweizer, T. (1990) 'A Century of Change in the Javanese Rural Economy: Contrasting Developments in Upland and Lowland Klaten', *Internationales Asienforum* 21, 1-2:259-277
Sethuraman, S.V. (1976) *Jakarta: Urban Development and Employment*, ILO, Geneva.
Tanter, R. and K. Young (eds) (1990) *The Politics of Middle Class Indonesia*. Monash University, Centre of Southeast Asian Studies, Clayton, Victoria.

28

The Inner Contraction of the Suharto Regime: a starting point for a withdrawal to the barracks

Ulf Sundhaussen

The New Order of General Suharto has now lasted for more than a quarter of a century. The question is whether the military-dominated system of government can outlive the eventual political or biological demise of its architect and steward without undergoing drastic modification.

Over time the legitimacy of all authoritarian regimes is likely to be questioned. Military regimes may be inclined to ignore their declining legitimacy for longer than civilian regimes; on the other hand, their legitimacy may decline more rapidly than that of civilian regimes. The reason is that military men, with some striking exceptions, are unlikely to have the skills required for political processes. This is largely due to the organisational culture of the military. Socialised into an organisation which depends on adherence to the principles of discipline and hierarchy, military men are accustomed to giving and obeying orders, and have difficulty adjusting to arguing and bargaining, the modes of operation in the realm of politics.

When military rulers experience legitimacy deficits they will be asked to move over to allow professional politicians to run politics (Sundhaussen 1984:545-7). After all, most coup-makers gain initial civilian acceptance, or at least toleration, by the assurance that military rule will only be temporary. Moreover, it matters little whether they have solved the problems which initially served as the justification of their intervention: if they have, indeed, solved those problems, they have worked themselves out of the job; if they failed to do so, there is no good reason for them to stay on.

In this situation several policy options are available. One option is to hang on to power no matter how much force this entails. But the cost in terms of accelerating oppression cannot be sustained indefinitely. Another option is to broaden the basis of the regime, retaining power but giving strategically important groups in society a real share of power. A more drastic step would be to vacate the seat of power, and either impose certain limitations on the civilian successor regime (which, almost invariably, leads to re-intervention); or throw the system wide open and allow for free elections to determine the course of politics (Huntington 1968:233-37). The choice as to which of these options to follow is not left solely to the discretion of the regime leaders; a range of factors which can be divided into *reasons* and *preconditions* for withdrawal, have to be taken into account. If a regime fails to face up to the challenges to its rule it may lose the capacity to influence unfolding events.

Reasons for military withdrawal to the barracks

There are three sets of *reasons* which compel a military regime to consider its policy options. Firstly, its legitimacy may have so declined over the years that civilian opposition to it begins to be articulated and activated. Such opposition may range from mere social pressure on the members of the armed forces by the general populace to armed resistance.

Secondly, regime legitimacy may have declined in the eyes of the outside world. This may take the form of loss of support by a patron state for a client military regime. Or a hostile country may resort to invasion. Tanzania's invasion of Idi Amin's Uganda is a case in point.

Finally, pressures endogenous to the military establishment may force the regime's hand. Factions within the officer corps may question the wisdom of hanging on to power for too long. The reasons for such soul-searching may be primarily moral, practical, or a combination of both. It may affect the regime leadership itself, resulting in a declining will to rule.

In an investigation of whether the Suharto regime will continue to govern Indonesia, and whether the regime will survive beyond the demise of its architect, the catalogue of *reasons* provides a useful checklist (Sundhaussen and Green 1985).

Civilian opposition to the regime

In Indonesia civilian opposition to the Suharto government has been so restrained that it has never caused the regime to re-consider its position. Partly, this has to do with the fact that the Indonesian Armed Forces (ABRI) have never promised that their intervention is limited in time; in fact, their doctrine of *dwifungsi* (as an agency for national defence and security, and as a socio-political force) postulates that its non-military activities are permanent.

As it stands, the government 'party' Golkar (Functional Groups) is firmly controlled by regime loyalists, mostly retired generals. There have always been aspirations within certain sections of Golkar to become less dependent on the regime leadership. But even if these dreams were to come true, Golkar, being part of the regime, may in the end not be willing to shake its own foundations.

The non-government parties, the all-Muslim Unity Development Party (PPP) and the secular and Christian Indonesian Democratic Party (PDI) do not clamour for power. As PPP Secretary General Mardinsyah once put it so succinctly, 'our purpose in an election is not to take control of the government but to participate in it' (*FEER* 20 Nov 1986). The PDI is not markedly more disposed towards challenging Suharto and the military-dominated system of government.

Of course, opposition may come from outside the formal party landscape. But the only truly dynamic party the country has ever experienced, the Communist Party of Indonesia (PKI), was crushed by the Army and its civilian allies in late 1965. Given the fact that this was achieved by slaughtering hundreds of thousands of communists (Cribb 1990) the Far Left may not become active for some time to come. Students have at times staged powerful demonstrations against the regime but they seem now to have run out of steam. Probably the greatest threat to the political *status quo* comes from sections of the salaried and professional middle classes — particularly academics, journalists and artists, but also retired Army officers — who have begun debating the prospects of political change. So far, these groups lack cohesion, organisation, and public support, but in the long run may provide the stimulus for a different system of government.

There is also armed resistance to the regime. In Aceh fundamentalist Muslims have been fighting 'secular Jakarta' since the early 1950s; in Irian Jaya, acquired from the Dutch only in the 1960s, a Melanesian Free Papua Movement has resisted incorporation into Indonesia; and in the newest province, the previous Portuguese colony of East Timor, invaded by Indonesia in 1975, freedom fighters have been waging a protracted guerilla war against the occupation forces. Notably, all these armed conflicts are played out in war theatres at the extremities of the archipelago and therefore do not directly threaten the regime. But they have, as we shall see, some bearing on the long-term directions of the regime.

External interference

Although Suharto's New Order obtained substantial aid from Western countries it has not exposed itself to the threat of loss of financial support from patron states. When the Netherlands, which chaired the international committee of donor countries to Indonesia (IGGI), tried to link aid to human rights issues, Indonesia dissolved IGGI and pointedly refused to accept any more aid from the former colonial power (*The Economist*, 4 April 1992).

Some observers see a greater possibility of foreign intervention in the form of United Nations actions over Indonesia's dismal human rights record, highlighted by its occupation policies in East Timor. But so far, the UN has demonstrated resolve only when one of its member states, Kuwait, was not only attacked by a neighbouring country, but incorporated into it.

Intra-military pressures

Given that civilian opposition to the regime is unlikely to assume proportions which would force the government to re-consider its policy options, and that decisive intervention from outside of Indonesia is even more remote, the discussion regarding regime survival must focus on the regime itself and its major pillar of support, the military. This requires, first, an analysis of the relationship between the government and the military establishment.

GOVERNMENT-MILITARY RELATIONS

The military is portrayed both by scholars and by the notoriously hostile Western press as brutish, corrupt and, of particular relevance in this context, divided. The notion of disunity sustains the cherished thesis that the 'coup' of 1 October 1965 which led to the mass slaughter of communists was not, as the Army was to argue, master-minded by the PKI but the result of intra-Army divisions. Since they came to power, every sign of disagreement between the military and the regime leadership has been exploited to the full in attempts to forecast the imminent collapse of Suharto's New Order.

It may, indeed, be argued that the diverse background of the Indonesian Armed Forces did make it prone to internal dissension. At the same time, no rebellion (with the exception of one mutiny against the Army headquarters in 1952/3) has ever succeeded. Rather, the purges which followed each act of radical dissent gradually made the military more cohesive (Sundhaussen 1971). By the time Suharto secured the leadership over both the Armed Forces and the country it had become clear that radical dissent was extremely dangerous; furthermore, there was the realisation within the officer corps that coups are highly undesirable since they only breed counter-coups and counter-counter-coups (Simatupang in Sundhaussen 1982:53).[1]

When Suharto took over, the four armed services (including the police), which, formerly had enjoyed considerable autonomy under separate ministries, were brought under the centralised Ministry of Defence and Security. Also, a new command structure deprived the once powerful regional commanders of their control over combat troops and vested it in central commands (Sundhaussen 1978:57-67). Even more important were the efforts to professionalise the military. Training facilities on all levels were improved and curricula gradually oriented towards the kind of training normally provided in Western military schools. This included changing the value system. In Western societies the military officer is 'subject to civilian control, not only because of the 'rule of law' and tradition, but also because of self-imposed professional standards and meaningful integration with civilian values' (Janowitz 1960:420). Moreover, the obedience of the new Indonesian military was also handsomely rewarded with political influence, social status, and material benefits. What Suharto aspired to and largely

---

1. . See also T.B. Simatupang (1954:102-5).

achieved was a military which because of the newly implanted professional ethos and the accompanying rewards, would unquestioningly obey government orders and passively support government policies. This is not to say that there are no opinions in the military different from those of Suharto: in an organisation as large as the 280,000 strong military such differences must exist. But once a decision has been made by Suharto no dissent is tolerated.

Indeed, there have been no serious challenges to Suharto from within the military for a quarter of a century. Yet, it could be argued that after such a long period in office a degree of regime fatigue must occur. There is, for instance, growing irritation about the business opportunities provided to Suharto's children, and this excessive nepotism undoubtedly has weakened his authority even amongst his most loyal supporters. But the President has kept firm control over military promotions and assignments, and has so far been able to side-line, or even sack, anyone who came to be seen as lacking in loyalty.

THE INCOMPATIBILITY OF EXISTING MILITARY DOCTRINES

The greatest threat to the longevity of the regime are unfolding contradictions in present military and political doctrines and a clash of class interests which may not be able to be contained beyond Suharto's stewardship of the New Order.

It has to be remembered that the Indonesian Armed Forces came into being not solely as the result of government fiat, but by popular spontaneity; and that the Army in 1948/49 kept fighting Dutch forces when the civilian government had given itself up to the colonial authorities. These factors not only made it more difficult to establish civilian supremacy over the military, but they led the '1945 Generation' of officers to see themselves as the true liberators of the country from colonial rule, and as 'shareholders of the Revolution' who had the 'historical right', if not the obligation, to protect the future of the nation. They were not professional soldiers subscribing to the ethos of the profession of arms, but patriots who had joined the struggle for national independence in the role of the 'fighting man'. Their sense of obligation to render service to the nation increased at the rate at which civilian politics came to be seen as having failed to provide 'good government'.

The Army entered the political arena cautiously, essentially filling the vacuums which emerged as the result of the ineptitude of civilian politicians. It was in the context of the inertia of both the sitting parliament and the Constituent Assembly that the 'Middle Way' concept was proclaimed in 1958 by then Army Chief-of-Staff Nasution, himself a Dutch-trained officer but also a patriotic freedom fighter. This concept stipulates that the military, apart from its normal function of defence, should also be given the opportunity to 'participate actively in non-military fields, and in determining national policies', as well as being represented in all state agencies (Penders and Sundhaussen 1985:133-34; Notosusanto 1979).

Moreover, the specific defence and security requirements of Indonesia were crucial in shaping the Army's political role. Obviously, an archipelago ought to be defended by a strong Navy and Air Force. Yet, Indonesia could never afford to build up these comparatively expensive services. Instead, it came to rely on the Army as the principal pillar of external defence which could also be deployed for internal security purposes. However, even the Army was starved of funds to the extent that it never amounted to much more than a light infantry force. While such a force deprives the country of any offensive capacity, it is ideal for guerilla warfare, an effective deterrent against outside invaders as the war of independence had amply demonstrated.

The key to success in a guerilla war is not military action as such but 'winning the hearts and minds' of the local people without whose support no guerilla movement can survive. When in 1953 Nasution summarised the lessons he had learned in the guerilla war of 1948/49 against superior Dutch forces, he concluded that

> The most important thing is to please the people.... For that reason we must make efforts at all times to improve their conditions in questions of economic matters, education, health and the like...[Therefore a guerilla war] is not only a military war but also a political, psychological, and socio-economic war.... (1965:273,293)

The principle of 'pleasing the people' applies equally when government forces face internal enemies. With guerilla warfare, or Territorial Warfare, adopted as the national defence doctrine, the Army moved to implement its insights from guerilla warfare to the wider field of national politics. It sought to put particularly economic rehabilitation higher on the list of national priorities than, for instance, 'regaining Irian Jaya' or 'crushing Malaysia', in order both to secure its own sustenance, and to be able to 'please the people'.

When General Suharto built his New Order the concept of the 'Middle Way' was replaced by *dwifungsi* (Dual Function). Both doctrines envisaged a political role for the military; but while the former confined the military to being *one* political force among many, the latter designated the military as the *major* pillar of the government. Although military leaders went out of the way to insist that the New Order was not a military regime, (*Kompas* 3 July 1969; and Priyosudarmo 1973:6) Nasution, now chairman of the People's Consultative Congress, soon came to warn of the 'excesses of militarism'.

Suharto's efforts to keep the military establishment tightly under his control by injecting military professionalism into the Armed Forces only accentuated the problem of the inherent contradiction between professional military norms and *dwifungsi*. This difficulty is two-fold. With professional specialisation becoming increasingly time-consuming it becomes almost impossible to train a person in two professions, namely as a military expert as well as an expert in non-military fields. But much more important are the difficulties experienced by professional soldiers, socialised into giving and obeying orders, when their next assignment places them in a political position requiring them to argue and persuade.

Such a proposition may be countered by the argument that for decades the Indonesian military apparently has fared rather well in the implementation of *dwifungsi*. This was, indeed, the case as long as the '1945 Generation' of officers ran a military which was not burdened by the restraint of professionalism. But once officers are successfully socialised into military professionalism they are likely to behave as professional soldiers regardless of what their assignment may be. This problem is understood well enough in Indonesia. As early as March 1972 an Army seminar discussed the problem of passing on the values of those who fought in the war of independence to the *Generasi Muda* (the younger generation of officers) which lacked the unique political experiences of their elders (Sundhaussen 1978:79). Yet the resulting document, the *Dharma Pusaka 45*, while recognising the problem, did not solve it. By now it would be difficult to find an officer of the older generation who would not lament the fact that the *Generasi Muda* has obviously lost the commitment to the welfare of the people, and regards *dwifungsi* as not much more than a formula by which they can retain political power and privileges.

One aspect of this change is the emphasis placed on maintaining internal security by often excessive means rather than by 'pleasing the people', an emphasis abundantly demonstrated in its brutal but inefficient handling of East Timor dissenters. Moreover, security is seen as an indispensable precondition for economic development. On the other hand, development requires that no unnecessary funds are lavished on the military; and in fact, in terms of population/military ratio, Indonesia has one of the smallest military forces in the world, and allocates a lower percentage of public expenditure to the military than any of its ASEAN neighbours except the Philippines (Lau 1987:42). By the same logic, the police, particularly the riot police, is under-funded and under-strength as the government assumes that soldiers can double as policemen. As a result of this policy security is enforced by bringing maximum impact upon anyone disturbing public order. This largely explains why peaceful demonstrators are confronted by combat troops — not just in East Timor or other regions in revolt, but in the capital as well. And if such troops feel that they have 'to do something', they make use of the implements they carry, namely automatic weapons.

MILITARY CLASS VALUES AND CULTURE

But it is not only the increasingly apparent contradiction between the professionalisation of the military and the values which gave birth first to the 'Middle Way' concept and then to *dwifungsi* which create tensions in the military and the existing political system. The blurring of class values provides another level of tensions.

There is a huge cultural and value gap between trading and manufacturing middle classes on the one hand, and the salaried and professional middle classes on the other (Sundhaussen 1991). While the former are easily enough identified by resorting to class analysis, the various groups which constitute the salaried and professional middle classes, are more difficult to isolate. It is even more difficult to identify the respective value systems, and the range and character of the possible political activities of the latter middle class groups. However, the military officer corps as a particular segment of the professional middle classes has been sufficiently investigated to allow some useful generalisations.

In terms of interests, military officers have aspirations similar to those of other salaried middle class groups in state employ, such as civil servants, judges or teachers, which is to earn an income allowing them a dignified, but by no means excessive, life-style. With the large majority of the Indonesian salaried and professional middle class derived from the *priyayi*, the old petty aristocracy (Mahasin 1990:139), traditional *priyayi* values have been transmitted to the modern middle classes. An important aspect of *priyayi* culture for our purposes is the nature of patron-client relationships practised from time immemorial. The patron in such a relationship expects respect and support but, on the other hand, has an obligation to secure the well-being of his followers. For the military this means that the material interests of the Indonesian officer extends well beyond his family to the people under his command.

The corporate interests of the military during the 'Revolution', i.e. the period of 1945-1949, were of minor importance: soldiers served without a regular salary. When Indonesia's independence was recognised Nasution tried to establish a leaner Army which would allow, at no extra cost to the state, decent wages for military personnel. But party politicians torpedoed these plans, and throughout the period of parliamentary democracy military salaries remained below subsistence levels. The introduction of Guided Democracy brought no increase in real military salaries but whole enterprises, usually Dutch properties nationalised as part of the Indonesian drive to wrest West New Guinea from Dutch control, were handed over to the military for its own sustenance. Unfortunately, the income from these properties could not halt the slide into corporate poverty: by the end of Guided Democracy the monthly salary of a full colonel amounted to the meagre equivalent of $US16. The officers never forgave civilian politicians for reducing their self-promoted image of the heroic defenders of the fatherland to those of beggars trying desperately to find sustenance for their families and their subordinates by often highly questionable methods. It took the New Order a number of years to lift salaries to a level sufficient to allow military personnel to survive on them.

Moreover, middle class groups share a commitment to development, equality of opportunity, and upward mobility through merit and education (Dick 1990:68), and the military is no exception to that. The commitment of the Indonesian military to economic development needs no elaboration: in fact, the legitimacy of the New Order rests quite simply on success in economic management. And upward mobility through merit is one of the prerequisites for a modern state and economic development.

The commitment to upholding the state ideology, the Pancasila, with its *sila*s on social justice and people's sovereignty, can of course easily be dismissed as hollow rhetoric; but years of indoctrination in these values may well affect the political attitudes of Indonesian officers. To this may be added the in-built military obsession with law and order which prompts the creation of institutions regularising procedures and processes. Obviously, imposing law and order may largely benefit the regime and muzzle its opponents; but if the law is observed it also provides a degree of security for the latter. Much of the criticism of the New Order, including that by retired officers, has centred on the fact that the law is not upheld thoroughly enough (Nasution 1989).

The ideal-type Indonesian officer is, then, a man with definite material interests reinforced by responsibility for his subordinates, someone committed to serving his country and bringing about modernity, development and the rule of law, and a skilled person who believes in education and the right to acquire information and knowledge in the pursuit of his career. As long as he can afford it, he will also entertain a sense of contempt for people who are primarily interested in making money, i.e. the trading and manufacturing middle class, which is a sentiment wide-spread in the traditional societies of Asia and among the educated throughout the world. Such, anyway, is the self-image nourished by the Indonesian officers, and while circumstances may cause some deviation from this image, the great majority of them feel that efforts ought to be made to maintain it.

But the New Order did little to sustain these norms. While official salaries improved, so did the opportunity for corruption. Many officers came to enjoy the accumulation of wealth. After a period of publicly-paraded austerity and notwithstanding regular proclamations against the ostentatious display of wealth and the occasional anti-corruption drive, corruption has become a hallmark of the New Order.

Other officers, however, take their commitment to service to the nation seriously. The question is, to what extent officers should be allowed to surrender the values typical of the salaried and professional middle classes, and adopt those of trading and manufacturing middle classes determined by the notion of profit maximisation? If this question is not resolved in the long run, it may seriously impair the unity and sense of purpose of the Armed Forces.

Preconditions for military withdrawal to the barracks

Reasons for withdrawing from government responsibility are not the only considerations which determine what policy option a military regime suffering from legitimacy deficit ought to take. *Preconditions* for doing so have to be considered as well (Sundhaussen 1984:549-550). The first *precondition* to be considered is whether regime leaders intent on retreating to the barracks have the backing of all military units capable of taking unilateral action. If there is substantial rejection of such a policy within the officer corps a counter-coup may oust the regime leaders.

A second *precondition* is the extent to which a civilian successor regime will respect the individual, corporate and ideological interests of officers. Regime leaders will seek assurances that there will be no drastic cuts in defence expenditure once they have vacated the presidential palace. Probably even more important is the issue of indemnity against prosecution for, say, corruption and human rights violations: obviously, regime leaders will not resign if their next appointment is with the public prosecutor (Sundhaussen 1985:274-5). Similarly, the military will not tolerate substantial deviations from their vision of the state.

But clearly the most important *precondition* for a hand-over of power to civilian forces is also the most obvious one: the existence of 'high-calibre' civilian leaders able to govern effectively and possessing public confidence. If a post-military government does not have these qualities military re-intervention is not only a possibility, but a high probability.

Consensus within the military

For the time being, the notion that a section of the military may oppose a possible retreat to the barracks is of little relevance to Indonesia. Neither Suharto personally nor the military collectively have any plans to retreat from political power. On 22 July 1992 Suharto warned that 'if ABRI is excluded from the process of determining state policies, it is feared that it may take up arms if it feels unhappy about certain legislation or strategies' (*FEER* 6 August 1992). It may, thus, be safe to conclude that Suharto is unlikely to alter drastically the role the military has been allocated within the framework of the New Order.

However, change is likely once Suharto has left the *istana*. Vice-President Try Sutrisno, his most likely successor, is on record as having said that 'government is not a military monopoly', and that 'future leaders may not necessarily be drawn from the ranks of the Armed Forces' (*Australian Financial Review*, 19 June 1986). Try is fully aware of the fact that the *Generasi Muda* has not the same legitimacy in the quest for power as the '1945 Generation' of officers. He is also familiar with the contradiction of being a professional soldier and a politician at the same time, and may come to conclude that the only solution to this intra-military problem is to change *dwifungsi*, or even abandon it altogether. When that moment comes the issue of convincing the Armed Forces that such steps have to be taken, may be one of the problems he will have to confront.

Military interests

When the moment has arrived for the military to consider foregoing political power, it is unlikely to agree to heavy cuts in the defence budget. It has to be remembered that the Indonesian military is a low-cost, small force which cannot be trimmed down much further. A civilian government in Indonesia bent on cutting military expenditure could only retrench the 'territorial' organisation of the Army as a major cost saving measure. However, this would require giving up 'Territorial Warfare' as the major defence doctrine, and strengthening the Navy and Air Force leading to drastic increases in over-all defence spending. Simply lowering the defence expenditure regardless of its implication for national security would entice the military to consider re-intervention.

Also, the military would refuse to cooperate in the civilianisation of the polity if the successor government would hold soldiers responsible for past human rights violations. Nor would officers like to be asked to account for wealth accumulated in the past.

Finally, the military would not tolerate any radical tinkering with the state ideology, the Pancasila. A discernible move towards, say, Islamization of the polity, or any form of socialism, would terminate all efforts to hand power back to civilian politicians.

Availability of civilian counter-elites

If, due to unforeseeable circumstances, General Suharto and the military were suddenly prepared to relinquish power, there would be no effective civilian leaders or parties able to command popular support. Golkar is still run by the military and so far has failed to acquire a political soul of its own, and both the PPP and the PDI still go out of their respective ways not to be seen to be clamouring for power. They certainly do not have the confidence of the people: in New Order elections they together capture usually about one third of popular votes. Moreover, the deep-seated antagonism between Muslims and more secular forces which has plagued Indonesia from its inception, has not been overcome yet, and may rule out any degree of cooperation or mutual toleration.

Of course, this situation is likely to change. In the process of *regenerasi* which affects the military and non-military organisations alike, the politicians of old are being eased out by younger activists who demand a greater say in politics. This process is under way within the PDI, and Muslim politicians within and outside the PPP have begun to probe what is politically feasible. Moreover, there are a large number of NGOs and activist groups which may well be the breeding ground for a new kind of politician. Last but not least, a variety of middle class activists have swelled the choir of those critical of permanent military rule. But so far, these groupings lack the capacity to challenge the regime.

Conclusions

A current world-wide trend towards democratisation has enhanced pressures for military rulers to withdraw to the barracks, as has the end of the Cold War which released the Super Powers from the 'necessity' to recruit allies in the Third World with whom they normally would prefer not to associate. As a result, military regimes have vanished in many regions of the Third World.

General Suharto's New Order has so far weathered all winds of political change. This truly remarkable regime resilience can partly be explained by the fact that there simply is no viable alternative to Suharto. Also, among the more important explanations is a traditional sense of authoritarianism which inclines people not to go against established authority. But the legitimacy of the regime is primarily seen as 'not due to the supremacy of their weaponry, but to their ability to solve problems.'(Fachry Ali, quoted in Liddle 1992:fn6) Whatever the truth of this assertion, no dissent has been tolerated allowing the Suharto government to begin solving the economic problems of the country; and while by no means everybody benefited equally from these policies, the standard of living of potentially vocal groups certainly improved. Ironically, successful economic strategies also strengthen the very societal forces which, in time, will challenge the political monopoly of civilian-authoritarian and military regimes alike. In any case, as we have noted already, the ability to solve problems is no guarantee against a popular desire for change.

As things stand, the legalised political parties do not clamour for power, and other critics lack the coordination and organisation to force the regime into a serious consideration of its longer-term options. Secondly, the chances of outside intervention with the effect of changing Indonesia's political structure, are more than remote. The most important *reason* for the regime to consider its long-term options, therefore, lies in factors endogenous to the military.

While Suharto remains at the helm of the government no substantial change in the distribution of power is to be expected. His unopposed re-election in March 1993, and the successive cabinet re-shuffle which eliminated from positions of power those officers who were seen by outside observers as being too independent of Suharto (Vatikiotis 1992:205), proves — yet again — that the President is in full control of the government and the military.

But his successor, most likely General Try Sutrisno, is unlikely to achieve a level of control similar to that of the incumbent president because he lacks the authority as well as political nous of Suharto. So the contradictions between military professionalism and *dwifungsi*, as well as the erosion of traditional military middle class values, may not be able to be contained beyond Suharto's departure from the apex of the system he created. Significant changes can therefore be reasonably expected for the post-Suharto era.

The biggest obstacle to the civilianisation of the Indonesian government is the non-availability of a civilian counter-elite which would not only undertake to recognise the individual, corporate and ideological interests of military leaders, but would also offer credible prospects of being able to provide strong leadership.

In these circumstances the political outcomes in the post-Suharto polity become more predictable. Because it will take considerable time and effort before civilian activists can meet the *precondition* of creating a viable counter-elite, the policy options of establishing in the short run a functioning democracy appear to be remote. The most likely outcome, then, is a broadening of the regime's base aimed at shoring up its legitimacy. This would involve a genuine sharing of power with other social forces until these forces are seen to be able to take over the government, and further professionalisation of the military has reconciled its officers to the view that the true military professional ought to restrict himself to exercising only the roles he is trained for.

References

Cribb, R. (ed) (1990) *The Indonesian Killings 1965-1966*, Centre of Southeast Asian Studies, Monash University, Clayton.

Dick, H.W. (1990) Further Reflections on the Middle Class, in R. Tanter and K. Young (eds) *The Politics of Middle Class Indonesia*, Centre of Southeast Asian Studies, Monash University, Clayton.

Huntington, S.P. (1968) *Political Order in Changing Societies*, Yale University Press, New Haven.

Janowitz, M. (1960) *The Professional Soldier*, Free Press, New York.

Lau Taik Soon, (1987) Defence Expenditures of ASEAN States: The Regional Strategic Context, in Chin Kin Wah (ed) *Defence Spending in Southeast Asia*, Institute of Southeast Asian Studies, Singapore.

Liddle, R.W. (1992) 'Indonesia's Threefold Crisis', *Journal of Democracy* 3 (4), October 1992

Mahasin, Aswab (1990) The Santri Middle Class: An Insider's View, in R. Tanter and K. Young (eds) *The Politics of Middle Class Indonesia*.

Nasution, A.H. (1989) *Sejarah dan Esensi serta Praktek Dwifungsi*, Jakarta.

_____ (1965) *Fundamentals of Guerilla Warfare*, Pall Mall Press, London.

Notosusanto, Nugroho (1979) 'Angkatan Bersendjata dalam Percaturan Politik di Indonesia', *Prisma* 8(8), August 1979.

Penders, C.L.M. and U. Sundhaussen (1985) *Abdul Haris Nasution, A Political Biography*, University of Queensland Press, St. Lucia.

Priyosudarmo, Sunandar [Major General] (1973) *Penyelenggaraan Pemerintah di Indonesia Berdasarkan U.U.D. 1945*, SESKOAD, Bandung.

Simatupang, T.B. (1954) *Pelopor dalam Perang, Pelopor dalam Damai*, Jakarta.

Sundhaussen, U. (1971) 'The Fashioning of Unity in the Indonesian Army', *Asia Quarterly* No. 2, 1971.

_____ (1978) The Military: Structure, Procedures, and Effect on Indonesian Society, in K.D. Jackson and L.W. Pye (eds) *Political Power and Communications in Indonesia*, University of California Press, Berkeley.

_____ (1984) 'Military Withdrawal from Government Responsibility', *Armed Forces and Society* 10(4), Summer 1984

_____ (1985) The Durability of Military Regimes in South-East Asia, in Zakaria H. Ahmad and H. Crouch (eds) *Military-Civilian Relations in South-East Asia*, Oxford University Press, Singapore.

_____ and B. Green (1985) Indonesia: Slow March into an Uncertain Future, in C. Clapham and G. Philip (eds) *The Political Dilemmas of Military Regimes*, Croom Helm, London and Sydney.

_____ (1982) *The Road to Power, Indonesian Military Politics 1945-1967*, Oxford University Press, Kuala Lumpur.

_____ (1991) 'Democracy and the Middle Classes: Reflections on Political Development', *Australian Journal of Politics and History* 37(1), 1991.

Vatikiotis, M.R.J. (1993) *Indonesian Politics under Suharto*, Routledge, London and New York.

29

Can all good things go together? Democracy, Growth, and Unity in post-Suharto Indonesia

R. William Liddle

Alternative approaches

In comparative political science, there is a substantial body of recent research, much of it East Asia-based, on the relationship between regime type (authoritarian versus democratic) and economic growth. There is no comparable literature on the relationship between regime type and national unity, though current events in East Europe may soon produce one.

The conventional wisdom in the East Asian growth-and-politics literature is that democracy is incompatible with rapid economic development, particularly of the export-led variety. Robert Wade's *Governing the Market* (1990) makes the case, mainly with data from Taiwan, that a prime cause of development success in East Asia has been the presence of an interventionist or activist as opposed to a passive-policeman state. An interventionist state in turn must be both authoritarian and corporatist. Stephan Haggard, in his widely-cited *Pathways From the Periphery* (1990), explicitly concludes that authoritarianism is not a prerequisite of successful export-led growth. His substantive argument, however, based on the Korea, Taiwan, Singapore, and Hong Kong cases, puts great weight on the degree of 'insulation' of the state from societal pressures.

In my reading of Haggard's book and many similar studies, the concept of insulation comes close to being a euphemism for authoritarianism. Insulation means the independence of state officials from the demands of social groups, and democracy implies the responsiveness of officials, through the electoral and policy-making processes, to such demands. There is therefore at the very least an inherent tension between the concepts of insulated and of democratic government.

For this reason, the concept of insulation seems to me to obscure rather than to clarify the nature of the relationship between regime type and economic growth. I prefer to build instead on the idea that politicians in all systems, democratic and authoritarian, accumulate and deploy in various combinations three basic kinds of political resources: coercive, normative, and utilitarian (Lehman 1969). This alternative approach offers, I think, a more appropriate frame for examining the connection between the political process and policy outcomes.

Coercive resources, in an authoritarian regime, are the principal stuff of insulation; in sufficient quantity, and effectively mobilised and deployed, they make it possible for government officials to deny and repress popular opinion. In a constitutional democracy governments also possess and use coercive resources, but as the ultimate sanctions behind the judicial process, not as uncontrolled weapons in the hands of the executive.

Coercion in democracies is an instrument of policy enforcement and of protection for officials from individuals and groups who are willing to use illegal or unconstitutional violence to achieve political ends. But it does not protect them from the retribution of interest groups who may mobilise against the government in electoral and other constitutional ways.

Normative resources are attitudes and beliefs such as recognition of a state's or a government's legitimacy, identification of state policy with a popular ideology, or the respect or awe accorded to a strong or charismatic leader. They may also be used for insulation in the limited sense that a government can obtain acquiescence in an unpopular policy if it has wider support for its general policy orientation, its adherence to a constitution, or its leaders' right to make authoritative decisions. But normative resources alone are not likely to provide effective long term support for major policy orientations that are at odds with widely popular demands.

Utilitarian resources are the more tangible, material ingredients of exchange, the policies, programs, appointments, contracts, and awards given by a government in return for political support. They are the predominant component of day-to-day politics in democracies, but can also be important in authoritarian systems (as in fact they have been in Indonesia's New Order).

It is the centrality of utilitarian exchange in democracies that raises fears about their unsuitability for rapid economic growth in developing countries. Many resourceful individuals and social groups may make demands on government for macroeconomic, sectoral, and other policies that run counter to the policies required for growth. If these individuals and groups are sufficiently influential, economic progress will be slowed or even stopped.

This argument is based on the notion of the dilemma of collective action — the proposition that the pursuit by individuals and groups of their private interests does not always or necessarily lead to the realisation of the good of the whole — central to the thinking of public choice theorists. The universality of collective action dilemmas suggests that, in the minds of many public choice theorists and other analysts borrowing from this tradition, like Wade and Haggard, democracy may nowhere be considered a suitable form of government.

To my mind, this is a sign for hope rather than despair, for the fact of the matter is that, despite collective action problems, democratic institutions have worked fairly well in most of the industrialised economies of the West for decades, in some cases centuries.

This brief excursus into theory has been designed to counter the mainstream scholarly view that authoritarianism or insulation is a prerequisite for growth, and to replace the conceptual framework of collective action dilemmas that undergirds it with a scheme that will enable us to look more directly at the variables involved. Within this context, how can a democratic government be created that does not threaten either continued rapid economic growth or national unity?

In this essay I will focus on two major obstacles to successful democratisation of this kind: the nature of politically mobilisable cleavages in Indonesian society and the resource gap between pro- and anti-democratic forces, the latter primarily in the military. I will then offer a distinction, borrowed from the Italian political scientist Giovanni Sartori, between centrifugal and centripetal party systems, and propose that construction of the latter is a *sine qua non* of an Indonesian democracy that does not undermine unity or diminish growth.

In the final section I will discuss a recent statement by Sarwono Kusumaatmadja, a leader of a faction within the state political party Golkar that has long appeared to be genuinely committed to eventual democratisation. My purpose is to begin a debate as to the value of Sarwono's strategy of reform for creating a centripetal party system and thus overcoming the two major obstacles to democratisation.

Groups and the politics of growth and unity in a democratic Indonesia

In this section I want to single out some key groups in Indonesian society that are potential supporters of democratisation and that might be brought into a new pro-growth, pro-national unity coalition or political formula. I will begin with economic interests, and then discuss ethnic/regional and religious groups.

Domestic and foreign professional economists, no matter how sympathetic personally they may be to democracy, appear to be at one in the view that Indonesia needs to be ruled by an authoritarian government for some time into the future (see e.g. Timmer 1992:12). They believe that to maintain rapid growth the government must continue to pursue an export-led growth strategy, and that the social forces in favour of such a strategy are much less powerful than those in opposition. The latter are said to include both the big conglomerates, most of whose profits still come from sales to domestic markets, and smaller entrepreneurs, who chafe under the restrictions imposed on them by high interest rates and other policies of the economists.

I have several rejoinders to this standard argument. First, there is today something approaching a Third World-wide, certainly an East Asia-wide, consensus on the preferability of the export manufacturing route to development. This consensus is backed up by the ability of the World Bank, the International Monetary Fund, and the Consultative Group on Indonesia to give or deny financial assistance depending on their evaluation of the Indonesian government's policies.

This situation differs considerably from that of the 1950s, when import substitution policies were advocated by many development economists as the best way to break the vicious circle of underdevelopment. It even differs from the mid-1960s, when it took great courage for General Suharto to adopt the policies of the economists. The current consensus and the World Bank/IMF/CGI institutional backup are powerful resources that can be used to build a winning coalition by either an authoritarian or a democratic politician. Conversely, they make it harder for a politician, again either authoritarian or democratic, to win support by challenging the consensus.

Second, Sino-Indonesians still constitute the large majority of successful business people. If Indonesia becomes a democracy, their way of articulating their political interests is not likely to change very much, at least in the short run. That is, they will still seek a personal relationship with high officials and to a lesser extent work through the business associations described so well by Andrew MacIntyre (1991). They will not form political parties of their own, both because they are suspect as insufficiently Indonesian, and therefore prefer a more private political style, and because political parties led by a 4% racial minority could not hope to attract enough support from the 96% majority to win many parliamentary seats. My point is this: if Sino-Indonesian influence in the New Order is not great enough to overcome the economists' control of macroeconomic policy, it is not likely to do so in a democratic regime either.

Third, fear of capital flight will be just as strong in the minds of the leaders of a democratic Indonesia as it has been to New Order authoritarians. If a new government lowers interest rates substantially, or in other ways destabilises or threatens the business climate, the resulting capital flight to Singapore, Hong Kong, and elsewhere will choke off investment and continued growth, and generate its own political backlash from a range of domestic interests.

Fourth, there is probably a growing number of groups that benefit from deregulation and export-led growth policies and that would therefore constitute a support base for a new democratic government adhering to these policies. Obviously, this base would include all those manufacturers who now export a large percentage of their production, the companies that have made the recent export boom possible. Many of the conglomerates, which contain both export- and import substitution-oriented divisions, are if not pro-export, at least in conflict (and thus politically immobilised or indecisive) on this issue.

The pro-export, pro-democracy base might be much wider than this. It might also include the millions of small farmers who have gained economically from the rice and rural development policies of the past quarter century and who increasingly deposit their savings in the rural banking system (Gonzalez-Vega & Chaves 1992). Small-town entrepreneurs may prefer lower interest rates so that they can expand their businesses, and would also probably not mind a mild debt-eroding inflation. But they would be opposed by anti-inflationary, pro-high interest rate savers, who might well be much more numerous today. Organised urban labour — that is, autonomously-formed labour unions replacing the current state corporatist SPSI — might also be attracted to this coalition, if it could be demonstrated to union leaders that manufacturing employment in the present and future is dependent on the continued growth of export markets.

Finally, both Ruth McVey and Richard Robison see an increasing regularisation of the Indonesian political process, in terms of the government's relationship with the business community, that may be a first step toward democratisation. McVey (1992:32) writes that 'Increasingly, what determines Southeast Asian policy-makers' strategic decisions will be the interplay of complex interests — bureaucratic, political, and business, national and regional — which will be expressed more and more through agencies, associations, and lobbies rather than through the dyadic relationships of patron-client networks.' Arguably, these relationships are more easily conducted in a Western-style (bourgeois, if you will) democratic political system than in a continuation of the New Order's patrimonial authoritarianism. Robison's analysis (1992) focuses more narrowly on the growth of the state, but also stresses a regularisation that includes strengthening the rule of law.

The continuing threat by ethnic/regional and religious groups to national unity is one of the principal New Order justifications for authoritarianism. In a democratic Indonesia, would there be a significantly increased opposition either to the boundaries or to the religious pluralism of the Indonesian nation-state? Alternatively, what regional and religious groups might become major supporters of a democratic regime?

One near-certainty is that East Timor, forcibly incorporated in 1975-76, would not long be part of a democratic Indonesia (see Liddle 1992a). Irian Jaya, whose modern history sets it apart from the rest of the country, might also see a resurgence of nationalist activity. Aceh, despite recent disturbances, is not a likely candidate for independence. Unlike the people of East Timor or Irian, the Acehnese did participate in the Indonesian nationalist movement. The memory of and pride in that participation remains strong, and there is today a modern, schooled elite solidly rooted in Acehnese culture and society and at the same time fully committed to the Indonesian nation-state. There are also many economic links that bind Aceh to the rest of Indonesia.

Beyond these three regions, separatism is not likely to be an issue at all. The ties of Indonesian nationalism, rooted in the movement and revolutionary years, appear to remain strong. They have been fortified for the elite and for an increasingly educated citizenry by common experiences in school, the spread and growth of modern *bahasa Indonesia* and the all-Indonesia culture whose values and struggles that language expresses and shapes, and by a pervasive political-economic network of institutions.

What is likely to be an issue is decentralisation. While few groups in the regions appear to have any thoughts of seceding, many would like to have a greater devolution of governmental power from the centre to the provinces. This is particularly true for business groups, whose members resent, for example, the restrictions imposed by the centre on exporting directly to foreign buyers (or importing from foreign sellers) instead of having to go through Jakarta or a major regional port like Medan, Surabaya, or Ujung Pandang. More generally, there is a close association between democracy and provincial autonomy in the minds of many members of the politically active or would-be active public who live in the regions.

Finally, there is the question of religious cleavages, and particularly of a politically resurgent Islam. Would Islamic groups in a democratic Indonesia constitute a threat to the maintenance of a religiously plural state? In the last two years much attention has been focused on the formation and activities of ICMI (Indonesian Muslim Intellectuals' Association) and the opposition to ICMI which has taken shape in Abdurrahman Wahid's *Forum Demokrasi* (Democratic Forum).

My view is that Islamic groups will not constitute a threat as long as they organise as interest groups only. Muslim political parties, however, are likely to be politically destabilising if not genuinely threatening to religious pluralism.

From one perspective, the political calculations of President Suharto, who blessed its creation and anointed its patron, Minister of Research and Technology B.J. Habibie, ICMI is a limited purpose, probably short-term tactical political instrument. It is quite possible, even likely, that both Suharto and Habibie will lose interest in it in the near future.

Muslims outside the government who have joined ICMI appear to have a stronger commitment. They can perhaps be clustered into three groups: clients, with an Islamic (*santri*) social background but without an Islamic agenda, seeking patrons in standard New Order fashion; *santri* social activists who see ICMI as an opportunity to advance an egalitarian agenda; and religious activists who see an opportunity to make Indonesia more Islamic, particularly but not entirely in the formal sense of greater conformity to the symbols of religious observance. Among the latter group there has been much talk about the possibility that ICMI might be the embryo of a new

Masyumi in a democratic Indonesia.[1]

The most important Islamic social and political leader who has not joined ICMI is Abdurrahman Wahid, since 1984 the head of *Nahdlatul Ulama* (NU), Indonesia's largest Islamic social and educational organisation, with a claimed membership of over thirty million. Abdurrahman is a social democrat who envisions a democratic Indonesia without religious parties. For that reason he pulled NU out of the Islamic political party PPP in 1984. Abdurrahman condemns ICMI as sectarian, as a step backwards toward political divisions based on religion. He believes that it increases the fear of Islam among others.[2] His own *Forum Demokrasi* includes many non-*santri* and non-Muslims.

Is Abdurrahman right? Would a new Masyumi — that is, an Islamic political party competing with non-Islamic parties in genuinely free elections — have a destabilising effect? My own answer is yes, though there are strong arguments on both sides.

Those in favour of an Islamic party (or parties, for surely there would be more than one) say that Indonesians are all now Pancasilaists. They claim that there is no longer a significant group of Muslim political activists or potential activists who favour an Islamic state, as that term was used in the 1950s. Some, indeed, argue that the Islamic state concept was itself never very clear or deeply held in the minds of its protagonists. They assert that a new Masyumi would be like the Christian democratic parties of Europe, a vehicle more of modern middle class than of traditional religious interests.

They also contend that there is a secular trend toward *santrinisasi* or Islamisation, so that the old *abangan-santri* polarisation has lost much of its meaning. And they conclude with the clincher that an Islamic party or parties is what most Muslims want. The issue is therefore not whether there will be Islamic parties in a democratic Indonesia but rather how many there will be, what objectives they will have, how big a share of the vote they will get, and so on.

My sense that Muslim parties are a bad idea is based on two considerations, one elite and near-term, the other mass and long-term. First, demands for an Islamic party made at the time of a democratic transition are bound to be opposed by most Army officers, who have been carefully recruited from non-*santri* backgrounds and/or socialised into anti-Islamic state military ideology.

Second, Islamic parties will inevitably have a polarising effect at the mass level. This is already apparent in the nervousness of non-Islamic groups concerning ICMI. There is a large constituency potentially mobilisable on issues suspiciously close to the old Islamic state idea. The enormous success

---

[1]. This idea is also very popular among small town Muslims in east and central Java. Field notes from a trip from Yogyakarta to Surabaya, November 1990.

[2]. See the long interview, 'Abdurrahman Wahid: Saya Presiden Taxi saja deh' [Abdurrahman Wahid: I'll just be President Taxi] (1992).

of ostensibly apolitical *muballigh* (preachers) like Zainuddin M.Z. is a sign of a popular hunger for guidance in personal life that may be put to political use. During election campaigns there is bound to develop a process of outbidding for the *santri* vote between Islamic and non-religious parties and among competing Islamic parties in which the rhetoric can easily become inflammatory.

On the other hand, persuading Muslims not to form parties in a democratic Indonesia does not mean keeping them out of politics. Like all other groups, Muslims have interests which require channels for articulation to government decision-makers. But these views can be effectively represented by organisations like *Nahdlatul Ulama*, the modernist Islamic social and educational organisation *Muhammadiyah*, and even the currently excessively timorous *Majelis Ulama Indonesia* (the state-created Council of Indonesian Muslim Religious Teachers) without touching the large and dangerous questions to which partisan battles often lead.

Confronting Leviathan

In the previous sections I have argued that, despite a scholarly consensus to the contrary, democracy, growth, and unity in countries like Indonesia are probably in principle compatible. I have also tried to show that many groups now exist that might be brought into a pro-growth, pro-unity democratic coalition. There is, however, a Brobdingnagian political force that stands in their way: ABRI, the Armed Forces of the Republic of Indonesia. What are the characteristics and resources of this leviathan, and how might it be induced to withdraw from politics?

Juan Linz and Alfred Stepan (forthcoming:42-45) propose a useful distinction between hierarchical and non-hierarchical military-based non-democratic regimes. In hierarchical regimes, the military acts politically as an institution under its commanding officers, while non-hierarchical regimes are led by lower-ranking officers who have come to power through coups against their seniors.

In a hierarchical regime, 'the officer corps, taken as a whole, sees itself as a permanent part of the state apparatus, with enduring interests and permanent functions that transcend the interests of the government of the day.' Linz and Stepan draw two important implications from this situation. First, democratic transition may be made easier by the organisational needs of the military, as articulated by its top leaders. Second, however, a hierarchical military poses serious obstacles to the consolidation of a democratic regime, after the transition has taken place. 'Precisely because the military ... is a permanent part of the state apparatus, and as such has privileged access to coercive resources, it will be an integral part of the machinery that the new democratic government has to manage.'

The New Order is a hierarchically-led military regime in two somewhat different and potentially conflicting senses. First, in a broad sense it is led by Suharto, a general who became *de facto* Army commander on October 1,

1965 by virtue of his official position in command of strategic troops and the strong support of his fellow officers, but who has long since retired and is now commander-in-chief only *ex officio* as president. Second, ABRI is currently led by officers — the commander, the Army chief of staff, and so on down — appointed by a hierarchical process controlled by seniors. At the top of this hierarchy is of course the President, who directly chooses the commander and other top officers and who also has final say over virtually all Armed Forces appointments and promotions of any importance.

What makes this arrangement a potential source of conflict is that two institutional (plus of course many personal) interests are at work: the interest of the presidency and the interest of the Armed Forces, both of which are seen by incumbents in terms of autonomy from and control over other institutions. Since about 1987 there has been in fact a growing gap between the two institutions. The principal reasons for this are Suharto's advancing age and apparent desire to stay in office until he dies, coupled with Armed Forces concern to retain control over the presidency and the political system in general in the post-Suharto period. I will pursue the implications of this point below.

What are the political resources with which ABRI has gained and maintained its present dominance over other state institutions and over society? Coercion does not exist in a vacuum. It requires unity within the coercing organisation, in particular a willingness all the way down the line to obey the leadership hierarchy. In the New Order, this obedience has been achieved through a combination of persuasion and exchange.

Persuasion means the promotion of the idea of a moral order within ABRI, emphasising ideals of nationalism, discipline, service, self-sacrifice, and so on, which justify the institution's internal decision processes and also its relationship to the larger society. Exchange means appropriating material and status resources — business opportunities, governmental positions — from society and using them to secure the support of subordinates.

President Suharto and senior ABRI officers have been expert persuaders and exchangers. For the most part, as I have already indicated, the two groups have worked in tandem throughout the New Order to achieve these results. It is probably true, however, that material resources have over time come more and more under the control of the President at the expense of the Armed Forces.

Effective use of coercion requires organisational networks for intelligence gathering and political supervision. Since the late 1950s ABRI has built four extensive Armed Forces-society networks: the territorial command system; the appointment of officers to positions within the civilian bureaucracy; appointed membership in the MPR, DPR, and DPRD at the provincial and district levels; and leadership in Golkar by retired officers.

ABRI's relationship with the larger society has not, however, been based entirely on its monopoly over the means of violence, its ability to extract resources from society for internal military consumption, and its surveillance and supervisory capacities. Processes of exchange and persuasion have been at work in other ways as well.

Most Armed Forces-society exchange has been economic, trading delivery of economic goods and services to many large and politically important civilian groups in return for acceptance of military rule. This practice has motivated the military, under Suharto's leadership, to build an alliance with the professional economists and the civilian bureaucracy. The economists provide the knowledge and skills to make economic growth happen, in return for which they are rewarded with high government positions, respect for their service to the nation, and business opportunities. The bureaucrats provide the organisation and personpower to implement development policies and programs, and they receive similar rewards. In the larger society outside the state, exchange has also probably — without opinion polls or open politics it is impossible to have more than an impression — gone a long way toward persuading people to accept military rule.

What counter forces might induce such a powerful and successful political organisation to withdraw from the political arena? That is indeed a very large question, to which I can sketch only a partial and unsatisfactory answer. A number of forces are now at work that lessen the future tenability of authoritarian rule. These include: the disappearance internationally of the threat of communism, which weakens ABRI's claim to be the chief defender against communism domestically; the growth internationally of pro-democratic forces; the emergence domestically of a network of pro-democratic non-governmental organisations; the absence of Islamic state fervour among members of the now large Muslim middle class; the rise of middle class, professional, and working class groups more generally; and the increasing competence of younger educated civilians to manage the economy, social organisations, and polity, in contrast to the narrower training and experience of their military opposite numbers, who are also many fewer in number.

In the shorter run, the greatest opportunity for reducing ABRI's political role, and perhaps for democratisation, will come with President Suharto's passing from the political scene. The Armed Forces' unity, internal and external exchange capacity, and especially legitimacy in the larger society are to a large extent the product of, derivative from, the leadership of Suharto. When ABRI is no longer led by Suharto, it will no longer possess these resources in the quantity or quality it does today.

Second, no other individual, military or civilian, possesses anything like Suharto's personal political resources as *Penyelamat Bangsa* (Saviour of the Nation), *Bapak Pembangunan* (Father of Development), controller of vast wealth in private foundations, master of the central bureaucracy, skilful political tactician, and so on. Indonesia's third president will have to amass resources of his own, and his control over the Armed Forces is by no means certain. This situation creates the possibility for change.

Political parties in a democratic Indonesia

In the preceding section I have argued that ABRI controls Indonesian politics and government today. In a democratic Indonesia, this role will have to be assumed by a party system — one or more political parties — that represents and mobilises popular demands and support and also holds the offices in which government policy is made. Parties appear to be a *sine qua non* in modern nation-state democracies. So far, at least, no other organisation or institution has been able to fill their role as the critical link between state and society.[3]

How can the creation of a party system be accomplished in such a way as to maintain growth and unity and at the same time to consolidate successfully a democratic transition? Part of the answer, I believe, has to do with a deliberate effort on the part of democratisers to devise a party system with what Giovanni Sartori, analysing the multi-party system of contemporary Italy in the European setting, has called a centripetal rather than a centrifugal tendency.

Indonesia in the 1950s did not have a large centre party. Sartori saw the absence of a large centre party as the cause of many of Italy's problems. What it did have was a multi-party system split along three axes — ethnicity/regionalism, religion, and social class — with marked centrifugal tendencies (see Feith 1962). In the 1955 elections, the only time nationwide free elections have been held in Indonesia, four parties — the nationalist PNI, the modernist Muslim Masyumi, the traditionalist Muslim NU, and the communist PKI — divided almost evenly three-quarters of the total vote, with the remaining quarter fragmented among dozens of tiny parties and other electoral organisations (Feith 1957). None of the four major parties had a strong commitment to democratic institutions, and there were deep differences among them as to how to achieve economic growth and national unity.

The centrifugality of the 1950s party system was manifested in the policy incoherence of multi-party coalition cabinets which tried to reconcile too many competing forces, the political instability of relatively rapid cabinet turnover, and the policy inconsistency from cabinet to cabinet. Partisan mobilisation of voters during the election campaign of 1955 and the regional elections of 1957 also led, according to Feith and other standard accounts, to a dangerous sharpening of the tensions among ethnic, religious, and class groups.

What would a party system with centripetal rather than centrifugal tendencies look like in a democratic Indonesia in the 1990s? One implication of Sartori's analysis — which contrasts the 'pathological' multi-party systems of contemporary Italy, Fourth Republic France, and the German Weimar Republic with the 'healthy' multi-party systems of contemporary

---

3. The classic statement of this position is Samuel Huntington (1968:Ch 7).

Sweden, Norway, Denmark, and Switzerland — is that multi-party systems are not centrifugal *per se*. The issue is not the number of parties but whether the parties in the system, especially the major parties, incline toward common positions and compromise of differences or not.

In the 1950s on the religious issue there was polarisation between Masyumi-NU on one side (though NU never took the uncompromising stand that some Masyumi leaders did) and PNI-PKI on the other. On governmental decentralisation, and on many economic policy issues, Masyumi as the party of the Outer Islands was basically in opposition to the Java-based PNI-PKI-NU. On class issues, the lower class-oriented PKI confronted Masyumi-PNI-NU, defenders of several different upper class groups.

The issue today, of course, is not simply how to restructure or recombine the interests of the 1950s, but rather how to respond creatively to the current range of actual and potential, organised and unorganised, interest blocs in Indonesian society. Three possibilities are the East Asian one-party dominant model, the American two-party system, and the European multi-party system.

The East Asian solution, of which Japan is the exemplar but which also includes quasi-democratic Malaysia and democratising Taiwan and Korea, offers the stability and predictability of rule by a dominant party that can count on being returned to office repeatedly by a large majority of the electorate.[4] Comparison with Taiwan, where the KMT is converting itself from a military- and bureaucracy-backed instrument of authoritarian (even Leninist) mobilisation into a broadly-based party capable of genuine contestation, is perhaps most interesting for Indonesians. It suggests the possibility of a similar conversion for Golkar.

The American solution would envisage two major parties divided primarily by economic policy: one adhering more strictly to the kinds of policies followed by the professional economists today, the other to a social democratic or welfare-state set of policies promoting more egalitarian distribution of the benefits of development.[5] The advantage of this arrangement is that conflicts over other issues, particularly religious but also ethnic and regional disputes, would take place within the two major parties and thus not polarise parliamentary debate.

European-style multi-party politics is anathema to New Order officials, who see it as a return to the chaos of the 1950s, and is perhaps thus unlikely to be put into practice. Nevertheless, it might well be the 'natural' outcome of a genuine opening-up of the political process and for that reason would enjoy great popular legitimacy. To the extent that Indonesians really are now all Pancasilaists — that is, they reject the Islamic state, communism, and separatism — it would also not be fissiparous in the manner of its 1950s avatar.

---

4. On one-party democracies in general, see T. J. Pempel, ed. (1990)

5. For a discussion, see Liddle (1992b)

A fourth possible model is Thai democracy, also based on a multi-party system. Despite considerable political instability, Thai multi-partyism has not posed a threat either to national unity or to the maintenance of pro-market economic policies. Recent Thai history also suggests two ways to gradually remove the military from politics. One is to reserve an institution for officers — the Senate in Thailand, perhaps the MPR in Indonesia — and then gradually to limit the institution's power. A second is to allow retired officers to become leaders of political parties and members of parliament, where at least some of them are likely to develop an interest in the strength and autonomy of democratic institutions.

Sarwono's path to democracy

As there may be many kinds of party system compatible with a pro-growth, pro-unity, consolidated Indonesian democracy, so there may be many possible paths to transition. In this concluding section I want to explore just one of these, the course recommended by Sarwono Kusumaatmadja, long term Golkar activist and currently Minister for Population and Environment, and his colleagues in the G stream in Golkar.[6]

In an interview in the business magazine *Eksekutif* (1992), Sarwono offered his own analysis of the changing character of Indonesian society and the implications of these changes for politics. According to Sarwono, the first quarter century of New Order development has produced a 'new strategic elite' in Indonesian society. This elite consists of four components: the business community, 'which is beginning to emerge politically in the broad sense: people who are able to influence the decision-making process, without having to become a member of a political party or Golkar'; professionals; 'leaders of social organisations (*ormas*) which are active and have a capacity to apply pressure'; and traditional leaders.

The three latter categories are not discussed further in the interview. By professionals Sarwono presumably means the doctors, lawyers, journalists, academics, and other highly educated Indonesians who dominate modern urban life. The social organisations are the non-governmental organisations or LSM (*Lembaga Swadaya Masyarakat*, Self-Reliant Community Development Institution) and LPSM (*Lembaga Pengembangan Swadaya Masyarakat*, Institution for Promoting Self-Reliant Community Development) that have become increasingly active in the past two decades in village-level development, environmental protection, consumer rights, human rights, publishing, and similar areas.

---

6. Journalistic accounts of the decision process within Golkar describe three *jalur* or streams: A for ABRI, B for the civilian bureaucracy, and G for Golkar. G is really a residual category for those party officials who do not directly represent the interests of either A stream (as articulated by the Commander of the Armed Forces) or B stream (the Minister of Home Affairs). Professional politicians who have made a career in Golkar, like Sarwono, are one important element in the G category.

Traditional leaders are a seemingly strange category to be included as part of a 'new strategic elite'. Almost certainly Sarwono is thinking here both of the traditional rural Islamic leaders or *kiai* who frequently pronounce on matters of public importance, and also of the genuinely new phenomenon of Muslim preachers who regularly attract enormous urban audiences. These preachers, as I have said, are so far apolitical, but politicians like Sarwono must be fascinated by their ability to connect with the masses.

Sarwono's central assertion is that Golkar and the political parties must attract these new constituencies if they are to survive into the 'Second Long Term Development Phase', the second quarter century of development in the government's current jargon. In Golkar's case, which is what Sarwono is primarily interested in, this means expanding beyond the military and bureaucratic streams that have been the backbone of the organisation since the late 1960s. He implies that all four of the new elite groups are potentially part of the Golkar family.

This political change is necessitated by the power of the new groups, which are already influential with government officials and are bound to become more so, especially if deregulation, de-bureaucratisation, and decentralisation continue. To Sarwono, the new groups do not need the parties so much as the parties need them. If Golkar and the parties do not take advantage of this opportunity and provide a channel for articulation of the new interests, they will become increasingly irrelevant to the political process.

Is this strategy a plausible route to pro-growth, pro-unity democratisation for Indonesia? I see four reasons why democratisers might want to join Sarwono's team, and one why they might not.

First, the strategy's gradualism and top-down quality provide for continuity in a leadership committed to both growth and unity. A major difficulty with more violent, mass-based, crisis-dependent strategies of democratisation is that the values and policies of the new leaders are harder to predict. There is also a higher probability that they will be tempted to rely in the struggle for power on simplistic populist or religious appeals. Once in power, if they deliver on their promises, they will undo the New Order's economic and social progress. If they do not deliver, they will de-legitimise the new democratic institutions.

Second, military support for democratisation — a serious obstacle, I have indicated, given the current gap in resources between civilians and the military — might be easier to obtain if Army officers have a place in the new system. They might in fact have two places: continuation of the ABRI stream in some form as a part of the Golkar structure from the centre to the districts; and an increased role for retired officers in the more powerful provincial governments that are certain to accompany democratisation. Third, many Muslim groups would be inside the tent, reducing the probability of religious polarisation in parliament. Golkar has in fact a long history of attempting to attract Muslim support.

Fourth, this path also lends itself to a transformation of state, or authoritarian, corporatism into societal, or democratic, corporatism.[7] State corporatism, domination by state officials of the leadership selection and policies of private interest organisations, has been one of the means by which the New Order government has tightened its grip over business, labour, professionals, religious people, students, youth, women, and many other groups. In societal corporatism, on the other hand, interest organisations enter freely into a privileged relationship with the state, trading some autonomy and freedom to challenge state policies for increased access.

Both Stephan Haggard and Robert Wade argue that state corporatism has been an important part of the East Asian development model, and that Korea and Taiwan are now moving in the direction of societal corporatism. Though Sarwono does not mention labour as a new strategic elite, there are several years of evidence, in the form of wildcat strikes and illegal unions, of increasing labour pressure on business, and of the failure of the government's state corporatist strategy to contain this pressure. Indonesia has not yet reached the income level of either Korea or Taiwan. A change in policy from state to societal corporatism may therefore be premature, but it is certainly a possibility in the medium term. A one-party dominant Golkar in a democratic Indonesia might also see the electoral advantage in doing so.

Finally, there are good grounds for scepticism about the Sarwono strategy. Perhaps the most important, to return to Juan Linz and Alfred Stepan, is the nature of the deal that would have to be struck with ABRI in return for any transfer of authority to a democratic government. At some point, Linz and Stepan argue, so many concessions are made to the military during the transition process that democratisation becomes meaningless.

The most powerful military regimes, they say, are led by unified hierarchical armed forces in societies where pro-democratic groups have few political resources. This description sounds very much like Indonesia today. Is it possible to imagine ABRI in this decade willing to give up, to any form of civilian governmental leadership, one or more of the following: autonomy of the Ministry of Defence and Security; the territorial command structure; the quota of appointed members in the MPR and DPR; final-say influence in Golkar; or access to major sources of patronage and position?

If it is not possible, Sarwono's strategy is unlikely to succeed, and we are back to square one. Are there other alternatives for pro-growth, pro-unity democratisers who recognise the tenacity of anti-democratic forces and understand the need for a strong party system?

---

7. The terms are from Philippe Schmitter (1974).

References

Abdurrahman Wahid (Interview) (1992) 'Abdurrahman Wahid: Saya Presiden Taxi saja deh', *Detik* No. 563, 2 November 1992, pp. 4-8.
'Current Data on the Indonesian Military Elite' (1992) prepared by the editors of *Indonesia* No. 53, April 1992
Feith, H. (1962) *The Decline of Constitutional Democracy in Indonesia*, Ithaca: Cornell University Press, 1962.
_____ (1957) *The Indonesian Elections of 1955*, Cornell University Modern Indonesia Project, Ithaca.
Gonzalez-Vega, C. and R.A. Chaves (1992) *Indonesia's Rural Financial Markets*, Rural Finance Program, Department of Agricultural Economics and Rural Sociology, The Ohio State University, Columbus.
Haggard, S. (1990) *Pathways From the Periphery*, Cornell University Press, Ithaca.
Huntington, S. (1968) *Political Order in Changing Societies*, Yale University Press, New Haven.
Lehman, E.W. (1969) 'Toward a Macrosociology of Power,' *American Sociological Review*, 34 (4), August 1969, pp. 453-465.
Liddle, R.W. (1992a) 'Indonesia's Threefold Crisis,' *Journal of Democracy* 3, 4 (October 1992), pp. 61-74.
_____ (1992b) *Pemilu-Pemilu Orde Baru: Pasang Surut Kekuasaan Politik*, Jakarta: LP3ES, 1992, pp. 142-153.
Linz, J., and A. Stepan (forthcoming) *Democratic Transitions and Consolidation: Eastern Europe, Southern Europe, and Latin America*, Yale University Press, New Haven.
MacIntyre, A. (1991) *Business and Politics in Indonesia*, Allen and Unwin, Sydney.
McVey, R. (1992) The Materialization of the Southeast Asian Entrepreneur, in McVey (ed) *Southeast Asian Capitalists*, Cornell University Southeast Asia Program, Ithaca.
Pempel, T.J. (ed) (1990) *Uncommon Democracies: The One-Party Dominant Regimes*, Cornell University Press, Ithaca.
Robison, R. (1992) Industrialization and the Economic and Political Development of Capital: the Case of Indonesia, in McVey (ed) *Southeast Asian Capitalists*.
Sarwono Kusumaatmadja (1992) 'Jangan Mengandalkan Aliansi Lama', *Eksekutif*, August 1992, pp. 45-46.
Schmitter, P. (1974) 'Still the Century of Corporatism?', *Review of Politics* 85, January 1974, pp. 85-131.
Timmer, C.P. (1992) "The Political Economy of Rapid Growth: Indonesia's New Development Model," paper prepared for delivery to the IPMI (*Institut Pengembangan Manajemen Indonesia*) 21 December 1992.
Wade, R. (1990) *Governing the Market*, Princeton University Press, Princeton.

Democratisation in the 1990s: Coming to Terms with Gradualism?

Marsillam Simanjuntak

Gradual: better slow but..[1]

Today's world is moving towards a common belief in the desirability of democracy, peaceful conflict resolution, respect for human rights, poverty eradication, protection of the environment, gender equality — and, by extension, into more specific, if problematic, variants like free market systems, industrialisation, free trade etc. But, in being committed to changes of this kind, people do not think in terms of revolutions and sudden turnabouts. They are content with small steps, piecemeal improvements. Where the system is not in question, fundamental change is no longer in demand. The keyword for change in the future is *gradualism*.

How does this apply to the prospects for change in Indonesia? There is certainly much dissatisfaction with the present political situation and many demands for change; but none of these, whether from intellectuals, more radical critics or from the officially organised groupings such as Golkar and the political parties, challenge the official ideology or the existing framework of power. Almost all such demands, in character and direction, fall within the same broad guidelines of state policy. Even where there is harsh criticism of policy implementation, the changes pursued are supportive and remedial rather than reformative and emancipatory. They call for improvement in performance while keeping within the rules laid down by the regime. And they display a readiness to accept step by step achievement. To any sign of

---

1. For helpful suggestions, I am grateful to A. Rahman Tolleng; responsibility for the contents is mine alone.

impatience shown there will be an immediate reminder of the Indonesian wisdom of prudence and the traditional canon of right timing: better slow but safe. Indeed, from the outward symptoms, quite an impressive number of progressive steps have been taken in the past decade. Apart from the celebrated success of economic growth, the list includes increasing bureaucratic leniency, a relatively freer press (in quantity, if not in quality) and concomitantly more courage amongst sociopolitical personalities to voice their critical and even dissenting views, and more tolerance of frequent labour strikes, the comparatively gentle handling of militant students and other non-governmental groups, the lifting of exit permit regulations for foreign travel, a new role for the parliament in allowing the expression of social grievances, etc.

Not only is it fashionable to talk about the need for more openness today, but it is easier to raise specific issues. For some these changes are mere appearances whose significance can be offset by other counter-indications, but they serve as a basis for optimism about the workability of gradual progress for Indonesia, rather than the pursuit of fundamental solutions. Adjustments and fine tuning are likely to be more effective, it would seem, than attempts to remedy abstractly-defined structural defects.

The avoidance of thinking in terms of fundamental solutions, in its turn, also affects the mental process: the way people state a problem affects their perception of possible solutions. Thus, many view the weakness of the DPR (parliament) as arising from the lack of personal capacity and the low intellectual quality of its members — a circular argument — rather than considering the possibility that a premeditated political lobotomy was performed on the institution causing its systemic paralysis. But the case for gradualism is not exhausted yet, given that there has been a certain progress in parliamentary affairs. The recent rise of more 'vocal' members of parliament, especially from the military faction, rekindles the hope for a chain of gradual reform. Notice, for example, the emerging demand, put in the form of a polite proposal, to reduce, though not to abolish, the number of appointed military deputies in the parliament. Some proposed, as a start, a reduction of 50 percent and others wanted to leave only 10 percent of the one hundred existing appointees. However no change was made before the 1992 election and presumably the status quo will therefore remain for the next five years. Any gradualist plan of change reflects a certain degree of moderation, very carefully formulated so as to conceal a longer term true intent. All share a common maximum end — a democratic parliament with no military appointees — but any broad agreement between the variety of gradual approaches has invariably become stalled. Why is this?

Consensus by coercion

For an explanation of the failure of the proposal to cut back military participation it is necessary to go back to the original entry of ABRI members into parliament. This part of the story has been neglected as compared with the more popularly known account of the New Order political consensus in 1968. That consensus, later embodied in legislation, is regarded, especially by then younger generation as the original basis for the inclusion of the military in the legislature. It is, perhaps, the fallacy of the gradualist to believe that it will simply take another consensus to revise or to revoke it.

In fact the New Order consensus was not the starting point of ABRI's dual function. Its formal entry into the legislature is rooted in the period of transition from the parliamentary order to the system of Guided Democracy, between 1957 and 1960, during what was later to be called the Old Order (*Orde Lama*). The military at that time, under General Nasution, developed the idea of the 'Middle Way' or the dual function of ABRI. Sukarno then made it part and parcel of his Guided Democracy plan which gave a central role to the functional groups as a means of cutting back the influence of the political parties.

According to Mohammad Yamin (1959:29ff), a close aide and supporter of Sukarno, the rebirth of the 1945 Constitution was based on what he called a trilogy of inseparable elements: Pancasila, Guided Democracy (*Demokrasi Terpimpin*), and the representation of functional groups (*golongan fungsional/karya*). He explained further that 'the invention of the functional group or *karya* group is simultaneous with the birth of Guided Democracy'. It was here that we find ABRI was officially placed under the rubric of 'armed (forces) core group' (*pokok golongan bersenjata*), as one of seven 'core functional groupings' comprising workers/civil servants, peasants, national entrepreneurs, ulama, the 45 generation etc.

The official entry of ABRI into politics and into formal political institutions was not the result merely of a voluntary consensus. It involved also a certain degree of coercion. As a preparation for it, Sukarno had included the military in the National Council in 1958. That was made possible only by the 1957 declaration of Martial Law which provided Sukarno and the Army with the legal means to use force and to take extraordinary measures. Sukarno and Nasution did not stop here, but together continued to use the situation to bring about a 'functional revolution' which saw the military enter not only parliament, but also the cabinet.

Sukarno, living up to his own revolutionary image, did not bother to observe constitutional formalities. Following Marx, he often said that constitutions are made for people, not people for the constitution. He did not feel bound by the letter of the 1945 Constitution which only mentioned the MPR, not the DPR, as the place for functional group representation. After dissolving the parliament in 1960 — Sukarno's first act in violating the 1945 Constitution — he did not call an election but composed his own parliament which he called the DPR Gotong Royong. None of the functional groups condemned the 'breach of the 1945 Constitution', and all accepted appointment on the tacit understanding that they were to carry out a two-fold task: to overturn the dominance of the political parties, and to mobilise the people in support of Sukarno as the leader of the Revolution. His theme of corporatism and mobilisation under a single command can still be felt today (Cf. Reeve 1990), although the term Guided Democracy has long been out of use. The political parties, whose representatives made the consensus with General Suharto to allot one hundred seats in the DPR for unelected military members, were practically the same parties which a few years before consented to, or did not oppose, the appointments made by Sukarno to his DPR Gotong Royong under the system of Guided Democracy. It can be concluded, then, that the history of the military's presence in the DPR runs continuously from the past, starting with Sukarno-Nasution's Martial Law supported Guided Democracy, via the route of the New Order's consensus, to reach today's legalised composition of the DPR/MPR. The consensus is merely a neat legitimising wrapping of the enforced military entry to civil political institutions some time before.

It is a question whether the gradualist demand for reform is limited to unfolding the outer wrapping only, or whether it also aims to reach the inside contents of the package, which in this case would be to question the military presence in politics as a whole.

This ambiguity seems also to apply to the proposal, staunchly advocated by the PDI, to limit presidential tenure to two consecutive terms. Is this merely an impersonal constitutional proposal or is it really intended to effect a transfer of power from the hands of Suharto?

Change: discontinuity of regime & leader

A quick review of the history of political change in Indonesia, may help to illuminate this hypothetical relation between gradual and more fundamental change. It will show that there are no examples of accumulated gradual changes leading smoothly to more fundamental reform. Almost all significant changes that have occurred have been of a drastic and an abrupt kind, marked with discontinuity, sharp turns, overall transformations involving a change of system and, most importantly, a change of leadership.

The transition from Sukarno's Guided Democracy to the New Order of the military under Nasution-Suharto in 1965 was clearly far from gradual and smooth. The discontinuity, in this case, was even physically apparent. There was a total overhaul of the political system and a complete turnabout of the state ideology. And, of course, a change of leadership. Sukarno was finished.

The change that took place in the last days of the parliamentary democracy system of the '50s, must also be regarded as representing a sudden break. The system was terminated by the dissolution — by decree — of the Constituent Assembly in 1959, and the re-instatement of the 1945 Constitution. The multiparty system and the parliamentary order, were regarded merely as western liberal democratic imports. The parties lost their position of leadership. Their political significance vanished, and Sukarno, supported by the military, seized the monopoly of power.

A similar pattern of abrupt change and discontinuity was apparent in the transition from the federal system (RIS, *Republik Indonesia Serikat*) to the unitary Republic in 1950. Or earlier still in the first days of Indonesian independence, when the system of a parliamentary cabinet accountable to KNIP (*Komite Nasional Indonesia Pusat*), acting as a provisional parliament, was introduced to replace Sukarno's first presidential cabinet. There were also hasty changes to the system of party politics, with the abortive proposal for a single 'state party' and the encouragement of a multiparty system. The familiarity of Indonesians with abrupt and wholesale change was no doubt assisted by the sudden shift from the Dutch colonial regime to the Japanese occupation, and the subsequent dramatic passage to independence. Each had its own extreme effect of cataclysmic turbulence.

The typology of changes in Indonesian politics suggests a persistent pattern in which political change has meant a replacement both of the system and the leadership. If the system sank, the leader was drowned. And this has worked both ways. When the leader ceased to hold power, the system also went down and could not survive him. This, then, raises two questions about the future. First, will it be possible to bring about meaningful political change without first changing the leader? And second, will it be possible for the system founded and maintained by President Suharto to survive without him?

The history of political change in Indonesia does not provide a comforting answer to these questions.

Those who assume the existence of political stability, and who rely on the possibility of gradual change, will give an affirmative answer to both questions. A difficulty arises if we have to define political stability, since the present regime has not been tested for survival under a different leadership. Suharto is the founder-builder and the only ever leader of the regime in question. Can it continue without him? To put it in a different way, stability under the regime might be already proven, but the stability of the 'system' itself is still to be proven. Is the system separable from its leader?

What we witnessed in the latest political development in Jakarta, the incontestable renomination of President Suharto as the sole candidate for the umpteenth term in March 1993, supports our view that the political condition has reached a point where now, paradoxically, it is the leader who has to be defended in order to stabilise the system. Usually it is the other way round. The system has become dependent on a person, or better still, the system and the leader has blended in one body, a sight common only to absolutist regimes. The picture is definitely unpropitious for the case for gradual change.

The constellation of democracy

At this point it is necessary to consider the aim of the change to be achieved. Change toward what? The occasion of this conference, if not the theme of it, helps to provide the answer. The change contemplated is directed toward the possibility of having a constitutional democracy established. Constitutional democracy in Indonesia during the 1949-1957 period, according to Feith (1962:xi) had six distinct features: civilians played a dominant role; parties were of very great importance; contenders for power showed respect for 'rules of the game' which were closely related to the existing constitution; most members of the political elite had some sort of commitment to symbols connected with constitutional democracy; civil liberties were rarely infringed, and, governments used coercion sparingly.

I propose not to analyse the existing political situation in the light of each of these features, but rather to consider the obstacles in the way of attaining them through gradual change or otherwise. To do that, we need to visualise, quite arbitrarily, the role of social activities in the making of political decisions. For this purpose we may consider that there are several interrelated realms of activity — of which we will be interested only in three — which have a close connection with how policies are determined in a certain political community, or a state.

The first among the three realms, is the public sphere where people concern themselves with the *management of 'truth'*. For lack of a better term we may call it here the *realm of public aspirations*. Second, there are those activities concerned with the necessities of life and the accumulation of wealth, the *economic realm*. And the third is the group of activities specifically exercised to maintain the integrity of society and the state by the use of force. This may be termed the *realm of coercion management*. These three realms of activity interact mutually and move in a certain dynamic constellation — from the shape of which one can judge what type of political system is at work in a given period.

In a democracy, this imagined constellation should be mostly determined by the realm of public aspirations. It is the realm open to all members of the society, or citizens of the state, standing on an equal footing and exercising their free will in the pursuit of 'truth' and other values for the common good. What is decided in this realm will affect the way things are done in other realms. This realm, then, occupies the uppermost position in the supposedly hierarchical configuration of a democratic society. All political decisions are to be made in this sphere. It is the central processing unit, to use computer jargon, from which commands are distributed to other receptors in the circuit. Illusory as it may be in reality, the logic of the economic realm should also be subordinate to the norms dictated by the activities in the realm of aspirations. This is even more the case with the realm of coercion management, since the nature of the activities here, unlike those in the two other realms, is not self-generated, nor self-determined. These are basically reserve activities, activated only in matters of contingency.

No society has ever succeeded in attaining this neat, hierarchical design. The inevitable imperfection varies, depending upon the realm where the movable *centre of gravity* is situated. States based on popular sovereignty will reflect a greater emphasis on the realm of public aspirations, while authoritarian or totalitarian states will be centred on the realm of coercion management. When we refer to democratisation, we are talking of moving the centre closer to the realm of aspirations. When we talk about constitutional democracy, it means that the imperatives of the constitution must run parallel to the idea of the supremacy of this realm. There is nothing, actually, in the 1945 Constitution of Indonesia which permits the realm of economy or the realm of coercion management to occupy the central position. Constitutional democracy would therefore require a change in the way in which the constitution is implemented.

Unity and the logic of coercion
The political history of post-independence Indonesia has had almost had no respite from the numerous conflicts that have threatened the integrity of the state and nationhood. It was not only because Sukarno, recognising the complexity of Indonesia's heterogeneity, made it a persistent plea from early in his political career, that union and unity must be given the highest priority at all times. The concrete experience of endless national crises since the first days of independence underlined the importance of unity.

The 3 July 1946 affair, the Madiun revolt of 1948, DI-TII of Kartosuwirjo and Kahar Muzakar, Soumokil and the Republic of the South Moluccas, a series of Army coup attempts in the mid-50s, the PRRI-Permesta rebellion, all posed immediate threats to national integrity and increasingly opened the way for the prominence of the realm of coercion management. Sukarno's Guided Democracy, which essentially emasculated the operation of the political parties operating in the realm of public aspirations, automatically boosted the influence of the logic of coercion management. Social mobilisation, mentally and physically, to increase awareness of the threat to the integrity of the state and the nation, was intensified in the aftermath of the abortive coup of 1965.

The usurpation of the realm of coercion management was done in two ways: by direct intervention of the state institutions using both military techniques (Cf. Tanter 1990 and 1991) and legal enforcement, and by implanting the predominance of its reasoning in the activities of the two other realms. The habit of giving priority to the considerations of union, unity and integrity had not only become widespread, but had also regularised and normalised its application in every other kind of social activity. Hence the blurring of the boundary between right and duty and between persuasion and compulsion.

The priority given to the maintenance of the integrity of the State, known popularly as the 'security approach', when rationally tuned to the much needed economic development, appeared in the less emotive garb of 'national stability'. The point of contention here is not with stability *per se*, the vitality of which is recognised as the bedrock for any national development plan. It is just that the business of producing this stability has not been determined in the realm of public aspirations, and is locked instead in the realm of coercion. The inherently plural character of the realm of aspirations is perceived to be a great risk to union and unity. According to the logic of coercion management, the public realm, which contains pluralism as a 'necessary evil', could never be trusted to handle matters pertaining to stability. Consequently, the centre of gravity is shifted deep into the realm of coercion management, which then functions as the hub of the constellation of all public activities.

From the goals of union and unity, there followed the application of power necessary to maintain it. Both together gave the realm of coercion management a position of autonomy and generated an authoritarian type of stability.

Streamlined authoritarianism

How then are we to envisage the probability of gradual change as a way of getting closer to constitutional democracy? The task is to push the centre of gravity back, gradually, to the realm of public aspirations. It is to turn the authoritarian type stability, also in piecemeal fashion, to a democratic type stability. Managing stability would be left to the ethics of the realm of public aspirations rather than to the logic of external coercion. How is one to do all this without altering the existing power system first?

The dilemma can best be clarified as follows. To give credence to the growing symptoms of openness cited above as representing a substantive gradual change, requires two assumptions. The first is that the actors in the realm of public aspirations have freed themselves from the ruling idea that social cohesion and national integrity are so fragile that they must be constantly protected by means of coercion. The second is that there is a sort of altruism on the part of the power holders, the guardians of the realm of coercion — i.e. the military — to relinquish voluntarily their position by a sustained and gradual release of their once strict control.

These assumptions may be tested by looking again at the proposal to reduce the military's seats in parliament.

First, a proposal to reduce the number of military representatives in the parliament while still maintaining a military presence in the parliament, is tantamount to accepting the need for some military role in preserving union and unity. Thus, the proposal — which came from the public realm — still accepts the overriding constraints of duty from the realm of coercion.

Secondly, even if we disregard the naïveté of the thought, there is no need to speculate about the possibility of a voluntary military withdrawal. It has plainly been rejected. Recent statements by senior officers indicate clearly the military's refusal to budge from the New Order consensus on the grounds that the military must safeguard the perpetuation of the state ideology and the 1945 Constitution.

This classical stalemate suggests that the case for the cause of gradual change is not very promising. The latest development of more openness was clearly *not* a gradual advance in the field of real democratisation, but rather a move towards employing subtler and more *streamlined* means of control and appeasement in order to preserve the primacy of the realm of coercion management. The progress made in the public realm is but a by-product of the progress made in the coercion realm. It is more of an intra-realm lubrication than an inter-realm relational change.

In the absence of genuine freedom to articulate demands and ideas, the public realm is, by strict definition, in a state of collapse. Indeed conceptually, it is impossible to speak of a public realm any more. It has already been swallowed into the black hole of authority.

Democracy first, succession later

There is another important overarching problem beyond the near futile struggle to restore the centrality of the realm of public aspirations as required by constitutional democracy. That is the question of the role of President Suharto which now has assumed control over the three realms together. Obviously it was the realm of coercion management that he used to extend his influence, rather indirectly, to other realms, especially at the early stage of his power. But now, as it happens, all activities in the three realms come immediately into the domain of his power. It is intrinsically a re-run of a much better copy of Sukarno's Guided Democracy[2] that Yamin dreamed about a good three decades ago: Pancasila as a foundation, 'democracy' with strong leadership, and the blooming of *golongan karya* (functional groups) including the Armed Forces.

The problem of change towards democracy, defined as the effort to recapture the hegemony in the inter-realm relation, then becomes secondary. It is superseded by the question of how to deal first with the all-encompassing influence of President Suharto's power.

As mentioned above, in this regime the 'system' has become embodied in the person of the President, that is in a structure dependent upon a personality. If the desire for gradual change is grounded on the assumption that the system should not be altered, the only logical thing to expect is democratic change under the guardianship of the leader, President Suharto. But we are going in circles here. If that is so, then gradualism is unwarranted, and any change in the direction of democratisation must mean dealing first with the succession of the President, an issue (still) omitted from the gradualist agenda. But the dictates of logic seldom find their way in politics, certainly not in authoritarian politics. Either by doggedly defying the logic of the prerequisites of change, or by simply just mistaking an unending status quo for an inevitably slow journey through a long winding road to democracy, the gradual change option is still preferred by many people today in Indonesia.

If that is so, and granted that all the impossibilities described above can be

---

2. See Liddle's argument (1992b:68) on the strong presidency as a legacy of Sukarno's era. Much of what is discussed in this paper Liddle (1992a) also covers.

totally disregarded, then gradualism can only be thought of in three ways. First, it can be regarded as a symptom of indecisiveness, or mere powerlessness. This is too amorphous to be described in detail; the range extends from innocent acquiescence to cunning opportunism. Second, is the more creative *'meanwhile-ism'* type. Realising that while nothing substantive can yet be done in the way of democratisation, why not make the most out of the time to improve other sectors of social life. This pragmatic approach, earnestly pursued by some, provides a convenient moral shelter by believing in the constructiveness of the choice. Third, there is the true believer of gradual change toward democracy under the leadership of Suharto. What needs to be done is to further 'deepen' the existing Pancasila Democracy system. The consequence of this is to give ample time to President Suharto's leadership to bring the national development process to full circle. The finish line, therefore, cannot be determined in advance.

All three types of gradualism, with their various degrees of commitment to democratisation, must rest their conviction on one common assumption: that the incumbent president is problem-free, or is not part of the problem of attaining democracy. And this is precisely the crux of the matter: to define whether the President is to be relied upon as the leader to solve the problem of democratisation, or as a problem, and a complex one at that, to be solved first. Succession politics might not be identical with democratisation, but at this point the question should be, is democratisation possible without dealing first with succession as a problem?

Conclusion

All in all, it seems impossible to draw a clean conclusion here. What we have been analysing so far is the idea of transformative change as an *intended* effort. But most of the quite drastic changes in Indonesia were ignited by historical accidents. There is no example of a meticulously planned and successfully organised transformation recorded yet (except for the change from RIS to RI in 1950, or can we include also the transition to Guided Democracy in 1959?). It seems that we lacked the aptitude for it. What we have proven up to this moment is that we are experts at 'crisis hitchhiking', jumping quickly at any unpredicted incident and doing what can be done. Perhaps it has become an incurable habit.

If there is a chance to break with our past record as gradualist reformers, this will have to be the time to do it. Can it be done through a steady, self-sacrificing policy of the power holder for the sake of democratic change? Deviating from the known manner of authoritarian system change, to deliver a centrally-induced metamorphosis under one leader? This is a rather tall order.

Nonetheless, does President Suharto deserve the benefit of the doubt, since in these circumstances it is only he who is logically capable of making it happen? He is the solitary horse on the track that gradualists may have to lay their bets on. And if committed, the stakes must be raised beyond just one more term for Suharto. Since the regime is just another breed of Guided Democracy, however, the odds are slim. The last Guided Democracy that we had did not make it. Change occurred only with the downfall of its great leader Sukarno.

References

Feith, H. (1962) *The Decline of Constitutional Democracy in Indonesia* Cornell University Press, Ithaca.

Liddle, R.W. (1992a) 'Indonesia's Democratic Past and Future' *Comparative Politics* 24 (July 1992).

_____ (1992b) 'Indonesia's Threefold Crisis', *Journal of Democracy* Vol.3 No.4 (October 1992).

Tanter, R. (1990) The Totalitarian Ambition: Intelligence and Security Agencies in Indonesia, in Arief Budiman (ed) *State and Civil Society in Indonesia*, Centre of Southeast Asian Studies, Monash University, Clayton.

_____ (1991) *Intelligence Agencies and Third World Militarisation: A Case Study of Indonesia, 1966-1989*, Unpublished Ph.D thesis, Politics Department, Monash University, Clayton.

Yamin, Moh. (1959) Tinjauan Pantjasila terhadap Revolusi Fungsional, in *Seminar Pantjasila ke I di Jogjakarta*, Panitia Seminar Pantjasila, Universitas Gajah Mada, Yogyakarta.

31

Afterword[1]

Anthony Reid

The Monash conference on Indonesian Democracy was called with a number of divergent aims, and was no doubt attended by hundreds of people with even more divergent expectations. Three aims at least would have been in the minds of most — to celebrate Herb Feith on his retirement; to re-examine the 1950s which were the subject of his most important research; and to discuss the possibilities for democratisation in the 1990s. Can anything be said when it is over about what it meant, and whether the conference and this resulting book were anything other than the sum of papers presented and contradictory views expressed?

The very holding of the conference and the surprisingly large attendance it generated, from Indonesia most importantly, is already very significant. It must have been the biggest conference on Indonesian democracy in the last 30 years, and perhaps ever. An academic conference of this sort convened by and at a foreign university would be of almost exclusively academic interest if it concerned Australia or the United States, evoking barely a mention in the domestic media. But in this case about forty prominent Indonesians attended, many at Indonesian expense, and many from the press. The conference was widely reported in the Indonesian media, as well as by Michael Vatikiotis in the *Far Eastern Economic Review* (28 Jan 93). It was perceived as more important than its convenors envisaged, or perhaps intended.

Mochtar Lubis, whose credentials cannot be doubted, was among those who complained that campaigns for political rights should be conducted within

---

1. These remarks originated as an introduction to the final session of the Monash Conference.

Indonesia. The Indonesian Front for the Defense of Human Rights sent a letter supporting the conference but calling for a similar event in Indonesia. Others in the Indonesian media were disappointed at the academic, multivoiced tone of the conference. Some were judging it as if it were an Indonesian event rather than a Monash conference. Though unquestionably a scholarly international conference determined to explore all sides of the issues, and conducted predominantly in English (though with some interesting Indonesian exceptions), it may also have unexpected repercussions in Indonesia. If so it was only one of many ways in which Indonesian debate interacts, and must interact, with international debate.

What was unique about this conference was its combination of discussion of the fifties and the nineties. Although the majority of papers were concerned with present developments, if the conference had been limited to this theme it would have resembled a number of other talk-fests that have been held in recent years about where Indonesia is headed. By trying to do two other things at the same time the organisers dealt themselves a hand which must have seemed at times unplayable — and which caused some confusion among invitees as well. Yet during the conference it did begin to appear that each re-evaluation of the fifties spoke directly to the nineties, while every point made about the nineties required us to rethink the fifties. At the same time Herb Feith himself, irresistibly combining roles as celebrant and celebrated, was a kind of leitmotif linking the two periods and the hopes they contained. Whatever the case in Indonesia itself, international scholarship will henceforth allow more centrality to a period of Indonesia's history when there was robust pluralism, a parliamentary system and a high degree of freedom of political and cultural debate.

What did the conference say about the 1950s? There were three points that have particularly struck me.

Firstly, the argument was strongly made that, in terms of political structure and intellectual climate, 1950-57 should not be separated from the preceding period of revolutionary struggle in 1945-1949. In the whole history of twentieth century Indonesia's engagement with modern political structures, there is no doubt that those twelve years represent a distinctive period of relative freedom, openness and pluralism, when governments were frequently changed to meet pressures from below. In 1945-49 there were four prime ministers and a change of government every 10.6 months; from 1950 to the end of parliamentary democracy in March 1957, six prime ministers and a change of government every 12.4 months. The revolutionary period was the best possible demonstration of how effective, indeed virtually indispensable, multiple parties, electoral processes and representative assemblies can be in moderating and channelling dangerous primordial conflicts and bringing them into a national forum where they can be debated. In that period, as later, parties could also institutionalise and deepen those conflicts, but in a situation of dramatically rapid change, democratic pluralism proved the only practical means for a government to govern. One thinks particularly of

November 1945, when the chaotic risings all over Indonesia against the Japanese, against the Bucho cabinet, and against traditional rulers and power holders at local levels, were channelled through the essentially democratic revolution engineered by Sjahrir and Amir Sjarifuddin, which legitimised the existing political pluralism and channelled it through a system of representative assemblies (KNIs).

The second point which emerged was how bad a press the parliamentary period has been given, not only by scholars and commentators reading the signs that the tide of history was flowing the other way, but also by New Order polemicists with their own specific agenda. David Bourchier described how systematically Indonesian children have been schooled, particularly since Nugroho Notosusanto's tenure of the education ministry in 1982-85, to believe that liberal democracy as practised in the fifties was un-Indonesian, divisive and anarchic. A number of other papers regretted the way in which the excessively negative image generated for political purposes, first by Sukarno and then by the New Order apologists, had extended into the world of scholarship. It was notably the political scientists who had written most about the fifties — Herb Feith himself, Ruth McVey and Dan Lev — who expressed this view most strongly and regretted the extent to which they had contributed to it.

In terms of scholarship in English, the negative image of the early fifties was best expressed in that Feith/Benda debate to which Ruth McVey's paper drew attention. Feith's *Decline of Constitutional Democracy in Indonesia*, as he reminded us in his paper, was affected by the pessimism of the time it was written, at the end of the fifties and beginning of the sixties, a period which, as he noted, made 'constitutional democracy seem a lost cause all over the third world'. Benda went further, arguing somewhat as Sukarno did that parliamentary democracy should never have been expected to work in the first place. It was simply inappropriate for Indonesia. Ruth McVey suggested that although Benda was widely seen to have won the argument in the 1960s, the Feith perspective made a comeback in the 1980s, making the Orde Baru look like a hold-out of anachronistic authoritarianism in a region of economic expansion and political experiment. The conference heard numerous hopes expressed that the nineties will provide a more favourable economic and international context for the kind of reforms that were defeated in the fifties. It also heard warnings against seeing the *arus sejarah* [tide of history], to use Ben Anderson's phrase, as irresistibly moving now in a democratic direction, any more than it was irresistibly moving in the opposite direction in Sukarno's time.

A third point frequently made was how much the fifties have been ignored since the writing of *The Decline of Constitutional Democracy*. Several speakers pointed out that the quality and detail of that fine book scared subsequent students away from any re-examination of the case. There is undoubtedly much truth in that, but it was not, I suggest, the primary reason for neglect. The contrast is remarkable with the period of revolution, 1945-

50, which we have seen to be linked with the fifties in terms of political dynamics. There was also a great book written on that period by George Kahin, but that classic account has not discouraged a couple of dozen subsequent books and theses on the revolutionary period in English, and hundreds of Indonesian studies.

At least two other factors must be taken into account. Firstly the revolutionary period was separated conceptually from the fifties; all Indonesia's failures were associated with the latter sub-period, partly so that the revolution could be seen, particularly in Indonesia, as the pre-eminent success. Young scholars are not attracted to failure; they worry that when they finish their PhD thesis nobody will want to hire them because they studied the wrong thing while time passed them by. Instead there were in the sixties a lot of studies of potential winners, particularly of the PKI but also of Sukarno, the Army, the Muslims.

The second reason for neglect of the fifties is that there are no new sources becoming available to allow the Indonesian voice to speak more vividly than it did in *The Decline of Constitutional Democracy*, which was already a completely convincing usage of newspapers, interview material and direct experience. In other countries the 30 year limitation on confidentiality of archives, and freedom of information legislation, make it possible to know what the cabinets, presidents and other political actors were thinking and deciding in the fifties, in addition to what they were saying for public consumption in the media. As I revise these thoughts in the new year of 1994, the Australian press is full of the new revelations from the 1963 archives titillatingly headed 'Secrets of '63'.[2] In Indonesia, by contrast, the archives remain silent. The ambitious young historian of today has basically the same sources that Herb used, except that informants are fewer, older and more forgetful, and even some newspaper collections have disappeared.

Part of this absence of information is the culture of fear and silence that elements in the Armed Forces and elsewhere have wanted to perpetuate, monopolising and manipulating the past much as communist parties have done elsewhere. The point was made in a number of papers how critical free access to the past is in creating an open society. One suspects that military historians probably do know where the PKI archives are, and perhaps those of other parties. Somebody must know the whereabouts of cabinet records and various other crucial documents of that period. The collection of early Republican newspapers which historians used in the sixties and seventies in the Perpustakaan Negara in Yogyakarta appear to have disappeared from

---

2. The choicest revelations about what the Menzies government knew in that year but had concealed from its people, according to your choice of newspapers, were that there was 'no practical alternative to eventual Indonesian sovereignty over east Timor', or that the American communications station at Northwest Cape was 'a likely target in Australia for nuclear attack' in the event of a global war; *The Canberra Times*, 1 January 1994; *The Sydney Morning Herald*, 1 January 1994.

public view during the time Professor Nugroho Notosusanto, former head of the Armed Forces History unit, was Minister of Education. Such apparently deliberate policies by people in power provide part of the explanation for the silence from the Indonesian side, but there is, I fear, an even more fundamental and troubling reason. Indonesian intellectuals, professional historians and journalists have shown little interest in demanding access to this part of their past; and foreign scholars have provided little support for their doing so.

The paper of Buyung Nasution, based on almost 10,000 published but ignored pages of the debates of the Constituent Assembly, demonstrates how much can still be learned by re-reading the public record with the new perspective of today. Greg Fealy and others showed that there is plenty of work to be done on neglected aspects of the existing record. Yet there was only one paper able to introduce hitherto unavailable new data about the fifties, and that was George Kahin's account of what the U.S. was up to in Indonesia. Excitement is generated, as he brilliantly demonstrated, when it becomes possible to know events and understand linkages which were only dimly perceived and poorly understood at the time. But the new data came from outside, just as the new data on the Revolutionary period has generally come from outside (notably Dutch archives). Indonesian history subsequent to 1950 can only be a strange distortion if all the primary sources about what the principal actors were up to comes from the records of foreign governments.

We might extend the melodrama of the title Ruth McVey used in the paper which opens this collection, to ask 'who killed the lovely heiress Constitutional Democracy' (aka Carmen Desiree, or CD)? Was she murdered, did she die of an overdose of aspirations or did her own diseased condition reach its natural end? CD had plenty of enemies with a motive for murder, about whom the conference has reminded us — Sukarno; the military; confessional Islam; the CIA which, as George Kahin showed, tried to rescue the lady with such brutal clumsiness that she was flung bleeding into the arms of other murderers; the PKI, involved in a fatal dance with the CIA, each exaggerating the other's influence; the revolutionary veterans (*bekas pejuang*) with excessive expectations of the rewards of independence; Dutch stubbornness over West Irian; and the underlying primordial sentiments which polarised and divided the countryside in Java and elsewhere. CD's friends seem an anaemic bunch when compared with this lethal gang into whose company she was thrown.

There is no question, in other words, that the environment was very hostile in the 1950s. Even if Jamie Mackie warns against thinking in terms of inevitability, and Ben Anderson protests against accepting that the current of history necessarily flows in a certain way, we have to acknowledge that there were very concrete threats to CD.

Much has changed since then: the international situation has seen the end of the Cold War; eastern Asia has undergone a period of extraordinary economic growth; Indonesia has had 20 years of stability, common education and centralisation in government. The two powerful forces which have opposed CD's rebirth, Suharto and the military, can no longer be assumed to be working together, and the first of them is mortal. Change is therefore inevitable.

The conference made clear that pluralism, open debate, and the accountability of leaders to popular constituencies are major parts of Indonesia's political heritage. Some papers argued that particular items of CD's estate — human rights, better representation of regions, workers and minorities, a free press, and perhaps even the 1950 Constitution — will be essential ingredients in any solution to the crisis which seems likely to be facing Indonesia with the succession of the 1990s. Others saw the demons of ethnic, religious and class conflict which emerged from the Indonesian Pandora's Box in 1945, 1948, 1958 and 1965 as still lurking there, likely to create havoc whenever fundamental questions about Indonesian identity are allowed to be openly raised.

A whole generation has been born and raised to political maturity since the last major trauma tore Indonesia apart, and they understandably question the caution of their elders. Is Indonesia really the same society it was in 1965? Even if fissures are still very deep and a sense of common purpose relatively weak, can these conditions ever be healed if they cannot be openly addressed? Is not one of the lessons of eastern Europe that to forcibly suppress ethnic and religious hostilities, in the name of a state ideology which is everywhere expressed but nowhere internalised, is to postpone these problems rather than to deal with them?

The conference reached no consensus on any of these issues, and the papers in this volume are similarly diverse. They do however reflect very well the state of discussion between Indonesian intellectuals and sympathetic foreign scholars about the major issue of the 1990s.

Index

abangan, 18, 133-34, 292
Abdurrahman Wahid (see Wahid, Abdurrahman)
ABRI (see Armed Forces)
Aceh, 7, 21, 54, 138, 211-12, 214, 216, 219, 225, 230, 274, 290
Afghanistan, 153
Afro-Asian Conference, 17, 21
Aidit, Dipa Nusantara (1923-65), 128-32, 135, 138
Air Force, 20, 56, 134, 277, 282
aliran, 5-6, 18, 23, 133, 135, 139-41, 143-44, 162, 249, 255-57
Anderson, Benedict R. O'G., 8, 11, 74, 120, 123, 172, 224, 315, 317
Anshary, Isa (1916-69), 18
Armed Forces, 29, 31, 76, 79, 93, 120, 134, 157, 159, 229-30, 273-84, 293-96, 298-300, 316-17; dual function, 51, 54, 84, 209, 244-45, 277-78, 304; and Islam, 160-67, 292; and Golkar, 238-39, 241, 244-46, 294, 299-300
Army, 7, 9-12, 18, 26, 76-78, 93, 210, 131-32, 185, 194-95, 218, 221, 226, 272-84, 308; role in regional unrest, 18, 28-33, 54, 67-73, 206, 208; political role of, 19-24, 28-32, 34-36, 39-42, 93-94, 108, 120-22, 220, 272-84, 293-96, 303-5, 308; political ideas of, 12, 54-56, 58-59, 77-78, 163, 209, 276-80, 304; economic role, 116-17; ethnic composition of, 227; professionalisation, 120, 275-77; possible withdrawal to the barracks, 272-73, 280
arus sejarah (flow of History), 129, 136, 138, 315
asas tunggal ('sole basis'), 164, 183, 186, 246

Benda, Harry J., 5-6, 11, 23-24, 27, 43, 315
Beureueh, Daud (1899-87), 21, 142
BFO (Federal Consultative Assembly), 76
Brunei, 116
Budiman, Arief, 24, 121, 234
Bureaucracy, 9, 18, 106, 153, 172, 262, 265-66, 294-95; effect of Revolution on, 75-77; regional administration, 204-5, 209-10, 214-21, 224, 227
Burma, 129, 131

Capitalism, 12-13, 101, 190, 200-1, 253
Chalid, K.H. Idham, 92, 94-95, 97, 144
Chiang Kai-shek, 65
China, 12, 36, 65-66, 75, 104, 128, 130, 134, 137, 139, 148, 262
Chinese (in Indonesia), 19, 21, 116-18, 130, 136, 142, 188, 230-31, 289
CIA, 19, 64-70, 72, 142, 317
Cikini affair, 30, 68-69
Civil servants, 17, 169, 204-5, 217, 266, 267, 279, 304
Cold War, 59, 65, 125, 128, 134, 142, 282, 317
Communism, 8-9, 11, 13, 128-42, 163; US containment of, 63-64, 66, 133-34; influence of Russian Revolution, 129; Comintern, 129-33. See also PKI.
Constituent Assembly, 4, 19, 35, 40, 41, 43-48, 55, 60, 92, 103, 152, 153, 172, 207, 208, 276, 305, 317
Constitution of 1945, 32, 34-36, 44, 51, 53, 55, 60, 100, 153, 246, 304, 308-9; reintroduction of, 19, 36, 41-42, 45, 47-48, 55, 92, 95, 208, 216, 305
Constitution of 1950, 53, 59, 91-92, 100, 103, 170, 318
Constitutionalism, 13, 24, 46
Consultative Group on Indonesia (CGI),

289
Corporatism, 305; state, 183, 190, 192, 286, 290, 300; societal, 300,
Corruption, 10, 17, 75, 206, 280-81
Cottrell, Sterling, 71
Cumming, Hugh S., 65-67

Dachlan, K.H. M., 96
Darul Islam (DI-TII), 7, 21, 40, 101-2, 216, 219, 308
Darusman, Marzuki, 110, 239
Darusman, Suryono, 100-1, 103, 109, 112
Decentralisation, 135, 204, 205, 207, 211-13, 214-22, 291, 297, 299
Decline of Constitutional Democracy, xiii-xiv, 5, 17, 21, 27-29, 33, 36, 65-67, 74, 236-37, 307, 315-16
Dharma Wanita, 177
Djokosutono (1904-65), 23, 40
Djuanda Kartawidjaya (1911-63), 29, 44, 47-48, 70-71, 142
DPR (People's Representative Council), 36, 58, 104, 111, 171-72, 218, 221, 236, 238-39, 242, 244-46, 294, 300, 303-5
Dulles, John Foster, 65-67, 69-71
Dulles, Allen, 65-67, 69
dwifungsi, 40, 51, 56, 84, 86, 164, 165, 209, 244-45, 273, 277-78, 281, 283-84

East Asia, 284, 286, 289, 317
Eastern Europe, 20, 128, 268, 286
East Timor, 127, 138-39, 219-20, 230, 274, 278, 290, 316
Economic growth, 6, 116-18, 126, 247, 261, 268, 286-88, 295-96, 303, 318
Effendi, Djohan, 144, 148-49
Eisenhower, President Dwight, 65-69, 71-73
Elections, 11, 59, 111-12, 121, 135-36, 172-73, 273, 292; of 1955, 3, 17, 19, 27, 34-35, 54-55, 59-60, 66, 77, 88, 101-2, 104-5, 124, 135, 171, 207, 215-16, 296; subsequent elections (1971, 1977, 1982, 1987, 1992), 59, 218, 231, 240, 244, 282; regional elections, 206

FBSI (All-Indonesia Workers Federation),
192, 194-95, 203
Feith, Herbert, xiii-xv, 5-6, 8, 11, 16-24, 26-28, 32-33, 36, 39, 65-66, 74, 77, 120, 123, 207, 224-25, 236, 307, 313-15
Floating mass, 35, 105, 175, 218, 261, 268
Foreign aid, 8, 125, 217, 274
Forum Demokrasi (Democratic Forum), 149, 157, 165, 291-92, 233
Free Papua Movement (OPM), 274

GAPI (Indonesian Political Federation), 76
Geertz, Clifford, 18, 223, 255, 259
Geertz, Hildred, 251
Gerindo (Indonesian People's Movement), 100, 104
Gerwani (Indonesian Women's Movement), 170, 175
Gestapu (30th September Movement), 27
Golkar, 105, 107, 110, 121-22, 140-41, 152, 177, 210, 218, 221, 227, 230, 267, 288, 297-300, 302; formation of, 217; relations with Armed Forces, 122, 238-41, 244-46, 273-74, 282, 294; composition of, 152, 177; election performance of, 231-32, 243-45
Guided Democracy, 3, 5, 7-11, 16, 43-45, 48, 88-89, 92, 128, 182, 216, 236, 255, 279, 310-12; explanations of transition to, 19, 22, 23, 27-37, 39-42, 75, 83-4, 94-96, 134, 207; character of, 16, 55, 123-24, 185, 304-5, 308

Habibie, Bachruddin Jusuf, 162, 165, 232, 241, 247, 291
Haggard, Stephan, 286, 288, 300
Harahap, Burhanuddin (1917-87), 18, 69, 225
Hardi (1918-?), 41-42, 103, 136
Hartas, Harsudiono, 164
Hasbullah, K.H. Wahab, 91-93, 95-97
Hasjim, Wahid (1913-53), 142, 147
Hatta, Mohammad (1902-80), 10, 18-20, 22, 27-28, 30-32, 35, 48, 52-53, 64, 70, 79-83, 87, 100, 131-33, 142,
Historiography; of the 1950s, 3-7, 22-23, 28-37, 44, 77, 88-89, 314-317; New Order ideology and, 3-4, 24, 50-60, 64, 139-40, 315; suppression of archives,

316-17; in school texts, 24, 51-57; and East Timor, 139; and literature, 140. See also *arus sejarah*, Nugroho Notosusanto, PSPB.
Hong Kong, 126, 286, 289,
Human rights, 43-48, 58-60, 106, 125, 159, 164, 183, 189, 233-34, 246, 274, 281-82, 298, 302, 314, 318
Huntington, Samuel, 6, 123
Husein, Colonel, 68-71, 73

ICMI (Indonesian Muslim Intellectuals' Association), 58, 157-67, 232-34, 241, 291-92
IGGI (Inter-Governmental Group on Indonesia), 209, 274
India, 24, 82, 116, 119, 129, 135, 141, 178
Integralism, 24, 58, 157, 163, 165
Integralist state, 45-46, 48, 58
Intellectuals, 86, 136, 156, 220, 232-33, 237, 239, 254, 302, 317-18; and nationalism, 79; attitudes of to 1950s, 4, 7; Muslim, 58, 121, 145-49, 152-53, 159-60, 162-63, 165-67, 241, 291. See also ICMI.
Intelligence, 13, 63, 66-67, 69, 294
Iran, 54, 153
Irian Jaya, 22, 30, 65, 68, 138, 208, 211, 213, 219, 230, 317, 274, 277, 290
Islam, 7, 21, 40, 102, 171, 317; under parliamentary system, 8, 18, 30, 45, 77, 88-97, 216, 219; under New Order, 212-22, 156-67, 227, 230; attitudes to state and politics, 89, 151-55, 291-93; developments in Islamic thought, 143-49; Armed Forces and, 162-65, 227, 292. See also ICMI, PPP.
Islamic state, 7, 45, 46, 91, 98, 160-63, 166-67, 292, 295, 297

Japanese occupation, 24, 52, 75, 79, 101-2, 104-5, 124, 131, 153, 306
Jones, Howard, 72
Journalists, 142, 183, 254, 274, 298, 317

Kadarisman, 100-1
Kahin, George McT., 39, 63-73, 74, 77
Kartodirdjo, Sartono, 79

Karyaputra, 100-1, 103-4, 107-8, 110-11
kepribadian nasional (see National identity)
keterbukaan (see Openness)
KNI (National Committees), 111
KNIP (Central National Committee), 76, 83, 100, 102, 131-32, 306
Konfrontasi, 27
Konsepsi, 36, 92, 94
Konstituante (see Constituent Assembly)
Kopkamtib, 59, 216
Korea, North, 128, 137; South, 37, 116, 118, 190
Kowani (Indonesian Women's Corps), 174
Kusumaatmadja, Sarwono, 24, 239, 288, 298-1

Labour, 30, 57, 118, 138, 170, 190-202, 258-65, 268; legislation, 172, 193; unionisation, 57, 118, 192, 194, 196-98, 232, 234, 269, 290; strike action, 57, 175, 192, 194-201, 232, 269, 303; state control of, 193-95, 198-200, 300
Lasjkar Rakjat, 132
Legge, John, 204-5
Legal Aid Institute (LBH), 152
Lev, Daniel S., 3, 11-12, 22, 34, 39-42, 208, 315
Liberalism, 50, 57, 152, 163, 165, 182
Liddle, R. William, 11-12, 22, 24-25, 145, 290, 297, 310
Liga Demokrasi (Democratic League), 96
Local government, 106, 132, 218-19, 221-22, 226
Lubis, Mochtar, 313

Mackie, Jamie, 22, 26, 317
Madiun rebellion, 64, 103, 130, 132-35, 308
Madjid, Nurcholish, 144, 147-50, 161-62
Malaysia, 27, 108, 140, 223, 277, 297
Mao Ze-dong, 36, 66, 128, 134, 137
Marcos, Ferdinand, 14, 236
Martial Law, 8-9, 30, 36, 182, 185, 207-8, 304-5
Masyumi, 18-20, 46, 64, 88-89, 93-94, 103, 141, 143-44, 215, 292, 296-97; participation in governments, 18-20, 77; role in regional resistance, 30-33, 67-70,

73, 136, 216, 297; banning of 73, 97
McVey, Ruth, 75, 129, 137, 255, 290, 315, 317
Middle classes, 11, 123-25, 147, 169, 174, 227, 258, 269, 292, 294; composition and character of, 117-18, 251, 254-55, 266-67, 278-80; and democratic development, 12, 37, 57-58, 119-20, 125, 229-37, 242, 246, 274, 282-84
Middle Way, 276-78, 304
Military (see Armed Forces, Army)
Moelyono, 100-1, 105-8, 112
Moerdani, L.B. (Benny), 120-21, 164, 229
Mohamad, Goenawan, 24
MPR (People's Consultative Assembly), 60, 107, 120, 151, 161, 163, 220, 229-30, 233-34, 237-38, 244-46, 294, 298, 300, 304-5
Muhammadiyah, 88-89, 110, 133, 241, 143-44, 293
Murba (Proletarian Party), 21
Musjawarah Nasional (Munas), 22, 30-31
Muso (1897-1948), 130-32, 134
Muzakar, Kahar (1921-65), 21, 308

Nahdlatul Ulama (NU), 19, 88-97, 141, 144, 149, 172, 256; as a political party, 19, 45, 48, 73, 88-97; religious thought of, 88-92, 146-47; role in transition to Guided Democracy, 19, 48, 92-96; under the New Order, 157-60, 164-65, 241, 292-93, 296-97
Nasution, Adnan Buyung, 4, 22, 41, 43-49, 59-60, 317
Nasution, Abdul Haris, 8, 19, 29-32, 67, 71-73, 76, 78, 132, 208-9, 279-80; and regional rebellions, 29-32, 67, 71-73; role in transition to Guided Democracy, 22-23, 32, 34, 39-42, 305; political doctrine of, 40, 208-9, 276-77, 304; Petition of Fifty, 231
National Congress, 22, 31
National identity, 35, 77, 155
Nationalism, 4, 17, 81, 129, 151, 185, 186, 224, 291, 294
Natsir, Mohammad (1908-93), 17, 30, 69, 136, 142
Navy, 20, 68, 72, 134, 277, 282
Neo-Modernism, 143-49

Nepotism, 276
NICs (Newly Industrialised Countries), 116, 190-191
Nicaragua, 168-69
Njono Prawiro (1922-66), 132
Notosusanto, Nugroho (1931-85), 24, 44, 51-52, 54-57, 139, 315, 317

Oil revenues, 20, 71, 138, 191, 209, 210, 217, 262, 264
Openness (*keterbukaan*), 121-22, 195-96, 220-21, 234, 239-40, 246, 303, 309

P4 (Pancasila Education courses), 51, 151
Parliament, 1945-50, 44; 1950s, 19, 21, 30, 36, 44, 76-77, 91-93, 102-105, 171-72, 208, 276, 314; Gotong Royong, 92-93, 95, 304-5; New Order 110-112, 122, 175, 216-18, 232, 236-242, 298-99, 303-4, 306, 309. See also DPR, MPR, Constituent Assembly.
Pamong Praja, 9, 20, 42, 204, 206, 215, 226, 244. See also *Pangreh Praja*.
Pancasila, 7, 18, 24, 40, 45, 47-48, 51, 55-56, 80, 86, 103, 112, 147, 151-52, 156-67, 186, 220, 229, 246, 280, 282, 304, 310-11
Pancasila Democracy, 16, 43-44, 107-9, 111, 123, 164-65, 192-94, 222, 236, 311
Pandora's Box, 7, 13-15, 318
Pangreh Praja, 101, 103, 105
PDI (Indonesian Democratic Party), 122, 140, 218, 231-32, 240, 245, 274, 282, 305
pemuda, 21, 100, 130
Permai (Union of the Common People of Indonesia), 18
Permesta rebellion, 7, 19, 30, 32, 34, 72, 134, 216, 226, 308
Persis (Muslim Unity), 89
Perwari (Indonesian Women's Association), 170, 172
Pesindo (Indonesian Socialist Youth), 132
Petition of Fifty, 17, 59, 121, 231, 233-34
Philippines, 14, 68, 72, 82, 119, 129, 131, 180, 236, 278
PID ([Dutch East Indies] Political Intelligence Service), 131

PKI (Indonesian Communist Party), 8-9, 14, 21, 71, 100, 106, 128-42, 194, 316-17; revolts of 1926-27, 129-30; Madiun Affair, 103, 132-34; under parliamentary system, 41, 45, 66, 73, 88-89, 134-36, 296-97; role in seizure of Dutch enterprises, 30-31, 33; under Guided Democracy, 27, 93, 96-97, 123, 136, 227, 248; 1965 'coup', 51, 137; destruction of, 137, 141, 274-75
PKK (Family Welfare Guidance), 86, 174, 176, 177
Pluralism, 24, 59, 143, 145, 147-49, 161, 182-86, 236, 239, 242, 290-91, 309, 314-15, 318
PNI (Indonesian Nationalist Party), 18-22, 32, 45, 77, 88, 100-1, 103-5, 136, 141, 215, 225, 296, 297
Police, 20, 64, 77, 85, 103, 105, 131-32, 266, 275, 278
Popular sovereignty, 58, 59, 76, 90, 139, 307
PPP (Unity Development Party), 121, 140, 151, 217, 229, 232, 240-41, 244, 149, 274, 282, 292
PPPKI (Agreement of Indonesian People's Political Associations), 76
Pramoedya Ananta Toer, 99, 112, 140, 142
Prawiranegara, Sjafruddin (1911-89), 30, 52, 69
Press, 121, 182-189, 230, 233, 303; freedom of, 21, 51, 57; censorship, 220
Primordial conflicts, 314
Proletariat, 80, 191, 202, 258, 263, 269
Provincial autonomy (see Regionalism)
PRRI (Revolutionary Government of the Republic of Indonesia), 7
PSI (Indonesian Socialist Party), 18, 20, 21, 28, 30-31, 88, 100-1, 105-6, 108, 136, 152, 216
PSPB (History of the National Struggle course), 51-53, 55-57, 60
Public realm, 309-10

Rahardjo, Dawam, 145
Rahman, Fazlur, 145-146
Rais, Amien, 160
Regionalism; provincial autonomy, 50, 58, 207-9, 213, 215, 218-19, 222, 225-26, 291; regional rebellions, 7, 17, 21, 30, 35, 54, 79, 93, 95, 124, 129-30, 207-8, 225, 227
Republic of the South Moluccas (RMS), 7, 21, 138, 308
Revolution, 8, 10, 17, 21-22, 28, 43, 56, 74-78, 81-83, 85, 123-24, 179, 204-5, 207, 225, 279, 315-16; experiences of, 18, 99-102, 129-32, 169; symbolic importance of, 4-5, 9, 28, 74, 237, 276, 305; changes in perception of, 52, 64, 139; social, 225
Robison, Richard, 117, 200, 224, 290
RUSI (Republic of the United States of Indonesia), 102-3
Russia, 108, 112, 130

Sakirman (1911-67?), 103, 132
santri, 18, 133, 284, 291-93
Sartono, Mr Raden Mas (1890-?), 21, 142
Sastroamidjojo, Ali (1903-75), 18-19, 36
Saudi Arabia, 153
Semaun (1899-1971), 104, 130-31, 141
Sexual division of labour, 169-70
Shiraishi, Takashi, 129
Siauw Giok Tjhan, 21
Siddiq, K.H. Achmad (1926-91), 91, 96
Siegel, Jim, 140
Simatupang, T.B., 78, 275, 284
Simbolon, Colonel Maludin (1916-?), 68, 73
SIUPP (Press Publication Permit), 186
Sjahrir, Sutan (1909-66), 80-83, 100, 102, 136, 142, 176, 180-81, 315
Sjarifuddin, Amir (1907-48), 64, 77, 82, 133-34, 142, 315
SOBSI (All Indonesia Central Organisation of Workers), 194
Soemitro, Gen., 24, 59
Soewignyo, 100-1, 106
SOKSI (Union of Indonesian Socialist Karyawan Organisations), 194
Soumokil, (1917-52), 308
Soviet Union (USSR), 8, 108, 125, 129, 132, 133-34, 137-38, 141, 223. See also Russia.
SPSI (All Indonesia Workers Union), 118, 192, 194-200, 232, 290

State of Emergency (see Martial Law)
State ideology, 56, 58, 151, 156, 158, 164, 220, 280, 282, 305, 309, 318
Students, 23, 51, 53-54, 57, 87, 100, 102, 110, 198, 227, 233, 237, 242, 268, 274, 300, 303, 315
Sudrajat, Edy, 164
Succession, 18, 25, 35-36, 92, 127, 202, 219-20, 240, 255, 310-11, 318
Sudharmono, 120, 229-30, 238-40, 243-45
Sudisman (1920-68), 131-32
Sudomo, Admiral (Ret), 195, 200
Suharto, President, 6, 10, 12, 16, 35-36, 40, 42, 51-52, 55, 58, 137, 140, 208, 216-17, 221, 229, 233, 289, 305-6; and the Army, 120-24, 166-67, 209, 230, 234, 237-42, 272-77, 281-83, 293-95, 318; and Islam, 121-22, 158, 160-63, 165-67, 291; business connections, 121; and reform, 36, 107-12, 125, 141, 305-6, 310-12
Sukanto (Said Sukanto Tjokrodiatmodjo 1908-?), 20
Sukarno (1901-70), 44, 52, 57, 60, 103-4, 106, 123, 131, 139, 186, 245, 305, 312, 315-17; and idea of Revolution, 9-10, 79-84; and Army, 18-19, 22, 304; and Islam, 18, 69-70, 92-97; and PKI, 64-71, 132, 134; and transition to Guided Democracy, 8, 19, 23, 27, 29-32, 34-36, 39-42, 44-45, 55, 92, 207-8, 216, 236-37, 304, 306, 308, 310
Sukiman Wirjosandjojo (1896-74), 17, 133, 193
Sumitro Djojohadikusumo, 9, 70, 136
Sumual, Colonel V., 72
Sunarto, 99-102, 104, 109-10
Sundhaussen, Ulf, 22, 34, 75, 120, 216, 272-84
Supersemar, 110
Supomo, Raden (1903-58), 48, 58
Suprapto (1897-?), 20
Sutrisno, Try, 60, 122, 281, 283
syari'ah, 91, 93, 153-54
Syansuri, K.H. Bisri, 96

Taiwan, 37, 68, 72, 116, 118, 286, 297, 300
Tan Malaka (1897-1949), 130-31, 135, 142
Tanter, Richard, 201, 242, 266, 308
Thailand, 37, 116, 122, 180, 298
Tiga Daerah, 100, 103
Tjahyono, Indro, 24
Tjokrodirdjo, Mustapha, 100-1, 111
TKR (People's Security Army), 100
Tolleng, Rahman, 22, 302
Trade unions, 22, 30-31, 58, 68, 131-32, 135, 172, 175, 190-203, 232, 234, 269, 290, 300. See also Labour.
Truman, Harry, 65

umat, 90, 93-95, 97, 144, 147, 158
United Nations, 64, 274
United States, 63-72, 102, 125, 133, 198, 205, 252, 313
Urbanisation, 13, 227, 248-251, 253, 261

Vietnam, 24, 63-64, 128, 137, 139

Wade, Robert, 286, 288, 300
Wahib, Ahmad, 144
Wahid, K.H. Abdurrahman, 24, 144-49, 151-55, 157-62, 164-67, 233, 241, 291-92
Wahono, 239, 244
West Irian (see Irian Jaya)
Wijaya, Putu, 140
Wilopo (1909-81), 17-18, 47, 88, 142
Wirosardjono, Soetjipto, 161, 243
Women, 46, 87, 168-79, 263-65, 300; organisations, 135, 169-79
Working classes, 57, 116, 118, 170, 190-92, 195-97, 200-2, 262, 269, 295
Yamin, Mohammad (1903-64), 48, 142, 304, 310
Young, Kenneth R., 201, 242, 266
Yugoslavia, 8, 128, 223

Zainuddin M.Z., 293
Zulkifli Lubis (1923-91?), 69, 70, 73